BIO LEWIS

GAS MONEY

by TROY LEWIS

Donated

In Memory of

DON TOMS

BY

KERRAN AND DEE RYAN

OCTOBER 2016

#23

OCT -- 2016

GAS MONEY

Printed in the United States

Cover design by Nicole Ganz
Interior design by Mick Wieland
Author photo by Dave Kramer
Proofreading by Pamela Fehl

First Printing, 2015

ISBN 978-1-5141-3594-5

www.GasMoneyBook.com

Gas Money is dedicated to Mumma,
who taught me that there was no such word as
"can't." Words can never express my love for
you. I regret that it took me so many years to
understand your struggles. You did the best
that you could. Thank you for being my first
and best teacher.

INTRODUCTION

"Life is a test every day." At least, that's what Mumma told me on March 24, 2012. Sometimes our lives provide us with moments of clarity when it all comes together and makes sense. Sometimes life doesn't make sense until we gain a little more perspective. Well, that's the way it was for me. Each one of us was tested every day. *I know I was.*

Gas Money is a book about the many people who offered me a nudge in one direction or another. Sometimes it was in the form of advice, other times in the form of clear direction, and lastly, in the luckiest of times, it took the form of a gift. Each of them offered *gas money* that took me from one destination to the next on my life's journey. In hindsight, it was as though other people knew where I should be going when I didn't.

The impetus for writing *Gas Money* resulted from back-to-back events. First, Mumma *(yes, I called my mom "Muh-muh")* suggested that I write about those people and how they impacted my life. The day after Mumma's suggestion, I ran into Molly Ward, a coworker that I hadn't seen in years, and she suggested I do the same. "Troy, you told me a story three years ago that I've never forgotten, and I've applied it to the rest of my life." She continued, "If you write a story nearly as well as you tell it, then you should write a book."

So that's how *Gas Money* took shape – back on July 8, 2009, when I wrote the first sentence, and finally, here it is. Actually, it began when I was born on April 22, 1961 – my Da, *(yes, I called my dad "Da," which rhymed with what a sheep might say, "Baa")* said that the 22nd day in April was the happiest day of his life, but he didn't tell me that until I was 34 years old. Often, I wished he had told me that much earlier, but later was better than never, I guess. As you read, you will experience the highs and lows that have taken place in my life. It was accompanied with joy, humor and sometimes, sadness. Throughout this book, I inserted the soundtrack to my life to help you understand the mood and the period in which I grew up. What follows is the way I remembered it. Perhaps you'll recall how others have shaped your life and all of the *gas money* you have been given – the angels and achievements, the devils and derailments that possibly influenced your life choices. "Experience was what you got when you got what you didn't want" was a phrase I learned when I was in the military. All of my wrong turns eventually taught me how to make right ones.

I felt that my life was often similar to my favorite character and movie, George Bailey in *It's A Wonderful Life*. Although I was never rich and often struggled, I was fortunate to have people who enriched my life with simply their presence. None of us have ever known where life would take us, but that's the beauty of it. And you know what? It was a pretty good life until I decided I didn't want it anymore. I never appreciated what a nice life I had until I quit living.

But, let's start at the beginning…

CHAPTER 1

By the time Mumma turned 16, she had five kids and was still a virgin. I became her sixth a little before she turned 19. My cousin, Sharon, who was older than me by four years, moved in with us in 1962, and that was the same year my little sister, Bridgette, was born. So at the age of 20, Mumma had a husband and eight kids to cook for, clean up after, read to and, last but certainly not least, take a belt to every day. I think her favorite part of the day was finding out who had misbehaved because she swung better than Willie Mays.

Sharon was the daughter of Mumma's oldest sister, and I wasn't sure why she lived with us. She used to be up in Philadelphia with her parents, my Aunt Grace and Uncle Jeff. I was 5 years old on Easter Sunday of 1966 when Uncle Jeff gave me the second best present I ever got, a stuffed animal I named Peter Rabbit. What was the best present I ever received? Well, that's another story.

I never asked Mumma why Sharon lived with us, but then again, I wouldn't dare do so. In our house, "Children were to be seen, *not* heard!" If I ever developed the boldness to ask her, it would have been met with, "If you've got a question about something you think you shouldn't be asking, then you'd better *think* it and not *speak* it." So I never knew why Sharon was there with us. *She just was!* Sharon was the oldest Latimore grandchild, and she reminded everyone of such at Grandpop Horace Latimore's funeral, just in case they had forgotten. She certainly didn't allow Bridgette or me to forget that she was older than us when we were growing up. Mumma often left Sharon in charge of Bridgette and me, and when the two of us failed to follow Sharon's "guidance," we paid a price for it. I wasn't particularly fond of Sharon as a disciplinarian, but there was nothing I was going to do about that. *Sharon was tough!* Her return to Philadelphia was something I eagerly awaited, but she never left Middlesex County, Virginia, until college came to pick her up. Sharon was more like a sister than a cousin, an older sister who took great pleasure in telling you what to do, when to do it and how to do it! Even when we were in high school, she took on all comers, male and female. Guys knew better than to mess with Sharon, and any girl who was brave enough to flirt with Sharon's "man" paid the same price as Bridgette and me. They got their butt kicked! In high school, I remember a few young ladies taking the school bus home with tissues up their noses to stop the bleeding after going toe to toe against Sharon. I never learned how her college "boxing" career went, but I *know* she retired from Middlesex High School undefeated!

My cousin, Sharon, 11; my sister, Bridgette, 6; and me, 7. 1968

CHAPTER 2

When Bridgette was born in 1962, Da and Mumma were 23 and 20. Looking back, I thought they did a great job in teaching the eight of us right from wrong, but their husband-wife relationship took more wrong turns than right ones. *Of course, when I was in my 20s and married, I did everything correctly!* Mumma and Da were probably too young for that much responsibility, but they tried and that was all anyone could ask. Neither had a day off unless you counted Sunday and even that involved church, cleaning and cooking. Mumma didn't go away on a "vacation" until she was 43 years old!

(Insert "Tune Up" by Junior Walker and the All-Stars) Mumma admitted to me that she and Da really loved each other when they first married, but the only time I ever witnessed anything resembling love was the manner in which they spun when jitterbugging to records in the living room. *They could do that!* I liked sitting on the living room steps to watch them because it was magical. They had perfect timing and rhythm. Watching them glide and swing across the hardwood floor to R&B music was pure magic, but the magic and their love for one another faded (died might have been a better description) a long, long time ago.

Da was a carpenter and handyman who fixed or built anything he put his mind to. Mumma started out washing windows and cleaning houses for various white people in the county. Sometimes she was a substitute teacher for grades 1–12, though she never set foot on a college campus until she picked me up after my freshman year of college. However, because she was a pretty good student when she was in high school, Mr. James Brinson and Mr. Charles I. Thurston, the "colored" elementary and high school principals, would ask her to come down the road to sub when a teacher called out sick. They knew Mumma could handle the curriculum and, more importantly, discipline the students. Mumma took no shit from *anyone*, with the exception of the man she married.

Me with the two best dancers I ever saw, Mumma and Da. 1962

CHAPTER 3

Mumma had five kids before she was a junior in high school because her parents decided that she would raise her one sister and four brothers. Four years later, Sharon, Bridgette and I were added to the brood, bringing her total to eight. Mumma had just turned 16 in June 1958, when her sophomore year of school ended. She may have thought her life would pretty much be the same once the school bell rang again in September. Improve her typing skills, pay attention in Mrs. Catherine Cameron's English class and hang on every word uttered by her favorite teacher, Mrs. Easter Holmes, who taught history. After school, work on her throw from short to 1st base (she was on the girls' softball team) or shoot free throws in the St. Clare Walker High School gymnasium or maybe flirt with Edward Yarborough (she didn't know then that Edward was a distant cousin) while waiting for the school bus to take her the two miles home. But while she washed dishes one August evening, Grandma Grace and Grandpop Horace Latimore changed the manner in which they *all* would live for the next 11 years.

Grandma and Grandpop Latimore's four-bedroom house was surrounded by about nine acres of cornfields and soybeans in Middlesex County, Virginia. It started being built around 1948 and was finished sometime in 1952. Mumma's oldest siblings, Uncle Dee and Aunt Grace, left Middlesex County as soon as they could – Uncle Dee before he even graduated high school. Both left for the hustle and bustle of Philadelphia. They wanted to get away from our sleepy, little town.

The Latimore front yard separated their home from two-lane U.S. Route 33. Cars and trucks and a few tractor trailers used 33 to head to Richmond, Newport News, Tappahannock or someplace else because there wasn't much reason to remain in Middlesex unless you lived there. Grandma and Grandpop Latimore struggled to make ends meet, and no one knew that better than Mumma because she had been balancing their checkbook since 5th grade. Grandma and Grandpop could read and write, but arithmetic was never a strong point for either of them. Both had quit school after 7th grade to work, and that was just the way it was for many black and white families in the late 1920s during the Great Depression. Grandma and Grandpop may have struggled with the nuances of a checkbook, but the decision regarding who would raise their family for the next 11 years was an easy one. They placed their dinner plates on the kitchen counter in August of 1958 and said to their 16-year-old daughter, "Jean, we're moving to Pennsylvania. We've found some new jobs up there. You're gonna stay here and take care of your sister and brothers."

At 16 years old, I would have been angry, upset and resentful with the type of responsibility my mother had thrust upon her. I was too selfish at 16 to be that kind of accountable. Aunt Grace told me, "Your mother was the perfect person to raise the family. God knew what He was doing. Jean was in the right place at the right time. Your mom was always older than her age. She was older than me, and I was her big sister!" Mumma felt an obligation to help her parents and, more importantly, her siblings who remained at home. So it was in 1958 that Mumma began raising Patricia, Edward, Randolph, Darnell and Anthony. A rising 11th grader raising a 13-year-old, an 11-year-old, a 10-year-old, an 8-year-old and a 5-year-old. To me, they were always Pat-Pat, Eddie, Ronnie, Darnell and Tony. They were my aunt and uncles, but like my cousin Sharon, they were more like brothers and sisters. Only eight years separated the youngest, Tony, from me. From my perspective, it seemed like Mumma took care of them forever, or at least she did so until Tony was a junior in high school. By then, Grandma and Grandpop Latimore had retired and moved back to Virginia.

As much as Mumma and I disagreed over the years, I always considered her the most selfless person I ever met. That being said, selfless was never to be confused with being a "softie!" Mumma was all business, all the time. When Pat-Pat or Eddie or Ronnie or Darnell or Tony or Sharon or Bridgette or I didn't do what Mumma wanted, she let us know about it! Mumma was capable of going on a rampage when any of us failed to follow her instructions. When I first learned of the term "spontaneous combustion," I immediately thought, "That's Mumma." She didn't *ask* you to do things; she *demanded* that you do them. "Sweep the steps! Dust the china cabinet! Set the table! The fork goes on the left, not on the right! Are you stupid or something? Clean the table! Rake the leaves! Cut the grass! Take out the trash! Go to bed! Get outta bed! And if you don't get up, I'm coming up there, and you don't fucking want that! Make your bed! Do your homework! Don't answer me with 'what'? Show some God-damn respect, say, 'Yes, ma'am.' It's only one more syllable than 'what', ya lazy ass!" None of us wanted to be on Mumma's "bad" side because it took a long time to get back on her "good" side.

Parts of Interstate 95 were still being constructed in the late 1950s when Grandma and Grandpop Latimore headed north for Pennsylvania on U.S. Route 17 that connected with U.S. Route 301 in Port Royal, Virginia. They stayed on 301 until it ran out in Delaware and worked their way over to U.S. Route 1 to begin work as "domestics" for the Peddle family. Domestic work for white folks was called "private duty." When you didn't have much education (which Grandma and Grandpop didn't), it was a good job. There were many black people from Middlesex who went off to do the same type of work. Da's mother, Grandma Pearl Lewis, would do the same. The children may have been left behind with the other parent or grandparents or an aunt or uncle to care for them, but no one that I knew of had a teenaged daughter raise the family. But that was precisely what Grandma and Grandpop Latimore did. Unfortunately, there weren't a lot of career options for blacks in Middlesex County in 1958. Grandma was a housewife, while Grandpop worked down the road about a mile or so at Len Davis' Cook's Corner gas station for about $30 a week changing tires, repairing carburetors and pumping gas. He and Grandma stood to make more money doing "private duty" work in Pennsylvania.

Grandma and Grandpop's decision to have Mumma raise *their* children might have been considered a poor choice in more recent times, but back then no one gave it a second thought. I liked to think that Grandma and Grandpop Latimore did the best they could, and who was I to judge my grandparents? "There wasn't enough money for us to survive," Mumma told me many years later. "*Something* had to change. Mom and Dad just did what they had to do for us to make it." While staring out the kitchen window that overlooked the cornfield, Mumma continued washing dishes after Grandma and Grandpop delivered their news. Somebody had to wash them. My Aunt Patty wasn't. I was pretty sure Pat-Pat found any way she could to get out of performing that duty. I know I did the same when I was her age because I never liked getting my hands dirty!

When Mumma was a 16-year-old kid, she began walking the two miles up to the Saluda Post Office seeking a Philadelphia postmarked envelope containing a check every two weeks. Her sister and brothers needed groceries, clothes, shoes, and the lights to stay on while Mumma needed more than the 24 hours in a day to do the countless things a "parent" needed to get done. But enough talk about Mumma, the former Jean Elizabeth Latimore, who married my Da, William Franklin Lewis. After Da left her and us, she married another man and took his name and became a Ferguson. There is plenty of time to talk about her.

(From tallest to shortest.)
Pat-Pat, Eddie, Ronnie, Darnell, Tony and Mumma's shadow. 1958
Mumma's "kids" who were my aunt and uncles.

The Latimore house they and I grew up in. 1977

CHAPTER 4

I grew up in the rural, farming part of Virginia that was Middlesex County, and I lived there until I was in the 8th grade. As an 8th grader, I was the junior varsity high school basketball manager. Sadly, I was the last "cut" from the JV team and that kept me awake every night for about six months. *Who was I kidding? That kept me awake for about 6 years!* I was never one to let things go. Da passed the "stubborn" gene on to me, but that's another story!

Respect, as in "Yes, sir" and "No, sir," was mandatory in my little community, but there was one member of the Hires family that moved to Middlesex around 1970 from Philadelphia that didn't feel the same way, and his first name was Pinckney. He was an outspoken, sometimes rude, teenager who I liked to hang out with. He always said what was on his mind. He spoke before he thought, and Mumma did not like people who did that! Although she liked his older brother, Gregory, and their younger sister, Cookie, she was never too crazy about Pinckney. He was an 11th grader when I was in the 8th grade in 1974. He was a starter on our varsity basketball team, and he and my cousin, Arnold Johnson, were the first guys to wear cornrows to school. They even wore them during basketball games and *that* was really crazy for those times.

On a team bus ride down to the Newport News area to play Poquoson High School, Pinckney and Arnold showed how "crazy" they

could be. They pestered Head Coach Thomas Walton about having the bus drop them off after the game at The Lemon Drop in
Gloucester County because they wanted to hang out with some
girls. Arnold and Pinckney kidded with Coach Walton and junior
varsity Coach John Clements about being dropped off at the little club. The Lemon Drop was a concrete building with a cement
dance floor that had sawdust sprinkled on it to make gliding easier.
It was a "hole in the wall" kind of place that black kids from Middlesex, Gloucester and Mathews counties went to on Friday and
Saturday nights to dance and drink and possibly "fool around" in
cars outside in the parking lot. Coach Clements said, "Y'all know
we can't drop y'all off at that place. If you go down on the bus, you
have to come back on the bus. That's the rules."

During the return trip, things took a turn for the worse. Pinckney
became more vocal and belligerent as the bus got closer and closer
to The Lemon Drop. Once he realized the bus wasn't going to come
to a stop to allow Arnold and him to hop off, he yelled, "God-damn,
Coach Walton, just because *you* ain't gettin' *none* don't mean *we*
don't wanna get *none*!" Only the rumble of the wheels against the
pavement could be heard because the bus occupants fell silent. In
Middlesex County in 1974, a teenager intimating that they wanted
to get "some" and that an adult wasn't getting "any" was unheard
of. Taking it a step further, a teenager uttering "damn" in the presence of an adult was out of this world. *"God-damn?" In front of
Coach Walton? That was worse than spitting in church!* Coach Walton
stared straight ahead from his right front seat and never said a word.
Seated next to him was Coach Clements, a tall, lanky man of more
than 6 feet and over 210 pounds. His deep, bass voice was thick
with a Southern drawl. He stood and turned to face Pinckney in the
darkness of the unlit bus. In a soft, even tone he said, "That's gonna
cossssst ya, Pinnnccckkk-nee!"

The remaining 30 miles or so seemed to take forever. The once-loud
teenagers were too shocked to talk anymore. *I know I was.* I sat next
to my best friend, James "Butley" Jarvis, who was a 10th grader.
He lifted an index finger to his lips to whisper, "This is gonna be a
long ride home. I can't believe he just said that to Coach Walton."
Neither could I! I don't remember Pinckney starting another game

or even getting much playing time after The Lemon Drop incident. That Friday night, I learned from Pinckney when, where and against whom to pick your battles. Many years later, Butley and I often wondered why Coach Walton and Coach Clements didn't throw Pinckney off the bus and let him walk the remaining 30 miles back to our high school. I think all of us on the bus, black and white, would have considered it fair punishment. When and where I grew up, no one cursed at a coach, teacher or parent, unless you wanted to lose some teeth! It just wasn't done, and if you were foolish enough to do so, you were going to pay a price for it.

CHAPTER 5

Most who lived in Middlesex County struggled to make ends meet. If you were fortunate, you found a "good" job in neighboring Richmond, Newport News or Yorktown, all about an hour away, or at the Pulp Mill in West Point that was 16 miles from Saluda, Middlesex's county seat. Others became farmers, fishermen or oystermen who worked on the surrounding Rappahannock and Piankatank Rivers. Those who remained in Middlesex to work were either self-employed or schoolteachers because other than river work, jobs were scarce. Around 1967, the largest town was Urbanna with about 300 inhabitants. *Forty years later, the U.S. Census showed that number had jumped to 793!* The county's annual highlight was the Oyster Festival held each November since the 1950s. It used to be called Urbanna Day, but I think some marketing people changed it to the "Oyster Festival" sometime in the 1980s. Attending the Oyster Festival was like showing up at a high school reunion; you saw people there you hadn't thought of in years.

There was only one traffic light in all of Middlesex County when I was growing up. It flashed red on the 17 side of the street and yellow on the 33 approach, moving traffic through Saluda past the Courthouse, the Tastee-Freeze and the Esso gas station where the Greyhound bus stopped twice a day. Sitting at the light across from the Saluda Courthouse, a left onto 17 North took you "up the county," and a right turn put you on 33 East to head "down the county." All residents were identified as living "up the county" or "down the county." At funerals and weddings, people that I hadn't seen in decades would say to me, "Who are you again?" "You know me. I'm Bill and Jean Lewis' son. Reverend Lewis' grandson. I used to live 'down the county,' now I live up in Jersey!" "Oh, yeah. Now I know who you are!"

A brick wall encircled the Saluda Courthouse that was built in 1852. When I was a little boy, there you often found older black men, whom Mumma called "no-count," sitting on or leaning against that wall while they waved at passing cars and sipped from brown paper bags. "Look at them. Making it bad for all of us. Just sitting up there doing nothing. Why don't they do something positive with their lives?" I was 13 years old when I decided that I was going to find out firsthand what it was like to sit on that wall with those men to watch traffic pass. I thought I was pretty cool as I sat there running my mouth with my new "buddies." About 20 minutes later, though, my coolness quickly turned to fear when Mumma pulled up to the light and saw me sitting on that wall drinking from a brown paper bag like my older friends. Although my bag only contained a Tahitian Treat soda that I picked up at Mr. Pokie Davis' store, I knew I shouldn't have been perched up there because I had been warned about the type of person who sat up there since my ears could hear. I was now on Mumma's "bad" side. I was surprised she didn't gun the accelerator of her four-door 1973 white Chevrolet Caprice with the maroon top to head straight for the wall to run me over! Instead, she parked across the street in front of the white two-story multi-office building where we went to see our dentist, Dr. Robert Barlowe, twice a year. I dreaded going to see him, but I loved the sweet scent that was in his office and every other dentist office I ever visited. *What was that smell anyway?*

Mumma motioned me to join her in the car. "Motioned" was putting it mildly. It was more of a hand gesture that said, "You better get your black ass off of that wall and in this damn car!" I heard my "buddies" laughing at my misfortune as they continued sipping from their paper bags that contained much stronger liquids than my soda. Slipping into the car, a tight-lipped Mumma said, "How many

God-damned times have I told you *who* sits on that wall?" Silence. "You better answer me, boy!" "A lot." "If you start sitting up there *now*, you'll end up sitting there *later.*" "Yes, ma'am." "Yes, ma'am, my ass! I dare you to let me catch your monkey-ass up there again." *She wouldn't, and I didn't.*

Even after the "new" traffic light was installed in the early 1980s, my Aunt Jenny still complained about it holding up traffic. "Whew, I sure hate that they put up that new light in Saluda!" "Aunt Jenny, there's probably only three cars waiting for the light to change, and it's been there for about 15 years now!" "Well, if that light weren't there, your Aunt Jenny could have made it home a *long* time ago!" She drove her four-door 1971 green, hardtop Chevy Impala from her home to the Saluda Post Office and back, roughly a one-mile trip that took about 5 minutes because she never went more than 25 miles per hour. She had that car almost 15 years, and it probably had about 3,000 miles on it when she quit driving. Who was my Aunt Jenny? She's another story!

There were three towns in Middlesex County: Saluda, Urbanna and Deltaville. Blacks didn't own any property in Urbanna and Deltaville when I was growing up, and some of the white people who lived in those two towns intended on keeping it that way. Saluda and Urbanna weren't "up the county" or "down the county." They were tiny black dots opposite each other on the Middlesex County map, separated by only a few hundred feet when traveling by small boat, but about 5 miles in a car. Each town sat on the Urbanna River, which emptied out into the much larger Rappahannock River that flowed into the Chesapeake Bay.

Although Middlesex County was a quiet, sleepy community, there was racial tension below the surface in most "social" interactions that took place between whites and blacks. *Who was I kidding?* When I was growing up, there were no "social" interactions between blacks and whites until we officially integrated schools in September of 1969 and even less interaction for the generations that preceded me. "Interaction" only occurred when money exchanged hands, but even then, lots of white people went out of their way to avoid touching a black hand. Mumma said they were afraid that the "black" would rub off on them. Many blacks tried to change things in our area, and some whites fought harder to keep things the way they were. Combine those racial issues with the tension that was the fabric of any family, and Middlesex County was just like any other place in America in the 1960s. Tension was always present in the four homes in which I lived. I was so accustomed to strife that as an adult, I found it strange when things were going well. *I was always waiting for something bad to happen.*

(Insert "He Ain't Heavy, He's My Brother" by The Hollies) Mumma's oldest brother, Uncle Dee, grew up in Virginia and lived with his maternal grandmother, Lenora Latimore. Because Grandma and Grandpop Latimore were seldom around during his formative years, Uncle Dee resented Grandpop telling him how he should live his life once he got older. They never saw eye to eye. After quitting high school, Uncle Dee took a garage job in Philadelphia and was later drafted into the Army as a mechanic in Korea. The Latimores were excited when he returned to Virginia for his infrequent visits. For whatever reason, even after "Uncle Sam" let him go, Uncle Dee didn't come home very often. I never knew why that was so, but I did know that he took much delight in teasing Bridgette and me about cutting our ears off with his pocketknife when he did visit. Despite his mischievous nature, his rare appearances provided Mumma with much happiness. I don't remember *anyone* making her smile as much as he did.

Uncle Dee and Grandpop looked so much alike that I thought they were twins when I was a little boy. One head was covered with wavy, gray hair while the other's wavy hair was jet-black. I once asked Uncle Dee, "Why do you call Grandpop 'Daddy' when he's your brother?" His deep bass voice chuckled at that thought and he whispered, "He *ain't* my brother." Then, he winked and moved on. Their father/son relationship was awkward, but I didn't know that then because I was just a little boy.

Uncle Dee had charisma and any room that he was in seemed to be brighter than the one he had just departed. Although I only met him a handful of times, I could tell he was a smooth character. *I wanted to be smooth like him when I grew up.* Mumma told me he could do no wrong as far as the ladies were concerned, but sadly, Uncle Dee was too smooth for his own good because he was dead from cirrhosis of the liver by age 46. After he died, he took a big chunk of Mumma with him.

Uncle Dee and Grandpop Latimore. 1970
They always looked like brothers to me!

The Saluda Courthouse that was built in 1852. 2012
The brick wall where I sat once and only once!

CHAPTER 6

It was funny how certain details in life were recalled. The first time you received a bee sting, the first person you kissed, the first beer you tasted or the person who sat behind you in 1st grade. Some memories never left, and some could never be evoked regardless of how hard you tried to conjure them up.

My earliest recollection was when I was almost 4 years old (or 3 years and 11 months, to be exact). Julie Andrews said in *The Sound of Music*, "When you read, you begin with A, B, C. When you sing, you begin with do-re-mi." Going to see *The Sound of Music* was my earliest memory. I didn't even know that was the case until I looked up its release date, March 2, 1965. I was close to turning 4 when Mumma and Da took Bridgette and me to see Ms. Andrews at the Tappahannock Theater. I remember that Da complained the entire drive. "Why do we have to drive all the way up there to see a dumb movie when it's playing over in Urbanna?" He was right. It was playing a couple of miles away in Urbanna, but Mumma wouldn't give in. As I got older, I always wondered why *did* we drive north on 17 for 29 miles to Tappahannock when we could have gone to the theater in Urbanna, so I finally asked Mumma. She said, "I thought it was such an important movie for you and Bridgette to see that I didn't want y'all to see it in a *segregated* theater. Tappahannock had already desegregated theirs." *Well, that answered my question.*

CHAPTER 7

Aunt Jenny, who hated the traffic light, lived up the road from us on 33, about a quarter mile away. She married one of Grandpop Latimore's eight brothers, Uncle Carey. He was a trim, light-skinned, almost white man with very "good" or straight hair. All Latimores had "good" hair, but Mumma married Da, so I inherited Lewis "hair," which wasn't quite as "good" as the Latimores!

Uncle Carey owned a considerable amount of farming land that he rotated with corn, wheat and soybeans. He wasn't a farmer though; he rented out his land to Mr. Frank Moore, a white man who had a large farm down the road about a mile away. Uncle Carey worked for over 30 years at the U.S. Naval Weapons Station down in Yorktown. Every now and then he reprimanded his brothers for their excessive drinking habits. Of Grandpop's brothers, Uncle Carey was the only one that I remembered who didn't drink a lot. Grandpop and his other brothers took great pleasure in raising a bottle to their lips. Some men made hunting or fishing or tinkering with cars or chasing women their pastime. The Latimore brothers made *drinking* theirs. Liquor eventually contributed to the death of most of them, but not Uncle Carey. He was 70 years old when a heart attack took care of him while he sat on the steps of his back porch puffing on a cigar in 1981.

Aunt Jenny was a petite, pleasant woman who always wore her hair in a bun and was the part-time babysitter for me, Bridgette and

Sharon. I had a crush on Aunt Jenny when I was a little boy, and as an adult, I grew to love her even more. She and Uncle Carey began seeing each other back in the 1930s. They had one son, Carey III, who lived on the other side of their shared vegetable garden when I was coming along. I never knew why everyone called him "Cakesy" instead of Carey, but Tony told me it was because as a little boy, Cakesy loved eating the cakes that Aunt Jenny baked, so the nickname stuck like icing to a mixing bowl! *If Tony told me the sun was the moon and the moon was the sun, I would have believed him.* Cakesy was close to Mumma and Da's age, and he had a very pretty wife, Gloria, that everyone called "Glo." From my little boy perspective, she always seemed bitter and grumpy. There was nothing "glow"-ing about her personality as far as I was concerned. As I got older, I asked Mumma what made Glo so sullen. "Troy, for every *peculiar* thing there's always a *reason* behind it." I was thinking, "Yeah, yeah, let's hear this one. Glo has a nice husband who doesn't smack her around (that was how I determined if you were a nice husband when I was a kid) with a decent job, two beautiful little girls (Kim and Kerri) and a nice house with "running water" (we didn't have that). What did Glo have to complain about, and why did she always smell like Grandpop Latimore, another admirer of Gordon's Gin?"

I shook my head, "Mumma, I don't get it. You're gonna have to explain that one to me." "Well, when Glo was around 39 years old, she found out that she had inoperable liver cancer, and I guess she just couldn't deal with it. Maybe she began drinking to speed up the process." In 1970, Glo was 39, and she wouldn't be around to see Muhammad Ali fight Joe Frazier in 1971, but Joe Frazier was another story. Maybe Mumma was right. *Was she ever wrong?* I guess there were reasons for peculiar things.

Aunt Jenny lived to be 94, and at the end of her life in 2005, she didn't know me or Cakesy or anyone anymore. Cakesy and his second wife, Ann, who played the piano for me when I sang at weddings and funerals, brought Aunt Jenny from across the garden to live with them. When my Uncle Ronnie stopped by to visit her, she whispered that she was glad that at least he came to see her because her son never did anymore. Dementia wasn't kind to Aunt

Jenny's once sharp mind because Cakesy was sitting 10 feet away in the kitchen.

When Aunt Jenny was still in her "right" mind, she and I used to sit on her front porch for hours and watch the cars pass by on 33. She explained how she and Uncle Carey began "courting" by attending each other's church when she was in her early 20s. Aunt Jenny's church was New Mt. Zion Baptist in adjacent Gloucester County, and Uncle Carey attended Antioch Baptist Church in Saluda just like every other Latimore. Sometimes Aunt Jenny ventured over to Antioch, and at other times, Uncle Carey made it over to her place of worship. Their courtship began with them leaning forward to peek and nod at each other from their pews. That was how they became acquainted. Peeking and nodding. After the sermon, they might exchange a few words if Aunt Jenny's mom let her go over and talk to him for a bit before heading back home. They had a week to think about seeing each other the following Sunday. Eventually, she invited him home to meet her parents for Sunday dinner. She told me that went just fine, but when Uncle Carey invited her home to meet his mother, Aunt Jenny said my great-grandmother gave her the "once-over" and turned up her nose as if to say, "You aren't good enough for my Carey!" Aunt Jenny chuckled at that thought almost 60 years later, and so did I. The thought of Aunt Jenny not being "good enough" for *any* man still made me laugh. When she was young, I'm sure lots of black men in Gloucester and Middlesex County sought her affection. Aunt Jenny was my first older woman crush, and there would be many more that followed. I even married one of them, but she's another story!

On Aunt Jenny's screened front porch, she and I often sat to talk about something and sometimes, nothing. As an evening breeze sent the aroma from her peach trees across the porch, she'd mention that her snowball bush was blooming late this year or her canned peaches weren't as good as last year's. She'd tell me that Kim and Kerri (whom she helped raise after Glo died) still called her every Friday night to let her know what was going on in their lives. Or that her house needed a new coat of paint and maybe, just maybe, the air conditioner in her bedroom would make it one more summer. Then one evening, as if she'd seen a rabbit munching on her petunias or begonias, she hopped from the outdoor glider sofa on which we sat and said, "How'd you like Aunt Jenny to bake you a chocolate yellow-cake right now? I know you like those!" *Aunt Jenny, I love your chocolate yellow-layer cake. Do you really think I'm gonna say 'No'?* "Aunt Jenny, it's getting late. You don't have to do that!" She leaned over and said, "Well, if your Aunt Jenny makes a cake, you'll have to stay a lil' bit longer now, won't you?" *How could I say no to that?* Then, she headed off to her kitchen to mix flour, butter, eggs, sugar, vanilla and whatever else went in a cake. That kept me in her kitchen another two hours, and I think that was exactly what she wanted.

When Grandma Latimore died in 1996, Aunt Jenny showed up to the funeral with a chocolate yellow-layer cake for me. I arrived early to practice for the solo that I would sing that day. Antioch Baptist Church was empty except for the funeral home personnel and Grandma Latimore lying in her casket. I didn't dare look at her or the casket because dead people scared me ever since I could remember. I had gone back outside to get a wintergreen Lifesaver (they were great for cooling a singer's throat) from my car when a car horn beeped. It was Cakesy and Ann pulling into the parking lot with Aunt Jenny in the backseat. "Hey, Aunt Jenny!" I hadn't seen her in about two or three years. "I knew you were singing today, and I figured you might get here early to practice, so your Aunt Jenny baked you a cake. I know you won't want to share it, so you can just hide it in your car!" "Aunt Jenny, it's Grandma's funeral. You didn't have to do that." "Well, you've been away for a long time, and Aunt Jenny doesn't get many chances to bake you a cake anymore." *God, I loved that lady!* I shared the cake afterwards at Ronnie's house "up the county," but I only got to eat one slice because Eddie, Ronnie, Darnell and Tony consumed it in about 10 minutes. They devoured *my* cake as though Aunt Jenny had baked it for *them!* I should have listened to her and left the cake in the car! Aunt Jenny taught me that even though funerals were gloomy occasions, some happiness could still be found during those sad times. The thought of her sneaking me a cake always made me smile. I missed Aunt Jenny's chocolate yellow-layer cakes, but I missed her a whole lot more.

Me and Aunt Jenny. 2000

Grandpop Latimore with two of his brothers, Uncle Carey and
Uncle Eddie. 1970

CHAPTER 8

"I can't wait 'til I get big so I can leave this place," was something I probably said every day as a youngster. "There's nothing to do here! This place is boring." Sharon and Bridgette were of a similar mind-set. Mumma's response to that was always the same. "Nothing to do? Go read a book!" That drew eye rolls from the three of us, but we *never* let Mumma see that. She would have gone berserk. "Did y'all just fucking roll your eyes at me?" "No!" "No, what?" "No, ma'am." "I thought not, if you know what's good for you."

Mumma had many rules and one of them was, "You *will* eat every-thing on your plate!" *We were poor and food was not to be wasted.* This applied even more so when eating at someone else's house, and that usually only happened once a year at Thanksgiving. *I wouldn't eat at a restaurant until I was a junior in high school - a Bonanza Steakhouse down in Newport News. We simply didn't have money for restaurants.*

I only remember one Thanksgiving dinner as a child. It took place at my Aunt Dot's house in 1970 when I was 9 years old. She was married to Grandpop Latimore's youngest brother, Uncle Eddie. Uncle Eddie didn't show up for that meal, but that's another story. There were probably a dozen or more of us at Aunt Dot's house for the big meal that came with the usual fixings: turkey, stuff-ing, mashed potatoes, sweet potatoes, string beans, rolls, broccoli, carrots, lima beans, squash and a ham. *I loved ham!* Her ham was decorated with sliced pineapples that were affixed with pink, blue and yellow toothpicks. Mumma fixed my plate with ham, turkey, mashed potatoes, stuffing, string beans and sweet potatoes. I never wanted any of my food to "touch," so I was really thankful she had separated them for me! I dug in and started with the sweet potatoes first because they weren't my favorite, so I wanted to get them out of the way! *Remember, I had to eat everything on my plate!* I saved the ham for last, but I couldn't believe that Mumma only gave me two slices. It turned out to be a blessing.

Before taking a bite of the ham, I thought the decorative toothpicks were there to enhance its flavor. I assumed, "Why else would toothpicks be on the ham if you weren't supposed to eat them?" I cut the ham with the toothpicks into tiny pieces. I looked around to see if anyone else had a problem and all seemed to be enjoying their meal. *I was not going to be the one who objected to Aunt Dot's toothpicks.* I raised my fork to insert the ham and toothpicks and swallowed. The ham tasted great, but the toothpicks were hard and dry. I sat at the dining room table staring at everyone and thinking, "Aunt Dot's ham is really good, but she doesn't know a thing about cooking toothpicks!" It took a few glasses of water to get those small slivers of wood down into my tummy. Swallowing wood was no easy task, but there was no way I was going to tell Mumma that I didn't like the toothpicks. I feared that Mumma would have given me "The Look," taken me out on Aunt Dot's back porch, yanked off the belt that held my pants up and given me a quick spanking! The Look said, "Please shut the fuck up before I smack the shit outta you. I really don't feel like dealing with your dumb ass today." All of us got The Look at some point, with the exception of Da. For me, it was easier to just swallow the toothpicks and act like nothing was wrong. That was how afraid I was of Mumma. *"You will eat everything on your plate."*

When we got home that evening, Mumma asked, "Didn't you like your Aunt Dot's ham? I'm surprised you didn't ask for some more!" I made a weird face. "What's wrong?" I shrugged my shoulders and lowered my head. "Mumma, I liked her ham, but I didn't like the way her toothpicks tasted." "What are you talking about?" "Well, the ham was really good, but I had a real hard time swallowing those toothpicks. They hurt my throat going down. That's why I didn't ask you for anything else to eat." "You *ate* the toothpicks?" "Yes, ma'am." "Oh, Troy. You weren't supposed to eat those! They were on there to hold the pineapple! Why did you do that?" I hung my head even lower and whispered, "Mumma, you always tell us we have to eat *everything* on our plate." I was terrified of Mumma and pretty much listened to anything she told me for fear of ending up on her bad side. Even when I was in my 50s, I knew not to cross her because she was crazy. *I experienced her craziness all of my life.*

CHAPTER 9

In the 1960s, the Middlesex County Public School System didn't allocate kindergarten funds for the "colored/Negro" children every year, but it did for the white kids. When I was coming along, black kids got it every other year, and that's just the way it was. I never asked Mumma or anybody else if they got a chance to go to kindergarten, but it didn't really matter if they did or not. All I knew was that I didn't, and Bridgette did because she was a year behind me.

(Insert "Say It Loud, I'm Black and I'm Proud" by James Brown) Around 1968, the term *Black* replaced *Negro,* and I think James Brown's "Say It Loud, I'm Black and I'm Proud" spurred that change. Well, at least that's what Tony told me when I asked him why we weren't called Negroes anymore! Grandma and Grandpop Latimore came home every couple of months from Pennsylvania, and when they did, Grandpop had me read to him from the daily paper out of Newport News that was called the *Daily Press.* "Man, my eyes can't see today, read me the paper. Start with the front page and work your way through. Just give me the headlines, and I'll tell you what story I want to know more about." Reading to him improved my vocabulary, although I didn't realize that was Grandpop's intent at the time. *I thought I was simply amusing him because I often struggled with words that were more than two syllables!* "Take your time and sound it out," he said. The stories that interested Grandpop the most were those that involved criminal mischief, and his first question about the evildoer was always, "Was he *white* or *colored?*" "Oh, Grandpop, we ain't 'colored' anymore. We ain't even 'Negroes' anymore. We are now called 'Black!'" He smiled and said, "Same thing!" Then, his smiling face turned serious and he said, "And if you use 'ain't' again, I'll knock you right in that big mouth of yours!" I knew he meant it. "Now, read me another story." "Yes, sir." I did so using more appropriate English. *I knew I shouldn't have been using "ain't" in the first place.*

First grade marked my first formal year of schooling. *Wasn't that crazy when you thought about it, your skin color determined if you got kindergarten or not.* If I thought I had it bad, it was mild compared to any "colored" generation that preceded me, so I couldn't complain. School began in September of 1967 at Rappahannock Central Elementary School, and I couldn't wait for it to start. Mumma had been going over my A-B-Cs, 1-2-3s, nouns and verbs since forever, and life at my house was a constant examination. When Eddie, Ronnie, Darnell and Tony were tired of my mouth, one of them ripped out a sheet of notebook paper, jotted down the 50 states and left blank spaces for me to fill in the capitals and state nicknames. They knew that would shut me up.

Indiana: <u>Indianapolis</u> – <u>The Hoosier State</u>
Iowa: <u>Des Moines</u> – <u>The Hawkeye State</u>

If I made a mistake, they grabbed my paper, balled it up and threw it in the trash. "Start over!" Tony took great pleasure in having me go all the way back to the beginning, starting with the As. If I complained, he placed me in a headlock until I said, "Alabama: Montgomery, The Cotton State. Alaska: Juneau, The Last Frontier. Arkansas: Little Rock, The Land of Opportunity!" That being said, I preferred my uncles quizzing me instead of Mumma. Having her grill you was akin to presenting oral arguments before the U.S. Supreme Court, and God forbid I misidentified *Baltimore* as Maryland's capital. *In case you didn't know, it's Annapolis!* I never, ever forgot the 50 state capitals because I was too afraid Mumma or one of my uncles would call and ask me to recite them over the phone just for kicks!

Sitting in front of the TV as a child, I often received a cross-examination on the important contributions of black people like Harriet Tubman, Sojourner Truth, Frederick Douglass and Dr. Daniel Hale Williams. When I failed to recall what made them noteworthy, Darnell or Tony told me that I could no longer watch *My Three Sons* with them, and they banished me from the living room. "Go get the *Negro History Book,* read some more and *maybe* we'll let you watch *Dragnet* in an hour. *Why does my family want me reading all the time?* Many years later, a coworker, Brian Gathen, challenged me to a contest of who could fill in the 50 state capitals the fastest, and that was like taking candy from a baby. Brian became a big part of my life, but he's another story!

Mississippi became my favorite word to spell. "M-I-S-S-I-S-S-I-P-P-I." When I was 5 years old and studying at the dining room table, Da would look over at me while taking a break from watching his favorite TV program, *The Red Skelton Show,* and ask, "Chopper (my nickname), what state is Jackson the capital of?" "Mississippi!" "That's right! Now, spell that for me!" I would and that made him laugh. He'd look at me and say, "Now, why did you 'pee pee' all over yourself?" Then he'd ask me to spell it again, and I'd giggle the entire time I was trying to spell M-I-S-S-I-S-S-I-P-P-I because I knew I was going to "pee pee" all over myself again!

It was September of 1967 that I learned a very important lesson. It was the first day of 1st grade for me, and I did not want to look stupid. But stupid was exactly how I felt a few minutes after I took my seat. I wanted to impress my teacher, Mrs. Melissa Jackson, and I didn't want to disappoint Mumma because she had done so much to prepare me for school. Even at 6 years old, I knew all of the 20th century U.S. Presidents, most of the junior and senior U.S. senators and presidential secession among other things. "Mumma, why do I need to know who *could* become president?" "Suppose another president gets assassinated. Don't you want to know who's next in line?" "Oh, I get it." She also had me reciting each president that was born in the state of Virginia, and there were eight of those! "Washington, Jefferson, Madison, Monroe, Harrison, Tyler, Taylor and Wilson!" Knowing all of the 20th century U.S. presidents was never required by Mrs. Jackson, but Mumma wanted me prepared just in case.

On that first day of school, I faced a dilemma that had little to do with naming the president who took office after Washington and Adams. Fortunately on that morning, my cousin, Renee Johnson, was in my class and more importantly, so was her mother, Mrs. Cynthia Johnson. She gave me some *gas money* that would last me the rest of my life on that September day.

CHAPTER 10

(Insert "It's A Beautiful Morning" by The Rascals) My seat was the first chair in the first row of Mrs. Jackson's class. *That* seat wasn't my choice. Mumma *told* me to sit there and disobeying her was simply out of the question. She mellowed as she got older, but I knew there was always a crazy person inside of her just waiting to come out and play. I learned over the years that when you dealt with a crazy person, you never knew what might set them off or what they were capable of doing. They could "lose it" at any time. That was my mother. She snapped like a twig at the slightest infraction.

I squirmed in my seat while Mumma, Renee's mom and a couple of other mothers spoke with Mrs. Jackson before class started. I needed to pee. I was considering my first encounter with the door that had a "Rest Room" sign on it. *I've never been inside of a Rest Room.* I thought I would find a "pot" behind that door. We didn't have "running water," so I had never used anything other than an outhouse or a "pot" to pee. "Pots" were white metal buckets that people without indoor plumbing kept in their home to use as toilets. Darnell and Tony couldn't wait to hand over the dumping and cleaning of pots to their 6-year old nephew. *I hated that job.* I collected the pots from each of the four bedrooms at Grandpop's house to take them to the outhouse when I got home from school. Darnell and Tony showed me how to clean the pots using a large bristle brush and water drawn from the well in the backyard. Turning over that responsibility to me was something that pleased them and displeased me. *Did I mention that I hated that job?*

Public rest rooms were still segregated in Virginia in 1967. When Sharon, Bridgette and I went shopping with Mumma, we were told to, "Use the outhouse, go pee in the pot or hold it until we get back." *I didn't know it then, but Mumma didn't want us using rest rooms marked "Colored."* Three to four times a day, the pots' contents needed to be emptied into the outhouse. Later on, Da built us a new home "down the county" that had indoor plumbing and *two* bathrooms, and that was when I thought we were *rich*! I had a bathroom that I could use anytime I felt like it and as much "running water" as I ever wanted!

Heading into the door marked Rest Room, I thought I'd find a pot inside. However, once I closed the door behind me, there was only a large, white porcelain bowl with a black lid and what seemed to be a gallon of water in it. *What the hell is this thing?* But I had to "go," so I unzipped my pants, took a chance and peed in that bowl. While I stood there urinating, I was thinking, "How on Earth am I going to get rid of my pee?" I washed my hands and closed the door behind me. *I'm going to find Renee's mom. She'll tell me what to do.*

Everyone called Renee's mom, C-Y. I never knew anyone who called her Cynthia. After Aunt Jenny, C-Y was my second "older" woman crush. She was around 29 in 1967, and I thought she was gorgeous! Even though she was my 3rd or 4th cousin, it didn't stop me from having an infatuation with her. She had lots of personality and was fun to be around, unlike Mumma who *never* seemed to be in a good mood. C-Y babysat Bridgette and me when Aunt Jenny wasn't available, and I learned later on that she did it for free. "C-Y, how much money did Mumma pay you to watch me and Bridgette?" "Are you crazy? I never charged Jean a dime! I did it as a favor to help her out." We loved staying at her place to play with Renee. Renee was sort of a tomboy back then, but blossomed into a pretty girl and an even prettier young lady. She retired from the U.S. Coast Guard as a Command Senior Master Chief, the highest rank that an enlisted person could attain in that branch of the military.

I grabbed C-Y's hand. "I need you to help me." "What is it, Honey?" "Come in this little room with me." We made our way into the small room, and I quickly closed the heavy door behind us. I pointed at the evidence in the white bowl. I whispered, "C-Y, I peed in that thing, but I don't know how to make it go away." She leaned against the door and sighed, "Troy, you just grab this little handle here, pull down on it and your pee will go away. Now, go ahead and you give it a try!" I pulled the handle, and in an instant, my pee disappeared. "Wow, I didn't know how to do that before!" She smiled. "Troy, there'll be lots of things in your life that you won't know how to do, but it's okay to *not* know how to do them. You'll figure it out. Just keep trying." I never forgot C-Y's *gas money* lesson from September of 1967. I promised myself that going forward I wouldn't panic when I didn't know how to do something, or worse, ridicule someone when they didn't. Her words of encouragement stayed with me forever. *"It's okay to not know."* Many things in life took me longer to figure out than it did others, but my cousin C-Y gave me the confidence to overcome obstacles, big or small.

In Middlesex County, everyone that I knew felt warmly about C-Y, with the exception of possibly one person. That exception was probably Reverend John Joshua Lewis, my paternal grandfather. He formed his opinion of C-Y around 1953 or so when she was pregnant and unmarried at 15. He embarrassed her in front of his church congregation because her tummy was slightly larger than it was a couple of months earlier, and her finger was missing a wedding band. In 1950s Middlesex County, if you were pregnant and unmarried you could attend church, but communion was off-limits. In order to partake in communion, you needed to stand before the congregation, admit your transgressions and ask the church for its forgiveness. And maybe, just maybe, "they" might accept you back into the fold. I could not imagine being a 15-year-old female and having to do that in 1953 or any year. One Sunday morning, Rev. Lewis spoke about those "trespassing against us" while glaring at C-Y from the pulpit, pressuring her to come forward. He intimidated her. Decades later, she never forgot the humiliation she felt on that Sunday morning as she recounted it with watery eyes. I felt awful for my cousin C-Y as she described that story to me almost 40 years later.

Mumma informed me that C-Y wasn't the only young lady that had to seek "forgiveness." There were others, and Mumma came close to being one of them! She was already two months pregnant with me when she and Da got married. "God, Mumma, what would you have done? Would you have gone in front of the church?" She said with a twinkle in her eye, "I was scared to death. I was just glad that I didn't have to go that route because your Dad and I got married before it got to that point!" In fact, Grandpop Lewis performed a triple wedding ceremony on October 15, 1960, for Mumma and Da and two other couples who were in similar circumstances. But, of course, Rev. Lewis didn't know any of that or that his son had gotten Mumma pregnant!

C-Y and Arthur, the young man who aided in her pregnancy, got married a few weeks later and they stayed that way for over 60 years until he died in 2014. Neither of them graduated from high school, but they raised three kids who did, Clinton, the aforementioned Arnold and Renee. The oldest child, the one C-Y carried in her tummy in 1953, became Arthur, Jr. He did not graduate from Middlesex High School. He quit during his junior year and that made his parents very unhappy.

Arthur, Jr. was called "Tubby" by most of us because he was slightly chubby. In high school, he got a job bagging groceries at Mr. Raymond Walton's Park Place grocery store in Urbanna. He saved enough money to work out a deal with Bareford Chrysler-Plymouth Motors to buy a two-door 1970 red and white Plymouth Duster 340. He had a girl somewhere down in Gloucester County, and he knew the red Duster with the racing stripes on each side would make her like him even more. He told C-Y and Arthur he was going to quit school to work full time at the grocery store to pay for the car. *I guess he thought bagging groceries for a living was a good job at 17. Well, at least it would pay for his car, and it was a cool car!* C-Y and Arthur wanted Tubby to go farther than that Duster would take him, but Tubby only wanted to go as far as Gloucester County after he was done putting groceries in the trunks of cars for the day. Like most teenagers, Tubby was hard-headed and short-sighted, maybe even more so than most. He certainly didn't want to listen to C-Y and Arthur, Sr. anymore. Instead of listening to his parents, Tubby decided to listen to his "Uncle." "Uncle Sam" told Tubby what to do for the next 30 years.

Unfortunately, Renee died the year she and I turned 53 from a rare bacterial infection that attacked her spine. In May of 2014, we made plans to attend our 35th high school reunion together, but Renee was dead by July 5th. She only lasted about 10 days after she went in the hospital. That year, C-Y lost her husband and her youngest child within 57 days of each other.

C-Y in the Latimore dining room at Christmas. 1967

CHAPTER 11

(Insert "My Girl" by The Temptations) After sliding back into my chair in Mrs. Jackson's room, I fell in love with the girl who sat in the first seat two rows to my right. She was the prettiest thing I had ever seen. When I first saw her in 1967, she was wearing a white dress decorated with blue and yellow flowers. She had long, pretty pigtails and was as cute as a button. Judith Lorraine Kidd had me at "Hello," but she didn't give me a second thought for another 13 years.

It was the summer of 1980 when I had completed my freshman year of college. I stopped by Rappahannock Central Elementary to see Judy's mom, Mrs. Catherine Kidd, the school secretary. I hoped she would let Judy know that I was around and that I stopped by to say "Hi!" *Much to my surprise, it got even better.* Mrs. Kidd gave me Judy's dormitory telephone number and suggested that I give Judy a call sometime. *Sometime? Mrs. Kidd, your daughter's phone will be ringing as soon as I see a pay phone.* Judy was attending summer school at the College of William and Mary in Williamsburg. Its campus was about 15 miles from where I now lived with Mumma and her new husband, Gerald Ferguson.

I called Judy and set up a date with her that was to be our first and last. We went to see *Macbeth* (who said that I didn't know how to show a girl a good time) that was playing at the Virginia Shakespeare Festival in Williamsburg where Mumma and Gerald lived along with me, Bridgette and Gentree, my little brother who was born in 1972. Where did this Gentree character come from? He was another story!

During *Macbeth's* intermission, I bought Judy some popcorn and a soda before we returned to our seats. I had read *Macbeth,* so I knew that the three witches were about to show up in Act 4, Scene 1 to say, "Double, double, toil and trouble; Fire burn, and cauldron bubble." After those words were uttered, I planned to make my first move! I reached for Judy's hand, and she held onto mine! I could have been struck by lightning later that night and died a happy 19-year-old. *I had been waiting for this moment since September of 1967, and it only took 13 years for it to happen!* In the 1370s, William Langland coined the phrase, "Patience is a virtue." He was never more correct!

Afterwards, I took Judy to Howard Johnson's Restaurant (waiting tables there was my summer job) for ice cream (Shakespeare and HoJo's in one night, I really did know how to show a girl a good time). When we finished our sundaes, I drove her back to her dorm room and opened the door of Mumma and Gerald's sky blue, four-door 1977 Volkswagen Rabbit to let her out. We hugged "good night" and that was the extent of our date. I never called Judy again. I was too afraid she might have said, "No." She never contacted me again, either. Maybe I should have called. Who knows? She might have even said, "Yes! Why didn't you call me sooner!" *But I wasn't willing to take that chance at 19 years old.*

Back when I was in the 8th grade, Judy was the 8th grade representative for the Middlesex High School Homecoming Court. Wayne Jessie was her escort and that broke my heart. I wanted to be her escort. *Maybe Wayne asked her. I didn't have much confidence at 13 or 19.* When I was in my 40s, I still had dreams that I was back in the 8th grade, and Judy and I were marching from the sidelines out to the 50-yard line. Her arm locked into the crook of my elbow with me showing all 32 of my teeth, but they were only dreams. Wayne was always nice to me when lots of other kids weren't in Middlesex. But my first thought of Wayne Jessie was that he took *my* girl out to the 50-yard line. I don't remember who was selected as Homecoming Queen my first and only year at Middlesex High School because I didn't watch the half-time ceremony. I had no interest in seeing Judy with another man!

When Wayne's mom, Mrs. Amy Jessie, passed away about 30 years later, I called to tell him that I wouldn't be able to attend the funeral. His mother was extremely nice to me the last year that I lived in Middlesex County. During 8th grade, Grandma Latimore made my school lunch each morning, a jelly sandwich. Every day it was the same thing, a jelly sandwich. I hated it, but it was all we could afford. Some days I was able to scrounge up 35 cents to buy a cafeteria lunch and a carton of milk. Mrs. Jessie was the cashier, and she knew that I wouldn't be able to come up with 35 cents *every* day. By the second week of school, I guess she had figured out I was sick of Grandma's jelly sandwiches. I was about to drop 35 cents into her open palm when she closed it, winked at me and said, "Thank you, have a nice day!" She "rang" me up as though I had paid. The next day, she did it again. She did it each time I came through her line for the entire school year. Some school days, Grandma's jelly sandwiches were enough for me and other days they weren't. I thanked Mrs. Jessie as she "winked" me through her line, but I didn't get around to doing that when I was older. I regretted that. Thanks to Wayne's mom, I didn't have to sit in the cafeteria and stare at my jelly sandwich or act like I wasn't hungry. *I never forgot Mrs. Jessie's kindness, but I never forgave her son for escorting Judy Kidd!*

I got out of the U.S. Air Force in the fall of 1995. C-Y's mother passed away around that time, and Mumma and I attended the funeral. I was standing in the churchyard and chatting with Renee, who I hadn't seen in a very long time. A woman approached us, and as she got closer, I realized it was Judy. She said, "You may not recognize me because I haven't seen y'all in so long. I'm Ju-" I stopped her before she could get the second syllable out. Fifteen years after *Macbeth,* did she think that I didn't know who she was? I said, "Judith Lorraine Kidd, I would know you anywhere, anytime, anyplace! I have loved you all of my life and always will. I *still* say a prayer for you every night!" That was the truth.

Judy was the smartest kid in my class from 1st through 8th grade, and nothing changed once I moved away. She became the 1979 Middlesex High School valedictorian. She graduated from William and Mary and eventually received a law degree from there as well. She spent her life caring for her parents until they passed away. Her mom, the elementary school secretary, had the most attended funeral in Middlesex County. Some said there were more people at her funeral than Lt. Gen. Lewis "Chesty" Puller's in 1971. Mrs. Kidd was a well-respected lady who had a kind word for every kid that came through Rappahannock Central Elementary School. I always loved her daughter, Judy Kidd. She was the girl with the pretty pigtails in the white dress decorated with blue and yellow flowers. She marked the beginning of an admiration and infatuation with beautiful women that would affect the rest of my life. *I always liked the pretty ones!*

Me, 1st grade. 1967

CHAPTER 12

As a boy, I got my hair cut at Mr. Sammy Key's barbershop about a mile outside of Urbanna on Route 227. It was a cement building painted white, with hedge bushes decorating its front. It was a fun place to be, and I loved going there with Da when I was 6, 7 and 8 years old. At Mr. Key's place, you could buy a candy bar, grab a Coke, get your haircut or pay your life insurance bill because Mr. Key was also the insurance man for pretty much every black family in Middlesex County. On the left side of the building was the "beauty parlor" for women to get their hair fixed. In the middle, there was a small snack bar area and on the right-hand side of the building were two rooms, one for barbering and one for shooting pool. In Mr. Key's barber room, there were two chairs, but I was never sure why he had *two* of them because *he* was the only barber that I remember. The male customers sat on two long, black leather couches that were nestled along the cinder block wall, or they shot pool while waiting their turn in Mr. Key's swiveling, leather barber chair. A snap of his apron signaled to the patrons, "Whoever is next in line, it's your turn!" WANN-AM out of Annapolis blared from the tiny radio behind his chair, and I loved listening to the "Hoppy" Adams Show. WANN was a black radio station at 1220 on the dial. Its low signal reached Middlesex County only during the day. At night, its signal faded, and most of the people that I knew changed their radio dials to 1510-WLAC out of Nashville. WLAC was a 50,000-watt clear channel AM station that reached the entire East Coast and much of the South and Midwest. At dawn, WLAC's

50,000 watts went faint, and most dials were returned to WANN or 850-WRAP out of Norfolk.

Walking into Mr. Key's barbershop at my eye level was a wooden counter with swinging doors where Mr. Key served treats to anyone desiring something for their sweet tooth. The counter held a Plexiglass encasement that contained many of the items that Mumma warned would kill me. Nabisco Cheese Nabs, Wise Potato Chips, Dentyne gum, Beechnut gum, Wrigley's Spearmint gum, Juicy Fruit gum, Doublemint gum and candy bars! There were all kinds of 'em: Mars, Mounds, Almond Joy, Hershey's, Hershey's with Almonds, Clark Bars. It seemed like there were a million of them. *Maybe death by candy bar wasn't a bad way to go!*

There were four wooden blocks that supported a bulky, red Coca-Cola soda cooler. *I loved that machine.* Unlike the soda machines that came later and dispatched a bottle by simply pressing a button, Mr. Key's machine required a little work on your part. "Mr. Soda Man" (that's what the black kids called the white men who drove the soda trucks that left the cold drinks at the barbershop, "Hi, Mr. Soda Man") stacked the crates full of soda against the rear wall of the snack bar area. Mr. Key removed the sodas from the crates as needed and placed them in his Coca-Cola appliance. A small electric motor chilled the water to keep the sodas cool. The water was just deep enough that only the caps on the tall 16-ounce glass bottles were exposed. Adults could easily read those caps with the brand name stamped on them to grab the soda of their choice. Kids could not. We had to tiptoe or stand on a crate that Mr. Key left on the floor and dip our hands in the nearly freezing water to grab a bottle by the neck to see what we had retrieved. It usually took me three or four stabs before I found the one I wanted, but it sure was fun watching the skin on my hand wrinkle like Prune Face's from the *Dick Tracy* comic book. Some kids liked Dr. Pepper. Some liked Pepsi. Some liked a chocolate soda called Yoo-hoo. My favorite was Nehi Grape. Sometimes, my buddies and I tried to see who could keep their hands in the cold water the longest. After 30 seconds or so, most of us pulled back with a shiver, but I don't ever remember Mr. Key yelling at us for playing in the cold water. He was a nice man with a very pleasant disposition. *I can still hear his laugh.*

Mr. Key's wife was Drucilla, and she fixed hair for the Negro women in Middlesex who lived "up the county." Ladies who lived "down the county" went to Mrs. Grace Roy. Mrs. Key died from breast cancer when I was about 5 or 6. The word "cancer" was taboo in the 1960s, and it was certainly *not* to be mentioned in Grandma and Grandpop Latimore's house. I found this out the hard way after receiving a smack in the face by some aunt or uncle when I said, "I heard Walter Cronkite say on the news that 'Cigarette smoking was dangerous to your health and could cause cancer'" after I saw someone light a cigarette in the living room. That was around 1966, and I didn't say that "C-word" for a long time. Grandma Latimore lost two sisters to breast cancer in the late 1940s, and later, Grandpop Latimore contracted colon, prostate and bladder cancer in 1964, and that almost killed him. Nonetheless, he lived for another 42 years. In fact, he lived two years longer than Da, and no one expected that. *I know I didn't.*

Mumma told me that I gave Mr. Key an awful time as a toddler. According to her, Mr. Key had the Patience of Job to put up with my shenanigans in his booster chair. Mumma and four of my uncles were needed to control me in that chair as I squirmed every which way to keep my curly hair away from Mr. Key's clippers. Mumma said I even foamed at the mouth! Each uncle was assigned a limb while Mumma did her best to hold my head still. I think it was the heat from the clippers and the crackling sounds that came from them that scared me. Every time we pulled into his parking lot, it became a sideshow for those present on the "male" side of the building, but Mr. Key only shook his head in amusement. Mumma said, "God bless Sammy Key, I don't know how he put up with you. I never saw anything like it! You were a Tasmanian devil in that chair, and he never complained!"

Around the time I started school, haircuts no longer required "limb" assistance. I was now a big boy with an even bigger head (at least Butley Jarvis said I had a big one). After my haircut, I swept snippets of hair from Mr. Key's linoleum covered floor into a dustpan and dumped the remains into the trashcan below the shelf that housed clippers and hair grease. My reward was a pack of Doublemint gum.

It was my favorite because Da liked it, too. "Mr. Key, you're gonna give me a *whole* pack of chewing gum for just sweeping hair? Can I do this *every* day?" *That* made him really laugh. One evening, C-Y's youngest son, Arnold, walked into the snack bar area to buy a pack of Doublemint. I offered him a few sticks of mine. "Mr. Key gives me a whole pack every time I sweep up!" He took a couple of sticks from my green pack of Doublemint and said, "Shoot man, that's stupid. That's *all* you get is a pack of gum? He's using you." Arnold was around 10 or so, and I was 6. From my perspective, Arnold was more worldly than I could ever dream of becoming. Whatever a 10-year-old said had to be the truth. *I think Arnold's right, Mr. Key is using me.*

On my next visit, I grabbed the broom and dustpan from the corner to begin my sweeping routine, but my heart wasn't in it. Once done, I sat and waited for Mr. Key to pay me. When he finished cutting Da's hair, he told me to wait for him at the counter. He placed the pack of Doublemint in my hand, then kneeled and said, "Chopper, last time you were here, I heard what Arnold said to you." I lowered my head. "Let me ask you this." "Yes, sir?" He paused for a few moments to stare at something on the floor and seemed to be deep in thought. "Are you happy with a pack of Doublemint?" I bashfully said, "Yes, sir." He stood and said something that I never forgot. "Son, if you are happy with what you're getting, that's all that matters. Don't let Arnold Johnson or anyone else tell you what makes you happy." Over the years, I never forgot Mr. Key's statement. He was right. I *was* content with a pack of gum. Why should I allow anyone to determine *my* happiness? It was 7 sticks of free gum, for God's sake! At that time, I was 6 years old, and later in life, others did influence me, but I always heard Mr. Key saying, "Don't let anyone else tell you what makes you happy." Mr. Key offered *gas money* for the rest of my life.

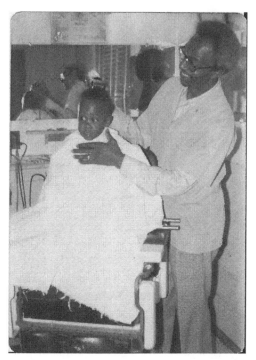

Mr. Sammy Key cutting his grandson's hair. 1974

A Coca-Cola machine like the one at Mr. Key's barbershop. 2012

CHAPTER 13

The Middlesex County Public Schools officially integrated in September of 1969, 3rd grade for me. My 2nd grade classmates and I were not looking forward to integration because we were afraid that the white teachers wouldn't be nice to us. We thought they would pass the white students whom they previously taught at all-white Middlesex Elementary and Wilton Elementary Schools and fail the black kids from Rappahannock Central Elementary. We wanted no part of integration. Things were fine as far as we were concerned. Plus, we felt the white players would mess up our high school basketball team that went undefeated the year before we integrated! However, 3rd grade marked the first time that we received new textbooks instead of "hand-me-downs" from the white schools. We also got a few new school buses, too, as opposed to the older buses that the white schools didn't want anymore. *Maybe this integration stuff wasn't so bad after all!*

As the first day of school began, I again sat right in front of the teacher's desk. Slowly flipping through one of my new textbooks, a white lady in her 60s placed her hand on my shoulder and asked my name. "Hello, ma'am. My name is Troy Lewis." Mrs. Ruth St. John smiled and said, "Well, I've heard a lot of good things about you, Troy Lewis. I'm glad you're in my class." She was off to introduce herself to the other black kids that didn't know her. I was confused. I thought these white teachers were going to be prejudiced. The black kids had been using that word repeatedly for the past year. *This lady seems kind of nice.* Mrs. St. John was nice to everyone. She treated me fairly, and that was all I could have asked for. That being said, she would kill me for placing a preposition at the end of a sentence!

Mrs. St. John was also the first teacher to send me to the principal's office. *There would be plenty more of those.* At recess, a bunch of 3rd and 4th grade boys, including me, climbed up on a large mound of dirt to play "King of the Hill." Becoming the King required climbing to the top and pushing or throwing others off. We knew we shouldn't have been up there, but that didn't stop us! Mrs. St. John was speaking with a couple of other teachers over by the big oak tree in the middle of the playground when she spied our bad behavior. She marched over and shouted, "All of you get down from there and head straight to Mr. Bass' office!" *Uh oh.* The five or six of us evildoers trekked down to the principal's office. Mrs. Kidd asked why we were there, and we all looked down at our sneakers like the answers lay within our Converse. She said, "Come on, let's hear it." I never looked at her, but I said, "We climbed up on the hill." She sighed and had us line up against the painted white wall of her office that she worked in for more than 30 years. She knocked on Mr. Bass' door. *Mrs. Kidd will never let Judy marry me now because I'm a bad boy.* Mr. Bass woke me from my brief daydream by calling each of us into his office one by one. Waiting turns to get our buttocks whacked by Mr. Bass' ruler seemed to take forever. I think the anticipation of his wallops was worse than the act itself. Each of us "bad" boys received about four or five of those from him. I *never* climbed up that hill again. Corporal punishment worked just fine as a deterrent for my behind.

Even though Mrs. St. John sent me to Mr. Bass' office, I wasn't mad at her. *To be honest, I was surprised that I made it all the way to 3rd grade before that happened!* I knew I was doing something wrong. I also knew that Mumma had a "hotline" to Mrs. Kidd's office, and she and Da were gonna hit me much harder than Mr. Bass did once I got home. But it was funny how sometimes things worked out. Sometimes, the people you think you won't like, you grow to love, and the people you think that you are going to love forever, after a few days or weeks, wind up driving you crazy! I thought Mrs. St.

John was going to be an unpleasant person simply because her skin was different than mine. She became my favorite teacher because she was unbiased at a time when I thought all whites would be unfair. It was what I'd been hearing at school for the past year. She taught me to not prejudge people, and when I got home from school, I ran to the dictionary to look up the word "prejudice." I learned that its definition was "to form a preconceived opinion without merit." That was what my fellow 2nd graders and I had done before we integrated. I often wondered how my thought process would have been altered had Mrs. St. John been what *we* thought she was going to be. How would *that* have impacted me? I learned to treat *all* people according to how they treated me. Most that I encountered were nice people, but there was always the occasional jerk!

In 1986, I married the older woman that I had been seeking since Aunt Jenny. Her name was Lori, and we were married for a little over 10 years. Things didn't work out (about 90 percent of that was my fault), but even after we broke up we remained very close friends. I'd do anything for her. She'd do anything for me. Around 1989, we were back in Middlesex County for a visit. While we sat at the light in Saluda that Aunt Jenny disliked, I said to Lori, "You know what? I'm going to stop to see Mrs. St. John." Lori shot me a look of disbelief. "Troy, that lady is not gonna remember you. She's got to be close to 80, 85 by now!" "Well, if she is alive, she'll remember me because I was always her favorite!" "Oh be quiet, you thought you were *everyone's* favorite, but I'll bet you a dollar she won't even know who you are!" We pulled into Mrs. St. John's driveway and walked through her yard to knock on her front porch screen door. A now much older Mrs. St. John slowly made her way to the front porch. "Hi, Mrs. St. John!" With the 20 years that had passed since our first encounter, she looked at me and paused for a few moments while trying to remember who I was. Then she said, "Well, Troy Lewis, where have you been? Come on in here and have some tea with me. Tell me what's going on in your life." Her eyes fixed on Lori and then returned to me. "Is that your wife?" "Yes, ma'am." Mrs. St. John then looked directly at Lori and said, "*He* was always my favorite!" As we walked into Mrs. St. John's living room, I grinned at Lori while she rolled her eyes. *She owed me a dollar!*

Mrs. Ruth St. John's 3rd Grade Class. 1969
Me, 1st Row, 7th from the left.
Judy Kidd, Basil Holiday, and Renee Johnson,
2nd Row, 4th, 5th, and 9th from the left.
Larry South, 3rd Row, 7th from the left.

CHAPTER 14

On Christmas Eve of 1969, we moved into our new home at Christchurch. The house was across the road from Christchurch Episcopal School, an all-white, all-male private boarding school for 9th–12th graders that opened in 1921. Lanny Stanley became its first black student in September of 1970. *That was a big deal when he enrolled.* He was a 17-year-old junior, and I clung to him like he was an older brother. He played on the football team as a wide receiver and kick returner and ran sprints for the track team. He was as close to a celebrity as we got in the black community at that time. Sometimes, he went with me to Middlesex High School basketball games, and the black girls stared at him like he was an early-day Denzel Washington.

(Insert "You're The Reason Why" by The Ebonys) After football practice, I followed Lanny up to his dorm room where he helped me with my homework while working on his. He liked listening to War, Santana, or The Ebonys who had a hit with the song "You're the Reason Why." In my falsetto voice, I sang the opening, *"Buh-buh-buh-buh-buh, buh-buh-buh-buh-buh-buh-buhhhhhh. Yeah!!!!!"* He crooned in his baritone voice, *"Baby, baby, baby. Baby, baby, baby."* I screamed, *"Just because of you, I'm a happy guy, you're the reason why!"* That was our song!

I often invited Lanny over to our place for dinner, and Mumma liked making him a home-cooked meal. I admired Lanny, but I never told him that. I thought he was brave in being the first black student, but I didn't know how to say *that* to him. That would have been awkward for a 9-year-old to tell a 17-year-old in 1970 (or today). I can't imagine what he went through. I never saw ugliness directed toward him, but I was sure it happened. Then again, I was only 9. *How much could I really see?*

Lanny didn't come to the school until my second year living at Christchurch. Until his arrival, other than the custodial and kitchen staff, I was the only black face on campus. That didn't stop me from having fun "across the road," the term I used to let Mumma and Da know my whereabouts. "I'm going across the road!" The day after Christmas, I looked out my bedroom window and noticed six white kids tossing a football. There were no black kids for me to play with living down at Christchurch, so I said to myself, "I'm gonna go play with them." That's how I met Ken and Dale Pollock, Eddie and Margaret Bunting, Jennifer Davies and Paul Kerr. Their fathers taught at the school, and those kids *and* their parents were very nice to me. Race was never an issue. Another white kid named Carl lived about a half mile away from the school. He was a local kid with no affiliation with Christchurch School. He was an 8th or 9th grader at Middlesex High School when I was a 3rd grader. He was no fan of black people or maybe he just didn't like me for some reason. One day, my new buddies and I were playing touch football when Carl rode by on his bicycle. He dropped his bike and trotted over to join us. He looked at me, then the others, and casually said for all to hear, "Since when did y'all start playing with niggers?" Ken, who was in high school, punched Carl in the mouth, making his lip bleed. After that, Carl never came around, but we always saw him riding his bike and staring at us. It was the first time I heard the "N" word. *I never did like Carl.*

My favorite expression became "Mumma, I'm going across the road!" My brand new Sears bike that I got for Christmas took me over to Christchurch. It was blue, green and yellow with a banana seat! I loved that bike, but I could never *ride* it across 33 to play. I wasn't proficient at looking "left, right and left again." That was what Da insisted I do when crossing any intersection, but I failed that exercise miserably when I was in the 2nd grade.

CHAPTER 15

In 1968, I was in 2nd grade, and we were still living at Grandma and Grandpop Latimore's house. I was late to the school bus one morning because, as usual, my outfit hadn't passed Mumma's inspection. As I ran to get on the bus, I paid more attention to the chill and fog than I did the road that I needed to cross. Had I missed the bus, Mumma would have to drive me the 2 miles to Rappahannock Central Elementary, and *that* would *not* have been a good start to a school day. That could be the *longest* 2-mile stretch in the county! "I told your ass to get up and wash your face and brush your teeth. Maybe tomorrow you'll get up on time, or you will *walk* to school!"

I sprinted from the front porch past the maple tree and the two evergreen shrubs that nestled the right side of our front yard. I didn't stop to *see* if headlights were approaching because I didn't *hear* any cars coming. I leapt from our embankment onto the asphalt that was 33 and almost died. In that instant, I heard tires screech and a truck horn blare while I inhaled the scent of burnt rubber. I stopped my forward momentum by planting a foot and lunging backwards onto the embankment. Schoolbooks and my Wild, Wild West tin lunch box that I begged Mumma to get me (because I didn't like the Bonanza one anymore) lay scattered next to me as I sat on the ground thinking, "Where did that come from?" It was Mr. Sam Miles in his lumber truck. He must have been going 60 miles per hour, and I never heard a sound! After coming to a complete stop a few more feet down 33, he craned his neck out of his truck window to ask, "You alright, boy?" "Yes, sir. I'm okay." "God-dammit, you nearly gave me a heart attack. I'll be back to check on you this evening." He put his truck in first gear and took off down the road. "Shit" was a new word that Darnell and Tony had recently taught me, and I said that aloud as I sat on the embankment praying that Mumma hadn't witnessed that scene. *How was I going to explain Mr. Miles stopping by the house that evening to check on me? Shit!* I gathered my books and my lunch pail and snuck a peek back at the house. I wouldn't need to explain why Mr. Miles was dropping by that evening. Mumma was standing on the front porch in her housecoat. She had seen everything! *Fuck!* That was another new word Darnell and Tony had taught me. She hollered, "Yeah, I saw it, and I will see your black ass when you get home from school!" *Shit! Fuck! Shit!* All day at school, I wished Mr. Miles had run me over instead of hitting his brakes. That certainly would have been better than facing Mumma *and* Da *and* Mr. Miles that evening. I think it was the worst spanking I ever got. But again, corporal punishment worked because I never failed to look "left, right and left" again. About a year or so later, a new friend came into my life who assisted me in crossing highways, but that's another story.

As promised, Mr. Miles stopped by the house that evening, and he gave me a couple of whacks across the butt for good measure because he was still mad at me for scaring him! When I was in my 40s, every now and then I ran into Mr. Miles at the Exxon gas station in Saluda, and he stared at me while trying to recall my face. His eyes went from me to my New Jersey license plates and then back to my face. "Ain't you Bill and Jean's boy?" "Yes, sir. I am. How you doin', Mr. Miles?" "You know, you scared the shit outta me back in 1968!" "Yeah, I remember, Mr. Miles. Sorry about that." I continued pumping gas while keeping an eye on him because I was always afraid he'd yank his belt off and give me a few more swats. Mr. Sam Miles was a *crazy* man. *I wouldn't have been surprised if he had tried!*

There was a guy who roamed the highways of Middlesex County, and I was told that he was related to Mr. Miles somehow. I often wondered if every community had someone similar to the Arthur "Boo" Radley character from Harper Lee's *To Kill a Mockingbird*.

A person everyone avoids. We certainly had our version of "Boo" Radley. His name was John the Baptist, and he walked the highways searching for discarded glass bottles and metal cans to put in his burlap bag for cash at the grocery store in Urbanna. John the Baptist was Middlesex County's boogeyman, as far as I was concerned. Darnell and Tony scared me to death with their stories of that guy. Even as an adult, I never stopped sleeping with a blanket or sheet over my head. I was still afraid that John the Baptist might snatch me in the middle of the night if my head was uncovered!

(Insert "Runaway Child" by The Temptations) My uncles told me John the Baptist snuck into homes in the middle of the night to steal children. He placed them in his burlap bag for various infractions like failing to do homework, not eating vegetables, receiving D's or F's on report cards, disrespecting elders or not doing a good job of cleaning pots. Whenever John the Baptist walked down 33 toward our house, Darnell yelled at me when I was planted in front of the television. "Hey, have you done your homework yet? "No, not yet. I'm watching TV!" "Well, you better get going because I think I see John the Baptist coming, and you know he likes picking up lazy, little punks that don't do what they're supposed to!" I crept toward the front porch and hid behind Darnell and Tony as John the Baptist marched closer. Tony said, "Man, he's strong. He's probably got two or three kids in that bag along with all of those bottles. Listen. I think I just heard a kid yell, 'I want my Mama!'" Then, he mimicked Eddie Kendricks of The Temptations singing "Runaway Child." I whispered, "I don't hear nothing." "He takes kids who don't speak good English, too. You just used a double negative." *Like I knew what that was!* "Plus, you still have way too much wax in your ears to hear good. You better go get a Q-Tip because John the Baptist likes to eat the wax outta kids' ears, too!" He then hollered out to John the Baptist from the front porch steps, "Hey, John the Baptist, how you doin' today? You got everything you looking for?" He tried putting me in a headlock before I escaped and ran back inside the house. John the Baptist kept walking. His eyes were focused on the asphalt ahead of him. He sometimes nodded in Tony's direction, but I don't ever recall him speaking. He just minded his business and continued on his way. He was harmless just like Arthur "Boo" Radley.

Tony Latimore. 1971
Anything he said, I believed!

CHAPTER 16

When we moved from Grandma and Grandpop Latimore's house, I moved away from my buddy, William Kemp, who lived across the road from us. The end of their driveway was where we caught the school bus, and that was where I met Mr. Miles' lumber truck in 2nd grade. William and I were born a few months apart, and we caught the bus with his older brothers and sisters who were closer in age to Pat-Pat, Eddie, Ronnie, Darnell and Tony. His oldest sister was Barbara Jean (but we pronounced it "Ba-ba" Jean). She named her sons William and Troy, because William and I were so close when we were growing up. We never fought. I guess she hoped *her* William and Troy would follow in our footsteps.

Waiting for the school bus on the morning of December 11th of 1967 was how I learned James Brown "killed" Otis Redding. Tony said that he heard on the radio that Mr. Redding's plane crashed in Wisconsin last night. *Capital: Madison! The Badger State!* He said, "Now, y'all know doggone well James Brown paid that mechanic to make his plane go down. He knew he wasn't gonna be 'Soul Brother No. 1' no more! Otis was starting to sell too many records." There were about eight of us waiting for the bus, and they all laughed at Tony, but I believed him because I believed *everything* Charles Anthony "Tony" Latimore ever said! Whenever James Brown came on the car radio, I asked Mumma or Da to change the station for years. One day, Da finally asked, "Why don't you like James Brown?" "I hate that guy. He killed Otis Redding!" "What?

Where on Earth did you hear that?" "Tony told me when I was in 1st grade. James Brown is a murderer. He paid that mechanic to crash Otis Redding's plane, but they could never prove it." It took a long time before I figured out that James Brown had nothing to do with Otis Redding's plane crash. *Tony Latimore was very persuasive!*

I wasn't sure if Mumma and Da worried about me riding my bike at Christchurch School. It was a private institution, and I had no reason to be over there. But there were no kids for me to play with for at least a mile in either direction except the white kids, so the Christchurch campus became *my* playground. I was 8 years old, and each day over there was an adventure. I said "Hi" to everyone, from the custodial and kitchen staff (all black) to the teachers and students (all white). The black staff already knew me as "Bill and Jean's boy from the new house across the road," but I was a new face to the white people at Christchurch.

I learned the layout of the campus and, whenever possible, introduced myself to incoming freshmen and their parents while providing them with a layout of the campus. "That's where the cafeteria is, over there is the P-X, and under the Old Gym they just put in some pool tables, some Ping-Pong tables and a weight room. Now, over there is the study hall and down the hill are the tennis courts. Go down that dirt road about half a mile and you'll find the swimming pool." I became an "unofficial" tour guide. I even sat in the rear of classes at night and during summer school to try to learn chemistry, algebra, English literature or whatever else was being taught. The New Gym was my favorite place to hang out. With my two-hand set shot, I pretended I was Oscar Robertson, and any shot that I took in the paint I imitated Lew Alcindor. Coach John Brown, the Christchurch varsity basketball coach, showed me how to turn on the lights, and his gym became my home away from home. "Just put the balls back in the rack when you're done." He let me have the run of place as long as there wasn't practice or intramurals going on, and even then, he let me sit next to him on the bench as he ran things.

(Insert "I'd Love to Change the World" by Ten Years After) Juniors and seniors lived in the New Dorm, and the freshmen and sophomores lived in the Old Dorm. Both dorms blasted music from their dorm windows; Led Zeppelin, Steppenwolf and The Moody Blues helped shape the music that I grew to like. For the rest of my life, whenever I heard the song "I'd Love to Change the World," it took me back to riding my bike around that campus, without a care in the world and doing whatever I wanted. I'm sure some of the white people may have thought, "Who in the hell is the little black kid roaming around like he owns the place?" I was oblivious and too naive to understand that I shouldn't have been over there. I had Mrs. St. John to thank for that. She helped make me feel comfortable around *all* people.

Mr. William P. Shields was Christchurch's Headmaster, and if I remember right, the 1969–70 school year was his first. One day, he motioned for me to come over, and asked, "Do you know who I am?" I said, "Yes, sir. I do." He put his hands on his hips and chuckled, "Okay. Who am I?" I said, "You're the B-M-O-C." He laughed even more. "Do you know what a B-M-O-C is?" "No, sir. But that's what I heard some of the juniors and seniors calling you." He got a kick out of that! He explained to me that B-M-O-C was an acronym that meant "Big Man on Campus." *He really was a big man!* "What's an a-kro-nim?" "Well, at least you know to put 'an' before a vowel. If you want to know what an 'a-cro-nym' is, go home and look it up, then the next time you see me, you can give me the definition." *God, he's just like Mumma!* He explained that he was the new headmaster, and if I didn't know what a "headmaster" was that I should also go look that up in the dictionary, too. *Good God, he does know Mumma!* He then bent down on one knee to get even with my eye level and softly said, "If you ever have *any* problems on this campus with *anyone*, you find me and let me know about it." "Yes, sir." He was gone. Our exchange took maybe 60 seconds. Looking back, I never realized all of the things that could have gone wrong for me at Christchurch School in 1969. *It was a crazy time, the 1960s and 70s.* Thankfully, nothing bad happened to me other than the incident with Carl, and Ken Pollock took care of that for me! Mr. Shields made me feel like *his* campus was *my* campus.

I didn't know what became of Mr. Shields and his family after we moved away from Christchurch a few years later. Mrs. Shields was

from England; well, at least she had an *English* accent. I didn't know
I was supposed to say it was a *British* accent until she corrected me
one day. *Are you kidding me, Mrs. Shields, I'm 8 years old! Aren't
British and English the same thing?*

The *Southside Sentinel* was the Middlesex County weekly paper
owned by Mr. Fred and Mrs. Gail Gaskins. Mrs. Gaskins was one
of my 7th grade teachers. She drove a 1970 yellow Opel like the one
Maxwell Smart drove in his TV show, *Get Smart.* Mrs. Gaskins was
a really nice looking lady. *God, she had great legs!* During the summer of 1970, an article appeared in the *Sentinel* announcing that
Christchurch School was offering free swim lessons for *any* kids in
the county who wanted to learn. The Christchurch School bus went
around the county to pick up black kids and bring them back to the
pool. No white kids came down for Mrs. Shields' lessons, and I was
sure they didn't want to set foot in the same water that we had been
in. What Mrs. Shields was doing was unheard of for that time in
Middlesex. There were only three pools in Middlesex County, one
in Urbanna, one in Deltaville and the one at Christchurch School.
The Urbanna and Deltaville pools were considered "public" pools
and were built with *everyone's* tax dollars, but not *everyone* could dip
their toes in the water. You had to be a town resident to swim in
Urbanna or Deltaville. Even if you didn't live there, as long as you
were white, you could just say you were visiting one of your white
town friends. None of *us* owned property in Urbanna or Deltaville,
so *we* had no swimming pools. We used rivers. If we wanted to go
"in the water," it meant going to the Rappahannock River, and even
parts of *that* were segregated. The "colored" sections were prone to
whirlpools and undercurrents.

I was sure some whites resented Mrs. Shields for opening the Christchurch pool to the black children of Middlesex County. I think she
was ahead of her time, or maybe 1970 was the *right* time for things
to start changing. What I did know was that she and her husband
were nice to me and other black kids when they didn't have to be.
With all of the craziness in the late 1960s and early 1970s, I had a
million positive things happen to me at Christchurch School. I was
sure Mr. and Mrs. Shields had a lot to do with that.

Headmaster Residence at Christchurch School. 2012
Still looks the same as the day I met the B-M-O-C!

CHAPTER 17

When we lived at Grandma and Grandpop Latimore's house, we had a Boxer named Sam. Sam was playful with Da and me, but everyone else pretty much stayed away from him. He could be mean sometimes. His mouth was always open with saliva falling from it. *I thought his wagging tongue was where Aunt Dot's ham came from.* I loved that dog, but heartworms stopped him from barking on December 17, 1968, when I was in 2nd grade.

That morning, I was eating a bowl of Kellogg's Sugar Frosted Flakes before heading out to catch the bus. *"They're great! That's what Tony Tiger says!"* Da left the dining room table to place his empty cereal bowl on the kitchen counter before stepping out to warm up his Chevy pickup. It was a light brown, 1958 beat-up old thing that shifted "on the column." Before Da walked outside, I said to him, "Sam's dead." Da looked at me and then at Mumma. "What?" "Da, Sam always barks when the sun comes up. I didn't hear him this morning." Da ran outside to Sam's doghouse where we kept him tied under the walnut tree in the backyard. I got up from the table, put my cereal bowl next to his and watched from the back porch. Da stood over Sam with his hands on his hips and turned to look at me standing on the back porch. *I told you he was dead.*

Once we moved to Christchurch, we got two more dogs. The first dog I really liked. The second one was one that I despised. The second dog was a Chihuahua named Cha-Cha. I hated that little dog because Bridgette and I always felt Da cared more about Cha-Cha than he did us. Fleas and all, he loved that little dog. Mumma agreed on his infatuation with Cha-Cha, and the three of us used to laugh behind his back about it. *Flea-ridden Cha-Cha!* Cha-Cha could go into the living room and sit in the bay window. We couldn't. Cha-Cha could sit on the couch. Bridgette and I couldn't and neither could Mumma.

(Insert "Wildflower" by Skylark) Mumma liked to sneak naps on the sofa after we left for school in the morning and Da had gone to work. She liked to unwind from her midnight shift at the textile plant down near Williamsburg by listening to the Zenith record player they had recently bought. *"Zenith! The quality goes in before the name goes on!"* Years later Mumma told me about the time that her internal alarm clock failed to go off before Da came home for lunch. He had nothing to eat, and he was pissed. His lunch wasn't ready, and she was still asleep on the couch that was lime green with a floral print. He stood over her and asked, "What the fuck do you think you're doing?" He grabbed her by the hair and threw her onto the hardwood floor. "You know your ass ain't supposed to be on the sofa." Pulling herself up from the floor, Mumma forgot *her* place and said to Da, *"You* didn't buy this God-damned couch, Bill Lewis. *My* mom and dad did, and I will lay on it if I damn well please!" Like me crossing the road without looking both ways, that was a bad move on her part. Da punched her in the head, and she went down again. She pulled herself up from the floor, gathered what was left of her composure and slowly walked to the kitchen like a hurt little puppy. My Da had a mean streak.

I think Da enjoyed making Mumma feel small because it made her more like him. He was tiny in stature all throughout high school, only 4'11" when he graduated. A year later, when dating Mumma, he had grown a foot to 5'11". I think Da had lots of animosity because of his previous small stature. Maybe smacking Mumma around made him feel better. More powerful. I didn't know what made him mean, but sometimes he was.

Da never showed much emotion other than laughter. His anger took place behind a closed door or down in the basement. I only saw him cry twice. The *second* time I saw Da cry was at the emergency room after he suffered a stroke in 1996. The *first* time? Well, that was when Da ran over Cha-Cha after she darted under the wheels of his maroon 1970 Chevy pickup as he was backing up in the driveway. Boy, did he cry on that day. Mumma thought it was hilarious. She came into my bedroom and whispered to me, "Can you believe he's crying over that dumb-ass dog?" She turned around and walked out. Cha-Cha dying could make him cry, but not much else. Mumma called him "strange." "Strange" as in when they lived at Grandma and Grandpop's house, he would avoid eating at the dining room table with Mumma and her siblings. She never figured out what made him tick. *Neither did I.* How could we? Asking Da a "personal" question resulted in a grunt, a shrug of the shoulders, and an "I don't know."

In the summer, he sat alone on the front porch to watch the cars pass as he ate his "day old" fried chicken wings. Not the breasts or thighs or legs, only the wings that *had* to be cooked the day before. Sometimes a small salad accompanied his meal, but there were always mashed potatoes and peas. *Always.* Same old thing. Mashed potatoes and peas. Mumma used a large spoon to form a "well" in the mashed potatoes for his peas. If there were any pea juice in there, he wouldn't have liked that, and he'd tell her to re-fix his plate. *Or else.* In the winter, he ate from a TV table in front of the living room television watching *Gunsmoke* while everyone else ate in the dining room. He wanted his hamburgers prepared the same as his chicken wings, a day early. He had a preference for miniature meatballs flattened to form small burgers, like an early-day precursor to "sliders." They were warmed up in Reynolds Wrap aluminum foil the following day just like the wings. If she overheated them, he'd beat her later on that night in their bedroom. If she put too much French's Mustard on them, then that was another reason to get punched or kicked in the stomach. Something went on in Grandma and Grandpop Lewis' house that made Da and his older sister, Aunt Virginia, not quite as friendly as their younger siblings, Faye, Portia and Michael. Sometimes, I wished I knew what it was but, then again, maybe I didn't want to know.

Between Sam and Cha-Cha, was a dog named Joe Frazier. Yes, that was his name. We found him in our carport begging for something to eat one day, but, on the other hand, it was more like he found us. Da took one look at him and said, "That dog is so ugly we should call him Joe Frazier." I thought that was funny then because I worshipped Muhammad Ali. *There was no bigger Ali fan than me. Ever.* However, as I grew older, I felt the way Mr. Ali taunted Mr. Frazier was cruel, and I thought it was even more mean-spirited that Da chose that name for our dog. But I was too young to understand all of that then. Our new dog was a big, ugly mutt that Mumma gave some scraps to, and he ended up staying with us for a few years. Never did I think he would become my constant companion. He helped me go "across the road" to Christchurch School, and he growled when I failed to look both ways. It was almost like he was a seeing-eye dog. He waited outside the gym as I played basketball, and jogged alongside my bike as I pedaled from the New Gym to the track to the earthen ditch that I crossed to get home each evening. Joe Frazier sat on the sidelines and watched me play touch football with my buddies. Joe Frazier and I watched the Christchurch football and baseball teams perform against other white prep schools like Trinity, Virginia Episcopal, Collegiate, and Woodberry Forest that made up the Virginia Prep League. Joe Frazier and I watched Colonel Nunn lead his track team through drills until it got dark.

Colonel William Nunn possessed the most booming voice I'd *ever* heard. He was a strict disciplinarian, and maybe that was why he was a former Army colonel! *I didn't know he was a "real" Colonel who served in the Army during World War II until I Googled him 40 years later. I thought the guys on the track team called him "Colonel" because he yelled all the time!* I never ran track, but I certainly learned the science of baton exchanges from watching him teach. At the time, Lanny was the only black track athlete in the Prep League, but Colonel Nunn yelled at Lanny just like he yelled at anyone else. He did not discriminate!

No one ever called Joe Frazier, "Joe"; he was always "Joe Frazier." He was a large dog with a brown coat. "Husky" better described him, and he wasn't a particular breed, more of a mongrel than a type.

He strolled rather than pounced and galloped more than he sprinted. He was the most laid-back dog I had ever been around, then or since. *He was my buddy!* But the neatest thing about him was that he liked to attend church on Sundays. *I'll say it again.* Joe Frazier liked to attend church on Sundays. Joe Frazier showed up at all-white Christ Church Episcopal Church every Sunday morning like he was a member of the congregation. He allowed church members to settle into their pews while he hung out in the vestibule as though he were an usher. He took a seat on the floor, laid his head over his front paws and listened to Reverend Jere Bunting preach on Sunday mornings. *Of course, I never witnessed any of this.* This is what was relayed to me by the white church members, like Rev. Bunting or Mr. and Mrs. Pollock and the Christchurch students. Grocery shopping with Mumma over in Urbanna, various white ladies (men didn't grocery shop back then, or at least not in Middlesex County) would say to me, "Hi, Troy. I saw your dog at church on Sunday. He is so well behaved!" Another would add, "He never makes a sound. Just sits there and listens to Rev. Bunting's sermon, and when the benediction is over, he gets on his haunches and heads home. I've never seen anything like it." It was weird and hard to comprehend.

Parishioners liked Joe Frazier, and he liked them too, I guess. After church, they'd pat his head, call his name and tell him what a good dog he was. He'd wag his tongue and tail in reply. I'd wait a distance away from the church as he slowly made his way back to our house for his Sunday dinner. I always stayed about 20 yards away, mind you. There was *no* way I would have gone *inside* that church or onto the grounds to retrieve him. I felt comfortable on the school's campus, but even I knew that I couldn't go into that church. It was forbidden. The white parishioners might accept a dog attending their church. They would not have accepted me or anyone else like me on Sunday mornings to listen to Rev. Bunting. Not in 1968 or 1969 or 1970 or 1971, anyway. Rev. Dr. Martin Luther King, Jr. was correct when he said, "It is appalling that the most segregated hour of Christian America is 11 o'clock on Sunday morning." Well, that's certainly how it was in Middlesex County when I grew up.

A dictionary will tell you that a mystic is someone who desires to know the deeper meaning of life through a more intense spiritual understanding. I wasn't sure what Joe Frazier was. At the time I thought he was just a dog. As I got older and reflected on Joe Frazier, I thought he may have been a reincarnated soul who came back to see the world from a different perspective. He certainly made my life better by helping me cross the busy highway. Joe Frazier was a lot better at judging the speed and distance of oncoming cars than I was. When it was safe to cross, he started and I followed. He certainly seemed content in all circumstances. Even at athletic events when the crowd was cheering, he remained calm. Even Colonel Nunn's starting pistol didn't faze him. He never barked, only growled. *He was just happy to be alive!*

I often wondered, if Joe Frazier was indeed a human in a previous life, was he black or white? Perhaps he came back to convince some that if it was okay for a *dog* to attend their church, just maybe a *black* person could one day as well. Maybe he was a man who came back as a dog and just wanted to watch some sports. He loved sporting events. He also liked attending the *all-white* Episcopal church. Maybe that was what he had done in a previous life. He certainly never ventured over to Calvary Baptist Church, the *black* church that was only 50 yards or so away. Maybe Joe Frazier was once a black man who wanted to see what a white church service was like. Maybe he took pleasure in the fact that he was a black soul trapped in a mutt's body, and he sat with whites in their church like it was *his* house of worship. *Who knew?* Joe Frazier was the most mild-mannered animal I ever came across, and Mumma agreed with that assessment. He was never animated or high-strung. He was a laid-back creature if we ever saw one. We had Joe Frazier for about two years and sadly, just as mysteriously as he showed up, he just as mysteriously disappeared. Vanished into thin air. Mumma, Da and I drove up and down 33 looking for him for a few days. We even searched the woods behind our property on Sundays after church. We thought maybe a car may have hit him, and he scampered off into the woods to lick his wounds. We never found him. He was gone. He came from nowhere and that was where he returned. We never took any pictures of Joe Frazier, but like most things, you don't need a picture to remember them. *I can see him now.* Maybe Joe Frazier went off to growl at some other little boy who failed to look "left, right and left again" before crossing the road. I hope that was where he went, anyway.

Christ Church Episcopal Church. Built in 1714. 2012
Joe Frazier's home away from home.

CHAPTER 18

Various people were in and out of my life, but one who never left was "Butley" Jarvis. His real name was James Monroe Jarvis, but anyone who grew up with him just called him Butley. We never lived more than a mile apart until I turned 13 and moved close to Williamsburg. Butley was only 2 years older than me, but he liked to think he was 20 years wiser. As a child, I never beat him at *any-thing* other than Ping-Pong, and that was only because I had a table to practice on, and he didn't! I never beat him at checkers, or games like Monopoly, Stratego, "dirt bomb" fights (I still had a scar on my scalp to prove it), or throwing a football. You name it, and I never beat him at it. Butley was injured in an accident at the Pulp Mill over in West Point when he was 29, and despite being paralyzed from the waist down, he could still beat me at shooting free throws! If I went 7 for 10, he'd go 8 for 10. If I went 8 for 10, he'd go 9 for 10. Out in his backyard, there we were in our 40s shooting free throws or playing "H-O-R-S-E." "Butley, I never play ball anymore. I haven't shot a basketball in years. Let's just go inside and watch the Carolina game." Always the good trash talker, he said, "C'mon, I'm in a wheelchair! What's wrong? Can't you beat a man in a wheel-chair?" As I said, I could only beat him at one thing.

Our parents were pretty close in age; Da even took Butley's mom, Rosetta, to the prom one year, but she's another story! Mr. and Mrs. Jarvis and their children often came down to our house, or we went up to theirs. Mr. Jarvis worked at the Pulp Mill for over 30 years, and Mrs. Jarvis drove Bus No. 25 for the Middlesex County Public School System for forever. Da remodeled the Jarvis house around 1970 by adding extra rooms and enclosing their porch.

Trey McLaurin was a kid who was a few years younger than Butley and me, and played with us whenever his parents stopped by the Jarvis'. I don't know how Butley felt, but I loved watching Trey's mother, Patricia McLaurin, walk because she had a great body and an even nicer butt! Well, I was only 9 or 10, but even then, I knew a nice butt when I saw one! Trey was 5 or 6 at the time, and whenever he was around, Butley and I were responsible for him. One day, I guess we weren't paying too much attention to him and before we knew it, Trey picked up one of Da's hammers to lift it over his head. It was too heavy for his little arms, and as he reared back, the hammer's claw became stuck in his scalp. Trey screamed! Da ran over to scoop him up, and whispered something in his ear that made him laugh as he slowly wiggled the claw from its awkward resting place. He handed Trey over to Mrs. Jarvis and Mrs. McLaurin for them to drop some Merthiolate into his wound. *I hated Merthiolate and Mercurochrome because they hurt more than the cut!* Ten minutes later, Trey was as good as new, running around and playing again like nothing ever happened!

Butley was fun to be around, but he enjoyed picking on me, and he never stopped! It was part of his personality. Mumma would say to me, "If ya don't like it, quit playing with him." I always went back for more. When we were in our 50s, we *still* got mad at each other over some sports argument or in the re-telling of a story from 1967 or 1974 or 2006. Often, we hung the phone up on each other like children. Then, three days later one of us would call the other like nothing ever happened. One of Da's sisters, my Aunt Portia, always said, "You and Butley? Both of y'all will always be 12!" We took that as a compliment!

Often in the evenings, Butley, his sisters Gwen and Kim, and Bridgette and I played Hide-n-Go-Seek in our backyards. For some odd reason, as darkness approached, Kim and I seemed to consistently have head-on collisions when trying to make it "home."

When the crying started, Mumma or Mrs. Jarvis would yell from the back window for us to stop and find something else to play because, "Y'all two clowns are gonna kill each other one day!" Kim and I staggered around the backyard seeing stars that hadn't yet appeared. We walked around in a daze with huge knots on our foreheads. In Middlesex County, we called those knots, "hickeys!" I later learned people up North referred to them as "eggs." *Eggs? That's what you eat!*

In the summer, Butley and I liked to catch lightning bugs in a Mason jar, punch holes in the tin top with a screwdriver for the bugs to breathe, then lie in his front yard and look up at the evening sky as the real stars began to dot the sky. Catching lightning bugs was fun or at least it was in Middlesex County. Using footballs as pillows, we lay on the grass with the jars on our chest and watched the lightning bugs flicker. Our conversations consisted of girls and sports, and those topics pretty much remained the same for the next 40 years! However, one evening, we began a "deep" discussion in the front yard that dealt with matters of geography and astronomy. Eight and six years old at the time, we gazed at the sky and contemplated what we were going to be when we grew up. Tiring of *that* serious conversation after a few seconds, I looked over at him and said, "You know what? Your head is as big as the state of Virginia." He replied, "Well, your head is as big as the United States!" I said, "Your head is as big as the world!" He responded with, "Your head is as big as the universe." I said, "What's a universe?" He said, "I don't know, but I hear it's pretty big!"

Gwen, Butley, and Kim Jarvis. 1966

CHAPTER 19

During the summer of 1971, I decided that I was "big" enough to ride my bike wherever *I* wanted. Since Mumma and Da finally trusted me enough to cross the road and ride my bike over to Christchurch, I figured, "Why not go a little farther than 300 yards?" At 10 years old, I decided to ride my bike about 2 miles up to Cook's Corner for some soda and a bag of potato chips. Cook's Corner was another "hole in the wall" joint that sold beer, had a couple of pool tables and a 15' X 15' square that served as a dance floor. In the 1950s and 1960s, it was one of the places where black people got together to have a good time in Middlesex County. I can close my eyes and still see the cars piled up in the small parking lot along 33 where their owners left them so they could go in and forget about their lives for a couple of hours. Mr. Len Davis owned the little honky-tonk joint, but it was called Cook's Corner because many Cooks lived in that area. I couldn't wait until I got old enough to hang out there, and I started doing that in the 8th grade. By then, Cook's Corner had seen better days.

(Insert "Drowning in the Sea of Love" by Joe Simon) It *wasn't* a smart move on my part to start hanging out there because I began doing dumb stuff with the people that I was "hanging" with. Stealing, gambling on pool, vandalizing. *Dumb stuff.* One day, Jimmy Davis, who was now running the place for his father, whispered to me as I was drinking a Mountain Dew and munching on Nabisco Cheese Nabs, "Why are you in here hanging out with *these* kids? You know you don't belong in here with *them*." He couldn't have been more accurate because those words ended my few weeks as a "hoodlum" before it ever really got started. For the few weeks of my criminal mischief, I constantly looked over my shoulder anticipating that the Middlesex County Sheriff would walk into Mrs. Tanner's 8th grade algebra class to arrest me. *What was I thinking?* For that matter, why would anyone want to lead the kind of life where they had to look over their shoulder all the time? A couple of weeks of doing that was more than enough for me!

In the 1960s, Cook's Corner wasn't the safest place to be. Fights took place there almost any night of the week, and there was no boxing ring. The intersection surrounding the Corner was just as precarious. Coming from Urbanna, State Route 227 ended as a triangular intersection. That little piece of road could kill you, and it did just that to a few unfortunate souls who failed to look "left, right and left again." Each lane of the 3-pronged fork compelled traffic to come to a complete stop with the oversized red octagonal stop signs that were posted. Very seldom did anyone do that; most chose a rolling stop instead. The left fork took you "down the county" and east on 33 toward Christchurch and Deltaville. If you took the middle road, you were headed towards Stormont, past Mr. Jake Kidd's house with its huge backyard where black men from neighboring counties came to play baseball against the Middlesex Blue Sox on Saturdays and Sundays during the summer. The right fork took you towards Saluda and west on 33.

Driving through Cook's Corner on a Friday or Saturday night was risky. There were cars creeping through searching for a spot to park and others backing up with occupants who more than likely were intoxicated. Nobody cared about drunk driving back then. Grandpop Latimore did that pretty much *every* day once he returned to Virginia. It was his drunk driving that allowed me to learn how to drive when I was 12, but that's another story!

People lined up to go inside Cook's Corner for a good time or they just hung out in the parking lot talking, smoking cigarettes (or something else) or pouring drinks from brown paper bags into Dixie paper cups. Once inside, they danced to music from the Wurlitzer jukebox or sat in booths to watch others on the small dance floor.

Every now and then, a small band might show up to play. Within Cook's Corner's walls, the slightest infraction could lead to a fist-fight. Looking at someone the "wrong" way or smashing an 8-ball in the "side" pocket when you had called for it to go in the "corner." Playing for money was taken very seriously.

About a half mile south of Cook's Corner on Route 227 took you to Herman Wake's Place. Mumma told me his Place was a little "classier of an establishment" than Cook's Corner. That may have been the case, but Darnell's buddy, James "Beaver" Curtis, got shot in the stomach at Mr. Wake's Place one night, and I couldn't believe that Da put a bloody "Beaver" in the backseat of his spotless GTO. *Why was James Curtis called "Beaver" anyway?* Mumma and Da drove him up to the hospital in Tappahannock to get him fixed up. Beaver survived. Every time he came over to our house afterwards, I begged him to lift his shirt and show me the bullet hole. *I had never seen one of those before!*

As a 10-year-old, I knew Cook's Corner was off-limits and that I should have not been riding my bike on 33 – too many vehicles and not enough shoulder room. *Bike paths? What the hell was a bike path in 1971?* Me riding on that road was an accident waiting to happen. So was attempting to go inside of Cook's Corner at 10 years old. Mumma didn't let Eddie, Ronnie, Darnell or Tony go in there until they were at least 15 or 16 to shoot pool. Why did I think it was okay for me to ride 2 miles up there on my bike? Grandma Latimore often told me that, "Boy, sometimes you don't have the good sense God gave you!" *She was right.* Mumma wasn't at home, so I figured I could scoot the 2 miles from Christchurch up to the Corner and be back before she got home. I hopped on my bike, got on the left shoulder and began my adventure up to Cook's Corner. Butley was outside shooting basketball as I pedaled by his house. I waved. He waved back and shouted, "Where are *you* going?" "Up to the Corner to get a soda and some potato chips," I yelled back. He had to be thinking, "I'm 12, and my parents don't let *me* ride up there, and it's only a quarter of a mile for me." I was thinking, "Take that, Butley Jarvis! I'm finally doing something you can't!" As the reddish orange flag attached to my bike waved in the breeze, I kept on pedaling! For about another 50 yards. The Corner was coming into sight at the same time as a brand new, lime green 1970 two-door Plymouth Duster 318 advanced toward me. *I know that car. It's the only one in Middlesex County that color. That's Mumma's car. Shit!* I came to a halt, straddled my bike and prayed that I would blend in with the scenery. *I didn't.* She pulled the car over onto the grass shoulder. The Duster was put in first gear, and she turned off the engine. A standoff ensued. She stared at me. I stared back at her. *My life is going to end right here on 33 all because I wanted a soda and bag of potato chips.*

Grandma Latimore *was* right. I didn't have the good sense that God gave me. I was pretty sure that Mumma had *two* thoughts on her mind. First, press the clutch, turn the ignition, release the clutch, step on the accelerator and run over me. Or, toss my bike in the trunk and beat the shit outta me when we got home. I would have liked it better if she had run me over! I think I would have rather been pulled over by a Virginia State Trooper for riding my bike on the wrong side of the road than by Mumma.

My feet were planted in the grass as I straddled the bicycle. I didn't budge. Finally, Mumma curled her index finger for me to come closer and open her car door because that was my job to open all doors for her. One of her favorite phrases was, "Your mother doesn't have any arms! Open it!" I opened her door, and she walked toward the rear, inserted the key and raised the trunk's lid. She never said a word. While I struggled to put my bike in the trunk, she plucked me in the back of my head. She returned to the driver's seat. I closed her door and walked around to sit next to her. I felt her eyes on me, but I wouldn't turn to face her. Total silence. She checked her side mirror, flipped the signal light lever and got back on 33. "Have you lost your God-damned mind? What the hell were you thinking?" were the first two questions. Many more followed in rapid fashion. My brain wasn't as quick as hers. I could only come up with one response: "I don't know." "Well, when we get home you will have plenty of time to think about it. I want you to put that God-damn bicycle in the storage room. Don't even think about going over Christchurch to play. Unplug the TV. Don't even touch a book. Just look at the four fucking walls in your bedroom and think about what you just did!" The breeze that once blew my bicycle flag had disappeared as had my anticipation of buying my first "drink" from Cook's Corner. The flag hung limply from the trunk. From the passenger seat, I saw Butley shooting basketball in his backyard out of the corner of my eye. He was smiling as he waved at Mumma's Duster as we passed by. I never waved back. *Butley Jarvis had defeated me once again.*

Although I would never defeat Butley at anything other than Ping-Pong, he would not allow anyone else to defeat me, either. A few years later, a few of my middle school buddies and I were in Butley's backyard shooting basketball. A couple of them asked me, "Hey, Troy? How's your Dad doing?" "What time do you think he's gonna come pick you up today?" They knew he wasn't coming. I knew he wasn't coming. Everybody in the county knew he wasn't coming. Da was gone and that was truly another story. It was sad knowing that my "friends" thought that was a funny situation. Maybe they were glad that I was in the same boat as them now. Fatherless. I had been close with most of them since 1st grade, but now in 7th grade, I found out that they didn't really like me after all. *That hurt.* Butley, who was bigger and stronger than all of us, looked at the kids who were making fun of me and said, "Knock it off. There'll be none of that shit today. And, if any of y'all have a problem with that, let's *talk* about it." He folded his arms, and it got real quiet. None of them wanted to tangle with Butley. Then, he and I played them "2 on 4" and killed them. Butley and I had perfected the "pick and roll" and "give and go" since he was in the 3rd grade and I was in the 1st. We learned everything we ever needed to know about basketball watching the Atlantic Coast Conference doubleheaders on Saturday afternoons and listening to Jim Thacker and Billy Packer call the games. Butley was a far better athlete than I ever dreamt of being, but he always said I was the "smartest" person he ever played ball with, and that was good enough for me.

As good as Butley and I thought we were, we could never beat his dad. He used to wear us out on that dirt court behind their house. Mr. Monroe Jarvis was a great player at St. Clare Walker High School in the mid-1950s, and I never knew that until the day he showed me his scrapbook filled with faded newspaper print. Each box score I read stated, "Jarvis, 44 points." "Jarvis, 38 points." "Jarvis, 40 points." "Wow, Mr. Jarvis, I never knew you were *that* good." "Troy, when you're good, you don't have to talk about it." *I never forgot that.*

Butley's accident at the Pulp Mill took place on May 12, 1989, a Friday night. I was in the Air Force stationed in Nebraska at the time when Bridgette called me at 8:00 on Saturday morning. I looked at the caller ID and knew it was bad news because *she* never called me. I picked up the phone, and my first question was, "Is Mumma dead?" "No." "Is Gerald dead?" "No." "Is Da dead?" "No." I said, "Good. Then I can handle anything else." She said, "It's bad news about Butley." I asked, "Is *he* dead?" She said, "No, it's worse. He's paralyzed from the waist down." My first thought was, "Wow, he'll never play basketball again." Butley played high school basketball and football and college basketball. The next day, my wife, Lori, and I drove from Nebraska to Virginia to visit him. As we pulled into the Norfolk General Hospital parking lot, I looked at Lori and said, "I can't do this. I can't go in there and see Butley like that." Lori looked at me and said, "Oh, grow up you big baby! This ain't about *you*, it's about Butley."

I prepared for the worst as we approached his hospital room door. I was very sad for what I thought awaited me, but I wasn't prepared for what I saw. Butley was sitting up in bed, playing cards with his sisters, Gwen and Kim, and his cousin, Niecey, like he didn't have a care in the world. He saw the sadness in my face and said, "Oh, Lord! Get out the Kleenex, here comes another crybaby!" Butley and I had never lost a basketball game of 2 on 2, 2 on 3, or 2 on 4 in our lives. We always knew what the other was thinking just by looking at each other since we were kids. He said, "Troy, I've got my whole life ahead of me. So what, I can't walk. I have a new wife, a new baby boy. I will be just fine. Niecey, hit me! I need another card."

Butley and his wife, Karen, raised their son and sent him off to college, and I never saw a better mother/son relationship than the one between Karen and Erik. The only thing that ever changed about Butley was that he never walked again. Stubbornness certainly never left him! Even though counseling was required for spinal cord injury victims, Butley wanted none of that. His motto was: "Just because I can't walk anymore doesn't mean my brain is paralyzed. It's no big deal." A few days after his accident, he was being wheeled down a hospital corridor for a physical therapy session. He overheard one physician whisper to another, "I'll give *that* one two weeks before he kills himself. He's in denial." That pissed Butley off. Before being allowed to go home, it was mandatory for Butley to speak with a psychiatrist. Butley wanted no part of that and that was why the physician had said that he was in denial. Aware that the hospital could outwait him, Butley finally gave in and went to see a psychiatrist. What ensued was a "staring down" contest between the two participants. Butley never said anything other than, "I'm fine." *Butley won again.* He hated losing. He never gave up on life. He was never depressed about getting "hurt." He and Mumma were the strongest people I ever knew.

Butley and me at a New York City restaurant. 2006

Butley and I were so much alike, yet so different. During most conversations, we finished each other's sentences for nearly 45 years. One time, when he was a 10th grade starter on the junior varsity basketball team and I was the team manager sitting at the end of the bench, the referee whistled Butley for "traveling" even though he hadn't lifted his pivot foot. Butley handed the ball to the official and stared at me. We both thought, "That's not a 'walk'!" We couldn't do anything about the ref's call, and I never forgot the look on his face. *Like I was going to get off the bench, take the ball from the ref's hand and correct him on the bad call!*

Butley dealt with his spinal injury and *never* complained about it. Even when he was going through rehabilitation, he told me that there were others far worse off than him. "I have nothing to complain about. Not one thing." Often, I wondered how I would have dealt with his type of adversity. Life provided me with my own adversity later on. I found out that I wasn't nearly as strong as Butley.

CHAPTER 20

(Insert "Let's Stay Together" by Al Green) Two things happened in the 5th grade that had a lasting impact on my life. First, I bought my cousin Renee a birthday present. It was Al Green's "Let's Stay Together." An expensive gift at 38 cents! I picked it up at Doc Marshall's Drug Store over in Urbanna. There were only two drug stores in Middlesex County, Doc Marshall's and the one "down the county" in Deltaville. Even though our family doctor, Dr. Harold Felton's office, was down there, we *never* spent money in the Deltaville Drug Store. If whites were mean to colored people in Middlesex, they were *really* mean in Deltaville. Well, at least that's what Mumma told me. "We don't use *our* money down there!" However, there were at least two white people who lived in Deltaville that I knew who were nice to colored/Negro/black people. One was Dr. Felton. The other? She's really another story.

"Are you sure you want to spend 38 cents on that record? That's a lot of money," Mumma said. But the look on Renee's face as she slid the 45 RPM from its jacket sleeve made it worth every penny. It was the first time I remember doing something nice for someone for no reason, and it made me want to do that for the rest of my life. Renee was my buddy. *Why wouldn't I want to do something nice for her?* She liked shooting basketball and throwing horseshoes and playing Hide-n-Go-Seek just like me. One time, the two of us read an article on tying knots and used our new skills to tie C-Y to the couch after she'd fallen asleep watching *The Edge of Night. Maybe that was why Renee joined the Coast Guard. I bet that branch of the military knew a thing or two about tying knots!* C-Y thought it was funny that she couldn't get up from the couch. Renee and I giggled for what seemed like hours until we looked out of C-Y's living window and saw Mumma pulling up. *All* of us knew that Mumma did not like kids *playing* with adults. C-Y said, "Y'all know you better hurry up and untie this rope before Jean walks in here!" *Renee and I hadn't thought about that.* When Mumma walked in she could tell by the expression on our faces that something was going on that shouldn't have been! "What have y'all been up to today?" C-Y laughed as she explained what we had done to her. Mumma barely smiled. She never let her guard down. Had we attempted to do something like that to her, it would not have been pretty. Mumma had plenty of bitterness to go around for anyone who came in contact with her. It took her a *long* time to let it go. She simply wasn't a happy person. *How could she be?* She had 8 freaking kids to take care of since high school and a husband who knocked the shit outta her if she put too much mustard on his hamburgers.

The second thing that had a huge impact on me in 5th grade was losing Mrs. Pollock. Her loss haunted me for the rest of my life and led me to never want children. Mrs. Jean Pollock lived at Christchurch School with her husband, Robert, an English teacher. They were Ken and Dale's parents. Dale and I were closer because only a year separated us. He taught me to play tennis and, more importantly, keep score, for which I was really thankful the first time I watched a tennis match on TV – Arthur Ashe defeating Jimmy Connors at the 1975 Wimbledon.

(Insert "Have You Seen Her" by The Chi-Lites) It was November of 1971 when Mrs. Pollock died in a car accident. She was only 37 years old. She was in a green 1972 Ford Squire station wagon with wood paneling when she was returning from a doctor's office visit in Tappahannock. I never found out what caused her accident. It could have been a tire blowout or she may have fallen asleep at the wheel. Maybe she overcompensated to avoid a deer. The cause didn't really matter. She was still dead.

Mumma called me into the dining room that evening and told me to have a seat. *Why is she telling me to take a seat now? We don't eat 'til 6:30! The CBS Evening News with Walter Cronkite* signaled that it was time to come to the dinner table, say the blessing, and see what was going on in the world on our Zenith television that sat on the wooden roll-away TV stand with clear plastic wheels. I only sat at the table to eat or do my homework, with the exception of Fridays. That was the day my weekly *Sports Illustrated* came, and Mumma placed it on the table with a glass of milk and a bag of Chips Ahoy Chocolate Chip Cookies she had picked up from the grocery store. *I liked Fridays!*

Mumma told me that Dale's mother had died in a car accident. "Your Dad should be home any minute now. Bill and I are gonna go over their house once he gets in. I want you to stay here and watch Bridgette. Y'all go ahead and eat. We'll see you when we get back." "I wanna go see Dale." "I think it's best if you see him tomorrow." "Okay." She gave me no further details.

When Da walked into the house from the carport, I crept from my room to listen to what else Mumma might tell Da as they talked in the kitchen, where Bridgette and I stood on our tippy-toes to wash and dry the dishes and splash each other with the sink sprayer. *We loved playing with that thing!* "Quit playing with that water and finish those dishes!" "Yes, ma'am!" Then, Bridgette would squirt me in the eye and giggle. Mumma thought that was funny and walked away. She liked "running water" as much as we did!

"Decapitated" was what I heard Mumma use to describe Mrs. Pollock's accident. Da offered a faint, "Oh, my Lord." I asked Mumma what "de-cap-i-tat-ed" meant when I walked back toward them in the kitchen. "If you don't know a word, sound it out and go look it up!" I did. *What the hell is "be-head-ed?" Do big words ever stop when you're 10?* This was a lot of work just to find out *how* she died. *Why won't Mumma or Da just tell me?* I guess they didn't know how to tell their 10-year-old that the mom of the little boy who taught him how to play tennis had literally lost her head.

Mrs. Pollock's funeral came a few days later. It was the second that I attended. My first funeral took place at 6 years old. It was for Mrs. Catherine Cameron, one of Mumma's high school teachers. She was another person who died from the C-word. Her open casket scared the shit outta me! I have no idea why I went, but Ronnie, Darnell and Tony were going so I wanted to show them that I was *big* like them. *Boy, was that a mistake.* I didn't sleep for weeks and became afraid of open caskets for the rest of my life. Dead people just frightened me. Leading up to Mrs. Pollock's funeral, I cautiously asked Mumma, "Will the undertaker stick Mrs. Pollock's head back on her body?" "No, Troy. Her casket will be closed." Now, I *really* knew her head wasn't on her body anymore and *that* scared me even more. Thus began the nightmare that haunted me for at least another 30 years.

> *It's dark when Mrs. Pollock's headless body slowly rises from her casket wearing a white gown. With head in hand, she makes her way from the Christ Church graveyard and floats toward our house. From my bedroom window, I see her approaching, and I know she's coming to get me! I'm terrified. In my pajamas, I run from the house and head "up the county" to escape her presence. But, no matter how fast I run, she has already been where I'm headed because each time I stop to catch my breath in front of the houses that dot 33, people turn their lights on and come out to their front yards and say to me, "Do you know Dale Pollock's dead mother is looking for you?" I take off running toward another home and yell back, "Please tell her you haven't seen me!" Then, it's on to the next house until I wake up screaming.*

Thankfully, Mrs. Pollock never "caught" me. Had *that* happened I might have had a heart attack at 10 years old, but I did wake up every night for the next few months perspiring like I had just stepped out of the Christchurch School sauna that the wrestlers used to melt away pounds to reach their weight limit. I couldn't wait for the sun to come up each morning because then I *knew* she had returned to her grave. I figured Mrs. Pollock's ghost was like *Dark Shadows'* Barnabas Collins and would avoid sunlight at all costs. Sunshine became my security blanket and the absence of it was frightening. Those nightmares consumed my daytime thoughts and began my first thoughts of suicide. Anything was better than what I was experiencing each night. After Mumma, Da and Bridgette had gone to bed, I grabbed my red, white and black checkered bedspread and my pillow to sleep in the hallway outside Mumma and Da's closed door. Around 1:00 or so in the morning, Da would come out of their bedroom to take me, my pillow and blanket and Peter Rabbit and Winnie the Pooh (and a miniature ceramic teddy bear that I got around the same time as Peter) back to my bed. I hated going back to *my* bed! I felt safer lying on the hardwood floor outside of their door. Even when I was older, I still slept with Peter Rabbit under my arm because he made me feel safe. *I never said I grew up!* What happened to Winnie the Pooh? Sadly, that's another story.

"Troy, it's only a bad dream, now go back to sleep. You'll be okay." However, no sooner had Da closed their bedroom door, I grabbed Peter and Winnie, my pillow and blanket to head back down the hall to lay on the floor. It was scary knowing Mrs. Pollock was buried across the road from us at the church Joe Frazier visited on Sunday mornings. I thought that our hallway might provide an extra layer of protection from her ghost like it might during a bad thunderstorm. Before Mrs. Pollock died, I liked looking from my bedroom window to watch the exterior lights over at Christchurch School flicker on automatically when the sun was settling, or watch the headlights and taillights of cars on 33 come and go. *Anything was better than doing my homework or listening to Mumma and Da fight.* After Mrs. Pollock died, I quit looking out of that window when it was dark outside. *I was afraid she'd be staring back at me.*

In 1971, Mrs. Carrie Peterson's 5th period math class was my last one for the day. I used to sit at my desk begging God to find a way to keep it from getting dark at night. I prayed that God would give the entire state of Virginia the "midnight sun" that we learned about in science class. I wanted to move to the Arctic or Antarctic Circle because their sun was up until at least midnight in those locations! I didn't care how cold it was in either of those places. If anyone needed sunlight, it was me as I was 10 years old. Mumma and Da didn't understand what I was going through. "Boy, it's just a bad dream. Now, go to sleep!" *I was losing my mind, but they couldn't see it. I was literally scared to death.* That nightmare hung around until I was 40-something. I probably needed to "talk" to someone, but "counseling" in the 1970s was for the truly insane. *The Bob Newhart Show wouldn't hit the airwaves for another few months.* No one sat on a couch to discuss personal problems. Problems were *private.* November of 1971 was when I first started losing my sanity, and that was when I first started thinking that dying was a better option than living.

I decided that I didn't want children because I didn't want *any* kid to suffer what I was going through sitting in Mrs. Peterson's class praying for the sun to stay up. I guess I was afraid I would turn into Mumma and Da and fail to listen to my kids if they were grieving like me in 1971 and 1972 and 1973. I would have been very disappointed in myself had that happened. To avoid that, I chose not to have kids. Lori didn't want any either, so it was a marriage made in heaven! *Or at least it started out that way.*

Beginning in my late 20s, I sometimes visited Christ Church's cemetery searching for Mrs. Pollock's grave. I probably did that eight to ten times over the years. *I wanted to make peace with her.* There were hundreds of headstones dating back to the 1700s in that graveyard, but I never found hers. In August of 2012, I got to the cemetery around 11 in the morning to walk the brick path Joe Frazier used to trot on 40 years earlier. "I'm not leaving here today until I find her," was what I said to myself walking onto the grounds. The granite and marble slabs displayed many Middlesex County surnames that I recognized from over the years, but none were inscribed "Pollock." About an hour into my search, I stumbled across Mrs. Cynthia Barlowe's granite headstone, my former elementary school librarian. I talked to her headstone as though she was still standing behind her desk pointing me to the right bookshelf. In the graveyard on that day, I was once again a little boy seeking her assistance.

For some reason back then, Mrs. Barlowe took an interest in me. I'm sure I wasn't the only kid she took an interest in, but she made me feel that way. "Talking" to her headstone, I thanked her for the many times she pulled me from class so that I could review the list of new books she was about to order for fellow classmates. Each June from 3rd grade through 7th grade, she pulled me out of class to help her. "Troy, do you think 6th graders would like that book? Would a 4th grader want to read a book with this title? What about this one?" *I couldn't believe she wanted my opinion on what others should read.* Seated together at one of the small desks in her library, we reviewed sheets of paper that contained a synopsis of each book in question. "Mrs. Barlowe, what's a 'sigh-nop-sis'?" "First of all, it's 'sa-nop-sis,' and if you want to know what that means you'll have to go look it up in the big dictionary next to my desk." *Good God, does Mumma pay people to torture me like this?*

At her gravesite, I told Mrs. Barlowe, "I still have every *Sports Illustrated* you ever gave me. Every single one and I read them all the time! Thank you for being so nice to me when I was a little boy. *You* were nice to lots of little girls and boys in Middlesex County, white *and* black. I never thanked you for being nice to me, but I'm thanking you now." I told her that I kept those magazines despite the fact that my ex-wife, my mother and my stepmother tried to get rid of them, but I could never part with them! I collected *SI* magazines for over 27 years. I "told" her headstone what was going on in my life and that I was sorry that I hadn't studied as hard as she urged me to when I was younger and that I was glad she was part of my life. I patted her headstone one last time and said, "Mrs. Barlowe, please help me find Mrs. Pollock's grave. I've been looking for that lady for a long time!" I got up to walk about 20 feet to the next headstone, and there was Mrs. Pollock's headstone as though she had been waiting for me all along! *I could not believe it!* I peered over my shoulder at Mrs. Barlowe's grave and said, "I see you're still teaching me how to look things up!"

I thanked Mrs. Pollock for welcoming me into her home when I was 9 years old and allowing her son, Dale, to be my first white friend. He often stayed at our house, and I stayed over at theirs. I guarantee *those* types of sleepovers weren't taking place anywhere else in Middlesex County in 1970. "Mrs. Pollock, I don't know what those dreams were all about. I know you would never have hurt me. I know you cared about me. In a way, I feel bad that I let you scare me because you were *so* good to me. But the brain can play all kinds of tricks on you when you're a kid. I don't know what else to say, but I'm okay now. I hope you're okay, too." And that was that. I thought it was ironic that Mrs. Pollock and Mrs. Barlowe were both born in 1934. I never figured out what that nightmare was all about. I continued to have them around two or three times a year until, thankfully, they stopped when I was in my 40s. Over the years when that nightmare "reared its ugly head," my bedroom light stayed on all night because I couldn't grab my pillow and blanket and go sleep outside of Mumma and Da's room anymore. But at least I still had Peter!

The latest version of Peter Rabbit. 2014
He's undergone 5 makeovers in 49 years!

The Barlowe and Pollock graves separated by only 20 feet. 2012

CHAPTER 21

Mrs. Bertha Taylor was a friend of Mumma's who lived "up the county." Her youngest child, Marilyn, was my girlfriend in 7th grade and halfway through 8th grade (until she dropped me for Rodney Hammond). I watched him and Marilyn "make out" on the bus when we were returning from a basketball game at New Kent High School one Friday night. I think she kissed him for the almost 40 miles back to Middlesex High School. *That hurt then, but it was funny much later!* Butley sat next to me on the bus, and he teased me for those 40 bumpy miles. He kept saying, "Troy, I think your girl has gone 'up the county!'" That was also where Rodney lived near a little town called Water View. It was a double whammy that particular night because I lost Marilyn to Rodney, and we lost to the New Kent Trojans.

When I came along in grade school, Mrs. Taylor was one of the teacher aides at Rappahannock Central Elementary School. The only other one I remembered was Mrs. Viola Scott who, during a 1971 summer arts and craft program at the school, caught me tie-dyeing a "good" shirt. "Troy Lewis, do you really think Jean wants you to tie-dye *that* shirt?" "Yes, ma'am. She said it's okay." *I lied.* She rolled her eyes in my direction. "Um hmm. We'll see when Jean picks you up." Later that afternoon when Mumma saw what I had done to that shirt, she wore my butt out before I even got in the car! Head lowered and pouting, I took a glance back toward the school office. Mrs. Scott happened to be standing there with a big smile planted on her face! Twenty, thirty and forty years later, *every* time I saw her, I thought she remembered the tie-dye incident. Finally, at Da's funeral, I asked her, "Do you remember the time I tie-dyed my shirt in 1971, and you told me not to do it because Jean wouldn't be happy if I did?" *She didn't know what the hell I was talking about!* She laughed. "Did Jean give you a spanking?" "Yes, ma'am. She sure did." "Well, you deserved it!"

Mrs. Taylor and Mrs. Scott were strict disciplinarians in the classroom and on the playground. "Troy Lewis, you better behave yourself and leave those girls alone. You hear? Do you want one of us to call Jean? Maybe we'll give you a spanking right here and now! Which one do you want?" "Yes. I'll behave." "Yes, what?" "Yes, ma'am! You don't have to call her." Most adults had *carte blanche* to spank kids where I grew up. Mrs. Taylor and Mrs. Scott had no problem doing that. They didn't mess around when it came to schoolwork either, and that's why I was very surprised on the day Mrs. Taylor slipped me *gas money*, but that's another story.

Like Butley, Mrs. Taylor's twins, William and Welford, were also two years ahead of me in school. They were the funniest people I'd *ever* met. I don't know what they ended up doing for a living, but I wished somehow they could have found a way to become comedians. They could make *anything* seem funny. The Taylor's house was about a five-minute walk from Mrs. Frances Johnson's two-story home. Mrs. Johnson gave piano lessons to black kids in Middlesex County. A thin woman with a "medium" complexion, she was a schoolteacher for forever, and Grandma and Grandpop Lewis used to go over to her house to watch TV back in the 1950s. Mumma gave Mrs. Johnson $5 apiece for me, Sharon and Bridgette to bang on her piano every couple of weeks. I pleaded with Mumma to let me quit taking those lessons, but it took a year or so before she came to the conclusion that I was no budding Ray Charles!

Sharon and Bridgette were pretty good at playing the ebony and ivory keys, but I was awful. "Mrs. Johnson, I'm no good at this! Sharon and Bridgette are just better." "Well, Troy, they are probably better because they practice a lot more than you do. You'll never be any good at *any* thing if you don't practice." I knew she was right, but all I wanted to do was go *play* with William and Welford, not *play* the piano! Out on our back porch, we had an old, broken-down upright, and that was what the three of us used for practice. *Well, Sharon and Bridgette practiced on it!*

(Insert "The Perry Mason Theme" by Fred Steiner) Each time I went over to Mrs. Johnson's for a lesson, I lied and told her that I had been trying my best. Sharon and Bridgette snickered when they heard that. They sat in Mrs. Johnson's parlor room watching *Perry Mason* and listening to my destruction of her piano. While she watched me stumble at reading half and whole notes, she also managed to keep track of the ongoing battle between Mr. Mason and his rival, District Attorney Hamilton Burger. What I couldn't understand was how Mrs. Johnson was able to *see* the action without seeing the TV and teach me at the same time. She seemed to know "who dun it" before the last bar of the Fred Steiner theme music had ended. That amazed me, but then again, I guess she didn't have to concentrate too much on my piano playing skills. All she needed was about 15 seconds to unravel that "mystery!" *No amount of practice was going to improve the nimbleness of my fingers!* I did master one song, though. It required using three fingers on my right hand, and striking "Middle C" and the key to its left and its right. That was as intricate as my piano playing ever got. Three keys. No more. No less. "Middle C will always show you the way home," Mrs. Johnson explained. *No, it won't, Mrs. Johnson! Just show me out the door so I can go play with William and Welford!* A year's worth of lessons and I only mastered one song that involved using all of three fingers! At the conclusion of my lesson, I often asked Mrs. Johnson to play a few bars of "Home on the Range." "Often" was an understatement, I asked her every single time! "Please, Mrs. Johnson, can't you play just a little bit?" She'd look at me like I was nuts. I just thought it was magical the sounds that she created with her fingers compared to what my three fingers did, but she obliged me more often than not. She would play two or three chords and then say, "Okay, that's enough of that. Bridgette, it's your turn!" "Bye, Mrs. Johnson!"

CHAPTER 22

Mrs. Taylor was the 1st baseman (or basewoman) on Mumma's traveling softball team. Mumma played shortstop and Ellen Beverley played 2nd base, and the three of them were a pretty good trio. The only other person I remember from their team was Gloria Johnson. "Glo" always treated me nice, and I was happy with that because not many adults took the time to be nice to kids, especially if they didn't belong to them. *Some weren't nice to kids even when they did belong to them.* Because Glo shared the same nickname as Aunt Jenny's daughter-in-law, I thought she might be as unpleasant as the first Glo that I knew. Glo Johnson proved me wrong. She was always a "nice" Glo! *But that's how my brain worked as a kid. If one Glo were mean, all of them would be was my thought process.*

Glo showed me how to "break in" the baseball glove that Milton Holmes bought me when I was in the 3rd grade. Milton was the youngest of Mr. and Mrs. Sherman Holmes' three sons. Mr. Sherman Holmes and Mrs. Easter Holmes were high school teachers at St. Clare Walker. Their two older sons went to school with Mumma and Da, and many years later, they became The Holmes Brothers, a blues band, that I sometimes went to see perform in New York City.

I was 9 years old when Mr. and Mrs. Holmes took me with them to visit the Big Apple. I guess they figured I had never really left the county more than a handful of times, and a trip to New York would be a good experience for me. Mr. Holmes marched over one August morning and told Mumma that he and his wife were going to visit her brother for a few days. "Maybe 'Troy Roy' would wanna go with us." *Mr. Holmes always called me Troy Roy, never Troy.* "He'll be ready in 20 minutes!"

We loaded up Mrs. Holmes' 1968 four-door, blue Ford Galaxie for the trip to head "up the county" and beyond. I can still see Mumma and Bridgette standing in the living room bay window staring at us as I waved "Bye" to them. *I was headed to New York City!* Mrs. Holmes drove about as far as Tappahannock until Mr. Holmes took the wheel from her because she would accelerate to 70 miles per hour, then slow to 45 miles per hour, then speed back up to 70 miles per hour and slow back down to 45 miles per hour! *There was nothing in front of her! Just drive!* Mr. Holmes said, "Easter, you're driving too erratic for this road. Pull over and let me have the wheel!" *I was glad he did. I loved Mrs. Holmes, but her driving scared me!* Mr. Holmes had a habit of slightly lifting his right hand from the steering wheel to check his speedometer, and when I started driving, I ended up doing the same thing. A smile came across my face *every* time I did that because it reminded me of our 1970 summer trip together.

Forever would describe how long it took us to get across the upper deck of the George Washington Bridge. I had never seen anything like the tons of cars and trucks fighting just to gain another inch. Drivers screamed and honked horns when someone wouldn't let them squeeze in. I even saw a couple of drivers "flip the bird." *How can anyone live here?! This place is a zoo!* Never did it cross my mind that one day I would become one of those animals fighting for an extra inch of asphalt! While we sat in that congestion, Mr. Holmes turned around to peek at me sitting in the backseat and said, "Troy Roy, do you know that we are about to get on a double-decker bridge?" "No, sir. I don't even know what you mean by 'double-decker?'" "Well, let me explain it to you this way. You take the bridge that's back in Urbanna and then stick another bridge just like it on top, and you've got a double-decker!" "Really? That's crazy!" I thought about that for a few seconds. "Mr. Holmes, which one are we getting on?" "The upper one." "Can I ask you a question?" "Go ahead, Troy Roy." "You said we are on the New Jersey side now and New York is on the other side, right?" "That's right." "Okay. How about once we make it to the New York side, we turn around and go back and get on the lower one so I can look up at the bridge that's above us!" I thought that was a reasonable request, but Mr. and Mrs. Holmes laughed like it was the funniest thing they had ever heard! Since it took us about an hour to get across the George Washington Bridge that afternoon, there was no way Mr. Holmes was going to sit in that traffic all over again so that the young clown in the Galaxie's backseat could stick his big head out of the car window to marvel at the upper deck!

Once we got to Mrs. Holmes' brother's apartment we were in for quite a shock! Throughout the two-bedroom unit, his walls were plastered with pictures of *Playboy* centerfolds and any other magazine that featured a naked woman! *They were everywhere!* I thought Mrs. Holmes was going to have a heart attack! I thought I might have one, too, because I had never seen naked pictures before, and trust me, I liked what I was seeing! *Do all single men in New York City tape naked women on their walls? If so, do all single men do the same thing all over the world? If that was the case, I couldn't wait until I became a single man because the only pictures Mumma and Da let me put on my bedroom walls were those of people like Lew Alcindor, Wilt Chamberlain and Jerry West. The three of them weren't nearly as exciting as what was in front of me!*

Mr. and Mrs. Holmes spoke in hushed tones with her brother in the kitchen while I sat on the couch staring at the "sights." Mrs. Holmes peeked from the kitchen to catch me sneaking glances at the centerfolds. Each time she did, I lowered my head and stared at my Converse sneakers. As soon as she turned her back, I went back to gawking. I know Mr. and Mrs. Holmes were embarrassed by his decorations, but I wasn't! We were in the Big Apple for a few days, and I don't recall any sightseeing excursions around the city. *I didn't need that!* I had come to New York City and seen things I *never* got to see back in Middlesex! I wouldn't get another chance to see breasts until I was in 7th grade, but that's another story!

On the way back down to Virginia, we stopped in Pennsylvania to pick Milton up from his summer job at Camp Susquehanna. Mr. Holmes and I helped him load his luggage in the trunk before we got back on I-95. As we headed south, Milton handed me a paper bag that contained an oversized shoebox. "Go ahead, take it out." It was my first gift from anyone other than Mumma or Da. Inside of the shoebox was a Ken "The Hawk" Harrelson MacGregor autographed baseball glove. I had never heard of "The Hawk," but he became my favorite ballplayer. Each morning I ran out to the paper box at the end of our driveway to check his stats from the night before in the *Daily Press*. The Hawk was a career .239 hitter, and although his numbers were never impressive, I pulled for him anyway. I had that glove for over 25 years until someone walked away with it after an Air Force intramural softball game. *I was sick when I lost it*. I bought a new one, but it never felt right. After someone took that glove, my heart went out of playing intramurals. I used to really look forward to softball season, but after that glove walked away, I guess my childhood went with it, and I didn't want to "play" anymore without it. *Did you ever really get over something that you loved and lost?* For years, I had dreams I found that glove, but it was gone forever. It reminded me of Milton Holmes and the 1970 New York City "Summer of Love."

Mumma's softball team played female teams from neighboring counties. Igloo coolers were packed and loaded with ice, and off we headed in caravans of five to six cars loaded with bats, gloves, ladies and kids to Gloucester, King William, Mathews, and King & Queen Counties. The games were usually doubleheaders, and if I weren't watching them play, I was grabbing a soda from the cooler that was in our red 1965 Pontiac GTO or a hot dog from the snack bar or playing Tag between parked cars in the grassy fields that served as parking lots. Once the games were over, Bridgette and I piled back in the GTO for the ride home. "C'mon Mumma, go faster! Find *somebody* to race!" Mumma liked to drive fast, and we wanted her to go even faster! I thought Bridgette and I got a bigger kick out of her burying the speedometer than she did! Every so often, she glided next to a Plymouth Roadrunner or a Chevy Camaro to give its driver a smile and a head gesture that said, "Wanna race?" Often, they obliged her and us.

Most races that Mumma participated in took place on the straight stretch of highway that ran in front of Grandma and Grandpop Latimore's house. Out there on 33, Mumma raced anybody for "side" money that she hid from Da. Bridgette and I knew to keep our mouths shut about it, too. Mumma didn't have to tell us to keep her extra income a secret. That was where she got the money to pay for our piano lessons. The spare cash she earned from the unfortunate men who didn't shift gears as well as she did for a quarter of a mile was *her* business. As she clutched the dollar bills that belonged to her, The Look was all we needed to remind us that this was to be kept quiet.

Mumma didn't need an opponent to drive fast. Speeding was her preference. She told me one night many years later, "I would just feel so free. The wind would take all my troubles away. The faster I went, the better I felt." I think she enjoyed it because it was probably the only way she knew to escape life for a little bit. Maybe speed gave her freedom for a few moments. Unfortunately, that freedom never lasted very long because of the obligations and responsibilities with raising her brothers and sister along with her own kids and the various other "strays" she took in over the years. Not to mention Da knocking her around whenever he felt like it. She wouldn't get to experience true freedom until she was in her 60s, and by then, she rarely exceeded the posted speed limit. I think Mumma drove fast because there was a lot in her life that dampened her spirits, and if going 85 miles per hour in a 55 miles per hour zone made her feel better, then so be it. From the backseat, I liked seeing the smile on her face in the rearview mirror of the GTO. The wind from the open windows whooshed her hair all over her head, but she didn't care. That was the only time Mumma didn't care how her hair looked! She was conscious of her appearance at all times, but I don't ever remember her complaining about her hair when she was flying down the road going over 100 miles per hour with the windows down! Back then, 70 miles per hour was pretty much her minimum speed, and later on, I inherited her heavy foot.

(Insert "The Girl Can't Help It" by Little Richard) Many men told me that Jean Lewis was the best driver they *ever* saw! One of those guys was a man named Philip Johnson. He was Glo's husband

(Arthur's younger brother) and worked as a mechanic over at Bareford Motors in Urbanna where Tubby bought his Plymouth Duster. Philip liked to play "chicken" with Mumma on the almost one-mile stretch between Grandma and Grandpop Latimore's house and Mr. Moore's farm. I was pretty sure Philip liked speed just as much as Mumma, if not more. *Nah, maybe not!* Sometimes, when we pulled out of the driveway, Mumma spotted Philip's 1965 two-door Plymouth Fury coming up the road and the "chicken" game was on. He crossed the double yellow line onto *our* side of the two-lane road and barreled toward us. "Go faster, Mumma!" Mumma punched the accelerator and the 389 cubic inches beneath the hood rocked the GTO toward Philip's Plymouth. Mr. Moore's farm had about 30 dairy cows, and as the two cars sped toward each other, I used to think one cow "mooed" to the other, "Look at those fools at it again. One day they're gonna kill each other!"

As we got closer to Philip's car, Bridgette and I got more excited. *This was fun!* Leaning forward from the backseat, we knocked heads to get a better view on who would be the first to "chicken" out. *Deep down inside, we both knew it wouldn't be Mumma because she feared nothing, except Da. That was something I never understood, but maybe it wasn't meant for me to understand.* Both cars bounced from the slight bumps in the pavement as they sped closer to the other, and just before we plowed into Philip's Plymouth, he turned his steering wheel a little to his right, and as though the "chicken" had never crossed the road, his car returned to the right side of the road. Mumma never gave in when "chicken" was involved; it wasn't her nature. When I really thought about it, I was pretty sure she was thinking, "I have nothing to lose, and if I'm gonna die, I'm taking my kids with me." I didn't care. Even though Mumma wasn't always nice to me when I was a kid, I would have been happy to accompany her wherever she was going if we died playing "chicken." That's how much I loved my Mumma. *That was really what went through my head when we were flying down 33 past those cows.*

"Mumma, that was fun! Let's go find Philip and do it all over again." "Nah, that was enough fun for one day." "Pleeease! C'mon, Mumma! Our car is faster than his, you can catch him!" She laughed and took a quick look at me through the rearview mirror, "You know, you shouldn't tempt Fate." *Huh?* "Mumma, who is Fate?" She offered a wry smile and said, "You'll meet her one day when you get older." *I will? Who in the hell is this Fate lady? It's gotta be a lady with a name like Fate, right? Why does Mumma think this is funny? Why do I have so many questions, and no one gives me straight answers?* A few moments later I asked her, "Mumma, how can you trust Philip like that?" She shrugged, "Oh, I don't know. I just do, I guess. Philip taught me how to drive when I was 16 after Mom and Dad left. He showed me how to use a gun in case I ever needed to protect myself or go hunting. Sometimes, when a check was late in arriving from Pennsylvania, I went out in the woods with Eddie, Ronnie, Darnell or Tony to shoot a deer, so that we would have something to eat. We had some rough days when I was growing up. It's kinda like Philip and I know what the other one is going to do on the road. So yeah, I trust Philip Johnson." She paused and looked at me again in her rearview mirror. "I don't know, Troy. It's like he and I can read each other's mind. You know how you and Butley do when y'all play basketball against other boys? That's how it is with me and Philip." Puzzled, I looked at her through the rearview mirror. "I've seen the way you and Butley look at each other and just through eye contact, y'all can figure out what the other one is gonna do. Cut this way or that way. Y'all are good at that." "Okay." "Well, it's the same way with Philip and me. I think we can 'feel' what the other one is gonna do on the road." *Now, it made sense to me.* I never knew she was aware of how well Butley and I fared against other kids. I guess Mumma paid more attention to me than I thought.

Pat-Pat standing next to Da's 1965 Pontiac GTO. 1965

CHAPTER 23

In 7th grade, Marilyn Taylor became my girlfriend after an evening of playing "Spin the Bottle" in Mr. Jessie and Eveleen Scott's basement (by the way, it was pronounced, "Eh-va-leen," not "Eve-leen," and don't ask me why). Eh-va-leen was Mumma's best friend. The Scott's oldest child was Gloria, who had been my 1st grade girlfriend after I finally came to the realization that Judy Kidd could care less if I lived or died! Gloria and I were "on and off" throughout elementary school until we finally drifted apart after entering middle school.

When Marilyn and I started "dating," she was a 13-year-old 8th grader at the high school, and I was a 12-year-old 7th grader who was 3 miles away "down the county" at the middle school. It was a long-distance relationship bound for trouble from the start, but I didn't know that at the time. All I cared about was convincing my cousin, Sharon, who was now a high school junior, to pass along my love notes to Marilyn at the high school before school started. Every now and then, Sharon charged me 10 cents for mail delivery, and sometimes an extra 5 cents to *not* read the contents. That all depended on what kind of mood she was in before she left Grandma and Grandpop Latimore's house that morning.

Marilyn was the first *older* woman that I actually kissed, and I was crazy about her. We mostly talked on the phone, or held hands at the movie theater in Urbanna. I had $1.50 for my movie dates with Marilyn to purchase our 50-cent tickets at the booth on the side of the movie theater reserved for blacks. We bought our tickets in a small entranceway on the left side of the theater and then we walked up a flight of concrete stairs to our seats. White people entered through a fancier, well-lit area that was equipped with red carpet. Their area was more spacious and cozier than ours. They had cushioned seats compared to the hard wooden ones that we sat on upstairs. Once I made it upstairs, I liked to sit right under the projector cutouts in the wall to watch the movie stream to the screen. *How a projector could take film and project it onto a screen 200 feet away fascinated me.* I liked looking up at the ceiling to see the movie streaming from the projector room. To my young eyes, it was mesmerizing. Every now and then Marilyn would elbow me and say, "Troy, did you come here to see *me* or the *movie*?" *Now, that was a tough question! I guess it was a little of both! Why were girls so complicated?*

The Urbanna Movie Theater was the place where Mumma didn't want Bridgette and me to see *The Sound of Music* back in 1965. Blacks sat upstairs and whites downstairs, and that's just the way it was. When we wanted to grab a snack, we headed down a narrow stairway. Once at the bottom, we turned right to place our order. Well, sort of. Our order was placed by speaking through a sheet of plywood that was painted an ugly shade of green that contained four cutout circles. Within it were two small circles at eye level, another to speak into and a larger semi-circular opening at the bottom of the shelf where you retrieved your order once you were served. You could look through and see that the white patrons were served quicker than we were, but there was nothing we could do about it. I guess the plywood was there to serve as some form of humiliation for us. I don't remember looking at it as discriminatory though; I didn't really give it a second thought. It was just how things were. Place your order, slide your money through, get your popcorn, go back to your seat and watch the movie. Then, pray that Sharon or Bridgette wouldn't tell Mumma or Grandma that they'd seen Marilyn and me kissing under the projector lights! After integration in 1969, I peeked through the cutouts and saw that the same white kids who were now my classmates didn't have a sheet of plywood separating them from their popcorn. Nor did they have to pile on top of one another in a crowded stairway just to get a soda. I just accepted it and didn't feel one way or the other about it. *We* liked sitting amongst ourselves anyway!

Marilyn moved in with her aunt, Mrs. Mary Thornton, after her uncle died from a sudden heart attack when he was only 40-something. Mrs. Thornton happened to be my 4th grade teacher, and she was never one of my favorites! Da didn't help improve my relationship with her, either. At that time in my life, my biggest hope was that Middlesex High School might find a way to defeat Charles "Duke" Thorpe and the Pointers of West Point High during the Tidewater District basketball "tuna"-ment. *College taught me that it should have been pronounced "tour"-nament, but everyone I grew up with in the South made that word sound like it was a fish!* Mr. Jarvis would ask Butley and me each year before the tournament started, "Do y'all think we got a shot at beating West Point this year in the 'tuna'-ment?"

We played West Point "home" and "away" after we integrated in 1969, and I don't ever remember beating those guys. *I hated West Point High School!* Their head coach was a guy named Norman Dinwiddie, and his teams were always solid fundamentally. The Pointers emerged from the locker room like they were going to punch in at the Pulp Mill as most of their fathers did; only they came to work with a basketball tucked under their arms instead of a tin lunch pail. I knew "Duke" Thorpe and his family, and I yelled, "Hey" at him as he ran by the corner bleachers. He acknowledged my presence with a head nod and that was it. They were not at the gym to make friends. It was like they were invading Normandy.

(Insert "Sweet Georgia Brown" by Brother Bones and His Shadows) The public address system blared "Sweet Georgia Brown" as the Pointers went through their pregame drills. The only drill Middlesex High ever ran was the layup line from the right side and then, the left. But even *our* fans liked watching the Pointers warm up. Despite the Harlem Globetrotters' theme music, nothing flashy took place with the West Point team. They went through left hand

and right hand dribble drills, chest pass drills, bounce pass drills, Figure-8 drills and between-the-leg dribble drills in preparation for their ensuing battle. All of their drills were well synchronized, and none of the Pointers took the task at hand lightly. Smiles were nonexistent. They came to the gym to kick your ass, and Coach Dinwiddie wanted them to look good while they were doing it. Their blue and orange pinstripe warm-up pants were matched with cream-colored warm-up jackets with each player's last name across the back. None of the schools in our low-income area of Virginia had warm-up uniforms (pants and jackets) with their names on the back! *Who am I kidding?* I don't remember any of the schools in our league even having warm-ups! West Point High was as close to a professional team as I saw when I was growing up. In 1973, they were at their finest, went 16-0, and won the Virginia State Group A Championship. *I never stopped hating those guys, but I respected them!*

Da did nothing to improve my student/teacher relationship with Mrs. Thornton. It took a turn for the worse at the Tidewater District "tuna"-ment held at the neutral court site at York High School in Yorktown. I was running around the gym goofing off between games with Butley when Da motioned for me to come over to the bleachers where he sat next to Mrs. Thornton. He laughed and asked, "Why do you come home every day and tell me how much you *hate* Mrs. Thornton? Why do you think she is so mean?" I stood in front of them not knowing what to say. *Why is he asking me this right in front of her? I wanted to kill him!* He and Mrs. Thornton graduated from St. Clare Walker High School in 1957, and they had known each other since they were kids. On the ride home, I didn't talk to Da for the 36 miles back, and although he kept trying to make me laugh, I wouldn't give in. I stayed mad at him for a few days. He finally apologized many years later, but that's another story. Almost 40 years had passed when I told Mumma how Da embarrassed me in front of Mrs. Thornton. Her reply? "I always said your Dad was an asshole!"

After Marilyn started living with Mrs. Thornton, she didn't have to share a phone with her brothers and sister anymore, thankfully. If there was one thing we loved doing, it was talking on the phone. *We were both miserable preteens and at one point, we even talked about running away together. Where in the hell were we going? Neither of us had an answer because we had no clue what lay beyond Richmond!* There were some days when Mrs. Thornton felt Marilyn had been on the phone chatting with me too much, and she wouldn't let her use it. When that happened, Marilyn walked about a mile down to Doc Marshall's Drug Store where there was a pay phone in the back with a sliding wooden door for privacy. *Bell Atlantic gave us 15 minutes for every dime!* On Fridays, I handed Sharon what little change I saved so that she could turn it over to Marilyn for our calls just in case Mrs. Thornton wouldn't let her use the phone over the weekend. Marilyn and I remained a "couple" for the rest of 7th grade and the first few months of 8th grade until Rodney came "down the county," and that was the end of that relationship! Butley contributed to the breakup as well!

It happened one evening after school when he, Marilyn and I were hanging out near the gym before basketball practice. As we stood around talking, Butley practiced his stand-up comedy routine. Marilyn never thought Butley was as funny as *he* thought he was, but I sure did. *I laughed at anything he said!* She warned, "If you laugh at any more of James Jarvis' dumb jokes, we are gonna break up!" Butley cracked another joke, I laughed and Marilyn left me standing outside of the gym wondering what happened! She headed off to cheerleading practice never giving me a second thought. Butley said, "C'mon, let's go to practice. Forget about her!" But I couldn't forget about Marilyn Taylor that easily. Later that night, I called and begged her to take me back. "No, Troy. It's over. Good-bye." She hung up. I dialed again. Click. A week or so later, she was kissing Rodney Hammond, so I guess it wasn't Butley that broke us up after all! But it wasn't so funny back then.

CHAPTER 24

Mrs. Taylor roamed the cafeteria during lunch period to keep boys from goofing off too much. She also served as a monitor when we took standardized tests in the school lunchroom. In 3rd grade, I was crouched over a sheet full of circles with my No. 2 pencil pondering a question. I don't remember the question, but I was pretty sure the answer was A, B, C or D! Mrs. Taylor came over to my table to lean in for a closer look and placed her arm on the back of my metal folding chair. She read the question and whispered, "Pick C." She then walked away as though nothing had taken place. I filled in the "C" circle and shifted in my chair to look at her. *Has Mrs. Taylor lost her mind? Adults don't give answers during exams. Well, at least they had never given me one!* During lunch period, she saw that I still had a confused look on my face. She came over and whispered again in my ear, "Troy Lewis, the *white* kids can't have *everything!*"

Before integration, the white kids did have a lot that was better. Better desks, better schoolbooks, better chalk, and better access to popcorn at the Urbanna Movie Theater! I think Mrs. Taylor saw that I had some potential and didn't want one question to hold me back from getting a better score. *Who knows?* Was it cheating? Some would say "Yes," but in the big scheme of things, I didn't think it really mattered. I think it was her way of giving me *gas money*. She gave me a nudge in the right direction and who didn't need that at 9 years old? I promised myself that when I grew up, I was going to help someone if they were in similar circumstances. The way I looked at it, it was not the question that mattered, but the person's potential to do greater things.

I got that chance many years later when working for a pharmaceutical company in the training department. One of my students was a young lady from Russia. Her name was Elena, and she struggled with examination questions that were "True/False, All of the Following, except" and so forth. In reviewing her missed questions, my coworker Matt Siegel and I determined that it was merely a language translation issue. Elena failed the exam a few times, and Matt and I saw the stress that it was causing her. We both recognized her potential, and, more importantly, that Elena maintained a positive attitude and gave her best effort at all times. Matt and I agreed on "passing" her! The next morning, Elena met me an hour early before class started for her exam retake. I asked, "Why are you down here so early?" She sadly said, "I'm here to take my test again." "Why? You already passed it." "No, I didn't. I have to take it again." I repeated, "Elena, you already passed it!" I smiled. She didn't catch on at first, but it slowly sank in around the same time her eyes started moistening. "Don't you dare start crying!" She dabbed at her eyes and said, "I promise that I won't disappoint you." She had a very successful career, and I was always proud of her.

Mrs. Taylor died in October 2010. I went down to Virginia for her funeral at Antioch Baptist Church, where her sons, William and Welford, and I used to cut up in the Junior Choir. I never knew how Mrs. Taylor managed to discipline those two knuckleheads, but Mumma gave me more than a few spankings for goofing off with them when I should have been listening to Rev. Fred Holmes' sermon! Many of those at the funeral provided accounts of Mrs. Taylor's life accomplishments. Honestly, I only knew two things about her life: She was the first basewoman on Mumma's softball team, and she told me to "Pick C" when I was in 3rd grade.

Mrs. Juanita Tabb shared with those in attendance more insight on Mrs. Taylor. Mind you, I thought Mrs. Tabb had passed on a long time ago, and when she introduced herself, I was quite shocked to see her still standing because she had to be close to 90! She and her husband, Mr. Pete Tabb, used to play "Bid Whist" with Grandma and Grandpop Latimore on the front porch nearly 40 years ago. Mrs. Tabb described how Mrs. Taylor helped desegregate the Middlesex County Schools by sending one of her children to the all-white elementary school in the early 1960s. She also explained that Mrs. Taylor helped with black voter registration during that time period. I learned that Mrs. Taylor lost her job as a county school bus driver when she sent Marilyn's older sister, Cheryl, to the white elementary school as part of the "The Original 13" black kids who integrated the white schools *seven years before* total desegregation occurred in 1969. *I wasn't aware of any of that.* On the day of Mrs. Bertha Taylor's funeral, I learned that she had been trying to help other black people long before she told me to "Pick C." She was an important part of Middlesex County's history.

CHAPTER 25

A year or so after we moved to Christchurch, Mumma started my *Sports Illustrated* subscription in 1971, and eventually, that got me interested in following horse racing, in particular the Triple Crown. Canonero II was the first horse I remember making the *SI* cover as he won the first two legs of the Triple Crown, the Kentucky Derby and the Preakness, but finished a disappointing fourth in the final leg, the Belmont Stakes. Two years later, everyone I knew was talking about a 3-year-old horse named Secretariat. After he won the Derby and the Preakness, in record time, even some of my female schoolteachers were talking about horse racing, and I never heard *any* of them mention anything sports-related. No horse had won the Triple Crown since Citation in 1948, and when *Grandma Latimore* asked me if I thought Secretariat had a chance, well, that's when I knew *everyone* was paying attention. The only other thing Grandma knew about sports was that Jackie Robinson had played baseball for the Brooklyn Dodgers. *Grandma Latimore is talking about horse racing? What the hell is going on!*

On the Saturday of the Triple Crown's final leg, the Belmont Stakes, I had three yards to cut, the Holmes', the Smith's and ours. The Holmes' property was about 100 feet away and the Smith's place was about 400 yards on the other side of our house. Cutting grass was how I made money. I received $5 for cutting each yard and when multiplied by three that came to $15, right? *Wrong!* Most Saturdays found me $5 short. The Smiths and the Holmes always came outside to pay me when I was finished. Da? Sometimes he paid me, and sometimes he didn't. "C'mon, Da! You owe me for 4 weeks now, that's $20, and that's not fair!" He smiled. "Why should I pay you for something you're *supposed* to do anyway? You live here for free! You're lucky I don't make you pay rent! The least you can do is cut the grass!" I guess he was right, but I didn't understand that then. *I wanted my money!*

I began cutting about 10:00 that Saturday morning. Each yard took about 90 minutes to mow, and I finished with the Holmes' yard and ours around 1:00 p.m. All I needed to do was motor over to the Smith's house on the used International Harvester riding lawn-mower that Da bought from Robert Greene's Hardware Store in Urbanna for $30 and call it a day. It came equipped with a Briggs & Stratton motor, and Da always told me that when I got big enough to buy my own lawnmower, to only buy one if it came with a Briggs & Stratton. I took his advice on that one and was never disappointed.

Saturday afternoons at 1:00 p.m. was also time for the *NBC Major League Baseball Game of the Week* on WWBT, Channel 12. At the time, it was the only baseball game we got on TV so I always wanted to watch it. The "post time" for the Belmont wasn't until 5:20 p.m., so I had plenty of time to watch the game. *Or so I thought.* I loved listening to the NBC play-by-play man, Curt Gowdy. Even though he passed away in 2006, he was always my favorite announcer. He also did play-by-play college basketball for NBC, and his favorite phrase after a made basket was, "Heeeee, hits it!" He and Joe Garigiola did the *Game of the Week* back in the 1970s. I liked Garigiola, too, but as I got older, I read somewhere that Garigiola and Jackie Robinson didn't get along quite so well, and just like that, I didn't like Mr. Garigiola anymore.

I quit watching the *Game of the Week* around 4:00 p.m. and headed over to the Smiths' house. Bouncing along on the International Harvester for a quarter of a mile, I began calculating the time need-ed to finish their yard and realized that I had a problem. *I wasn't gonna make it home in time to see the horse race. I was a big dummy! I'll just have to read about Secretariat in next week's Sports Illustrat-*

ed. The greatest inventions ever created, the VCR and DVR, hadn't yet been created so missing the race was the price I paid for watching baseball. Even revving up the engine to its highest speed wasn't going to help me make it home by post time.

The Smith property was a large one with many obstacles: walnut trees, an oak tree, a maple tree, azalea bushes and rose bushes, to name a few. I was in such a hurry to get home, I even chopped off some of Mrs. Smith's purple petunias she planted just a few weeks before! About an hour into it, she met me out in the backyard to offer me a glass of lemonade. *I wouldn't be able to pick Mr. Smith out of a police lineup, but I never forgot what Mrs. Smith looked like. She was a good-looking lady!* A brunette in her early 30s with legs that seemed like they went "up" and "down the county!" She always engaged me with small talk about school and such, but I always tried to end that conversation as soon as possible because I was scared to death that she would catch me gawking at her! "Yes, ma'am. School is almost over, and I'll be glad to do nothing but cut grass and play basketball all summer!" I gulped down her lemonade, thanked her and headed back to restart the mower and sit on its hard metal seat. Da strapped a cord around a wad of foam cushion from an old car seat to make it a little softer on my butt, but the metal was still hard to sit on for more than 10 minutes! Pulling the cord to restart the mower was always a struggle for me, and I used to lie in bed at night praying to God for the strength needed to make the mower "catch" on the first try. *I was a skinny kid with no muscles!* A couple of more "pulls" on the cord and still nothing. *I hated our mower sometimes!* Just when it was about to start, I looked up to see Mrs. Smith standing next to me. "Hey, Troy. I know you're a big sports fan. Why don't you come inside and watch the horse race with me?" *Are you kidding me?* I wasn't going to miss the race after all!

Mrs. Smith and I watched Secretariat destroy the field while his owner, "Penny" Tweedy, flailed her arms like a crazy woman in the Belmont stands. It was a wild scene. When Mrs. Smith and I watched racing history together in 1973 in front of her TV in Middlesex County, *never* did I think I would be at the Belmont one day. *Why would I dream something so crazy?* Thirty-one years later,

I squeezed into the grandstand with 120,139 others who hoped to see racing history. It was the largest crowd the Queens, New York, racetrack had ever seen, and I was part of it. Into the second turn, I felt Smarty Jones "went" too early, and I said to the lady standing next to me, "He can't hold on. He's no Secretariat." Smarty Jones failed in his bid to win the Triple Crown; he lost to a thoroughbred named Birdstone at the 2004 Belmont. Smarty ran out of gas.

I parked the lawnmower in our carport and ran into the house. Mumma couldn't wait to tell me about Secretariat. I stopped her before she even got started. "I already know what happened! Mrs. Smith let me watch it on her TV!" Her face went blank. *Uh oh.* She was *not* happy with that admission. Visiting Dale Pollock's house and playing over at Christchurch School was one thing, *this* was something completely different. I had been inside someone's home without her permission, and that was a mandatory requirement. To compound the situation, Mrs. Smith was a young, attractive white woman, and Mumma didn't trust white people. She was always cautious around them. She expected the same from me. She had been raised that way. Every now and then, I heard Grandpop Latimore whisper stories about two of his brothers, Elmore and Grant, who moved away, "lost their minds and never came back." Their disappearances took place in the 1920s or 30s, and I always thought it was the liquor that made Grandpop talk out of his head. Much later, I discovered their departures had more to do with seeing white women than just wandering off. "Losing their minds" was Grandpop's way of saying they were crazy for sneaking around with white women, but that's another story. Mumma used to tell Tony and his best friend, Milton, "Y'all better leave those white girls alone" after integration took place in 1969. They laughed it off, but I could tell she was serious.

Interracial relationships were taboo in Middlesex County and every other county in the South back then. Mumma's experiences with white people were far different than mine or Tony's or Milton's. Like when she attended Middlesex County School Board meetings to ask for more funds and resources for the black schools because the black teachers were afraid of losing their jobs if *they* asked for more supplies and materials. Instead, she and a few other St. Clare Walker High School students attended those meetings to meet with the man whose signature appeared on the back of my elementary school report card, Superintendent Mr. William T. Christopher. They might ask for a new school bus for the upcoming year to replace a battered one or some new textbooks for the 9th graders. Mr. Christopher granted some requests and denied others, but once he grew tired of their demands, Mumma told me he swiveled in his chair to face the wall behind him and turned his back towards the stunned students. That was his way of telling them he was done hearing their requests. It was time for the students to go home.

I think my venture into Mrs. Smith's house may have signaled to Mumma that maybe I was growing up a little too fast, and she didn't have quite the same control over me anymore. I knew that I was not to go into *any* person's home without her permission, yet I did it anyway. Maybe she worried that if something came up "missing" from the Smith home, I could have been blamed for it. But at 12 years old, I didn't think like Mumma did; I never gave it a second thought because I trusted *everybody* back then. I stopped trusting *everyone* a short 5 months later.

When Sharon, Bridgette or I misbehaved, Mumma used a wooden paddle that was emblazoned with red and black letters that displayed a drawing of a little boy with sparks flying from his bottom; its caption read: "Heat for the Seat!" I was very familiar with that paddle, and it was very familiar with my butt cheeks! My bottom was reintroduced to it after I revealed I already knew the race's outcome. Much later, I loved watching footage of Secretariat; yet, it was a pleasant and painful memory at the same time. It was "pleasant" because June 9, 1973, became a notable day in horse racing, and anyone old enough to remember it never forgot where they were. *I know I didn't.* I watched the CBS broadcast "live and in color" on Mrs. Smith's Zenith television. Had I not seen Secretariat cross the finish with 31 lengths to spare in record time, I would have been sick. I would have missed Chic Anderson's call, "Secretariat is widening now! He is moving like a tremendous machine! Secretariat by 12, Secretariat by 14 lengths! He's out there almost a sixteenth of a mile away from the rest of the horses!" He won by 31 lengths, setting a track record of 2 minutes, 24 seconds for the 1½-mile course, a record that still stands.

Recollections of that day in 1973 were also "painful" because I learned a new word that Saturday evening: Procrastinate. As Mumma swung the Heat for the Seat paddle against my butt, each syllable from her mouth was accompanied with a whack. "If-*whack*-you-*whack*-did-*whack*-not-*whack*-pro-*whack*-cras-*whack*-ti-*whack*-nate-*whack*-so-*whack*-God-*whack*-damned-*whack*-much-*whack*-you-*whack*-coulda-*whack*-watched-*whack*-the-*whack*-race-*whack*-at-*whack*-home-*whack*-NOT-*whack*-at-*whack*-that-*whack*-white-*whack*-lady's-*whack*-house!" I didn't even have to look up "pro-cras-ti-nate" to figure out that it had something to do with waiting until the last moment! From then on, I got Mumma's permission before going anywhere, but I was still glad I went inside of Mrs. Smith's house on the 9th day of June in 1973!

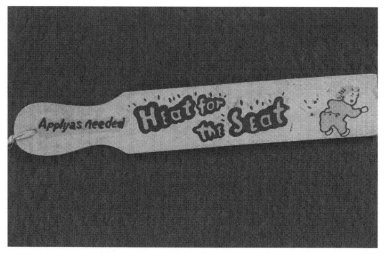

Mumma's weapon of choice. 2014

CHAPTER 26

St. Clare Walker Middle School was about a half mile up the road from Christchurch. The school had an interesting history as it was the "colored" high school in the 1940s, 1950s and 1960s, but became a middle school for all students in 1969. It was named after Mr. John Henry "St. Clare" Walker, the man deemed by many as most responsible for bringing formal education to blacks in Middlesex County. His nephew, Sherman Holmes, Jr., told me, "Uncle Johnny added 'St. Clare' to his name because it provided more flair than just 'John Henry Walker!'" *I thought that was funny!* Mr. Walker was born about 12 years after the Civil War (the war Mrs. St. John referred to as "The War Between The States"). Mr. Walker fought in the Spanish-American War and later received his undergraduate and graduate degrees from Hampton Institute. He named the first school he started for black students in Middlesex County after the poet Paul Lawrence Dunbar and later became principal for the "colored" Middlesex schools.

After we integrated in 1969, Middlesex High School retained its original school nickname: "The Saxons," a Germanic tribe reference. The basketball, football and baseball teams had "Saxons" emblazoned across their uniforms. It remained the Saxons for about a year until the black high school students complained about being referred to as Anglo-Saxons or white Germans. I didn't know what Saxons or white Germans were in the 3rd grade, and I didn't understand why the older black kids were complaining about being referred to as "Saxons." It was the talk around the county and in the *Southside Sentinel* until it was changed to "Chargers" the next year. At 8 years old, I thought, "Well, it was *their* school. They should be allowed to keep their nickname." But, one day while shooting basketball with Milton in his backyard, the 6'4" starting center on the Saxon/Charger basketball team broke down the controversy for me by saying, "I ain't no fucking German. Saxon is a white name. Our school name shouldn't be black or white, just a name." When we were done shooting, I ran into the house to look up Saxon in the dictionary, and then I understood what he meant.

The 1950s, '60s and '70s were challenging times throughout the South. Black and white families were impacted by the changes brought on with desegregation. The term "desegregation" is now just a history lesson, but it was real life for my family and me and others that I came to know. Two people, who later became a big part of my life, were affected by a decision in 1952 that cut funding for their "colored" high school in West Point. Beverly Allen School was the school for black students (grades 1–12) at the time, and when a new high school was built, the Town of West Point chose not to fund classes for the 29 students in Allen's grades 9–12. The black students thought they would attend the new school in the fall, especially after the local government quit subsidizing *their* high school. They were mistaken. When the 29 of them attempted to register in September of 1952, the new West Point High School principal, Mr. H. A. Humphreys, met them at the front door and turned them away.

The NAACP took up their cause, but in the meantime, the black high school students were still without a school. If they wanted to continue their education, they were forced to attend other black high schools in the area or move out of state. Some dropped out of school because they didn't see a better option. Parents of the black students were fined and threatened with jail time for keeping their kids out of school; they felt their kids should be allowed to attend the West Point High School just like the white kids within the town. They paid their taxes in West Point, and they wanted their kids educated in West Point. It was an ugly conflict that lasted over a decade.

West Point High School didn't open its doors to black students until 1969 – 15 years after the historic *Brown vs. Topeka Board of Education* lawsuit that officially desegregated schools throughout the United States. Thankfully, Rosetta Dobbins and Clarence Jackson left West Point in 1953 to catch a ride in a 1951 Plymouth station wagon heading to Middlesex County. It was driven by Mrs. Delores Tuppence who was heading to St. Clare Walker High School to become its new female physical education teacher. Each morning, Rosetta, Clarence and five others piled into the wagon for the 20-mile ride to become St. Clare Walker High "Wolverines."

Four years later, Rosetta Dobbins was a senior sitting in Mrs. Easter Holmes' history class preparing for the SAT. Mrs. Holmes tapped her on the shoulder and asked, "So Rosetta, what will it be for you? College or cottage?" Rosetta looked up and said, "Mrs. Holmes, I think it'll be the *cottage* for me." Mrs. Holmes knew Rosetta had been dating Monroe Vernon Jarvis, who had graduated two years earlier, and Rosetta knew that *she* wasn't going to college. *She* was going to get married and start a family. Her second child became James Monroe "Butley" Jarvis. *I was glad she chose the cottage!* Mrs. Jarvis made the best chocolate chip cookies in the world, and she used to send them to me when I was away at college and the Air Force. She always treated me like I was one of her own. Mr. Jarvis slipped me money every chance he got after Da left, and he told me that no one needed to know. I kept that information to myself until now. *I loved Mr. and Mrs. Jarvis.*

In high school, Clarence Jackson became Da's closest friend, but everyone called him "Dickie." He and Da were like Butley and me as kids: Inseparable. Dickie played basketball and baseball under my Uncle Eddie and after graduating from high school, had a tryout with the Pittsburgh Pirates as a pitcher. He was a pretty good left-hander and even in his 70s was still in really good shape at 6'5", 220 pounds. But after high school, his heart wasn't in playing baseball because it lay elsewhere, with a girl named Delight McGill. "Troy, all I wanted in life was to come back to West Point and marry Delight." In the fall of 1960, Rev. Lewis married Dickie and Delight Jackson, and Emmitt and Ruby Reed, and Mumma and Da in a triple ceremony in his living room. Each couple was "with child" at the time, but no one knew that except Dickie and Delight and Emmitt and Ruby and Mumma and Da!

Sometime in the 1970s, Dickie became the first black person elected to the West Point Town Council. I asked him, "When you were growing up and you had to go all the way to Middlesex just to go to high school, when there was a high school a couple of blocks from your house that you couldn't even *walk* into, did you *ever* think *you* would be on the West Point Town Council?" "Never, ever! Troy, after school, I was just trying to get enough money to buy a car. I worked at the Esso on the corner of Main Street for $25 a week. In 1957, I bought a '46 Plymouth for $100 from a white schoolteacher whose car I used to work on. She let me have it for a $50 down payment, and I paid her $5 a week until I was in the clear. I stopped by the Pulp Mill looking for a better job all the time. They finally hired me as a janitor, and I worked my way up to Plant Foreman and ended up supervising over 60 people. I got Butley's dad a job at the plant, too. I took him an application that he didn't want to fill out. He just wanted to drive that tractor trailer for the Urbanna Lumber Company for the rest of his life. Rosetta filled it out for him, forged his signature and dropped it off at my house the next time she came over to West Point. That's how Monroe and Rosetta were able to put Gwen, Butley and Kim through college."

I told Dickie about something I did when I came home for Grandma Latimore's funeral in 1996. Mumma had sent me to pick up a few things from the Food Lion grocery store in West Point. Walking ahead of me in the parking lot was an attractive black lady, and I thought to myself, "That's a good-looking older lady!" I "stalked" her up and down the aisles; and then she and I happened to check out at the same time. *Perfect timing on my part!* As we headed to our cars, I looked at her personalized license plate that read: "DELITE." *Uh oh. Could this be Delight Jackson? Oh, Lord.* "Excuse me, ma'am, are you Delight who's married to Dickie?" "Yes, I am." "Hi, I'm Troy, Bill and Jean's son!" She hugged me. I hadn't seen her since I was a little boy, and I felt really stupid that I was trying to flirt with someone as old as Mumma and who also happened to get *married* alongside her! We chatted for a couple of minutes, and on the drive back to Mumma's house, I thought how foolish I must have looked "stalking" Dickie Jackson's wife in the Food Lion!

Dickie retired from the Pulp Mill around 1995 and took up golfing in his spare time. Playing on a course that wasn't open to him or any other black person until 1980 or so became something he looked forward to after Delight passed away in 2008. Dickie and Delight (I always thought that had a nice ring to it) were married for 48 years, and after she died, he visited her grave every day. Once or twice he admitted to me that he'd forgotten to do so as he was getting ready for bed. He put his clothes back on, drove the mile or so over to her grave to tell her about his day, said "Good night" and headed back home. While recounting this, he stared off into the distance for a bit. "Dickie?" Nothing. "You okay?" More silence. Finally, "You know Troy, she's not coming back to me, so I have to go to her. I'm sorry for crying. I just miss Delight so much." I always liked Dickie Jackson. He was always nice to me, and he was my Da's best friend. *He certainly owed me no apology for crying.*

West Point students protesting segregation. 1952
*Mrs. Rosetta Dobbins Jarvis is holding the "No School,
No Town Taxes" sign.*

CHAPTER 27

In 5th grade at Rappahannock Central Elementary School, Mrs. Linda Tjossem was my music teacher. She and Da passed their love of music on to me. When it was time for the annual elementary school play, Mrs. Tjossem selected me as the lead in *Johnny Appleseed Comes to Town*. It was the highlight of my young life, and as I grew older, sometimes sadly, I thought it still was. A lot of the songs from that school play, I never forgot. Some of the lyrics were, "I've been rovin', up and down, here and there from town to town. And wherever I may go-o, from New York to O-hi-o-o, I plant trees, apple trees!" My favorite song was, "The slip of the tongue, the blot of the pen, the lapse of one's memory. The slight aberration, the miscalculation, they're common to you and to me! We make our daily quota of little absurdities. Maybe there's an explanation for all these senseless mysteries! But ole Alec Pope, whom you know I hope, has left us an immortal line. He said that, 'To err is human, but Sir, forgiveness is truly divine!'" *I always had a pretty good memory!*

I didn't know the meaning to most of the lyrics or who 18th century poet Alexander Pope was at 10 years old. *I certainly didn't know he was quoted nearly as much as Shakespeare or Tennyson, and not that I knew who those two guys were either at 10 years old!* I thought he was a "Pope" and not that I knew who or what a Pope was because I didn't know what a Catholic was because I didn't meet one until I went to college in Pennsylvania!

Mrs. Tjossem gave me the chance to be a "star" for one Friday and Saturday night in 1971. After the Saturday night show, Mumma and Da took Bridgette and me up to the Tastee-Freeze in Saluda for ice cream. Mumma and Bridgette stayed in the car while Da and I walked up to the sliding screen window to place our order. The woman behind the counter slid the screen back to ask what I wanted. Da looked down at me and said, "I am so proud of you tonight, you can order *anything* you want." *Whoa! This is a first!* Da or Mumma never let me order *anything* I wanted. They always *told* me what I wanted. Not that we went anywhere other than the Tastee-Freeze or the Burger King in Richmond on U.S. Route 60 near Byrd Airport. *I loved Whoppers!* "Da, I can order anything?" "Yup, you can." *What did I tell the woman behind the screen window?* "I'd like a *large* strawberry sundae with whip cream and a cherry on top." *I didn't learn that it was called "whipped" cream until I was in college.* Da sternly said, "Aren't you forgetting something?" "I'm sorry, ma'am. I forgot to say, 'Pleeease!'" *I thought he might change his mind when I forgot to say that!* Through the large glass window, I read the red, white and blue Pepsi-Cola menu with the black letters that hung from the ceiling by two chains. A large sundae went for 35 cents. A small was 25 cents. *Wow. I guess Da was really proud of me!* He spent an extra 10 cents. It was the first and *only* time he told me he was proud of me. No one had said that to me before. Now that I think about it, I only heard that two other times in my life, when I was 11 years old and 31 years old, but those are other stories! *I could not complain, some people never heard those words their entire life.*

When I went across the road to St. Clare Walker Middle School for 6th grade, we lost music because there was no funding for a music teacher. The next year, Mrs. Sandra Walton joined our school as the 7th grade English teacher, and she also volunteered as a music teacher. She started a choir for anyone who wanted to sing, and as much as I liked doing that, after a couple of weeks into it, I told Mrs. Walton I didn't want to be in her choir anymore. Her practice took place during the "free" 30 minutes before lunch period, and the boys and girls that weren't in choir were sneaking kisses and holding hands during their "free" time. *I wanted to be in on that kind of fun!* Mrs. Walton gave me such a look of disappointment when I told her that I wanted to quit that I didn't have the heart to do so. I didn't want to see that look on her face again (or any woman's), so I stayed. *It was the right decision.*

In English class, Mrs. Walton challenged us with her reading assignments and none was more challenging than the classic, *Beowulf.* She gave us a few days to read it, and I felt a lot better when Judy Kidd admitted she didn't understand it either because she was the smartest person I knew.

Another reading assignment was learning about the Mt. Vesuvius volcanic eruption that killed almost 16,000 Romans in 79 A.D. For extra credit, Mrs. Walton had me do a book report on Pompeii. Finding more information on what took place there wouldn't be easy. I was pretty sure Mrs. Barlowe wouldn't have a section of books devoted to Pompeii in her tiny library. I knew there was a Civil War (or a "War Between the States") section, a Virginia history section, a dinosaur section, a rock section, a chemistry section and a U.S. Presidents section and so forth. A Pompeii section? I doubted I would find that in Mrs. Barlowe's library! "Mrs. Walton, can I read about some other place for extra credit?" "Why?" "Getting more information on that Pompeii place is going to be too *hard.*" Mrs. Walton sighed. "Well, Troy, what will you learn if it's too *easy?*" *I've got no response for that one, Mrs. Walton!* She then looked at me and said, "Who knows, Troy? You may end up going there one day!" *Yeah, right. The only place I was going in life, if I was lucky, was to get a job at the Newport News Shipyard or the Pulp Mill in West Point like every other black man from Middlesex County or, through some minor miracle, go to college and become a schoolteacher.* I couldn't build houses like Da. Shoot, I couldn't even figure out how to pump gas because there were too many knobs to twist! Working at the Shipyard or the Pulp Mill was all I ever thought I would do, and since I had no mechanical ability, I worried throughout childhood that I wouldn't get one of those jobs, either. I certainly didn't think I would leave the Commonwealth of Virginia for more than a week. Mrs. Walton and the book report did give me something to think about, though. *Maybe I could go visit Pompeii one day.*

A couple of harmless comments from Mrs. Walton gave me *gas money* at 12 years old: "What will you learn if it's too easy?" "Who knows, Troy? You may end up going there one day!" I took the easy route often in life, but I always heard Mrs. Walton's voice reprimanding me for doing so. More importantly, she was the first person (other than Mumma) who made me think that I could see faraway places one day. Your parents may tell you that you can go anywhere and do anything, but Mrs. Walton was the first person outside of my family that made me think it might be possible.

In the summer of 2003, Mumma and I took a Mediterranean cruise where she picked the destinations. Each day I asked her, "So what are we going to see tomorrow?" "We're docking in Naples and taking a bus up to Pompeii." "Wow, Mrs. Walton had me do a book report on that place in 7th grade!" As we headed back to the cruise ship, I grabbed a postcard and mailed it to Mrs. Sandra Walton back in Urbanna. *"Hi, Mrs. Walton. It's Troy Lewis from your 1973 7th grade English class. I wanted to let you know I finally made it to Pompeii, and I owe so much of that to you!"* When I got home, I had a two-page letter from Mrs. Walton thanking me for the postcard. She wanted to know if I still sang, what I was doing with my life, and so forth. She went on to say that my postcard inspired *her*. She wrote how kids were different than when I came along; they weren't as polite and the parents weren't as involved, either. If I misbehaved in 7th grade, or *any* grade, Mumma *wanted* to know about it, and she'd *do* something about it. Mrs. Walton impacted my life almost 30 years earlier, and I had a slight impact on hers 30 years later. *I thought that was pretty neat.*

During our cruise, Mumma and I stopped in The Vatican to see St. Peter's Basilica and marvel at the sights within St. Peter's Square. While strolling through the country within a country, she asked, "Do you still go to church?" "Oh, Mumma. I used to go every Sunday. Now, I go about once every two months." "What? Boy, you better start going back to church." "Yeah, yeah. I know, I know." We stared at the panoramic view of the Square, the Basilica and the Obelisk. There were more than a hundred statues surrounding the Square, and as we stared at the breathtaking site, I know we were both thinking, "Never thought we'd get outta Middlesex County to see something like this!" We didn't say a word for a few minutes. Finally, Mumma pointed to one statue in particular that stood slightly taller than the others. "Why do you think that one is so much taller than the others?" "Mumma, are you kidding me?" "What?" "Look at it! That's Jesus!"

Later that afternoon, we stopped at an open-air market for a snack. I bought a white paper bag filled with white grapes from a merchant while Mumma admired the streets of Rome. I took a seat on the concrete wall surrounding the market, ate my grapes and admired the women who strolled by seemingly without a care in the world. Mumma walked over to me and said she was going shopping. "Take your time. I'll be right here eating my grapes when you come back. I've got plenty to keep me busy," pointing at the beautiful women walking by. "Boy, you better quit looking at those girls and pay attention to those grapes in your bag. The condensation is gonna make those grapes fall right through if you don't hold it from the bottom! Quit holding the bag from the top!" "Mumma, I am 42 years old! Don't you think I can eat a bag of grapes without you telling me how to do it?" "Okay, you never want to listen to your Mumma!" She was gone about an hour, and I continued plopping grapes into my mouth while admiring what Italy had to offer! She returned overloaded with shopping bags, and when she got within just a few feet of me, the grapes fell through the bottom of the bag! *Are you kidding me?* "I told you to hold that bag from the bottom!" *Mumma was right again!*

Mumma at The Vatican. 2003

Jesus just slightly taller than the others! 2003

CHAPTER 28

Mr. Howard Soucek (pronounced So-check) was my 7th grade social studies/history teacher, and he was the coolest and sharpest teacher I *ever* had. That's how much of an impression he made on me. He and his wife, Linda, who taught at the high school, drove a yellow 1972 Volkswagen Beetle, and that was the car that I wanted when I grew up. Mr. Soucek was the first and only teacher I had who wore sneakers to class every day. He wore the Jack Purcell brand that was originally manufactured by B.F. Goodrich until Converse bought the trademark rights in 1970. Those sneakers had a navy blue semicircle line across the toe that resembled a "smile," and anytime I saw those shoes they reminded me of Mr. Soucek, and that made *me* smile.

Mr. Soucek had an uncanny ability to keep everyone involved in class because you never knew when he was going to call on you. None of us wanted to disappoint him because we felt that he cared about us. In the summer of 1972, he loaned me *The Autobiography of Malcolm X* written by Alex Haley. He told me to read it at my leisure and to drop by during summer school if I wanted to discuss it. I doubt there were any other *white* teachers in Middlesex County or in the entire state of Virginia who were reading *that* book, let alone handing it over to an 11-year-old for him to read. I don't think Malcolm X was a very popular figure in Virginia in 1972. And I'd never even heard of Mr. X until Mr. Soucek gave me the book. I knew about people like Ralph Bunche, Thurgood Marshall and Dr. Charles Drew, but I had never heard of this "X" guy. Mr. Soucek taught me a lot that summer, and I wasn't even *in* his summer class.

The lesson that I learned best from Mr. Soucek came when he gave us a short writing assignment on a topic that I've long since forgotten. I was always a good speller and classmates sometimes asked me to proofread their homework before they turned it in. *There was no such a thing as "spell-check!" All you had back then was a dictionary and your brain.* Basil Holiday was in my class, and he asked me to read his two- to three-paragraph paper before handing it over to Mr. Soucek. I suggested a few spelling and grammatical changes before he placed it on the teacher's desk. When Mr. Soucek returned our papers the next day, Basil received an "A", and I got a "C." I couldn't understand that because I had read Basil's, and I knew my report was *better* than his! I was irritated. After class, I asked Mr. Soucek why Basil got an "A," and I didn't. *I never forgot his reply.* "Troy Lewis, this kind of stuff is easy for you, and in what you wrote, you didn't give it your best effort. For Basil, this kind of stuff is a bit harder, and he tried harder. So, that's why *he* got an 'A' and *you* didn't." I opened my mouth to complain, but no words came. *There was no "arguing" with teachers back then, anyway!* "Do you have any *other* questions?" *Well, I guess not when you put it that way, Mr. Soucek!* I was mad, but he was right. I hadn't given it my best. I'd just done enough to get by, and a "C" was what I deserved. I eventually discovered that I only cheated myself when I gave a lesser effort, and if you wanted "extra," you needed to give "extra" effort. Mr. Soucek also got me thinking that if I didn't know about that Malcolm X guy, there might be a *few* more people in the world that I needed to learn more about. And Mr. Soucek taught me the importance of keeping everyone involved in classroom discussions and rewarding the person who gives more effort than one who doesn't. Years later that lesson came in handy in my professional life.

When I was in the Air Force, I coached youth and squadron intramural sports. One year I was the coach for my supervisor's 10-year-old son's basketball team. His name was Raymond, but his nickname was "Bear" because his mom said he "growled" as an infant. So that's why he was called "Bear!" Even when he was in his 30s, I still called him by that nickname. There were two girls who also wanted to participate in Bear's 10- to 12-year-old league. In the early 1990s, the Air Force had no youth female leagues. After tryouts,

I overheard other coaches saying that they weren't going to pick either one of those girls. "Me, neither," I thought to myself as I was leaving the gym after watching them try out. *They were awful!* I told Lori about those two girls, and she wanted to know which of my draft picks I was going to use to select both of them. "Are you nuts? I ain't giving up picks for either one of them!" She looked at me as though *I* was the one who was nuts. "What? Why are you looking at me like that?" "Oh, I don't know, have you forgotten about Basil Holiday and Mr. Soucek, and how some things were easier for some and not so easy for others. Didn't you tell me that you and Butley used to go to a baseball clinic in Middlesex, and y'all never got picked for Little League because y'all were told you needed to 'work' on something to get better and maybe next year y'all could play?" *I forgot I had told her that story.*

All Butley and I wanted was a chance to play. Each year as little boys, he and I attended the clinic; yet, he and I still needed to *improve* in one area or another before we could make a Little League team. To be totally honest, as a 7-year-old or 8-year-old kid, I thought we *weren't* good enough to play, but as I got older I realized it wasn't that we weren't good enough, we just weren't *wanted.* Every *white* kid who attended the clinic ended up playing for the Saluda, Urbanna, Deltaville or Church View teams in the county.

I drafted both girls to be on my youth league team. Between the two of them, they probably scored 8 points in our 14-game season. Neither of them was that good, but they had fun playing. *Wasn't that what it was supposed to be about anyway?* One of the girls, Amanda, had a hard time understanding the nuances of the 2-3 Zone Defense. She usually wound up playing "man-to-man" or "woman-to-man" instead! I think the "area" responsibility of a zone defense was just too much for her brain to grasp at 10 years old. Our team finished 2nd in the league of 8 teams. We lost badly to the 1st place team from Council Bluffs, Iowa, by about 40 points during the regular season. *Those Iowa kids were like 10- to 12-year-old West Point Pointers!* We played Council Bluffs again in the league championship on a Saturday morning and lost by only 6. I stayed up all Saturday night trying to figure out a way to get those 6 points back! However, what I remember most about that game was that Amanda played the 2-3 Zone perfectly! She boxed out, rebounded and managed her area of the zone like she had been doing it since the day she was born! During a time-out, I looked at her in disbelief. "What are *you* doing?" With a big smile, she said, "I finally figured out this zone thing you've been trying to teach me all season!" Amanda didn't *get* it initially, but she kept trying and eventually, she did. Both of those girls tried and that was all I could ask for. It took me about 20 years to fully appreciate Mr. Soucek's lesson. It took Amanda the whole season to learn the 2-3 Zone, but she gave her best effort. *I never forgot her smile during that time-out.*

CHAPTER 29

The year horse racing was altered with Secretariat's run for the Triple Crown in 1973, three Middlesex County families' lives were drastically altered in the fall. I was part of that change, and the lives of the Lewises, the Latimores and the Merediths were never the same. The Merediths were a white family that lived "down the county" in Deltaville, and Da was in the process of remodeling their home. Mr. Robert Meredith was also the new St. Clare Walker Middle School principal, and he and his wife, Sandra, had three kids near my age or a little younger.

Lots of families went through divorce, but my parents were the first that I knew of to do so. Divorces may have been going on elsewhere in the U. S., but *not* in Middlesex County. People may have "separated" or "lived apart" in our county, but no one "divorced." Within the classified section of the *Southside Sentinel*, the battle played out. I was mesmerized and embarrassed to see *Jean Latimore Lewis vs. William Franklin Lewis (in absentia)* play out on Page Six of the seven pages that made up the *Sentinel*. The "play" went on for about 8 weeks and every Thursday when the paper came out, I didn't check out the sports section to read about the Chargers or the Pointers; I headed straight for the Classified Section where various land transfers and purchases were also recorded. It was also where I could see Mumma and Da's name in the paper for the first and only time in my life. It was a one-sided fight because Da remained "in absentia." The phrase "in absentia" frightened me, and I didn't want to look it up but eventually did. Its definition provided me with the finality that Da wasn't coming back, and that made me really sad.

The Middlesex County Court divorce case moved along without Da's presence. Like slowing down to look at a car accident, I tried to avert my eyes away from the *Sentinel's* Classified Section each Thursday, but I didn't. I was ashamed that Mumma and Da were no longer together, but I knew it was best because Mumma didn't have to get beat up anymore. In a way, I was glad Da was gone. I loved him, but I didn't like a lot of the shit that he did to Mumma. I know she never thought she'd be free of Da, but now she was, and I was happy for her. I was sad for Bridgette and me but happy for Mumma. The circumstances that surrounded their breakup were difficult to explain. Surreal or unreal were two words that came to mind, but that's another story.

CHAPTER 30

Coach James McCleary also came to Middlesex County in 1973, and he became a big part of my life. He was the new physical education teacher and replaced Coach James Dickens. Coach Dickens was a terror and scared the bejesus out of most St. Clare Walker 6th and 7th graders, but he did let us play dodge ball, so I loved him for that! That being said, I never thought I'd learn to open a Master combination lock under his tutelage. "C'mon, Troy Lewis, I heard you were supposed to be smart. Can't you figure it out? Is a *lock* smarter than *you?*" *You know what, Coach Dickens? It is!* Coach Dickens didn't come back after the Thanksgiving break, for some reason. So when I walked into the gym for 6th period, there was a new P.E. teacher shooting jumpers with a perfect Afro and even more perfect form on his jump shot; I liked him as soon as the ball fell through the net. I learned that he had recently graduated from Morgan State University in Maryland. The only thing I knew about that school was that there was a guy up there named Marvin "The Human Eraser" Webster, and *Sports Illustrated* had written an article about him.

(**Insert "City, Country, City" by War**) Coach McCleary was a fan of the funk group War, and over the next few months he let me borrow some of his albums. My favorite became *The World is a Ghetto*, whose album cover depicted urban life where people lived close to one another like what I saw when I visited New York City. Many nights I stared at the jacket cover wondering how people lived that way, and I knew *that* was no life for me, but much of my adult life found me living right there in Manhattan. Eventually, I used some of my grass-cutting money to buy my own *The World is a Ghetto* album "down the county" at Rich's Supermarket for my 13th birthday for $3.29.

Coach McCleary was from Beltsville, Maryland, and drove a 1968 green Dodge Dart. A military brat, his father served 20 years or so in the Army. Coach McCleary had a younger brother and sister, Henry and Cheryl, who were about my age. *How do I know so much about Coach McCleary and his family?* I went to live with them in Maryland.

After Mumma and Da broke up, Coach McCleary took me away to stay with his family during Christmas break of 1973 and the entire summer of 1974. Sometimes I stayed with him and his girlfriend at their apartment, but most of the time I stayed at his parents' Beltsville home, where I hung out with Henry and Cheryl and the other kids in their neighborhood. Beltsville was a quiet, suburban community of Washington, D.C., and although it was only about 3 hours from Middlesex, it seemed light-years away. The McCleary split-level home reminded me of where Mike and Carol Brady and their *Brady Bunch* lived on television. At the McCleary house, there was no yelling, no cussing and no fussing. Everyone got along. *What's wrong with these people!*

During the Christmas holiday, Mr. and Mrs. McCleary threw a party upstairs for their friends, and there was a downstairs basement dance party for all of the kids. Down in the carpeted basement, I sat on a couch and watched television. The TV was where I found refuge during the dance party. *Dancing was not for me!* Clicking from channel to channel, I stumbled across an old black and white movie. Something entitled *It's A Wonderful Life*. I settled back on the sofa. *This seems pretty good.* Never did I think that it would become a holiday staple that I could watch anytime. Never did I dream that VHS tapes and DVDs would come along either! Certainly, I never thought I would end up like George Bailey teetering on my own version of the Bedford Falls Bridge contemplating ending my life.

At the end of the movie, though, I hoped that Mr. Potter would be held accountable for "stealing" the bag of money from Uncle Billy, but he wasn't, and that made me mad. Many years later when I found out there was a Motion Picture Production Code that governed movies from 1930–1968, and it mandated that "all criminal action had to be punished," I got even madder! *How could Mr. Potter take money from the Bailey Building and Loan and get away with it?* Each time I watched it, I waited for a "Deleted Scene" to be added to the end of the movie, allowing Bert the Sheriff to head over to Mr. Potter's office and arrest him after the singing of *Auld Lang Syne*. It would have given me a great deal of satisfaction to see mean old Mr. Potter and his wheelchair hauled off to jail. Now, that would have been a truly merry Christmas for anyone watching! Good was supposed to conquer evil was what I thought the first time I saw *It's A Wonderful Life*. Maybe, at 12 years old, it was best that I learned life wasn't always fair in the movies or in real life.

(Insert "Mr. Big Stuff" by Jean Knight) While I waited to see if George Bailey would escape his precarious circumstances, the other kids were "bumping" on the dance floor to "Mr. Big Stuff" by Jean Knight and "Keep on Truckin'" by Eddie Kendricks. I had one eye on the TV and the other on the dance floor, but there was no way I was venturing out there to join them. A dance floor was something I avoided until I was a freshman in college, and after my first time finally getting on it, it was hard to keep me off of it! *I should have been doing this a long time ago!* But when I was 12 years old, I remained glued to the couch, sipping eggnog and watching Jimmy Stewart and Donna Reed on the TV. As George Bailey and I slowly came to the realization that his life wasn't so bad after all, a girl close to my age joined me on the couch. "What are you watching?" I hardly looked up. I didn't want to miss anything, but I gave her a quick *synopsis* since I now knew what that word meant. When the movie went to a commercial break, I took a peek at who was next to me. *She's cute!* I gave *more* details about the movie, and hoped that she would stay and watch with me. About 10 minutes later, when George and Mary started kissing while they had a phone conversation with Sam "Hee Haw" Wainwright, the girl sitting next to me kissed me. *Or, maybe I kissed her!* Honestly, I don't remember the details of who started the kissing game, but it wasn't important who started it! Her name was Towanda. Each time an adult came down to check on us, Towanda and I quickly separated. Once the coast was clear, she and I went back to kissing, holding hands and watching the movie. It was, indeed, a wonderful life for George Bailey and a wonderful night for me that evening! Towanda and I saw more of each other over the Christmas holiday and even more so the following summer. *Whatever happened to her?*

Thankfully, at the McCleary home away from home, there was no Bridgette for me to fight, and there was no Da fighting with Mumma. In the month or so since Da had been gone, I thought it would have made Mumma a nicer person, but that wasn't the case. *She was now angrier than ever.* I assumed that once Da was out of her life, her disposition would have become sunnier, but everyone knows what happens when you assume. My temporary life with the McCleary family was great, and that was all I cared about. All I had to do in Maryland was help out around the house, play ball, and stay out of trouble. *I could handle that.* That's all I really remember about my time with my 7th grade P.E. teacher and his family. I knew returning to Virginia was inevitable, but I wasn't looking forward to going back to a crazy mother, no father, an alcoholic grandfather, a grandmother who listened to Mahalia Jackson records all the time, a know-it-all, bossy cousin, and a sister who hated my guts. Frankly, after spending Christmas break and the following summer with *"The Brady Bunch,"* my family resembled *"The Munsters"*!

The McCleary family was different than any family I had ever been around. They all seemed to get along and genuinely care for each other. Their home was a loving environment. I got along great with Henry and Cheryl, and they both were really nice to me. I had never been around something like that before. It seemed like my family merely *tolerated* each other and that was only some of the time! Why Coach McCleary chose me to go home with him, I never understood. I don't think he was even sure himself, and he never asked for Mumma's permission. After gym class on the Friday before Christmas break, he walked up to me and said, "Why don't you come home with me for Christmas? Go tell your mother. I'll pick you up around 6." I walked into Grandma's house, and told Mumma that Coach McCleary was taking me away for Christmas. "Ok, go pack your stuff." Those were different times, and in the 1970s, it wasn't a second thought. Teachers helped students in need. *I was definitely someone in need.* I was just happy that Coach McCleary took an interest in me because it didn't seem like anyone else did. My family was busy living their *own* lives, and I understand that now, but I didn't then. There wasn't a lot of love on display in any of the homes that I lived in as a boy, but then again, I did have a family that kept a roof over my head, and fed and clothed me every day, so I guess that was their way of showing me love. *I just wasn't smart enough to figure that out at the time.*

Coach McCleary, his sister Cheryl, and me. 2015

CHAPTER 31

The growling Bear didn't stay with Lori and me for months at a time like I did with the McClearys. However, Bear was with Lori and me almost every weekend. If we were going out, he was going with us. Not that we went anywhere special, only to the mall or out for pizza or the movies and back home. Many years later, I found out that he liked being at our house sometimes more than his. *Kind of like me with the McClearys.*

The most money I ever made when I was in the Air Force was about $17,000 a year. I was "enlisted," and enlisted people never made a lot of money, so I worked a number of part-time jobs to help make ends meet. Telemarketing, loading boxes at UPS and working at Homer's Records and Tapes, a local chain music store, were a few of the jobs that I worked to make extra cash. Another opportunity fell in my lap while watching a local TV sports feature on the Omaha Racers, a Continental Basketball Association team, and Greg Shea, their Public Relations Director. When the segment was over, I ran to the Yellow Pages to call Greg and ask him if he needed an intern. *I had nothing to lose!* Greg told me that they had never had an intern, and he couldn't promise anything, but said he'd be willing to chat with me if I drove down to the arena. I became an "unpaid" intern who received a $50 bonus each Christmas; I copied score sheets, ran the 24-second expiration clock and called in scores to local radio and TV affiliates. I was nothing more than a "gofer," but I enjoyed it and figured that I could put it on a resume one day. Another of my duties was to pick up referees from the local Hampton Inn and drive them to Ak-Sar-Ben (Ne-bra-ska spelled backwards) Arena. Once the game was over, I sometimes took them back to their hotel or to Eppley Airfield, the Omaha airport, to catch their flight. I saw a bunch of those refs make it to the National Basketball Association, and I thought it was neat that I was able to tell Butley, "Yeah, I know that was a bad call, but I used to give that guy a ride to the airport!"

As the intern, I was usually the last to leave the arena after calling in scores and stats to the local media outlets. One night after the Racers had played the Quad City Thunder, I called in the score and headed to meet Lori in the parking lot where she was warming up the car. We noticed an older couple standing outside of the arena after it had been secured for the night. The "older" white couple appeared to be in their late 50s (*that* was ancient to me when I was in my 30s). It was about 10 degrees outside, so I pulled up to ask if they needed help. They told us they had been waiting for their limo for over 30 minutes, and they had no access to a pay phone. *There were no cell phones back then.* Lori and I were their only option. They needed a ride to Eppley to catch a flight. We offered. They accepted.

We began the 20-minute ride to the airport, made small talk, and as we got closer, they said they needed to be dropped off over at the *private* side of the airport, not the *commercial* side. "I'm confused. Why do we need to go over to that side?" "Well, we flew in from Illinois on our *private* jet." I looked over at Lori and then in my rearview mirror and said, "Who *are* you guys?" They were Mrs. Anne Potter DeLong and her husband, Ed, the owners of the Quad City Thunder, and they had their *own* personal jet! Well, I was in the Air Force, and I didn't know anyone who *owned* a jet; our Offutt AFB four-star general had use of a *personal* plane, but he didn't *own* it. America did! As the DeLongs exited our red two-door 1989 Ford Probe, they thanked us for the ride and handed us $50. We tried to give it back, but they wouldn't take it. My base pay at the time was $1381.80 a month, and for Lori and me, $50 was a *lot* of money. We fell asleep that night discussing all of the things that we would be able to do with that $50 bill!

I had an official Omaha Racers pass made for Bear that he wore around his neck. It read "Bear." He wore that pass around our house all the time. "Boy, are you ever gonna take that thing off?" "No!" The Racers were as close to an NBA team as we got in Omaha, and I guess Bear felt like he was in Chicago Stadium watching Michael Jordan and Scottie Pippen. He retrieved loose balls during warm-ups and at halftime, and helped me make copies of score sheets to hand out to the coaches and the local TV sportscasters. When we got a break, we headed over to the concession stand to buy Dove Bars from Steve, the ice cream vendor.

As time went on, I concentrated more on graduating from college, my own priorities and less on Lori and Bear. *I could have been a much better husband, but I wasn't. I was a real selfish, self-centered jerk.* Bear grew up, Lori and I broke up, and after a couple of years, we both lost touch with him. He was now a teenager finding his way. One weekend while working at the record store, Bear walked in, and I barely recognized him. He had become part of the "grunge" scene. He looked more like Kurt Cobain than Kurt Cobain ever did, and from my perspective, it was a terrible look for both. I could tell Bear was "high" on something, and I headed to the break area to gather my composure. *It hurt to see him that way.*

This was the same kid who would lie on one end of our L-shaped couch watching Jordan and the Bulls with me. The same kid who I took to The Scorecard Bar and Grill on Cornhusker Road to watch North Carolina–Duke on ESPN2 when no one in America got ESPN2, but the Scorecard's satellite dish did. This was the same kid who I taught to love Carolina and hate Duke! This was the same kid who would sit on the couch with me and watch the same Carolina game over and over on a summer weekend when there was nothing else on TV because we knew in the end Duke was going to lose. After he and I cut the grass on Saturday mornings, Lori would ask Bear what we were going to do the rest of the day. "We are gonna watch another Carolina–Duke game!" "Haven't y'all seen that about 80 times?" "Yes, we have! Let's make it 81!"

I returned to the store floor and said, "Hey, Bear." He strained his eyes to recognize me and replied, "What's up, dude?" and kept walking past me like he had never seen me before. I guess that was the part that hurt the most. He may not have recognized me at that point. *Whatever happened to Bear?*

Even after Lori and I broke up, we still remained very good friends. After moving from Nebraska, it took a while to track Bear down, but Lori helped me find him. He was living in Texas, and I met him at a restaurant while traveling for work in 2011. Prior to that, the last time I had seen him was almost 20 years ago when he was doing his impersonation of Mr. Cobain. He told me that he was sorry about *that* day at the record store. He recognized me but admitted that he was too ashamed to talk to me. He told me that even when he was doing things he wasn't proud of, he could hear Lori and me in his head saying, "Quit being a knucklehead." We spent a couple of hours catching up, and as we left the restaurant and headed to our cars, he told me that hanging out with me at the Racer games was his favorite childhood memory. Coach McCleary helped me for no reason, and I tried to do the same for Bear. He and I began texting during North Carolina basketball games, and that made me very happy. You never know how you'll impact someone's life. *I always loved that kid who growled, and I still do.*

Lori, Grandpop Latimore and me. 1983

CHAPTER 32

Right after Da left Middlesex County and just before Coach Mc-Cleary arrived, I did something that got me into *a lot* of trouble. Luckily, Da's middle sister got me out of it. Her name was Faye, and she was only 15 years older than I, making her more like an older sister than an aunt. When I reached my 50s, she told me that she and I had been "partners" since the day I was born. *Nothing made me happier than hearing that!* When I was 14, Faye allowed me to drive her from place to place, and once the Commonwealth of Virginia made it official for me to drive, I became her unofficial "chauffeur" taking her to NAACP meetings, weddings, funerals or anywhere else she wanted to go.

Faye was one of "The Original 13" colored students who integrated the Middlesex High and Elementary Schools in 1962. Although *mandatory* integration in the county didn't take place until 1969, those 13 kids started *voluntary* integration seven years earlier. One county in Virginia, Prince Edward, fought so hard against integration that it closed *all* of its schools, black *and* white. For five years! At Middlesex High, Faye was the single "colored" junior. "If I had known I was going to be the *only* one in my class, I wouldn't have done it," she told me. But then again, she couldn't have stayed at the black high school, either. Someone was there who made her life miserable when she was in 8th, 9th and 10th grade. She had to get away from *him*. That person was the St. Clare Walker High School principal, Mr. Charles I. Thurston. He and Faye were oil and vinegar. At the "colored" high school, there were probably 20 to 25 students in grades 8 through 12, and of those roughly 100 students, Faye was probably Mr. Thurston's least favorite. Faye was no "angel" as a high school student, but he was on her case all the time. "Faye Lewis, get to class!" "Faye Lewis, why didn't you do better on your English exam?" "Faye Lewis, leave those boys alone!" I thought Faye may have exaggerated his dislike for her, but multiple sources provided confirmation. "Charles I." had it in for Faye. *Some people were just that way. I had two supervisors who acted in similar fashion, and I could never figure those two clowns out, either!*

Faye was sassy and didn't take anything from anyone, even at 14 years old, and she certainly wasn't going to take it from Mr. Thurston. "I figured I'd take a chance with the integration stuff because those white kids couldn't have been any meaner to me than he was," Faye told me. During a phone conversation with her when she was in her 60s, I asked her to explain her integration experience in one sentence. There was a pause of about 30 seconds. "Faye, are you there?" She was choosing her words carefully. "I'm thinking. Shut up and be quiet." More silence. "Here's what I'll say – in each race, creed and color, there are good people and bad people. That was my integration experience. Was that enough for you?'" *Yes, Faye. It was.*

The following school year, Faye's younger sister, Portia, started 8th grade as Faye entered her senior year. I remember a couple of my uncles disagreeing with Faye and Portia and the colored kids up at the white schools. They felt those kids should have kept attending the black school. I really liked Faye and Portia, and I really liked my uncles Eddie, Ronnie, Darnell and Tony. I never said anything, but I was confused why my maternal uncles didn't like what "the integration people" (a term I heard used to describe them) were doing. I was an infant when the integration experiment began, and it continued with a sprinkling of black kids going to the white schools until complete integration occurred in September of 1969 when I was 8. As a youngster, I was also confused as to why the dozen or so black kids didn't want to attend the "colored" schools that my uncles and I were attending. *Were our schools not good enough for them?* It was all very confusing for my young mind. I didn't want my maternal uncles saying unkind things about my paternal aunts. They were *all* related to me. I just thought *we* were supposed to love one another. Maybe my uncles couldn't see that Faye and Portia and those other kids were trying to make it "better" for everyone in the long run. "Separate was equal" according to the *Plessy v. Ferguson* case of 1896, but it really wasn't. Fortunately, the *Brown v. Topeka Board of Education* decision in 1954 reversed that doctrine. When I got older, I asked Portia if she ever thought about leaving Middlesex High and returning to the "colored" St. Clare Walker. "Every year I told myself I wasn't coming back to Middlesex High School. But I didn't want to give the *white* kids the satisfaction of knowing they'd run me off, and I didn't want to give the *black* kids the satisfaction of saying, 'You couldn't stick it out.' So I stuck it out." That was a lot of pressure on a teenager. I couldn't imagine what it was like for Faye and Portia and those other kids. *They were a lot braver than I think I would have been.* Middlesex County didn't have the rioting and violence that took place in Alabama or M-I-S-S-I-S-S-I-P-P-I, but I could tell that some ugly things went on that Faye and Portia didn't want to reveal to me. *I was positive that I didn't want to hear it.*

Around 1972, Faye got a job as a secretary at the Middle Peninsula-Northern Neck Mental Health Center in Saluda. It was a two-story house that was converted to an office building. Psychiatrists used it to conduct their sessions as they rotated between Middlesex and neighboring counties. As a 7th grader, I became a Mental Health Center client after being labeled a "sexual pervert" by my Aunt Dot. That label was given to me for what I did one day in gym class. After Mumma and Da parted ways, some in my family thought that I was well on my way down a path that was far more sinister.

While Coach Dickens was setting up the volleyball net, a girl (her name wasn't important) came over and whispered, "If you follow me in the girls' locker room, I'll let you see my breasts!" I wasn't going to miss that opportunity because I hadn't seen *any* breasts! I took about two steps into the girls' locker room before Coach Dickens snatched me by the back of my neck, "Troy Lewis, where in the *hell* do you think you're going?" *Uh oh.* I was marched up to the principal's office to see Mr. Meredith, and he had Mrs. Arnetta Kidd, the school secretary, call Grandma Latimore for someone to come pick me up. *I guess they felt like they had to get me off the school premises as quickly as possible!* To make matters worse, Mumma was at work, so Grandma Latimore took the phone call from Mrs. Kidd. *Was there anything worse at 12 years old than standing in the secretary's office listening to her explain to your grandmother that you are being sent home from school because you were caught sneaking in the girls' locker room to look at a half naked 12-year-old girl?* Grandma Latimore lived for another 23 years, but I sincerely thought she would be dead when I got home from school. Faye came down to pick me up, and she wasn't happy as we walked toward her car. For each step, there was a smack to the back of my head! After starting the car and getting on 33, she gave me one more smack for good measure.

Aunt Dot lived across the field from Grandma and Grandpop Latimore's house. When she saw Faye's car pull up, she got in her tan 1970 two-door Chevy Malibu to see what was going on. It was unusual for Faye to stop by that early in the afternoon. Aunt Dot came in and asked, "Why are you home from school early? Why did Faye have to come pick you up? Are you sick?" "Sort of," said Faye, as she explained what I had been up to while puffing on her Parliament cigarette that came in the royal blue and white pack. Aunt Dot's contempt for me was evident when she said, "What are you? Some kind of sexual pervert?" I didn't even know what a "pervert" was, but her face told me it wasn't good. She went on, "There aren't any perverts in the Latimore family, and you *aren't* going to be the first." She turned her head in Faye's direction. "It's obvious this boy needs some help, and isn't that what that new Center in Saluda where you work is supposed to do? *Help* people? Let one of those psychiatrist people talk some sense into his big head! I don't know what's wrong with him! I think he's lost his mind."

Counseling may have been on the verge of becoming commonplace throughout the U.S., but it was cutting edge for Middlesex County in 1973. Anyone who "talked" to someone about a problem was considered "weird" or worse, "insane." *Counseling worked for me about 40 years later, but that's another story.* At the time, psychiatry was something that took place on television, not in Middlesex

County. And if people happened to drive by the Middle Peninsula-Northern Neck Mental Health Center and saw your car in the tiny parking lot, you might as well have posted it in the *Southside Sentinel* that you had a mental health problem because it was going to be all over the county by the next day. *That's just the way it was in a small town.*

Faye made an appointment for me with Dr. Jack Billups the following morning. *Looking back, I was surprised Faye and Aunt Dot didn't set up an emergency appointment for me the previous evening!* Faye picked me up at 7:30, and we drove in silence for the 2 miles up to the Mental Health Center. *She was still mad at me.* We pulled into the driveway of the Center, and I followed Faye inside. She took a seat at her desk, and dismissed me by pointing her index finger in the direction of Dr. Billups' office. *That was my signal to get away from her!* Dr. Billups greeted me at the top of the stairs and ushered me into his office. "Have a seat on the couch and tell me why you are here." *Wow, this really is like The Bob Newhart Show!* I sat down on his couch. "I'm here because I am a sexual pervert." A smile creased his face as he sought more information. *Why is he smiling? This isn't funny! I'm a pervert!* "Please explain to me why you think that you're a pervert." "Well, I was in 6th period gym class, and a girl walked over to me and told me that if I followed her into the girls' locker room she would let me see her breasts. I followed her in there, and Coach Dickens caught me." "Is that it?" "Yes, sir." He asked if I touched her. "No, sir." "Did anything else happen?" "No, sir. There wasn't time for anything else to happen." "Okay, here's my opinion. You aren't a sexual pervert." "Really?" "No, I don't think you are. I think you're going to be okay." "I'm not a pervert?" "No, you're just 12! Let's go downstairs and get your Aunt Faye to take you to school." My counseling session lasted all of 5 minutes, but Dr. Billups' assessment wasn't good enough for my family. They wanted continued counseling for the first pervert in the family!

Faye picked me up Monday mornings at 7:30 for the next few weeks, but we never stopped at the Center. At least *she* realized I wasn't a pervert! We drove from one end of Middlesex County to the other in her grey 1972 Datsun 240SX for an hour. As we drove "up and down the county," she puffed on her Parliament cigarettes and drank coffee, while we talked about life, family, girls and homework. She then dropped me off at school, winked and said, "Remember, this is our secret and don't you tell anybody!" It took about 2 months to be officially "rehabilitated." Our secret remained just that until I revealed the truth to Mumma some 40 years later. "Are you kidding me? I'm gonna kill Faye!"

CHAPTER 33

After Da left us on a Tuesday night in November of 1973, we moved back into Grandma and Grandpop Latimore's house. Our house down at Christchurch remained vacant until Faye saved enough money to buy it from Mumma. Mumma couldn't afford the payments, but Mr. Walter Major, the Bank of Middlesex president, let her pay what she could, when she could, because he didn't want to foreclose on her and ruin her credit. *Different times.*

Grandpop Latimore made us move in with him and Grandma because he was afraid for us living down at Christchurch. He worried that someone might firebomb the house or worse. Mumma, Bridgette, Gentree and I moved in with Grandpop, Grandma and Sharon. I guess he felt there was safety in numbers, but to be quite honest, it was our only option because Mumma couldn't pay all of the bills. Although the racial climate was improving in our area, Grandpop was still concerned about our safety. He knew firsthand the ugliness that could result from interracial relationships, but that's a story to soon come.

After Da left the county, there were a few unpleasant phone calls, and sometimes, men honked their horns from their pickup trucks to remind us that *they* hadn't forgotten about us. Faye told me that a few rednecks threw beer bottles in her yard or yelled in the direction of her house as they drove by during the nights that followed. Some nights, the Middlesex County Sheriff parked in the median on 17 to keep an eye on her place. She told me that she was prepared and kept a loaded gun in her bedroom just in case it was needed. "Yes, indeed! I wish one of those fools had come on my property!"

Monday night, November 12th, was our last night in the house down at Christchurch. I know when I woke up on that Tuesday morning to get ready for school, *never* did I think it would be my last night sleeping there. *Does anyone ever know when it's the last time they'll do something?* I thought Mumma and Da would be together that Tuesday afternoon when I got off the school bus. Bridgette and I would do our homework, and then I'd head over to Christchurch to play. Wednesday would be followed by Thursday. Friday would be there before I knew it and along with that would come a new *Sports Illustrated* and a bag of Chips Ahoy cookies and a glass of milk. On Saturday morning, Da and I would get up to wash the car and truck (technically, I could only rinse because my washing never met Da's satisfaction). On Sunday morning, we would pile into the Caprice, head up to Antioch to hear Rev. Holmes preach while I fought to stay awake. *I liked Rev. Holmes. I just found church boring!* Despite the constant fighting between Mumma and Da, I thought they'd *always* be together. I didn't know any husband and wife tandem that got along all of the time until I met the McClearys. As much as Mumma and Da fought, I still wanted them together even though that was selfish on my part. On the other hand, I wanted them to break up because I thought Mumma would be happier without him. It was a constant dilemma for me at that time. I went back and forth. Break up or stay together. Stay together or break up. I didn't have the answer at 9, 10, 11 or 12 years old, but I knew something had to change.

Mumma's life was never easy. I think her fights with Da made her bitter and angry with many that she encountered because she didn't see her situation getting any better. I don't think she had much to look forward to. Regardless of circumstances, I learned *everyone* needed at least one thing to look forward to each day. When you didn't have that, it made it hard to get up and face each day. *I learned that the hard way when I ran out of reasons to wake up.* The more I learned about Mumma's life, I was embarrassed to admit that I ever complained about mine.

Mumma and Da were my routine. That Tuesday evening, I thought I would be doing my homework or reading a *Sports Illustrated* magazine until dinnertime. The dinners that were hamburgers, french fries and a salad (that I only wanted to eat if it consisted of lettuce, tomatoes and Kraft French dressing, nothing more) were my favorite. I got mad at Mumma when she bought Wishbone French dressing instead because it was on sale or when she sliced onions and cucumbers into the large wooden salad bowl and scooped some into my smaller one. "I don't like Wishbone. I don't like onions or cucumbers. They smell funny." "Boy, you better eat that and shut up." *Once I started living on my own, I usually had my own burgers and fries and salad routine on Friday nights, but there were never any onions or cucumbers!* After dinner, Da and I would go out in the backyard to burn the trash in an old, rusted oil barrel that was a few feet from the basketball goal that he erected for me. Mr. Holmes might come over to chat with us about his day and ours. After we doused the flames, Mr. Holmes headed back through his apple orchard to turn in for the night. Da went down in the basement to work on cabinets he was building for somebody's kitchen. I watched TV and flipped between Channels 6, 8 and 12 or tinkered with the Panasonic radio to find a station on the AM dial that was playing a "good" song. That was my routine.

AM radio took me places I thought I'd never get to see. *Nobody listened to FM then, and if someone had told me in 1973 that there would be something called satellite radio, I would have told them to have a seat on Dr. Jack Billups' couch!* College taught me about the Kennelly-Heaviside layer and its effect on amplitude modulation, thus enabling me to hear distant radio stations at night. On the Panasonic, I picked up stations like WLS out of Chicago and WJR in Detroit and WHO in Des Moines and CKLW somewhere in Canada and WKBW in Buffalo and **(Insert WABC chime time)** WABC in New York with George Michael and Chuck Leonard and WBT out of Charlotte with Rockin' Ray and the Sunday Night Hall of Fame. All of those stations entered my bedroom through the Panasonic AM/FM radio that I "stole" from Mumma and Da's bedroom each night until they finally gave up and let me keep it next to me in bed. It was a heavy, bulky, wooden monstrous sort of thing that weighed about 4 pounds. I often tried to sleep with it next to my pillow, but Mumma was always afraid its 90-degree wooden edges would knock a tooth out! We compromised. I slept with it atop my bookshelf headboard, but sometimes, I still snuck it under the covers with me! I wanted to see Chicago and New York and those other cites one day just to say that I had been there, but I never dreamed that would happen. *I would see them all.*

And *never* did I dream that Mumma and Da wouldn't be together on the Tuesday evening that was November 13th. I didn't know it, but my life changed while I shot basketball in 6th period gym class. Mrs. Kidd walked in and told me that Mumma wanted Bridgette and me to take the bus up to Grandma Latimore's house instead of going home. None of us knew that Da would be leaving Middle-sex County that night with the *white* wife of Mr. Meredith, my St. Clare Walker Middle School principal. *No one saw that coming, not even Da and Mrs. Meredith.*

We never spent another night down at Christchurch, and as time went by, we only went down to remove stuff to bring it back to Grandma and Grandpop Latimore's house. I loved living at Christchurch, but I didn't like going into our house anymore. With the electricity off, it was cold inside. As far as I was concerned, it wasn't even a house anymore; just a brick building with three bedrooms. The moving of boxes and furniture could only be done during daylight. While Mumma, Sharon and Bridgette packed boxes, I went down in the basement to play Ping-Pong on the "butterfly" table Mumma and Da gave me for my 1971 Christmas present. I never thought about going over to play with the kids at Christchurch anymore. Just as Da was no longer part of my life, they were no longer part of mine. Although only 3 miles or so separated Christchurch from Grandma and Grandpop Latimore's house, it might as well have been 200 miles. It was my hope that somehow Mumma would find a way for us to move back to Christchurch, but deep down, I knew we were stuck at Grandma and Grandpop's. Mumma couldn't afford anything else.

I had always looked forward to Christmas, but I knew that the com-

ing holiday would not be nearly as nice as others. For sure, it wasn't
going to be like the Christmas of 1970 when Mumma found my
favorite Christmas present of all-time! A game called Drive Ya Nuts
that I saw during a television commercial. It was a pattern puz-
zle that was sort of a precursor to a Rubik's Cube. Mumma started searching for it before Thanksgiving and didn't find one until
Christmas Eve. I was watching a football game in my bedroom on
the used console Zenith TV when Mumma burst in and pulled
Drive Ya Nuts from a shopping bag. It was the first time I got a
Christmas present *before* Christmas. *I think she was happier than I
was when she found it!*

Christmas of 1973 offered me only one present: A yellow sleeping
bag dotted with red and blue little boys and girls on it. Mumma
bought one for Bridgette and me. *I wasn't sure what we were supposed to do with those things. We had a bed to sleep in.* I was mad at
Mumma because that was all we got that Christmas. I felt like she
walked into a department store, bought the first thing within arm's
reach and walked out. I knew nothing about being thankful for
food, shelter and family. *Nor did I know that Da left her with only
$28 in Mr. Major's bank on November 13, 1973.*

The Panasonic radio that took me to places that
I thought I'd never see. 2014

CHAPTER 34

Faye bought our house from Mumma in 1974. Her monthly payment was $214.94. "Faye, how can you remember that 40 years later?" "*You* pay something for almost 20 years and tell me if *you* don't remember how much it cost you!" *That made sense to me!* When she got the loan from the Bank of Middlesex, Mr. Major told her that there was a man who sat on the Middlesex County Board of Supervisors who hoped that she would miss a few payments because *he* wanted the house. *That wasn't going to happen.* Mr. Major was fond of Faye, and he wanted her to keep the property. Even after Faye and her 2nd husband, Willie, divorced, Mr. Major assured Faye that if she were going to be late with a payment to let him know, and he'd make sure it got paid. Banks weren't in the habit of extending loans to women in Middlesex County, or anywhere else back then, but Mr. Major took a chance with Faye. She made 235 consecutive, on-time monthly payments and was 5 months short of owning it when the Commonwealth of Virginia figured she was due for another mortgage. A new dual highway was planned for "down the county," so the Virginia Department of Highways' bulldozer tore down Faye's house and Mr. and Mrs. Holmes' house. Smashed and hauled them away in just a few days. The new 33 also tore down the three pine trees Da and I planted on Christmas Eve 24 years earlier. They had grown in height to around 40 to 50 feet. Every now and then, when Da took a chance in coming back to Virginia, he'd call me up and say, "Let's go down to Faye's and look at the pine trees!" Now, they were gone.

Da was hard enough to figure out when I was in my 40s and even more so at 8 years old living at Christchurch. He built us our Christmas present in 1969 – a new brick house with a full basement to play in, a room for me, a room for Bridgette and plenty of "running water" for all of us. Sharon didn't make the move with us, though, for two reasons. One, Grandma and Grandpop Latimore were returning to Virginia for retirement, and they would need Sharon's help around the house. The other reason was that Da wasn't too keen on having another mouth to feed down at Christchurch. Sharon was then a 7th grader, and she cried and cried when she found out she wasn't going with us (so did Mumma when she told me how hard Sharon took the news). Sharon had been with us since she was 4 years old, and although we would only be 3 miles apart, she wouldn't be *with* us anymore. Da could be the most selfish and (at times) selfless person you ever wanted to know, but I guess everyone carried those two traits. *I know I did.*

We piled stuff into the back of Da's olive green 1968 Chevy pickup a bunch of times to move our stuff into the new house. We weren't supposed to move in until sometime in January, but Da got it in his head that we were going to move in on Christmas Eve, and when Da got something in his head, it was there to stay. *He was stubborn until the very end.* While I helped Da unload the truck, Mumma and Bridgette unpacked boxes and began setting up the house. They worked as a team to hang curtains, make beds and arrange what little furniture we had. Faye and Eddie, Mumma's brother, stopped by later on that evening to help out. Because of the suddenness of the move, Mumma and Da had forgotten to pick up a Christmas tree. Faye and Eddie drove off and came back an hour later with a 7-foot evergreen they pilfered from a field "down the county!" Just before bedtime, I remembered staring up the living room chimney shaft. Mumma walked in and asked what I was doing. "I don't think Santa Claus can fit down this thing!"

Other than the rush of moving in on Christmas Eve, there was one other thing that always stayed with me. I thought it was silly then, but so many years later, it still made me shake my head when thinking about Da. I was in my new bed trying to sleep and trying not to think about what Santa Claus might leave under the Christmas tree. A few minutes before 9 o'clock, the mandatory bedtime for Bridgette and me, Da locked his hands against my bedroom door-jamb, leaned in and said, "Chopper, put your coat on and come go with me. We're gonna go plant some pine trees. *What? It's almost 9 o'clock. You and Mumma have been telling me since forever that if we aren't in bed by 9, Santa Claus will know and won't leave any presents. He's gonna see that I'm not in bed and Bridgette is, and she will get all of the presents. Are you losing your mind? Plus, it's nighttime, why are we planting trees?* Those were my unspoken thoughts because there was *no* debating Mumma or Da. "Ok, let me get my coat on." "Chopper, just throw it on over your pajamas and put your boots on. I'll meet you in the carport."

Da handed me a shovel and a spade. In the darkness, his flashlight created a path for us and the three pine seedlings housed in burlap bags. The air was chilly, and the frost on the ground crunched under our boots as we half-trotted, half-walked down the hill to the edge of our property line and the Smiths. *Why are we doing this? This is crazy. Why didn't Da think about doing this while the sun was still up?* Maybe Da simply forgot to do it earlier, and the thought just popped in his head. Maybe he wanted to bond with me, but I don't really think Da ever gave the word "bonding" much consideration. I never knew why he waited so late. "Da, we have to hurry up and plant these things. Santa Claus might fly by here and see me out here doing this. Shoot, he's probably only gonna leave presents for Bridgette now." He laughed. *This isn't funny.* "Don't worry, it'll be okay, Chopper!" As we dug, he told me, "You know, son. One day these trees will be taller than the Five and Dime over in Urbanna." *Now, I was sure Da had lost his mind.* There was no way those puny things would ever be taller than me, and I was only in the 3rd grade! The Five and Dime had to be about 50 feet high. *But he was right.* Each Christmas Eve night that followed, we'd go down to look at the trees, and I was amazed at their growth. Da would say to one tree, "Your big brother is a little taller than you. You better catch up with him this year!" Then to the other, "You better slow down and wait for your little sister!" I thought he and I would lumber down the hill to look at them for the rest of our lives, but as things turned out, we would only spend three more Christmases together. *I learned early on that there were no promises in life.*

After the new 33 highway came through in 1993 and wiped out those pine trees, we couldn't even drive down to our old house that used to belong to Faye to look at them anymore. *I think Da was sadder to see the trees go than the house he built.* As he grew older, he sure talked about losing the trees more than he did losing the house. The new highway cut down the trees, and eventually, a heart problem carved Da out of my life. While he was lowered into the ground in 2005, I glanced at the pines surrounding his burial plot and thought about Christmas Eve in 1969. I thought Da would have been happy with the patch of ground the former Mrs. Meredith selected as a final resting place for him. Pine cones were scattered throughout the small cemetery, and each time I visited Da's grave, I placed three of them on his headstone to let him know that I still remembered what he and I did together that Christmas Eve. Even after his death, I found it hard to believe that he was gone. *Maybe that was something you never got used to. I know I didn't.* Pine trees always reminded me of Da and of what he and I shared on that Christmas Eve night when I was 8 years old and scared to death that Santa Claus wouldn't leave me anything. *One thing was for sure, despite Da's dark side, I never stopped loving him.*

Our house at Christchurch. 1970

CHAPTER 35

In 1975, when I was in 9th grade, I started screwing up in school. In 10th grade, things got worse. Mumma and her new husband, Gerald, were sick of dealing with my sullen attitude. They asked Faye to come down and "talk" to her nephew. It was one of the most regrettable nights of my life.

I was lying across the edge of my bed listening to the same Panasonic radio that had been next to my head since elementary school (it lasted almost 20 years before it finally died of old age) half-heartedly doing homework. Faye walked into my bedroom and asked, "Hey there, you old skunk! What's going on?" "Not much, Faye." *What does she want?* "Well, your mom and Gerald asked me to talk with you about your school problems. Don't you wanna go places one day? Why aren't you studying harder? Are you just gonna throw your life away by goofing off in class? Don't you want to go to college? Don't you want a better life for yourself than Jean or Gerald or I have?" *I thought she was gonna talk "with" me, not "at" me.* I just stared at her hoping that she could feel all of the anger that I had towards most people in my life at that time. I wanted nothing to do with Faye or anyone. I was just an angry teenager. I tried to ignore her, but she was persistent. Finally, I let go. "Who are *you* to tell me what to do with *my* life? Just leave me alone." "Troy, you know I care about you. I don't want you to struggle, and if you don't get a good education, you *will* struggle." I looked up at her and unleashed with the 15 years of wisdom I had gained. "Faye, get outta my life, I'm not your little boy anymore." I felt awful as soon as the words escaped my lips. Faye looked so hurt. I wished that she had slapped me to take some of the sting away. Instead she turned and walked away to drive the 40 miles back to Middlesex. Bridgette came into my room and said, "I can't believe you said that to *Faye* of all people." *Neither could I.*

Even though Faye and I had a million conversations afterwards, I never apologized to her for being a rude punk. She was only trying to help me. Faye wasn't getting any younger, and I didn't want to be "staring down" at her one day regretting that I never said, "I'm sorry." It took 35 years for me to apologize for my bad behavior. I was on the other side of the country staring at the Seattle Space Needle from my hotel room when I finally picked up the phone to ask for her forgiveness. "Hey, Faye Wray, how you doin'?" "I'm okay, Troy Roy. Where are you this week?" "I'm in Seattle for work. I just landed about 30 minutes ago." "Boy, you fly all over the country, don't you?" "Yeah, pretty much, but I love my job. Faye, there's something I need to tell you, and it's taken me forever to do it. So, here it goes. Back when I was in the 10th grade and really screwing up in school, you tried to talk some sense into me and straighten me out. Of course, I didn't want to hear it. It has really bothered me for a long time how mean I was to you that night, and I'm sorry for it. You were *always* nice to me. I felt awful for telling you that I wasn't your little boy anymore when all you were trying to do was help me do better in school." It was difficult to get those words out. I cried the entire time that I was apologizing to her, but I was glad to get it off my chest. I felt much better after I voiced something that I had held onto for 35 years. Faye didn't remember any of what I remembered from 1976, and that made the conversation go a little easier. However, she did remind me that, "God never gave you the good sense that He gave a skunk, but I still love you, love you, love you!" *Aw, Faye!* She wanted to ask a question. "Go ahead, Faye." "How did I react when you were being a jackass?" "You just walked out of my bedroom and got in your car and went home." "You kiddin' me! You're lucky that I didn't go upside that big head of yours!" I *was* lucky! *Faye was only slightly less crazy than Mumma!*

I once told a coworker, Brooke, about my apology to Faye many years later during a dinner meeting, and she related a similar incident in her life. Over the years, she and her mother had their share of disagreements when Brooke was a teenager, and she too felt bad that she never apologized to her mom. "Wow, Troy. If you can apologize after such a long period of time then I can, too." Before we began our training session the next morning, I asked how the conversation went with her mother? "Troy, it was great! We talked for hours! I got it all off my chest just like you did." *Brooke and I both learned that it was never too late to tell a mother or an aunt that you were sorry.*

Faye Lewis. 1964

Faye smoked two packs of Parliament cigarettes a day ever since I could remember, sometimes three. *She was the reason why I never smoked cigarettes.* I hated that smell, but loved being around Faye, so I inhaled a lot of her second-hand smoke over the years. Eventually, she gave up the royal blue and white carton of Parliament cigarettes, not for health reasons, but because of their cost. It was more than what she was willing to spend, so she took up generic cigarettes. *I didn't even know generic cigarettes existed.* Sadly, the smoking side effects caught up with Faye in 1987 after she suffered a brain aneurysm. Her recovery was a long process. She needed to learn to redo everything. When her mind thought, "I want some water," her mouth said, "Pajamas got in the car." It was kind of funny, but I was just glad she was still alive. Gibberish became her new language, and even 20 years later, she still mixed up her words every now and then. Faye was a tough, old bird. It would take more than a brain aneurysm to keep her down.

CHAPTER 36

Once we moved to James City County, I never thought I would admit it, but I missed Middlesex County. I became a little fish in a big pond. Middlesex High was a single "A" school while Lafayette High was triple "AAA" in the Virginia High School system. I knew about five people at the new school, whereas I knew anybody and everybody at Middlesex High. It was a difficult period for me. Thankfully, a number of teachers helped make my life a little easier. One, in particular, was Mrs. Jackie Prater, my music teacher. She's another story.

After 7th grade, school became harder for me, and unfortunately, I tried even less. From 8th grade through 11th grade, I didn't care about school anymore. I barely managed to get by, but I did enjoy Advanced Placement history class. Another kid named Andre and I were the only black kids in that class. We got along pretty well, but we were never close. *I wasn't really close with anyone in high school.* He had tons of personality, was pretty smart and didn't apply himself in class, just like me! He was a really good athlete who played baseball, football and basketball and, if I remember right, got a full ride to college. He was a nice-looking kid, and his girlfriend was the 2nd prettiest girl I ever knew (second to Judy Kidd). Her name was Toni. She was petite, light-skinned, had beautiful teeth, short curly hair and a little mole on her cheek like Marilyn Monroe's. As far as I was concerned, she was a woman at 15! *That girl had the whole package.* We even kissed *once* until she came to her senses and never allowed that to happen again! But, at least it happened once, and that memory served to make me smile for over 40 years. If there were one word to describe Toni, I think it would have been "Exquisite." She and Andre dated off and on throughout high school, and I was often jealous that it was him and not me that got to kiss her more than once! I often wondered what happened to the two of them. Later, I learned Toni married and moved to Maryland and had a couple of kids. Andre? Well, he's another story.

In looking back, I liked to blame the insanity in my life for not doing well in 8th grade and 9th grade and 10th grade and 11th grade. I liked pointing a finger at Da for leaving, at Mumma for screaming and being tough on me, at Gerald for doing the same, at Grandpop Latimore for drinking, at Sharon for being a nuisance, at Bridgette for just being my sister, but to be completely honest, I should have been pointing the finger at myself. Accepting responsibility for your circumstances can be a pretty humbling experience at any age. Mumma and Da had separated and divorced, and in less than two years, both had new spouses. I wasn't crazy about either Sandra V. Meredith or Gerald L. Ferguson. Eventually, time proved me wrong about both of them because I grew to love them (and I never thought that would happen).

In fact, there were four things I was quite certain would never happen in my lifetime: First, Nelson Mandela would never get out of that jail in South Africa *(I went there!)*; second, the Berlin Wall would never come down *(I went there, too!)*; third, Mike Tyson would never lose a fight *(I met him in the parking lot of the Molly Pitcher Rest Stop on the New Jersey Turnpike when Lori and I stopped to take our 4-year-old niece, Teraje, to the rest room. She was hoisted on my shoulders with her legs bouncing against my chest as we walked toward the building. Mike Tyson was standing next to his Bentley signing autographs and shaking hands with anyone who passed by. He winked at Teraje, and she smiled back at him. "Hey there, pretty little girl, do you know who I am?" She was armed with a quick reply, "Yeah, you're the man that bit that other man's ear off!" He shrugged and said, "Yeah, that's me!")*; and lastly, there would never, ever be a black President of the United States. Obviously, I was never to be confused with Nostradamus. The night President Barack Obama was elected, Mumma stayed awake all night. She was worried that, somehow, "they" would find a way to keep him from being voted in. When the election returns started coming in and it appeared as though he was going to win, she called me every hour until about 3:00 a.m. to make sure I was still watching. *Yes, Mumma. I'm still watching. How can I not be? You keep calling me!* I was sure there were a number of black people who didn't sleep that night. I was also pretty sure there were a number of white people who didn't sleep too well that night, either! I worked with a few of them, and *they* weren't happy at all. That made me sad. *Equal opportunity. Wasn't that what America was supposed to be about anyway?*

Moving to James City County offered a new start for all of us, I guess. Bridgette certainly needed a break from Middlesex because she nearly lost her mind at 11 years old. After Da left, she moved in with a family over in King & Queen County because the girls at our school wouldn't stop teasing her about Da leaving with a white woman. I didn't know an 11-year-old could suffer a "nervous breakdown," but if there ever was a kid close to it, it was my sister. I never realized it at the time, though, and thinking about that many years later made me disappointed in myself. I should have been a better support to her, but I wasn't. *We never got along since the day she was born.* Never figured out why, but when she admitted that she threw my Winnie the Pooh (that I'd had since I was a toddler) out in the yard to be run over by the lawnmower, that cemented our precarious relationship.

It was 1995 when she revealed that information while passing a bowl of mashed potatoes at my first Thanksgiving dinner at Mumma's house in almost 15 years. The conversation turned to Peter Rabbit and Winnie the Pooh. I said, "I still don't know how Winnie ended up in the backyard getting run over by the lawnmower." Bridgette laughed and explained that she got mad at me for something when I was in college, so she decided that I was too old to have a Winnie the Pooh anymore. *Now I knew how the blades of the lawnmower crushed my small ceramic toy. I "killed" Winnie by slicing him up, and now, I wanted to kill her! Winnie had been with me since I was*

5 until I ran over him with the lawnmower when I was 20. Bridgette ruined that Thanksgiving for me, and I was angry enough to want to place my hands around her throat, but I didn't. Instead, I pushed my chair away from the table, grabbed my backpack, said good-bye to Mumma and Gerald and headed back to New Jersey. Winnie had once helped protect me from Mrs. Pollock's ghost when I was a little boy and a big boy, too. *Well, to be honest, I guess I was still a little boy because I continued to sleep with Peter Rabbit!*

Bridgette always had a temper, and if I stayed at Mumma's house that evening, I was going to lose control of mine. It upset me knowing that she deliberately destroyed Winnie. Granted, I was 34 years old when she revealed it, but it still pissed me off. She knew how much that little toy meant to me then, but she didn't care. Bridgette could be that way sometimes. *Indifferent.* I was surprised to learn that even at 34 years old, Bridgette could still hurt me. But, then again, hurt could happen at any age.

On the Sunday morning after Da left, Mumma took Bridgette and me up to Antioch Baptist Church for the 11:00 a.m. sermon. I was 12 years old, and I felt like all of the 30 to 40 souls that made up the church's congregation were staring at the three of us as we slid into our wooden pews. The older folks in the Senior Choir were up front on the right-hand side of the church singing "Bringing in the Sheaves" as we opened our hymnal to join them. *What was a sheave anyway? That was one thing I never got around to looking up!*

Bridgette and I hung our heads because we were ashamed that Da wasn't with us, and *everyone* in the county knew he wasn't coming back. But Mumma's head was held high, and she didn't give a shit what *anybody* thought. The Sunday morning that Mumma took Bridgette and me with her to church, Mumma curled her index finger to bring us a little closer. She whispered, "Y'all keep your heads up and sit up straight! Y'all have nothing to be ashamed of. Do you hear me?" "Yes, ma'am." *We sat up straight.* Mumma was like one of the two-by-fours Da left behind in the basement. Solid and sturdy. I think she was glad he was gone because now *everyone* in the county knew that Bill Lewis wasn't quite the saint they all once thought he was. *No one* knew how much he cheated on her except the ones he cheated with, and *they* knew who *they* were. I *know* she had to be glad that he wasn't around to knock her around anymore. Over the years, I thought that Mumma might have revealed to Faye at some point that Da used to beat her, but she never told anyone except C-Y and Eveleen. It was I who told Faye about Da's abuse almost 40 years later during a phone call. She went silent. "Faye, are you okay?" More silence. Finally, she said, "I can't believe Jean never told me that. Oh, my Lord. I never knew. Why wouldn't she have told me that a long time ago?" Long pause. She said, "I gotta go." She hung up on me. About 20 minutes later, she called back. "I have a question for you." "Yes, Faye?" "Do you think he beat Sandra, too?" I laughed. "Of course, he did. Why are you asking me that?" "Because, in a weird way, I feel better knowing that it wasn't just Jean that he was abusive with." "I get it. I know what you mean." My childhood taught me that you *never* knew what went on in someone else's house.

I don't ever remember Bridgette and me talking about Mumma and Da breaking up, but we became like baby turtles that seldom ventured from our shells. I don't know why we were embarrassed by Da leaving, we just were. I suppose it was because although we knew there were lots of other families with an absent father, we never thought it would happen to *us*. Once Da was gone, I think we realized that if it could happen to us, it could happen to any family. As unstable as Mumma and Da were, their stability was what we depended on, and that was now gone from our lives. When Da left, I was 12 years old, and from that point on, I started expecting the worst in life, not the best. *The glass became half empty for me, and I didn't even know what that meant at the time.* Being teased by "friends" taught me not to trust people. In a way, I guess it was better for me to learn that at a younger age than a later one. Bridgette came back to Middlesex from King & Queen after about a year or so, but I don't think she ever really recovered from that period in her life. *I wasn't so sure I recovered, either.*

CHAPTER 37

Puberty changed my voice, and once that happened, I quit singing. I liked my former falsetto voice, and the new one had become this deep thing that I didn't know what to do with. It sounded weird, and I wasn't comfortable with it, so I didn't use it. But, I got some *gas money* in 10th grade when I took an "elective" class: "Introduction to Music/Mrs. J. Prater." On the first day of her class, she placed a number of us on risers to see if any of us had any talent. While I reluctantly went through the warm-up exercises, "Do-re-mi-fa-so-la-tee-do" and "Be-la lu-go-si, lu-go-si be-la," I thought, "What am I doing in here? I just wanna go back to Middlesex High School and hang out with Butley and Pinckney." I watched Mrs. Prater tilt her head as though she were searching for something while walking between the rows of choral students. Finally, she stopped in front of me and said, "It's *you* with that big voice!" Embarrassed that she singled me out while the other kids snickered, I lowered my head. "What's your name?" "Troy Lewis." "See me after class, Troy Lewis." "Yes, ma'am."

After class, I waited out in the hallway until she beckoned me back inside. "Troy Lewis, get in here!" "Yes, ma'am." She was seated at her piano with perfect posture. *I knew proper pianist posture when I saw it. Mrs. Frances Johnson tried to get me to do that, but that didn't work out so well!* "So, why haven't you tried out for my Concert Choir?" "Oh, I dunno." "First of all, 'I dunno' isn't proper English, and when you are around me, that is what you will use.

Understood?" "Yes, ma'am." "So, let's try this again? Why haven't you tried out for my Concert Choir?" Shyly, I said, "Well, Mrs. Prater, to be honest, I don't like my voice anymore. *It* changed on me after we moved from Middlesex a couple of years ago, so I just don't use it anymore. It's too low now and sounds funny. That's why, I guess." She took a few moments, and then she let me have it. "Well, Troy Lewis, that's just plain silliness. You have a beautiful voice. God gave you some talent, and by God, we are going to do something with it." *The short, black lady with her hair in a bun is nuts. I don't have any talent. What the hell is she talking about?* "Yes, ma'am." "Plus, I'm sure you don't know this, but I'm from Middlesex County, too! I was a Polson before I got married. I know who your mother and father are and what happened over there. I don't care about that. Plus, there's nothing either one of us can do about that now is there?" "No, ma'am." "So, let's get started and move on. I'm going to teach you some vocal technique. Now, will you let me help you?" "Yes, ma'am." "Okay then, I'll see you tomorrow for class, and I better see you at my next Concert Choir practice after school on Tuesday. Is that clear?" "Yes, ma'am." "Now have a good remainder of your day!" *Why does this lady even care about me?*

Anyone who grew up in Middlesex knew the Polson family, Dr. G. H. and Mrs. Arnetta Polson, a dentist and a teacher and their two daughters, Jackie and Patricia. Pat Polson and Mumma were best friends in high school. She went on to be a judge somewhere up in The Bronx. Dr. Polson? He was the first black man I knew who drove his *own* Mercedes-Benz, and even though I knew a number of people who drove a Mercedes-Benz for *other* people, like Grandpop Latimore for the Peddles, Dr. Polson was the first black person I knew who drove his *own*. Mr. and Mrs. Peddle used to let Grandma and Grandpop Latimore borrow their Mercedes or Cadillac or Buick Riviera (or whatever car the Peddles owned that year) and drive it down to Virginia for holiday visits. But Dr. Polson? He could drive his luxurious vehicle whenever he felt like it! He and his family lived in a Colonial-style brick home with Dr. Polson's brick office building right next door. Everything was brick, even their garage. Now, they *were* rich! *Well, at least I thought they were!* Their compound was surrounded with trimmed hedge bushes that were as neatly manicured as their lawn. They lived about 100 yards from

Butley's house, and if I remember right, Mrs. Polson was Butley's first grade teacher.

By the time I stepped off Middlesex County Public School Bus No. 8, Mrs. Polson had retired. Butley told me she retired because she heard how "dumb" I was and figured since she wouldn't be able to teach me anything, she'd retire instead. *Well, that's what Butley told me!* Whenever I saw her in the grocery store pushing her cart, I told Mumma that I wanted to go back outside to sit in the car because I was afraid I might overhear her saying, "Hi, Jean. I'm so sorry your little boy isn't too bright." I didn't want to hear them talk about me as if I weren't standing right in front of them, so I went back out to the car whenever I saw her anywhere! I thought it might be better if I could watch that conversation from the safety of our GTO! I avoided Mrs. Polson for the rest of my life because Butley had me convinced that she thought I was dumb. *I believed every single thing Butley ever told me when I was growing up and, often, when I was an adult!*

Tony told me a story about Dr. Polson that I always thought was pretty funny, but I was never quite sure if it was true or not. It involved his buddy, Milton Holmes, punching Dr. Polson in his mouth when Milton was about 8 years old. As the story went, Dr. Polson hurt Milton while doing some dental work, so Milton socked him in the jaw, bolted from the dental chair and ran down 33 for a mile or so until he made it home! I always wondered if Milton really punched him or maybe it was another story Tony made up. *He was good at that!* After Mr. Holmes' funeral in 2003, I saw Milton for the first time in almost 30 years. *God, was I happy to see him!* I got around to asking him if indeed that was a true story, and he said, "Yeah, I punched him, and I ran all the way home with the bib still around my neck!"

When we lived at Christchurch, I used to hang out with Milton every chance I got. He was 17 when I was 9, and he was like a big brother who taught me how to cut grass patterns into a yard, how to ride a horse, and how to climb trees, which I was never really good at. I didn't like taking risks, and I felt climbing trees was a sure way to end up dead or with a broken limb. *No pun intended!*

(Insert **"Slippin' into Darkness" by War**) Every now and then, Milton smoked some marijuana, and when I was around, he asked me to keep an eye out for Mrs. Holmes' 1968 blue Ford Galaxie 500 or Mr. Holmes' olive green 1970 Mercury Marquis pulling into the driveway. He trusted that I would keep his smoking a secret. I liked serving as his "lookout." *But, I don't know how Mr. Holmes or Mrs. Holmes couldn't smell that stuff because it sure didn't smell like cigarettes coming out of Milton's bedroom!* On birthdays, Mr. Holmes used a pencil and ruler to mark the inches Bridgette and I gained each year since we were little kids. He etched a "T" and a "B" into the doorjamb of their den to mark our growth as he put a ruler on the top of our heads. When the new highway came through and took their house away, too, I felt bad that Mr. Holmes would lose that doorjamb.

(Insert **"Them Changes" by Buddy Miles**) Once, and *only* once, was I stupid enough to ask Milton to let me try one of his marijuana cigarettes. He was seated on the edge of his bed exhaling through the window when I said, "Hey, Milton, why don't you let me try some of that?" *That may have been the dumbest question I ever asked anyone.* He went nuts! "If I *ever* catch you smoking *anything,* I will fucking kill you! Do you *understand* me? I will fucking kill you!" "Okay. I'm sorry." *That scared me.* "Tell me right now, you will never smoke anything." "I promise." *Why is it okay for him, but not me?*

(Insert **"Me and Bobby McGee" by Janis Joplin**) A couple of weeks later, Janis Joplin died, and if there was one song I was crazy about, it was "Me and Bobby McGee." I was seated on the edge of my bed doing homework on a Sunday night in October of 1970 when Mumma walked in my room to tell me about her death. "You know that song you like by that Janis Joplin lady?" "I love her!" "Well, she died today." "How could she die? She's only 20-something?" "She died from some kind of drug overdose. I think they said on the news it was heroin." *Like I know what heroin is. I'm 9 years old.* "I'm never gonna get to hear her again. How could she do that? I promise you I will never do drugs." For the longest time, I thought that if I did do *any* drug, I'd end up like Janis Joplin. Dead. So I stayed away from them. I also thought that if I ever sipped any alcohol, I'd end up an alcoholic like Grandpop Latimore, so I avoided that, too, until college, where I found out that moderation was the key to life! In college, I smoked half a joint, nearly choked to death on each puff, and decided that was a waste of time. Later on though, I became more like Grandpop Latimore than I ever thought was imaginable. But that's another story.

One day, Milton and I were shooting basketball in his backyard when he threw a chest pass to me that sprained one of my fingers. *That pissed me off.* He was a senior in high school and stood about 6 feet 4 inches and weighed about 200 pounds and was the center on the Middlesex High School basketball team when I was a 4th grader. He said, "Look, if you wanna play with the big boys, they ain't gonna throw you easy passes." I stared at my throbbing finger and glared back at him. I had picked up some new choice words from the white students over at Christchurch School. When they were frustrated after missing a free throw at basketball practice or swinging and missing a curve ball at baseball practice, they used certain words to express themselves. I followed in their footsteps on this particular day.

"Milton Holmes, you're a son of a bitch," I shouted at him. He shot me a puzzled look. "What the fuck did you just call me? Are you calling my mother a 'bitch'?" *Uh oh.* I didn't even know what a bitch was, but I knew it wasn't good because he brought Mrs. Holmes in the conversation, and there was a crazy look on his face. He rushed toward me, and I threw the basketball at his knees causing him to stumble. I headed for Mr. Holmes' apple orchard that divided their yard from ours and ran as fast as my little legs could carry me. With each glance over my shoulder, Milton gained ground. *If I can make it to our brick storage shed and lock the door, I'll be safe. If I don't, he's gonna fucking kick my ass.* Throwing the ball at his knees gave me the head start I needed to finish about 10 feet ahead of him as I slipped into the shed and locked the door behind me! I peered at him through a crack in the door as he stood in the carport and yelled. "C'mon out, you little muthafucker! How dare you call my mother a bitch! You little 9-year-old punk! I will kick your black ass. You've been hanging around those white boys over at Christchurch too much, and you don't even realize what the fuck you said, but you said the wrong God-damn thing now!" *I'm gonna die at 9 years old in Da's storage shed for calling Mrs. Holmes a bitch, and I didn't even know I had called her anything or what a bitch was. I was mad at Milton, not Mrs. Holmes!* I waited in the shed hoping Milton would cool off, but then I started thinking that it might be better if *he* killed me instead of Mumma pulling up in the driveway and finding out that I had called Mrs. Holmes, or anyone, a bitch. *Mumma loved Mrs. Holmes.* At least Milton, in his rage, would kill me quickly. *My death at the hands of Mumma would be slow and painful.* Finally, Milton gave up and went home. I stayed in the brick shed for what seemed like an hour until I heard Mumma's car pull up. I walked out. "What are you doing in there?" "Nuthin." "You better put a 'g' on the end of that word." She paused and stared. "Nothing." "That's what I thought you said. Now, get over here and help me get these groceries in the house since you're doing 'nuthin.'" She unlocked the trunk, and I grabbed the groceries and held the door for her.

I really thought Milton Holmes was going to kill me that day. I avoided him for a few days, and when I saw him again, he acted like nothing ever happened! When I saw Milton at his father's funeral, I thought for sure the "son of a bitch incident" would have been first and foremost on his mind, but I was wrong. He couldn't have been happier to see me. We hugged, and he introduced me to his teenaged sons. He said to the two of them, "This here is my little brother!" I never thought Milton considered me anything more than a little pest who lived next door to him. I was extremely pleased that he didn't say to his boys, "This here is the little muthafucker that called your Grandma over there in the wheelchair a bitch back in 1970!"

Dr. Polson was one of only two black professionals in Middlesex County. The other was Dr. Toney, a family physician. My family didn't visit either of their offices because Mumma wasn't crazy about them for some reason or another, and I never asked her why. Maybe they slighted her at some point, and once you got on her bad side, you usually stayed there. *Her memory was like that of an elephant.* Instead, we went to Dr. Barlowe, the dentist, and Dr. Felton, the physician. Dr. Harold Felton got me through episodes of poison ivy, chicken pox and tonsillitis. In fact, when I was in 5th grade, he wanted to remove my tonsils, but I became terrified when I learned a tonsillectomy would require an overnight stay at the Tappahannock Hospital, about 10 miles from where Mrs. Pollock had her car accident. I was afraid her ghost would snatch me in the middle of the night from my hospital bed. Granted, she was buried right across the road from us at Christ Church Episcopal Church (and it would have been easier for her ghost to just snatch from my *own* bed), but the thought of lying in a hospital room with no Mumma or Da across the hall scared me. Dr. Felton tried to entice me into having them removed by telling me that I could eat all of the ice cream that I wanted, and even though that was tempting, I did *not* want to be away from the security of my bed and our house. A hospital bed? Mrs. Pollock's ghost could roam the hallways and seize me anytime she wanted! I didn't tell Dr. Felton about the nightmares, but I did ask him if there was any medicine that could help me avoid the tonsillectomy because I didn't want to miss any time from school. He fell for it! He gave me something to relieve the inflammation, and I didn't have to sleep at the hospital with one eye open. *A hospital and the mind of a child could be scary places when you were 10 years old.*

For Mrs. Prater, I became a baritone in her Concert Choir and Madrigal groups. She took an interest in me when I thought there was nothing interesting about me. She helped me with my diction and tonality and convinced me to try out for the Virginia State Choir competition, where I fared rather well. Two to three times a week after school, we worked on a number of songs in preparation for the state tryouts. When I failed to maintain a whole note for the proper duration or mispronounced a word, it was met with, "Practice makes perfect, Troy Lewis. Back to the beginning!" *Why did she always call me by my full name?* I never knew the answer to that question, but I called others by their full names when I grew up as a tribute to her. Often, when I was frustrated, I asked her, "Mrs. Prater, don't you wanna get outta here for the day? Can't we start all over tomorrow?" "Let me ask you this, Troy Lewis." *Uh oh, here it comes.* "If you quit now, how are you going to get better later?" "Yes, ma'am." "No one is going *anywhere* until we get this right!

Now, start over and quit procrastinating!" "Yes, ma'am." *Good God, Middlesex County women were difficult!*

When I moved to Pennsylvania to live with Da in 1978, I joined the Coatesville Area Senior High School choir and did pretty well there. But the thing I wanted most was to be named the high school's "Honor Soloist" for the upcoming Christmas concert. The winner got to sing "O Holy Night," and I wanted to win that honor. At Lafayette High School, Carrie Swift, who was a fellow 10th grader, sang it at the Christmas concert, and I never heard anything sung better. Ever! Anytime I heard anyone sing anything, I compared that person to Carrie Swift. There really was *no* comparison. She was a soprano with unbelievable range. At Coatesville High, I finished as the runner-up to the Honor Soloist, and I knew even then, that no one remembered the runner-up for anything. I had more than 30 years to get over finishing second, but I never did.

When I went off to college, a kid named Jay Pellman gave me *gas money* on a Saturday night while he was peeing in the urinal, and I was singing at the top of my lungs in the dorm shower. I don't remember what I was singing, but I'm positive it was something loud! He yelled, "Since you sing so damn much, why don't you go sing at the basketball game tonight?" I peeked out of the shower. "What are you talking about?" "All they do is play that old-ass tape recording of the National Anthem and stick it next to the microphone. You can do better than that!" *I never thought of that before. You know what? Maybe I will go sing at the game tonight.* I ran from the shower to change into one of the two good pairs of pants I had, slipped on a jacket and shirt and got Jay to tie my necktie. I sprinted over to the gymnasium, arriving five minutes before tipoff. I went up to the old guy who hit the "Play" button on the tape recorder, and told him that I wanted to sing the National Anthem tonight. He shot me a baffled look and said, "Are you sure you can sing?" "Yes, sir. I can." "Okay. You go ahead, but no one's ever done that in here before. Don't screw this up!" I was scared to death as I strolled out to half-court. I sung *a cappella* while focusing on the oversized U.S. flag that hung at that end of the gym, and it was the first time I thought that you really could hear a pin drop because

Shippensburg State College's Heiges Field House was eerily silent. I received a huge ovation, and as I walked back towards the bleachers, the Head Coach, Roger Goodling, shook my hand and said to me, "I want you here singing that damn song every night from now on. I am so God-damned fired up right now!" "Okay, Coach Goodling." I walked by Cheyney State's bench, whose Head Coach at the time was John Chaney who went on to coaching fame at Temple University. He also shook my hand and said, "Young man, that was excellent!" "Thanks, Coach Chaney." *I felt important for the first time in my life, and that night changed my life.*

At Shippensburg, I sang the National Anthem at all sporting events after that. I became a minor celebrity because of my voice and sang at all types of on-campus and off-campus functions. That helped me meet a lot of people in the community, and most importantly, a lot of those people were girls! I sang everywhere: birthday parties, dorm lobbies, and local churches. You picked the location, and I was there to sing at it. *I loved the attention because attention was something I never had.* Right before Christmas break, the Head Football Coach, Vito Ragazzo, asked me to sing his wife's favorite songs, "Oh, Shenandoah" and "O, Holy Night" and other Christmas carols at a party that he and his wife were throwing. I took Tammy Potts as my date, and I will *never* forget how beautiful she looked coming down the steps when I met her at the McLean Dormitory to walk over to Coach Ragazzo's house. After closing with "Oh, Shenandoah," Coach Ragazzo thanked me for coming and placed a crisp $50 bill in my palm. I had $15 to either take Tammy to McDonald's or Pizza Hut, and now I had $65! Unbelievable! It was one of the best nights of my life. The air was cold and crisp as Tammy and I strolled a half-mile hand in hand to McDonald's. *Whatever happened to Tammy?* I never found out, but she was drop-dead gorgeous on that night!

Singing gave me a great deal of exposure, and I sang for a number of military dignitaries and civic leaders. All of those opportunities came because I signed up for an elective class: "Introduction to Music/Mrs. J. Prater." She died in 1999, and I never thanked her for changing and shaping my life, but I didn't know she was giving me *gas money* at the time. I was just along for the ride. I was a "lost" Lafayette High School teenager in the mid-1970s, and because of Mrs. Prater, I felt like there was *one* person who cared about me. She saw something in me that I hadn't seen in myself and boosted my confidence when I had none. "Well, Troy Lewis, that's just plain silliness. You have a beautiful voice. God gave you some talent, and by God, we are going to do something with it." I never forgot those three sentences, and I could still hear her in my head 40 years later. *Thank you, Mrs. Prater.*

CHAPTER 38

Da and Sandra moved to Pennsylvania after they left Middlesex in 1973 and settled in the steel town of Coatesville. I joined them there in June of 1978 to work with Da and his carpentry business for the summer. I really thought that I could learn the nuances of woodwork just by observing Da and the two guys who worked for him, Donnie and Tommy (they were two funny characters). *I could not have been more wrong!* That work wasn't something that just *anyone* could do. *I know I couldn't.* God gave me 10 fingers, but with a hammer and nails, I was all thumbs. I tried to do whatever Da told me, but I failed in most of those assignments. Hanging doors, hammering nails and drilling cabinet hinges just wasn't my strength!

Initially, I thought that by working with him, I might be able to learn from him, and one day, maybe, build homes like him. *Who was I kidding?* I quickly learned that wasn't going to happen when you were born with 10 thumbs! The main reason for me leaving Virginia though was because Mumma was sick of me, and the feeling was mutual. Mumma was mean, and I knew she didn't like me. She may have loved me, but there was no way that she liked me at that time. You can tell when someone dislikes you. *I know I could.* I really think at that point in our lives, one of us was going to kill the other. *Seriously.* I contemplated various ways to make it happen, and although I never attempted to do so, I sure wanted to when she went off on me for something. We had a few guns lying around, but

I could never find a plausible scapegoat that the James City County Sheriff might want to blame it on, so I let Mumma live. *If you think I was kidding, I wasn't. At that time in my life, I hated her, and I would have bet good money that the feeling was mutual.* Who knows? Maybe she thought about getting rid of me, too! We had good days and bad days, but it seemed like the bad ones outnumbered the good ones. Nothing seemed to work for the two of us. Maybe I reminded her too much of Da. I had a lot of his personality and mannerisms. *I sounded like him, I walked like him, I thought like him, I was sarcastic like him.* From Mumma's perspective, I guess I was *him.* A double dosage of Bill Lewis could be too much for anyone.

After Mumma and Da broke up, I took a turn for the worse. School got harder. I got lazier. I don't know why I became a "brooder" in high school. I just didn't fit anywhere or with any group. I was a loner and stayed that way as an adult. I was bitter and it showed. One day I was pleasant and the next day, unpleasant. *Was kinda like that when I got older, too!* I guess Mumma and Gerald grew tired of my mood swings and my poor choices. I did stupid things like getting a speeding ticket the week after I got my driver's license because I wanted to see if our Chevy Caprice could keep up with the Amtrak train zooming along U.S. Route 60. I got suspended from school for being late to class because I walked this girl or that girl to her class and couldn't make it to mine before the tardy bell rang. I was probably suspended from school two to three times a year for that infraction. *I was an idiot.*

"Go live with your Dad. Maybe he can talk some sense into your rock head" is what Mumma told me at the end of my junior year of high school. I was happy to get away from her and Gerald. Sometimes a change of venue offered a different perspective. I know it did for me. I was a teenager who knew everything but, yet, knew nothing. I wanted no responsibilities in life, and responsibility was all Mumma had ever known. I was sure she couldn't understand my sullenness. At 17 years old, maybe she thought, "Why in the hell is my son so moody? He has no one to take care of but himself." She didn't understand me, and I didn't try to understand her. I didn't blame her for suggesting that I go stay with Da for the summer. *She didn't know what else to do with me.*

Although I never felt at home with Da and Sandra and their two-year-old daughter, Jennifer, Pennsylvania became a good move for me. Initially, I had much apprehension regarding Sandra Meredith. She had assisted in changing my life in a negative fashion, but over time, Sandra slowly became "Sandra V." ("V." was an abbreviation for Vaughn, her maiden name), and she was a convenient buffer between Da and me. I was looking forward to spending time with Da. I missed him after he left Virginia. I thought working with him for the summer would have been a good thing. *It wasn't.* In fact, it wasn't fun at all. After a couple of weeks, I knew I'd made a bad decision. If I thought I was moody, Da was even worse. I don't know what I would have done without Sandra V.

Over the course of that summer, Sandra V. changed my life when she asked a very simple question. We talked a lot about all kinds of stuff, but most importantly, she *listened* to me, and no one had ever really done that before. My opinion didn't matter to anyone in my family. Every other adult in my life had always *told* me what to do, think, say and eat. So I guess that's why I began to trust and like her. One August evening as my "work vacation" was quickly coming to an end, Sandra and I washed and dried the dinner dishes; Da was in the driveway washing his van, and Jennifer napped upstairs. I had just dipped another plate in the dishwater when Sandra V. asked, "Troy, what are you gonna do after high school?" *What? I really don't know what the hell I'm going to do. I'm a mess, Sandra V. No one likes me. I have no friends. Only one girl wants to go out with me. I'm better off dead. I have no direction in life, Sandra V. There's my plan!* That's what I wanted to tell her, but my reply was, "Oh, I don't know what I'm gonna do, Sandra V. Go back to school in Virginia and see what happens, I guess." "Well, I'll tell you this. From what you've explained to me, your grades weren't that good in Virginia, and I don't really think you have that much to go back to. I could be wrong, but that's what I think. If you stay up here, you'll get a new start, and I promise you that if you buckle down and study hard, I will do my best to get you into a college somewhere." I soaked my hands in the dishwater for a bit and stared at the hedges that separated Da's house from the house next door. *College? That was a thought I gave up on a long time ago. You know what? Maybe I will just stay up here and finish high school. There certainly is no reason for me to go back to Virginia. I just might end up killing Mumma if I do. Or worse, she'll kill me!* "Okay." "If I can get you into college, do you have any idea what you may want to major in?" *Major in? I didn't even know what a "major" was!* I didn't want to let her know that I had no idea what that word meant so I said, "I don't know, Sandra V., you kinda know me. Why don't you pick a major out for me!" She did.

I ended up staying in Pennsylvania with them, and just like that, Sandra V. took my life in a different direction. She changed my life while I washed dishes and stared at the hedges. Sandra V. kept her promise by doing everything she could to get me into college despite my poor Virginia grades. God knows she gave Bell Atlantic enough money every month with the number of minutes she spent chatting with financial aid staff, admission officers and administrative secretaries at colleges all over Pennsylvania.

When I was in the 7th grade, Sandra V. helped tear my family apart and five years later she helped put *my* life back together. Our relationship wasn't perfect, but she was nice to me and always had my best interest at heart. She was a little quirky, but weren't we all in some form or fashion? I grew to love Sandra V., and I knew people in my family couldn't or wouldn't accept why that would be the case, but Sandra V. got me into college and gave me *gas money* when I was 17 years old with no direction. I never thanked her enough for all of the phone calls she made on my behalf. She changed my life for the better when I had no idea what I was going to do with it after 12th grade. I finished my senior year with all A's and B's which hadn't happened *since* 7th grade. *Why didn't I do that sooner? I was such a knucklehead!* I ended up becoming a Communications Major at Shippensburg State College all because of Sandra V. Was there ever a way to thank someone who *truly* changed your life?

While Sandra V. made me feel welcome, Da made me feel like an intruder. Not that we were ever close, but Da had become more and more withdrawn. Prone to crazy mood swings, he could be charming one instant, and in the next moment, say something to really hurt your feelings. You never knew what kind of mood he was going to be in. I avoided him. Our morning rides to construction job sites in his maroon 1975 Chevy van usually took place in silence. *Thank God for the radio!* The return ride in the evening was even quieter. So I guess that's why Sandra V. and I became closer. We both needed someone to talk to. Da didn't talk much, but he sure must have "talked" to someone because about 600 people showed up at his funeral when I thought there would be about 60 people in the church. But that's another story!

Da with Sandra V. 2002
The lady who changed my life at 12 and 17!

Me and Jennifer. 1980
Da and Sandra V.'s
daughter

CHAPTER 39

Greyhound brought me home to Virginia for the summers going forward. I never worked with Da again. *One summer of that was enough for both of us!* Each summer after college, I returned to Virginia where Mumma got me a job working at the Colonial Williamsburg Foundation's Information Center. It was there that I met Mrs. Evelyn Fobian during the summer of 1981. At the Information Center, I sold tickets to visitors who wanted to visit the Historic Area's living history museum that John D. Rockefeller, Jr. and his wife, Abby Aldrich, and Rev. Dr. W. A. R. Goodwin began restoring in 1926. Mrs. Fobian was a visitor to the Historic Area who happened to stop at my booth while I explained her ticket options. While discussing her options, she asked questions about my life. "Are you a college student? Where are you going to school? What do you plan to do with your life?" "Yes, ma'am." "In Pennsylvania." "I don't know, ma'am. All I really want to do is graduate from college and get a job making $30,000 a year! Maybe one day that'll happen." "Well, young man, I have no doubt that you'll be successful at whatever you do. You take care of yourself." She purchased her ticket to head over to the escalator and hop aboard the tour bus. *She seemed like a nice lady.* I motioned for the couple that was next in line to come forward so that I could explain their ticket options. "Excuse me." I looked up. Mrs. Fobian was back. "Yes, ma'am? Is something wrong? Did you miss the bus? There'll be another one in 8 minutes, Mrs. Fobian." "No, I came back to talk to you." I looked at the couple, and they motioned for her to go ahead. "Yes, ma'am?"

She looked at my blue and white plastic nametag. "Troy Lewis, I want to see where your life is going to take you. Would you like to become pen pals with me?" *How could I say "no" to the 60-something-year-old white woman from Wisconsin?* I grabbed a pen and sticky pad. "Here's my name and address, Mrs. Fobian. Let me have yours." And that began an almost 10-year letter exchange between the two of us. We wrote about four to five times a year for almost a decade, but lost touch around 1992 or so. *I always wondered what happened to that lady, but I never forgot the name of her hometown, Wau-wa-to-sa, Wisconsin.*

In June 2009, I was driving through Wisconsin for work when I passed a Wauwatosa road sign. *That's where Mrs. Fobian lives. I'm gonna call that lady!* I was also heading up to Green Bay because I wanted to see Lambeau Field, the home of the Green Bay Packers. Directory Assistance put me in touch with the only "Fobian" in town. A woman picked up on the other end. "Hello?" "Hello, ma'am. My name is Troy Lewis, may I please speak to Mrs. Evelyn Fobian?" "Excuse me?" "Ma'am, bear with me. Again, my name is Troy Lewis, and I am from Williamsburg, Virginia. I met Mrs. Evelyn Fobian around 1981, and she and I used to be pen pals." "Oh, my God. You really exist!"

I was speaking with Jane Fobian, Evelyn's daughter, and she told me that, sadly, Evelyn passed away in 1997. "Troy, I can't believe you're a real person. Mom talked about you all the time!" *She did?* Mrs. Fobian's daughter explained that Evelyn developed Alzheimer's disease during the last few of years of her life, but she talked about me "incessantly." "Troy said he was gonna paint the house this year." "Troy said he would come over and shovel the snow." "Troy is coming to take me to the doctor this morning." "Troy is gonna rake the leaves this fall." Over the years, Jane grew sick of hearing about the "fictitious" Troy. *I would have, too!* She told me that I was very important in her mother's life, and the continued existence of me in her mother's mind made it easier for her mother to cope when her mind was no longer part of the present. *I was stunned.* After we hung up, I pulled over to the side of the road to think about how our chance encounter in 1981 impacted her life and now, mine. None of us ever knew the impact that we might have on another's life. *I certainly had no idea that when she was in the late stages of her life, she would remember me.* I had only met her once for about three minutes.

I pulled back onto I-43 to continue to Lambeau Field, and after a few minutes, Jane called back. "Troy, I know this is gonna sound weird, but I have a favor to ask of you?" "Yes, ma'am. Go ahead. I'm listening." *I had no idea what would follow.* "I know I'm not getting any younger, and I know I'm no 'catch' so no man is going to ask me to marry him now that I'm in my 60s." "Okay." She went on. "I really don't have any friends. All I do is go to church and the grocery store and the post office." "Okay." "Could you do me a favor and just call me every now and then and just talk to me?" *I had no idea that would be her request.* "Of course, I'll do that for you, Mrs. Fobian." She yelled. "Don't call me Mrs. Fobian! That was my mother! I'm Jane!" "Okay, Jane. I will save your number in my phone, and I promise I'll start calling you!"

That began my friendship with, Jane, the daughter of Mrs. Evelyn Fobian. We usually talked two to three times a week, and pretty much every Sunday when I figured she was home from Mass. In the beginning, I wasn't sure what to talk about but kept dialing whenever she popped in my head. She would tell me about church, the weather, her roof needing repairs, her windows being replaced, the fence that was falling down or what she ate that day. It didn't matter what the topic was, she just wanted to talk to someone. She was on a fixed income, went without cable television and the Internet, but did visit her local library as often as possible to stay in touch with the world. She drove, but never in bad weather. Eventually, she began talking to me about her fears of growing old alone, her health issues and other personal matters. When her mother was alive, she told me that they fought often, but now that she was gone, she missed her a lot. Jane slowly became my friend, and I hoped that I was hers, too. Her mom used to be my pen pal, and now, Jane and I were phone pals.

During one of our phone conversations, Jane asked if I liked to watch football. *That was a dumb question!* She said that she loved watching the Green Bay Packers play, but she didn't really understand the game. "Do you think you can explain to me what's going on?" "Jane, that's gonna be kinda complicated over the phone, but I'll try!" Our Sunday ritual became watching Packer games together with me in New Jersey and her in Wisconsin. I explained "down and distance" situations, penalties, the significance of the jersey numbers and so forth. I could watch Packer games on DIRECTV while she tuned in on her local Milwaukee affiliate. It took some time, but eventually, she started catching on to my explanations. Late in the 4th quarter during one Packer game, I knew she finally understood "down and distance" when she screamed, "It's 3rd and 14, why are they *running* the damn ball?" After a 2010 Packer playoff loss to the New Orleans Saints, she asked, "Okay, who do the Packers play next week?" "Jane, it's over." "What do you mean?" "When you lose in the playoffs, there is no next week." "Oh, no!" She had her heart set on watching another Packer game. "Now, what am I gonna do?" "Well, we can watch another playoff game together." "No, I only care about the Packers!"

Eventually, Jane wanted to know what I looked like so I sent her a picture. I asked for one of her and her mother. Although I had forgotten how Mrs. Fobian looked, as soon as I opened the envelope that contained their photos, the familiarity of her face returned. She was a thin, older, graying woman with a kind face. Jane very much resembled her mom, Evelyn. I called Jane when I got the pictures, and I told her how attractive I thought they both were! *That made her giggle.* Over the years, we talked about her life and her parents' lives. During one such conversation, she mentioned that her father didn't get along very well with black people. I said, "Well, some people can be that way, but at least your mother wasn't that way and neither are you." She paused. "Jane, what's wrong?" "I used to not be too crazy about black people either." She started crying. "It's okay, you don't have to cry." I tried to lighten the mood. "There are some black people that I don't like, either!" *That made her laugh.* "Jane, I have to ask you, though. You said you *used* to not like black people? What made you change?" "When I got your picture. All of this time that we've been talking, I thought you were white." *Oh.* She said that she had been praying for God's forgiveness. She asked me to forgive her as well. I said to her, "Hey, I don't care who you like as long as you like me!" She said, "I find it ironic that here I am in the latter part of my life, and I haven't gotten along with some people just because of their skin color, and now, my one true friend is a black person."

It was hard to determine the impact that a kind word or deed, or for that matter, an evil one will have on a person for the rest of his or her life. *Who would have thought that Troy Lewis from Middlesex County would impact anyone? Not me.* I found it hard to fathom that Mrs. Fobian remembered me when she couldn't remember much of anything else. I was glad she came back up the escalator to see where my life would take me. *It took me to Wau-wa-to-sa, Wisconsin, one day in June 2009.*

CHAPTER 40

The year before I moved to Coatesville, Pennsylvania, was one of the coldest winters ever recorded on the East Coast. In fact, the winter of 1977 was the coldest along the Eastern Seaboard since 1856. *I looked it up!* At that time, I had an after-school job working at the Williamsburg Pottery Factory greenhouse. I worked there all through high school until I quit because I didn't like my supervisor telling me what to do! *I told you I was an angry teenager!* Working at the greenhouse taught me a lot about plants, and I felt that girls, and more importantly, their mothers, would be impressed if I could offer some advice on house plants when I visited their homes. Not that I ever dated anyone other than one person after we moved to James City County. Her name was Brigetta, but she's another story.

Mumma used to pick me up from the greenhouse in the Caprice. Da bought that car before he left Mumma with the car payment. After he took off, she got new "30-day" tags on it because it had to be re-registered in her name. Mumma dropped me off at Grandma Lewis' house one afternoon and when I stepped inside, Grandma asked me, "Why did your mother put new tags on Bill's car?" *Bill's car? Grandma? Your son? Bill? He ain't here anymore, and it's not really his car because he ain't making the payments! Plus, I'm 12 years old. Why are you asking me? Why don't you ask Mumma?* I wanted to say those things, but I never would because she was my Grandma. I would never disrespect her. I became a "go-between" for the Lewises and the Latimores. With the exception of Faye, neither family had much to say to the other for a few years. *Faye and me? We loved to talk! To anybody!*

The mediator role was nothing new for me because I had been serving as a negotiator for Mumma and Da ever since we moved to Christchurch. Their disagreements sent Da outside to smoke cigarettes while he stared at passing cars from the front porch. I came out to sit next to him. "What's wrong, Da?" "Ah, your mother says she's gonna leave me." He took a drag from the same cigarette that I saw the Marlboro Man smoking in full-page ads in my *Sports Illustrated* magazines. "Oh Da, it'll be alright. Don't worry about it. I'll go talk to her. She's not gonna go nowhere." He plucked me in the back of my head. "Use the English you learn in school! Don't say 'not gonna go nowhere.' That's not right." "Yes, sir." I went inside and tried to make Mumma feel better by helping her with the dishes (which I hated doing) or just talking to her and trying to cheer her up. As much as they fought, I didn't want them to break up. I wanted them to work things out, but too much damage had been done over the years. *But I didn't know that then.*

It got increasingly colder during January of 1977. One evening, Mumma picked me up from the greenhouse and said, "I'm gonna drive us over to look at the York River. I hear that one is frozen too." A couple of days before, Mumma and Gerald took Bridgette and Gentree down to see the frozen James River at Jamestown. They even had a competition to see which one of them could fling a rock the farthest on the frozen body of water. In the South, frozen rivers just didn't happen. Mumma had never seen one before and neither had I. That winter broke records in the Tidewater region of Virginia as the mercury hovered around 25 degrees for weeks. As we left the Pottery Factory and headed down Virginia State Route 607, Mumma said to me, "You'll never see this again in your lifetime!" Coming down Croaker Landing Road we saw a river of ice that was indeed a sight to see. The York River was frozen solid from where we stood all the way down to West Point about 10 miles away. We probably could have *walked* across the York, but neither of us would have done something that crazy! We stood outside of the car for a couple of minutes and took it all in. We saw puffs of smoke rising from smokestacks over at the Pulp Mill. We shook our heads and got back inside the car to head home. It was only about a five-mile drive back to our place, but it was the longest and scariest ride we would ever take.

Going down the one-mile road that was called Croaker Landing was one thing. Coming up it became quite another. I guess neither one of us thought the conditions were so bad that we wouldn't be able to make it back up the incline. The gradient of Croaker Landing Road wasn't very steep, but with a touch of snow falling and the Chevy in need of new tires, we ran into trouble. With Mumma as the driver and me sitting beside her, the Caprice was all over Croaker Landing Road. The 1973 Caprice came with 400 cubic inches under its hood and that powered its rear-wheel drive. That kind of power was not made for snow and ice. As the temperature began to drop that evening to about 14 degrees, it brought more snow and the more it snowed, the harder it became for Mumma to keep the 19-foot-long, small block, V-8 moving forward. The slightest pressing of the accelerator sent the Caprice sliding toward the road's edge. Mumma took her foot off the pedal, and the rear end eased itself back onto the road. Another tap on the accelerator might take us five feet forward, but the car still would slide three feet backwards on the black ice. On the right-hand side of the road, an 80-foot ravine waited for us to fall into its arms and join the other 10 to 15 cars that were scuttled and junked at its base.

Twenty minutes into it and I think we had gone 50 feet. A one-mile stretch didn't seem very far until you began to think your car wouldn't make it that distance. *That's exactly what I was thinking.* The Caprice wasn't going to make it up the hill, and if it didn't, neither would we. I thought we would die on Croaker Landing Road. No one would even know where to begin looking for us. Mumma brought us down there on a whim. Who knew we would be down there? No one. Who else would be driving down this stretch of road? No one. Who was going to get us out of this mess? No one. But I was sitting to Mumma's right praying that she would. I thought we would use all of our gas just trying to get to the top of Croaker Landing Road, and the Caprice only got 12 miles to the gallon.

"Tragic End to Mother and Son" was the headline I envisioned in the *Daily Press*. If you ever drove in icy conditions, you sat a little straighter and a little closer to the steering wheel. *I know I did once I started driving in the snow with my own car.* As I looked over at Mumma, she was sitting taller and gripping the steering wheel a little tighter. But her face never showed panic. She concentrated on the task at hand. Panic? It was absent. It probably took us an hour to travel that piece of road before we made it to level ground and safety. Should we have noticed the conditions sooner? Yes. Did we? No. What I did know was that I learned *never* to show panic even when it might be warranted. Panic was contagious. In retrospect, had Mumma panicked she may have lost her concentration and lost control of the car. Nothing good would have come from that. Many years later, she admitted to me that she was "scared to death, but I couldn't let *you* see that!" I was in a few scary situations in my life, like the night Da dropped dead at my feet, but I didn't panic. Had I succumbed to that, Sandra V. may have become even more distraught than she already was. *I learned how to remain calm on the day Mumma and I went to look at the frozen York River.*

CHAPTER 41

My paternal grandparents were Rev. John Joshua and Pearl Ramona Jeter Lewis. Grandpop was a Baptist minister and preached at various churches in the counties of King & Queen and Middlesex for over 60 years. He also taught at the segregated schools in the 1930s and 40s. I really admired Grandpop Lewis, but he wasn't kind to teenagers who got pregnant before they were married. *It was a good thing he never knew about Mumma and Da!* I guess *all* ministers were that way back then. They weren't in the pulpit to be your "friend." They came to church on Sundays to put the fear of God in you, and they and God didn't think you should be pregnant when you *weren't* married in 1953. All you had to do was ask my cousin C-Y about that.

Grandma and Grandpop lived in a white, T-shaped, three-bedroom wood house. Like the Latimores, the Lewises didn't have "running water" either. They had pots and an outhouse just like we did before we moved down to Christchurch. I think Grandpop Lewis' house got indoor plumbing sometime in 1971. His home wasn't fancy but was always tidy. He took great pride in keeping his yard in the same fashion. Hedge bushes encircled his place, and within his yard were crepe myrtles, umbrella trees, pear trees, apple trees, rose bushes, gladiolas and fire bushes that my cousins and I used for Hide-n-Go-Seek, Tag, Easter egg hunts and any other game we could think of.

Grandma and Grandpop Lewis had five children over a 21-year span: Aunt Virginia, Da, Faye, Portia, and Michael. Aunt Virginia was

born in 1935, Da in 1939, Faye in 1947, Portia in 1951 and Michael
in 1956. Grandpop Lewis was the total opposite of my maternal
grandfather, Horace Latimore. Grandpop Latimore would have put
the A.B.C. store out of business if he had his way. A.B.C. was Virginia's way of demonstrating that it had Alcohol Beverage Control
over all intoxicating liquids within the Commonwealth. It was comical, yet sad, to see men and women with a drinking problem rush to
the only A.B.C. store within the county before its 6:00 p.m. closing
time. Sometimes, Grandpop Latimore was one of those "runners"
after Grandma Latimore had gone on a scavenger hunt to pilfer
his hidden cache of Gordon's Gin and Seagram's Whiskey bottles
he strategically placed throughout the house, basement or garden.
Grandpop Lewis never had to hide anything he drank because the
Welch's Grape Juice that was used on Communion Sundays was as
close as he ever came to having a drinking problem!

As a preacher, Grandpop Lewis' favorite expression was, "Hmm."
He used that to get his point across much like Arsenio Hall did
many years later on his television talk show. Grandpop wasn't the
"fire and brimstone" type of minister as were many Baptist ministers
in the South. He was more soft-spoken and clever when interpret-
ing Matthew, Mark and Luke. When I would return from college
during the summer, I liked driving over to hear him speak at the
church where he later married Lori and me in 1986. We were late
to our own wedding because we were watching the NCAA Final
Four! The second game ran late when the trailing team kept fouling
to put the other team on the free throw line. Lori kept saying, "We
are gonna be late." "Lori, I don't care, it's the Final Four. I told you
not to pick this Saturday!" *We both laughed!* We finally made it to
the church around 7:20 p.m. for the 6:00 p.m. ceremony, and there
was Grandpop Lewis *sitting* on the pulpit steps asking anyone in
attendance if they wanted to get married or remarried!

When I was a little boy attending his Union Prospect Baptist Church
on Sundays, I couldn't wait for Grandpop to ask youngsters to gather at his feet while he recited a prayer that began with "Suffer little
children to come unto me for theirs is the Kingdom of Heaven." All
of the other assembled children were hushed, but not me. Before

Grandpop Lewis closed his eyes and lowered his head to pray, I elbowed my way to the front of the pack to tug on his white robe and whisper, "Hi, Grandpop!" I wanted the other kids to know that he may have been Rev. Lewis to them, but he was *my* Grandpop! He smiled and patted me on the head. Thankfully, he never reprimanded me. Whenever Grandpop Lewis popped in my head that was my first thought of him, towering over me from the pulpit and me tugging on his robe. *"Hi, Grandpop!"*

Grandpop Lewis demanded that his grandchildren speak properly. "Ain't" was as bad as cursing, but no one ever did *that* around him. Shoot, no one really cursed back then except for Mumma when she was mad at me or Milton when he was trying to kill me or Grandpop Latimore when he was intoxicated! I was pretty good at butchering the King's English, and when I did, Grandpop Lewis warned that if I couldn't speak correctly, then I needed to, "Just hush!" Well, that wasn't gonna happen because I always had a lot to say! "Troy, people will *always* judge you by the words you use, so you need to use them wisely." "Grandpop, I'm just a little boy." "Son, good habits start early." "Yes, sir." I wanted Grandpop to lighten up on my usage of subjects and predicates, but he never did. He was right though. People judged you by the way you spoke.

Grandpop Lewis graduated from Virginia Union Seminary sometime in the 1920s, and after that, he began preaching and teaching. When I was around 5 years old, he showed me a letter that he had received from some guy named Rev. Dr. Martin Luther King, Jr. I never forgot his excitement as he showed me the envelope stamped with an Atlanta return address. All I knew about Atlanta was that it was the capital of Georgia and that a Union soldier named Sherman marched through there. I had never seen Grandpop as happy as he was on the day that he let me hold that envelope. I stared at it for a bit before returning it to his weathered hands that were battered from years of yard work. Sometimes I stared at the cracks in his palms and wondered what kind of stories *they* could have told me, but I never asked him any questions about his life or things he experienced. To me, he was just Grandpop. I wasn't as impressed with the envelope from Atlanta as he was, so I went outside to play. As far as I was concerned, it was just an envelope. I had never heard of this King guy. I remember heading outside thinking, "If this guy is a King, why isn't he called King Martin? I never heard of any king called Doctor. Or was it King Doctor? Or Doctor King? Who would name their child Doctor? Or was it King Junior? I'm really confused. Plus, why on Earth does this King guy have six names, for God's sake?"

Grandpop was always in a white long-sleeve or a white short-sleeve dress shirt and necktie unless he was doing yard work, and even then, he still wore the same outfit only minus the necktie. He was a serious guy but sometimes poked fun at himself. One such day, I was helping him snip cucumbers and tomatoes from their vines in his gigantic vegetable garden. He and Michael had rigged a huge scarecrow and placed it right in the middle. I tried to avoid looking at Mr. Scarecrow's eyes because I thought they were going to follow me from row to row! *I had to look! Yikes! It was staring back at me!* That makeshift man on a stick certainly scared me more than it did the crows that pecked at Grandpop's vegetables. Grandpop was teaching me to hoe and pull weeds from the vegetables when he came to a complete stop. He stood erect with his pitchfork and said, "Look at your Grandpop! He's the colored American Gothic man!" He couldn't stop laughing, and I laughed along with him, but I had no idea what a *colored* or *white* American Gothic man was!

At various times in his life, Grandpop Lewis was a schoolteacher, carpenter, painter and chef, but I didn't care what he did for a living as long as I could play Tag in his front yard or snatch tadpoles from the stream "out back" from his house. "Out back" there were a couple of apple trees, a pear tree, a walnut tree, and a Concord vine with grapes that he constantly tried to keep away from me. "Son, I need those grapes for my jelly and jam preserves this winter. Now, shoo and leave them on the vine and out of your mouth!" I walked away thinking, "Grandpop is nuts! How is he gonna turn a grape into jam or jelly!"

(Insert "I Heard It Through the Grapevine" by Marvin Gaye)
After plopping a few more in my mouth, I took a seat on a tree

stump near the grapevine and tried not to think about the grapes that were hanging just a few feet away. I stared at it and tilted my head back to stare at the blue sky. Grandpop stepped away to fetch something from his work shed, but when he returned, he could see that my head was leaning toward the grapevine as though a magnet was pulling me toward it. "Troy?" Nothing. "Son? What are you doing?" I lifted my index finger next to my lips. "Shhh, Grandpop. Tony told me if I sat close to your grapevine I would be able to hear Marvin Gaye sing "I Heard It Through the Grapevine." Grandpop wiped his brow with the handkerchief that he pulled from his pants pocket and walked away laughing to himself. *What was funny?*

Food was always plentiful at Grandpop Lewis' house, although I never quite figured out *how* he made that happen because he never made a lot of money. Yet, there were always three meals each day that he made from the wood stove in his kitchen. Supper was a big deal at his place. There was roast beef or pot roast or chicken that usually came with mashed potatoes and gravy, peas, string beans, corn on the cob or lima beans. All beans ended up tucked in the cuffs of my jeans! I never learned how Grandpop became such a good cook, but his homemade rolls were excellent and his lattice crust apple pie was even better. He knew his way around the kitchen.

Grandpop had a 30-minute religious radio show on WDDY-1590 AM over in Gloucester County, and he often loaded me and Bridgette in his two-tone green and white four-door 1963 Pontiac Tempest with him for the drive over to the radio station. We sat in the back eating Barnum & Bailey Animal Crackers, drinking from miniature Pet milk cartons and reading Dr. Seuss books. *Life didn't get any better than that!* After pulling into the angled parking spot next to the small brick building that was WDDY, Grandpop placed his Tempest in "Park" and turned to face us. He placed his fedora on his head and grabbed his Bible from the front seat. He looked at the two of us munching on crackers and covered with milk mustaches, "I'm going in there to give a sermon on the radio. I'll be back in an hour. I won't be able to *see* you two, but I'll be able to *hear* you through the radio as long as you keep it on WDDY. Now, there'll be no foolishness, and you two behave yourselves!"

As soon as I saw the radio station's door close behind him, I leapt over the front seat to push the radio pre-set button to WRAP-850 AM, the soul station in Norfolk, to listen to "Daddy" Jack Holmes, "Wake up, wake up, get up from there. You're gonna be late for work" his high-pitched voice screamed at listeners. I didn't want to hear Grandpop talk about *Genesis*! **(Insert "Cry Baby" by Garnet Mims)** I wanted to hear The Dells or Wilson Pickett or The Four Tops or Garnet Mims who had a hit song called "Cry Baby" that I told Bridgette was written just for her! Now, this was good living: WRAP, Barnum & Bailey Animal Crackers, a carton of milk and Bridgette in the *backseat*!

I loved Grandpop, but I didn't want to hear him on the radio. That was boring, and listening to "Daddy" Jack Holmes and WRAP wasn't! Bridgette was convinced that Grandpop could hear us through the radio, and he would know if I changed the dial. She leaned over the front seat and turned the radio back to WDDY's pre-set button. I returned it to WRAP. She pushed the pre-set again, and so did I. We went back and forth. Our game continued until she shouted at the dashboard radio, "Grandpop!" "What are you doing?" "I'm letting Grandpop know that you aren't listening to him!" "He can't hear you!" "Yes, he can!" "No, he can't!" "Grandpop, Troy's listening to WRAP again!" I wanted to strangle her.

When I saw Grandpop exit the radio station, I climbed into the backseat as though nothing happened. Bridgette couldn't wait to tell Grandpop what I did during his absence. "Grandpop, I was trying to tell you that Troy kept turning the station, but you didn't say anything back!" He returned his fedora and Bible to their resting place next to him on the front seat. He glanced at Bridgette through the rearview mirror and said, "Now, Bridgette, I'd heard the two of you carrying on, but I had a sermon to give. Was I supposed to stop in the middle of it and come out to the car and deal with the two of you? Would that be fair to the people listening who are too sick to come to church? Would that be fair to the radio man who was recording me?" We hung our heads knowing we had disappointed him. "No, Grandpop. We're sorry. We won't do it again." Well, not until the next time he took us with him, and it was the same thing all over again! Back then you could leave a 5-year-old and a 4-year-old in an unattended car for an hour, and they could drink their milk without ending up on a milk carton. *Well, at least that's the way it was where I grew up.*

Grandma and Grandpop Lewis' house. 1972

CHAPTER 42

Grandma Lewis left Virginia in the late 1950s to become a house-keeper for Dr. William Haynes in Bryn Mawr, Pennsylvania. She came back to Virginia around 1972. One of Dr. Haynes' patients liked her so much that he sketched an 8" X 10" caricature of her. He was an artist/cartoonist named Mr. Ted Key, the man who created the comic strip *Hazel*. His sketch was entitled *Love That Pearl*. Faye kept it for years, and then she passed it on to me.

Grandma and Grandpop Lewis' oldest child, Aunt Virginia, was married to Uncle Buddy, and they lived in Pennsylvania. They had four children: Gayle, Marilyn, Lynette and Chip. Marilyn was a sports fan like me, and in 1971, when Lew Alcindor changed his name to Kareem Abdul-Jabbar, she showed me that I wasn't nearly as smart as I thought I was! *What in the hell was a "Moose-lim" anyway?* Well, that was how the local Southern sportscasters pronounced the word "Muslim," and they probably knew about as much as I did about Islam and "Moose-lims," and I was only 10! When Marilyn came down from Pennsylvania that summer, we talked about Mr. Alcindor's name change. I insisted that his name should be pronounced "JAB-ber." Marilyn corrected me. "That's not the way to pronounce it, you clown! It's "Jar-BAR!" "Marilyn, shut up! You'll never know as much about sports as I do!"

Mr. Ted Key's tribute to Grandma Lewis. 1968

CHAPTER 43

Grandma Lewis was born Pearl Ramona Jeter and came from Caroline County, Virginia. If I picked up half of her personality, I would have been happy. Most enjoyed being around her, with the exception of Mumma, but that's another story. Grandpop Lewis was quiet and soft-spoken, while Grandma was the complete opposite. I often wondered how the two of them got together. Maybe I should have asked them that question years ago, but that chance passed me by. Based on the few pictures I saw of Grandma Lewis as a younger woman, I would have bet good money she had more than her share of young men chasing her. Maybe she and Grandpop met at church like Aunt Jenny and Uncle Carey to peek and nod. Like many Jeters, Grandma was fair-skinned and could easily have passed for white. At Uncle Willie's funeral (her brother), it was hard for me to tell who was a family member and who wasn't, because few of them looked like me. Heading into church, I thought, "What are all of these white people doing here?"

Grandma often said *all* Jeters were related because, according to her, we disseminated from *one* slave family in South Carolina. I never paid much attention to that because I thought it was just something she made up. Many years later at a work meeting, I saw a young black woman displaying a nametag that read "Shani Jeter." During a break session, I introduced myself and asked about her family background. I mentioned the *one* slave family story to her, and she told me that she had heard the same from her family over the years. Her family roots were based in Maryland. I knew many of my relatives settled there, so I called Faye (the unofficial Jeter/Lewis family historian) to ask a few questions. I explained the particulars to her and she said, "Put me on the phone with that girl!" Within a few minutes, they were talking as though they were long-lost friends. Shani was a cousin, and Faye knew her parents. Maybe Grandma Lewis was right after all.

I was stubborn as a kid and as an adult, and I attributed that to being a *Taurus*. Mumma once told me, "You couldn't help being stubborn. It was part of your DNA. All of those Jeters were stubborn. Your Dad was stubborn. *I'm* stubborn. You're three times stubborn!" I guess there were stubborn people in every family, but the stubbornness I possessed was minor compared to my third cousin, Mildred Jeter. She married a white man, Richard Loving, and they battled state and federal authorities for over nine years to live as husband and wife in the Commonwealth of Virginia. She was 18 years old when she started her legal fight, and I have no doubt that I would not have been as strong-willed as she was at that age or any age. Mildred was also from Caroline County, and in that county, as in many others throughout the South, blacks and whites and Native Americans had interpersonal relationships for years but kept them discreet. But a black person *marrying* a white person simply wasn't tolerated in the South during those times.

I never quite understood the dynamics of why the Caroline County Sheriff wanted to make an example of Mildred and Richard. He broke down the door to their house while they slept at 4:00 in the morning to arrest them for violating Virginia's *miscegenation* law. Mildred pointed to the dresser that held their 1958 marriage license that was obtained in Washington, D.C., but the Sheriff said, "Not here, you're not." He handcuffed them and hauled them off to the local jailhouse. Mildred and Richard had married in the District of Columbia to avoid Virginia's *Racial Integrity Act of 1924* and returned to Caroline County to live and raise their family. *Miscegenation* came from the Latin words *miscere "to mix"* and *genus "kind."* Mixing of different "kinds" was contrary to Southern law, and like pretty much everywhere else in the United States, it was frowned upon. Nothing exemplified that more than the fact that 22 other states concurred with Virginia's miscegenation laws. Mildred and Richard were convicted by the Caroline County Circuit Court on January 6, 1959. Their sentence was one year in prison that would be suspended for 25 years on the condition they leave the state. They settled across the Potomac River in D.C., but they did not like city living conditions. They were country people who wanted to come back to Virginia to be near their families. For birthdays or holidays, they snuck into Caroline County to visit, and when they got near the county line, they pulled off of 17 for Mildred to slip into the trunk of their car to hide. *Hiding in the United States because you were married to someone you loved? Crazy.*

I compared Mildred's plight to that of a slave on the run in the *1860s*, only it was the *1960s*. Usually after a few days, a malcontent who spotted them called the Sheriff to have them rearrested. Exhausted from the constant arrests, a relative suggested to Mildred that she write newly appointed U.S. Attorney General Robert F. Kennedy. "That's what he's up there for. To help us," Mildred was quoted as saying in an HBO documentary. Civil rights was prominent on the Kennedy Administration's agenda, more so than previous presidential administrations, so I guess Mildred figured she had nothing to lose and everything to gain. She wrote Bobby Kennedy in 1964, and he suggested that she reach out to the American Civil Liberties Union. Their case was eventually heard by the U.S. Supreme Court, and it ruled in their favor in 1967. The Court determined that Virginia's expulsion of the Lovings was contrary to the guarantees of equal protection of citizens under the U.S. Constitution's Fourteenth Amendment. Mildred and Richard were free to live in Caroline County just like anybody else.

I met them for the first time at a family reunion when I was 6 years old. It was held the same year they won their case, and I remember everyone being really happy to see Mildred and Richard and their kids, although I had no idea who they were or why they were so popular. All I remember thinking was that these Jeter people were some of the *whitest* black people I've ever seen in my 6 years of living! *Not that I knew that many white people.* In fact, at that time, I knew only four: Dr. Felton, Dr. Barlowe, "Doc" Marshall, the druggist, and Mr. Herbert Apsley who ran the laundromat in Urbanna. Mr. Apsley was a nice man, but his laundromat had the hardest plastic chairs I ever sat on in my life.

Mumma and Da introduced me to Mildred and Richard and had me shake their hands. Mumma leaned over to whisper, "These are very important people." I waved, said "Hi," and turned to Mumma to ask her, "Can I go eat some more potato salad now?" The significance of meeting Mildred and Richard was lost on me at 6 years old. I was more concerned with getting back to one of the picnic tables because back then I was a potato salad–eating fiend!

Later on, a bunch of kids headed off to an adjacent field for a game of softball. I kept staring at the *very* light-skinned kids with freckles and straight hair (Mildred and Richard's children). Bat and glove in hand, I ran over to Mumma to tell her where I was headed, but before I ran off, I pointed at the Loving kids and asked, "What *kinda* kids are those over there?" I didn't know if they were white, black, Indian, or Hispanic (not that I knew what a Hispanic person was because I didn't meet one until I was in the Air Force at Basic Training).

(Insert "Lyin' Eyes" by The Eagles) His name was Reynaldo Martinez, and he became one of my best buddies in the military. He played the guitar, and I sang with him on "The Highwayman" by The Highwaymen and "Lyin' Eyes" by The Eagles. We loved singing together! One time I said to him, "Martinez, I didn't think a Puerto Rican would know this kinda music!" "TL, I ain't Puerto Rican. I'm Mexican!" "Puerto Rican? Mexican? What's the difference? They ain't the same thing?" "You think you're so smart. You don't know shit! You dumb ass, a Puerto Rican is from Puerto Rico. A Mexican is from Mexico!" (I hadn't been exposed to very much in my life!)

My mother said, "Troy, does it really matter what *kind* of kids they are? Aren't they just *kids*? Now, shut up and go play." I guess she was right. It didn't matter what color they were. I only had to play with 'em! Mumma gave me *gas money* on race relations at 6 years old (and so did Martinez at 21) when I couldn't figure out what color my cousins were. Over time, I learned to pretty much like everybody unless they were assholes. I found out *they* came in all colors.

In honor of Mildred and Richard, June 12th became Loving Day, an unofficial holiday celebrating interracial marriages. HBO produced a documentary detailing their story and premiered it on Valentine's Day in 2012. They must really have loved each other to put up with all the crap they went through. Arrests, threats and hiding in trunks. Love coupled with stubbornness could make you do crazy things. Mildred wrote to a *Kennedy* and with Bobby's help and her persistence, she and Richard and their lawyers changed U.S. legal history. In the 1960s, the Kennedys were icons with most black Southern families (maybe in the North, too, but I wouldn't have known that because I didn't live up there). Pretty much every black home I ever visited had at least one J.F.K. or R.F.K. or M.L.K. picture framed on a living room wall. Most homes had all three. *I know Grandma Latimore's house did!* Knowing one of them played a role in one of my family members' lives was fascinating. Unfortunately, those three men didn't make it out of the violent 1960s, and Richard Loving only made it to 1975 because a drunk driver killed him when he was 41. Mildred lost a husband and an eye in that car crash. She passed away in 2008, and her obituary was featured in major newspapers throughout the country. Her death even made the front page of *The New York Times*. She was a brave woman, but from what I learned, all she ever really wanted was to be married and left alone.

CHAPTER 44

Grandma Lewis' favorite expression was "ain't that a killer" when she found something amusing. And *she* was a "killer" in more ways than one, but that's another story. Men throughout Middlesex, King & Queen and Caroline Counties were enchanted with her charm and good looks. Mr. Holmes adored her. He practically gave us the property next to his, and that's how Da acquired the land to build our house where we planted the pine trees. One hundred dollars for three acres in 1968? Maybe having a cute Grandma was a good thing!

Mumma was in a car accident on a Friday night, April 30, 1973. Her accident totaled our 1970 lime-green Plymouth Duster 318 with the black racing stripe down the side, the same one that carried my bike home after I tried to sneak up to Cook's Corner for a soda and some chips! She worked the midnight shift at a textile plant in Toano about 8 miles west of Williamsburg. Officially, it was pronounced To-ah-no, but if you were from around there you made it two syllables and called it "Twa-no!" Mumma told the insurance company that when she came around a curve on Virginia State Route 30, an approaching car crossed the double line, forcing her into a tree. It wasn't until years later that Mumma admitted to me that it wasn't a car, but a catnap that "came around a curve and forced her into a tree." *I couldn't believe Mumma fell asleep! She was such a good driver!*

The Saturday morning after the accident, I remember waking up and walking out to the kitchen in my pajamas to plop two Kellogg's Strawberry Pop-Tarts in the toaster. Strawberry was the only flavor I ever ate even though Mumma sometimes bought the cinnamon-flavored ones because she wanted me to try "new" foods. Those Cinnamon Pop-Tarts never made it into the toaster because I didn't like trying new food. Ever.

On my way to the kitchen I stopped dead in my tracks when I saw my aunt, Portia, and her best friend, Carolyn, sitting at the dining room table with sad faces. They were *never* at our house on a Saturday morning. "Where's Mumma and Da?" Portia started to explain. I stopped her in mid-sentence and cautiously said, "Are they dead?" She told me that Da had gone to the hospital because Mumma had been hurt in a car accident. I said to Portia, "Well, if she's only *hurt,* then she'll be okay!" Then, I hopped up onto the kitchen counter to grab the Strawberry Pop-Tarts box, plopped two of them in the toaster, poured a glass of milk and read my latest *Sports Illustrated* magazine! I guess that was my way of dealing with stress at 12 years old. Strawberry Pop-Tarts were my version of "comfort food." Mumma wasn't "okay." She was hospitalized for a number of weeks, and after her discharge, stayed with Grandma Latimore for the remainder of the summer until regaining her strength. Mumma didn't like talking about that accident, so I never asked many questions about it. What I did know was that the Duster's gas tank ruptured, and its leaking contents caused a great deal of skin damage. The gash in her scalp required 36 stitches. Her long hair that blew in the wind when the car windows were down was now gone. Her "good" Latimore hair was now as close cropped as mine and beneath it lay a long scar to remind her of that night. Mumma didn't like looking at mirrors for a long time. Two decades of headaches was the price she paid for falling asleep at the wheel.

Mumma was released sometime in June, and she stayed with Grandma and Grandpop Latimore until she could take care of herself. So that summer put me at Grandpop Lewis' house while Da went to work. Aunt Virginia and Uncle Buddy's oldest daughter, Gayle, was now married, and she brought her new husband and a buddy of his to Grandpop's house from Pennsylvania to stay for a bit during the summer. Like Aunt Virginia and Uncle Buddy, they came down to fish and crab at Alexander Burrell's Marina (everyone in the county called him "El-ick") about half a mile down the lane from Grandpop's place. Much later, I found out that Mr. El-ick was probably the richest black man in Middlesex County. He loved hearing me run my mouth, and I was always pretty good at that! His cement building that sat on an inlet of the Rappahannock River contained a snack bar where he and his wife never charged me for anything, but they opened their cash register to receive dimes and quarters from my buddies. *I never complained!* Da did oystering work for Mr. El-ick when he was growing up so maybe that was why they took a liking to me. All I knew was that I never complained about keeping my change in my pocket!

(Insert "Frankenstein" by The Edgar Winter Group) Gayle's husband, Jimmy, and his friend (I think his name was Johnny) were both in their early 20s. I only met them once, but I never forgot either of their faces. Grandma Lewis sent the three of us over to Urbanna to pick up a few things for her. Some mail from the post office, groceries from Mr. Walton's Park Place store and a couple of items from Doc Marshall's Drug Store. It was only a 3-mile trip. Heading back to the house, I was sitting in the backseat of Portia's blue 1970 Volkswagen Beetle that Jimmy was driving. I was humming along to the Edgar Winter Group's "Frankenstein" on the radio. I think it was Dick Clark who said, "Music is the soundtrack of your life." Well, hearing "Frankenstein" always reminded me of *that* day, and in a way, what they did to me was pretty monstrous. I was explaining to Jimmy and "Johnny" that "Frankenstein" and Deep Purple's "Smoke on the Water" were battling for the top spot on Casey Kasem's *American Top 40*. I guess they were tired of hearing my mouth because it had been running since we left Grandma's house. They told me to "shut up," and I wasn't about to do that because I had entertainment information to pass along! "Y'all can't tell me what to do!" They looked at each other while I continued babbling, and what they did next caught me totally off-guard. "Johnny" reached back, grabbed my wrist, and pulled my arm forward with the palm facing up. I didn't know what he was doing or about to do. While continuing to drive, Jimmy took the lit cigarette from his mouth and started burning the inside of my arm. It was done so nonchalantly and with such teamwork that it seemed like they had done this kind of thing before. He repeatedly jabbed the butt into my forearm as though he was a doctor searching for a "good" vein. In that moment, I was so shocked that I didn't do anything. I initially thought they were just going to twist my arm to shut me up. I never thought they'd burn me with a lit cigarette. I ended up with four or five burn marks when they were finished. "Johnny's" grip was too strong for me to pull away from, so I guess they figured out a way to shut me up after all. The two of them laughed and laughed like it was the funniest thing they had ever seen. After "Johnny" finally let loose of my arm, they had the silence they sought. I stared at the blisters starting to form on my forearm in a state of shock. I couldn't believe what had just happened. It was done so quickly, but seemed to take so long. I didn't cry because I felt that would have given them even more satisfaction. I wanted to kill them. Why did those assholes do this to me? I know I talk a lot, but I didn't deserve to be burned with a cigarette.

When we got back to Grandma's house, they had me take her stuff inside, and they continued on down the lane to Mr. El-ick's place to go fishing. I put Grandma's stuff on the dining room table and ran upstairs to change into a long-sleeve shirt despite the 90-degree temperature. I didn't want anyone to see what had been done to me. *I felt like it was my fault.* When I came downstairs, Grandma stopped me and asked where I thought I was going in a long-sleeve shirt. "It's too hot outside to be wearing that! Go put that tee shirt back on!" "I'm okay, Grandma. I'm kinda cold." "Oh, please. How can you be cold? It's burnin' up outside! You can't go outside and play unless you change your shirt. And that's that." I went upstairs to change again and when I came back down, she saw the burn marks. "Who did this?" I wasn't going to lie to Grandma Lewis.

Later on that evening when Jimmy and "Johnny" pulled into the driveway, Grandma went outside to "greet" them. I watched from the front porch as she did most of the talking, and when she was done, they backed up and that was the last I saw of the two of them.

I never saw them again. *I guess Grandma told them they were no longer welcome in her house.* Grandma turned to head back toward the house, and when she did, I saw her slip a small pistol in the front pocket of her housecoat. Sometimes, I thought I imagined the whole thing because I never knew her to have a weapon. Many years later Faye confirmed that Grandma kept a .22 pistol around just in case. *I guess it wasn't my imagination after all.* Grandma Lewis really was a "killer!"

What she did for me on that day was my first indication that maybe somebody actually *loved* me. No family member ever *told* me they loved me until I was 31 years old. All of those years, I thought my family merely tolerated me because I was a son, grandson or nephew. Grandma Lewis never *told* me she loved me either, but she *showed* me when I was 12 years old. I guess all of my family loved me. It just took me another 38 years to come to that realization.

A few weeks later, Grandma and I were headed back to her place after leaving Mr. Walton's grocery store. We were cruising along Urbanna Road a little before dark when she looked at me and winked. "Do you wanna drive?" *Are you kidding me?* "Yes!" She hoisted me onto her lap, and I "drove" the four-door 1969 silver Chevy Impala for about 3 miles. That was fun, and those lessons came in handy for me and another grandparent, but that story will come later! Grandma operated the pedals, and I directed the car down the highway. Keeping the car within the dotted dividing line and the white boundary line proved harder than it appeared! It became our routine whenever it was just the two of us in the car. "Concentrate, think about what you're doing. Ease it back to the right. There you go, now you're doing good!" She let me steer until there was an oncoming car, and then she scooted me over onto the passenger side. Once the car passed us, she pulled me back onto her lap. *I loved Grandma Lewis!*

Sometimes Grandma let me "drive" at night, and during one of those drives, she gave me a lesson in "magic." Her Impala's headlights (as with all cars during those times) were adjusted by depressing a floorboard button to the far left of the brake pedal. I couldn't figure out how Grandma dimmed the headlights each time a car approached and then was able to brighten them once that car had passed. "Grandma, how do you make the lights go high and low like that?" She looked over and said, "Oh, you don't know how Grandma does that, do ya? You just keep watching Grandma's eyes and I'll show ya!" The dashboard lights and the oncoming car's headlights illuminated her face, allowing me to get a closer look. Grandma blinked, and the Impala's headlights dimmed. The approaching car moved past us. Grandma blinked again, and the headlights returned to high beam status brightening the road ahead of us. *Grandma controlled the headlights with her eyes!* Wide-eyed and curious, I asked, "Grandma, how did you do that?" She winked and whispered, "It's magic!"

Eventually, I learned that anyone could control the headlights by depressing that button built into the car floor. I liked it better when I thought it was Grandma Lewis' magic. As time marched on, the flicker of headlights changing from high to low (and vice versa) *always* reminded me of her. I felt as though it was her way of saying "Hi" and "Bye" to me. Like a nightly check-in to remind me she was still around. During those instances, I was again sitting on her lap guiding her big Chevy Impala down Urbanna Road. "There you go, now you're doing good!" Maybe flashing headlights was Grandma's way of showing me that she was still performing magic somewhere. *Well, at least that was how I thought about it.* She left all of us in December of 1984, but she remained in my heart forever. I was constantly reminded of her presence every single time I saw headlights flicker high or low. To me, that was magical.

CHAPTER 45

Grandma Lewis and Mumma didn't get along very well, and I never knew the real reason behind it. Who knew what sent *any* relationship into a tailspin, especially when in-laws were involved. Maybe their bumpy ride began on the Sunday morning that found me screaming and kicking as an infant. I was seated on Mumma's lap while she and Da sat in church listening to Grandpop Lewis preach. (I cried more than any baby in the history of Middlesex County so I have no idea why they thought bringing me to church was a good idea!) The only thing that quieted me was a drive in Da's 1959 Volkswagen. It was like sticking a pacifier in my mouth. That was how my 13-year-old Uncle Ronnie learned to drive. Practically every day Ronnie was thrown the car keys to take me for a spin from one end of the driveway to the other. I bet that when Ronnie was teaching himself to drive Da's Volkswagen with me strapped in the backseat crying and screaming like a maniac, he never imagined that he would go on to receive a B.S., an M.S. and a Ph.D. But he did. I think our bond began with those drives back and forth in the driveway.

However, on the Sunday morning that I was screaming in church, nothing was going to quiet me while I bounced on Mumma's knee except, maybe, Grandma Lewis who sat behind us. She leaned forward, tapped Mumma on the shoulder to whisper in her ear, "Jean, let me have him. You don't know what you're doing!" Maybe that wasn't the nicest thing to say to a new mother, but that was the way Mumma told me it happened. To make matters worse, as soon as I was in Grandma's arms, my crying stopped. Mumma said, "I turned around to look at Mrs. Lewis as she leaned back in her pew. She was so satisfied. She was rocking you on her knee and smiling. Boy, that pissed me off! But, that didn't last too long because about two minutes later you threw up all over Mrs. Lewis' new dress. I was so proud of you! She handed you back to me, and I said to myself, 'Well, I guess *that* Mrs. Lewis didn't know what she was doing, either!'"

After Da left us, the tension between Grandma and Mumma intensified. Da's departure didn't help matters, but something else put a stranglehold on communications between my mother and my paternal grandmother. The source of that sour note was a clarinet that belonged to Portia. A musical instrument became the major root of discord between Mumma, Grandma Lewis and Portia for a number of years. The three of them rarely spoke because of a woodwind. Or so it seemed, but nothing was ever that simple.

Bridgette began using the clarinet in 6th grade when she joined the middle school band and continued playing into high school. Portia and Grandma Lewis let Bridgette "borrow" the clarinet because Portia was no longer using it. But since Da was no longer around, Grandma wanted the clarinet returned, and there was no way Mumma was going to do that! Only once did I ask Mumma about returning the clarinet to its rightful owner. I was about 15 or so, and her reaction scared me so bad that it made me think twice before asking her anything again. "Fuck Mrs. Lewis *and* Portia! They can both kiss my black ass. If they want that clarinet back so God-damned bad, they can come down here and try and take it!" At the time, I thought Mumma's response was over the top, and I didn't understand why she reacted so angrily. But as was often the case, the passage of time offered more insight on all parties' perspectives.

The clarinet affair was a "no-win" situation. I thought Grandma and Portia were wrong because even though Da was gone, Bridgette was still a granddaughter and a niece. She should have been allowed to play it as long as she wanted. I thought Mumma was wrong too, because Grandma owned the clarinet. I didn't like Mumma bad-mouthing Grandma or Portia. It made me very uncomfortable. I'd see Grandma at church and she'd say, "Has your mother said anything about the clarinet?" "No, Grandma, she hasn't." *Can we please change the topic?* When I got home, Mumma wanted to know, "What did Mrs. Lewis have to say this time?" I loved Grandma. I loved Portia. I loved Mumma. I loved Bridgette. I hated being in the middle of a woodwind war. Like the Arabs and the Israelis, it was a conflict that wasn't ever going to be settled amicably. When I was in my 50s, I asked Mumma, "Whatever happened to that clarinet?" "It's still sitting out in the garage in its case!" Forty years later, Mumma managed to hang on to that thing as though it were composed of gold instead of wood. Simple matters could often cause a rift in families and after the tempo slowed, it all seemed so trivial. Communication was the key to solving any conflict, but with no extension of an olive branch from either party, there was no point in sitting at the peace table. *That being said, I was glad Grandma and Portia never tried to take that clarinet from Mumma!*

Despite the bitterness, almost 10 years later, Mumma and Gerald aided in arranging a surprise party for Grandma and Grandpop Lewis' 50th wedding anniversary in 1984. Faye told me, "Jean jumped right in, just like it was her *own* mother. Yes, indeed, she did." Mumma helped prepare some of the items to feed the 20 or so people in attendance. She even had one of her friends bake a commemorative cake for the occasion that she and Gerald transported 40 miles back to Middlesex. All of this was done for an *ex*-mother-in-law who wanted her clarinet back. "Why *did* you do that for Grandma and Grandpop Lewis?" "Because it was the right thing to do. They were getting old. Let bygones be bygones."

As was often the case, Mumma gave me *gas money*. She showed me how to do what was "right" even when you felt you hadn't been treated fairly. I was pretty sure there were disagreements other than the clarinet issue, but those things didn't keep Mumma from "taking the high road." *At least not on that occasion!* I wasn't sure if I would have done the same. *Or, maybe I would have.* One thing was certain, an *ex*-mother-in-law was never to be confused with an *ex*-husband because I don't care how many months of Sundays slid

by on the calendar, there was no way Mumma was going to help
Sandra V. throw a party for Da!

I didn't tell Mumma about Grandma Lewis and the cigarette-burning incident until I was 50 years old. It was the first time I *ever* saw
Mumma speechless. She looked at me, searching for the right words,
and they didn't come quickly. It took her a few minutes to gather
her thoughts. Finally, she said, "I never knew Mrs. Lewis did that."
It was an emotional experience for Mumma. She placed her head on
her forearms on the small dining room table and sobbed for a minute or so. Maybe she was thinking that she was sorry that *she* wasn't
able to protect me from those two clowns that day. Or, maybe she
was thinking Grandma Lewis wasn't quite the person she thought.
"Mumma, are you okay?" She shook her head from side to side and
wiped her eyes. Finally, she said, "You know, this has changed my
whole opinion of Mrs. Lewis. I'm so glad she was there for you. I
can't believe she did that." "Well Mumma, that's why it bothered
me so much when y'all were fighting over that damn clarinet. I always loved Grandma Lewis because I knew she cared about me. I
just wanted y'all to stop it. I was torn because I loved both of y'all."
A few more minutes passed before I asked how *she* might have han-
dled that cigarette-burning situation if she weren't in the hospital
that summer. She laughed, "Well, I guess God meant for me to be in
the hospital that summer because I woulda killed those two moth-
erfuckers, and this conversation would be taking place behind bars!"

Grandma Lewis' note to Mumma. 1984

Jean,
We certainly cannot forget
it was you, who saw to
it that we had that
beautiful and delicious cake.
Thanks again.
With Love
Pearl L.

Grandpop and
Grandma Lewis
at their 50th
wedding anniver-
sary. 1984

CHAPTER 46

Bridgette stayed with Mumma while she recuperated at Grandma Latimore's during the summer of 1973. I stayed with Grandma and Grandpop Lewis during the day while Da worked. In the evenings, I looked forward to seeing his maroon 1970 Chevy pickup with the white top coming "down the lane" toward Grandpop's house. He usually showed up around 6:00 p.m., and I waited down at the end of Grandpop's driveway for him each day. Sitting on the edge of Grandpop's yard next to the lane, I did something that I was constantly told not to do. I threw rocks because I loved throwing rocks! *Mumma and Da hated when I threw rocks!* Other than "clean your room" and "take out the trash" and "be nice to your sister," their other favorite phrase seemed to be "don't throw the rocks!" But that's what I did each evening while I was waiting for Da at the end of Grandpop's driveway. I loved picking up pebbles and tossing them. It was like I was compelled to do it. I just had to pick them up and throw them at a pole, at an apple hanging from a tree, at Butley, or at an ear of corn across the road from Grandpop's house. I couldn't contain myself! *I'm gonna aim for that ear of corn. Okay, now I'm gonna try to hit the top of that cornstalk. Oops, here comes Da! Put down the rocks!*

(Insert "Are You My Woman?" by The Chi-Lites) I leaned against his driver side door and said, "Hey, Da!" The Chi-Lites blared from the speakers connected to his 8-track tape player. I ran in to tell Grandma and Grandpop, "Bye! I'll see y'all tomorrow. Thanks for letting me stay!" Hopping in Da's truck, I sang along with him. Our favorite song from The Chi-Lites 8-track was "Are You My Woman," (a song Beyonce "sampled" almost 40 years later. Well, at least that's what some people told me because I quit listening to new music when the 1980s ended). I alternated between singing the falsetto male lead and 2nd tenor parts while Da sang the baritone and bass sections. The chorus of "Are You My Woman" featured one of The Chi-Lites asking the group to give him a *"Yeah!"* When the others returned with*"Yeah"* in response, Da shouted along with them, and when he did, he removed his hands from the steering wheel and threw them in the air! The truck swerved slightly to the left or right until his hands returned to the wheel, but when it was his turn to shout *"Yeah"* with The Chi-Lites, the truck was on its own again. Allowing the pickup to make its way down the highway for those brief seconds scared me, but I giggled each and every time he did it! "Da, stop it! You're gonna kill us!"

Many, many years later, whenever I listened to "Are You My Woman" in my car, I removed my hands from the wheel just like Da did when I was a boy. It was instinct. It took me back to sitting next to him in his Chevy pickup, but sadly, Da wasn't sitting next to me anymore. That one moment in time was the *best* period of my life with him. I never thought about it until in my 50s, but I only had a total of 13 years with Da under the same roof. Not a very long time. Then again, some people never got to spend any time with a parent, so I had a lot to be thankful for. During the darkest and saddest moments of my life, I often thought, "Regardless of where Da ended up, Heaven or Hell, I would have been happy spending eternity with him singing that song in his maroon 1970 Chevy pickup with the white top. That would have been just fine with me." On the other hand, as Mumma often warned, "You better be careful what you wish for!"

CHAPTER 47

Some evenings that summer, I spent the night at Grandma and Grandpop Lewis' house, and other nights, I went home with Da. Either was fine with me because Grandma spoiled me to no end and would cook anything I asked for, and if I went back with Da, he did the same. Da became slightly more lenient while Mumma was recuperating. Maybe he felt sorry for me. Maybe he was just happier without her around. I felt sorry for him and Mumma. I could tell they were both unhappy, yet they were stuck with each other.

Despite Da's nicer disposition, my bedroom still needed to be orderly, and that often caused friction between us. Da wanted my bed made in the morning, my magazines put away before I went to sleep, and my shoes tucked neatly under the bed. It *never* stopped with him. He was an absolute "neat freak" although that phrase wasn't commonly used in the 1970s. For him, there was a place for everything, and everything needed to be in its place. He was maniacal. He probably had obsessive-compulsive disorder, but that term hadn't yet been invented, either! I once heard Mrs. Holmes say, "I don't keep house. The house keeps me!" Well, that was how I felt about cleaning!

When I went home with Da in the evening, we ate hamburgers or hot dogs and french fries or TV dinners. Mumma never cooked TV dinners. She said they were "garbage", but I could never figure out if TV dinners were "garbage," why were they in the freezer section

at Mr. Walton's grocery store! I once asked her that, and The Look
was her response. I was sure that sometimes she considered me the
dumbest child in the Commonwealth of Virginia. *Sometimes, I guess
I was!* Mumma's dinners were usually baked, broiled or fried chick-
en with two vegetables, a salad and bread. C-Y's husband, Arthur,
liked to fish, and sometimes he dropped some off at the house for
Mumma to fry. Mr. Cox was another man who lived close by and
found any reason he could to drop fish and oysters off at our house.
He was an older black man who had a slight crush on Mumma. Mr.
Cox was close to 70 years old when Mumma was around 30, but
that didn't keep him from flirting with her whenever he got the
chance. He lived in a house that was falling down all around him,
and I never paid him any mind. From my perspective, he was just
a nice old man who dressed shabbily. Many years later, Mumma
told me he was a very wealthy man who owned tons of waterfront
property over in Lancaster County. I would never have guessed that,
but what did I know at that age? Mr. Cox was living proof that you
couldn't judge a book by its cover. I was often reminded of that
going forward, and I had Mr. Cox to thank for it.

Mumma sometimes overcooked her fried chicken, so it was never
my favorite. Seated at the dining room table, I might have wanted
to say, "I don't want *that*, it's burnt." I liked living, so I kept those
thoughts to myself. I learned to say, "I'm not really hungry tonight, so please don't put too much on my plate, thank you" when I
sniffed food that may have been slightly overcooked. Mumma's *en-
trées* consisted of meat loaf, roast beef and, sometimes, steak (about
twice a year if we were lucky). I never heard the word "entrée" until
I made it to college, and that was where I learned that word was
used to describe the main portion of a served meal. The first time
I heard "entrée" used, I thought it meant that the meal would be
served "on a tray!" Sadly, I was very naïve when I arrived at college.

Sometimes Mumma cooked duck, but I wouldn't eat that because I
thought those animals were too cute. There was a duck farm down
the road behind Christchurch School, but I never thought they were
killing them down there. I thought they were *raising* them! I spent
some nights at the refurbished antique dining room table (which

Da found for $40 at a yard sale) until 9:00 p.m. as punishment for not eating my duck "entrée." *Ducks waddled and quacked, for God's sake. They had little orange beaks. Donald Duck had three nephews named Huey, Dewey and Louie. Why are Mumma and Da trying to make me eat them?*

Like Mumma, Da's frying skills weren't the best. On Saturday mornings, his scrambled eggs were often dry, brown and over-cooked. *Who wanted that for breakfast?* Not Bridgette and me! Instead of frying french fries, he baked them on a cookie sheet in the oven. Then, he busied himself with vacuuming the car or working in the basement, before one of us yelled, "Da, something's burning in the oven!" He was not the most attentive person in the kitchen, and he got mad when we pushed the fries around on our plates because they were too crispy and charred. "Don't y'all know there's kids starving in Ethiopia? You better eat that food." *Like any of us knew where E-thee-oh-pee-ah was!* That being said, Mumma and Da's inability to master frying taught me that attentiveness was the key frying ingredient. Over time, I perfected french fries, scrambled eggs and grilled cheese, and I never really learned to cook much of anything else! I was content with those three items and an occasional salad. Thankfully, grocery stores began offering rotisserie chickens! *Who cared about cholesterol? None of us were going to get out of here alive anyway!*

The one meal Da couldn't mess up was a TV dinner, and I absolutely loved the Swanson ones that came with turkey and gravy, mashed potatoes with a dollop of butter, peas and carrots and some apple cobbler in the middle of the aluminum tray. Da preferred Salisbury steak dinners, but not me! *What the hell was Salisbury steak anyway?* The summer Mumma wasn't around, Da and I ate TV dinners a lot. He also had a craving for fried meat skins. Most people called them fried pork rinds, but in our house, they were called "meat skins." He scooped up three or four bags of them when the two of us went grocery shopping. Mumma limited him to one bag per week, but she wasn't around, so Da ate what he wanted! Half a bag of those and a bottle of Miller High Life got him through *The Tonight Show with Johnny Carson.*

Mumma didn't allow me to watch Mr. Carson for a couple of reasons. First, his show came on at 11:30 p.m. and that was well past my bedtime. Secondly, she felt Mr. Carson's humor was for adults, not children. Despite that, I made attempts to watch *The Tonight Show* whenever I could. I loved Johnny Carson, and when his last episode appeared on May 22, 1992, I recorded it, cried a lot and fell asleep holding Peter Rabbit. Lori thought I was losing it, but I didn't care. Johnny Carson was Da and me eating meat skins on a Friday night in the summer of 1973.

Mumma's wrath didn't keep me from creeping over to the TV set in my room to turn the knob to hear Mr. Ed McMahon say, "Frommm Hollywood, it's the Tonight Show starring Johnny Carson!" Even though I had the volume set as low as possible, Mumma still managed to pick up Mr. McMahon's voice. *Why God blessed mothers with excellent hearing was a thought I often pondered.* She burst into my bedroom, "You better turn that TV off before I throw it outside!" "Yes, ma'am." As soon as she closed my door, I turned it back on, this time lying at the foot of the bed to hear Mr. Carson's monologue. A few minutes later I heard Mumma's foot stomp the hardwood floor. *How did she know?* I think it was the TV's flickering light from underneath my door that gave me away! She and Da sat in the dining room discussing their day until she shouted, "If I come in your room one more God-damned time and that TV is on, your ass is mine!" Television remotes hadn't been invented yet, so there was no way for me to flick it off if she decided to pop in again. I took the safe route and finally turned the TV off. But Mumma's summer absence allowed me to watch *The Tonight Show* or *The CBS Late Night Movie* or anything else I wanted (whenever I wanted), and that was fun! Maybe it was fun for Da, too.

The three TV stations out of Richmond signed off at midnight or at the latest, 1:00 a.m., so with Mumma gone, I was a free man that summer! However as English literary icon Geoffrey Chaucer said, "All good things must come to an end." The summer fun for a father and son did come to an end when the wife and mother returned in August. Da pulled me aside one night to say, "Now, when your mother comes back, she doesn't need to know that we ate TV dinners all the time or that you stayed up late watching TV." "Da, I'm not stupid!"

August brought 7th grade and the start of school closer, and Da took me over to West Point to do some back-to-school shopping. All summer long I begged him for a pair of new sneakers. "Okay, okay! We'll go buy them before school starts." I wanted a pair of blue suede Converse. The blue suede was adorned with two white stripes on each side of the shoe with a Converse star sewn in the middle. Da's brother, Michael, who was five years older than me, had recently bought a yellow suede pair of them. He was the first person in the county with those suede shoes! Butley got the second pair, and I wanted to be the third! Long before Michael Jordan made Nike the athletic shoe to wear, a pair of Converse were the sneakers everyone wanted. The suede variety was a notch above the regular canvas style. Suede was a status symbol (not that I knew what a "status symbol" was). I just wanted those sneakers because Michael and Butley had a pair, and I wanted to be like them.

The pair of Size 7s fit perfectly, and I could not have been happier when Aunt Dot put them in the Leggett's Department Store shopping bag for me to take home. She was the first black person to work at the Leggett's in West Point when she started there in 1963, and she couldn't believe Da was spending that much money on a pair of sneakers for me. "Hmph, hmph, hmph, Bill Lewis, I can't believe you're gonna spend *22 dollars and 98 cents* on some shoes for that boy!" In 1973, $22.98 was about what Mumma spent on groceries per week!

Mumma finally came home a couple of days before school started. She was tired and weak from the accident, but when she came into my bedroom that morning and saw me sliding on my new suede shoes, she was like *Popeye* eating spinach. All of her strength returned! She screamed, "Where on Earth did you get *those?*" I quietly mumbled, "Da got 'em for me a couple of weeks ago." "How much were they?" I remained quiet and that irritated her. "Answer me!" "Umm." "Umm, my ass! You know how much those damn shoes cost! Don't sit there and act like you don't know. I'm so mad at you and your dad right now." More silence from me. "I don't even want to know how damn much they cost. I *know* they weren't cheap, and now that I think about it, you asked me for a pair of those Converse before I had my accident, and I told you 'No' because they were too expensive. Then, you have the *audacity* to get your daddy to buy them for you while I'm gone." *Who in the hell is Orr Dasidy? I didn't have Orr Dasidy do anything. I don't even know anyone named Orr Dasidy!* "You must have lost your God-damned mind!" She screamed, "I changed my mind. Tell me how much those damn shoes cost!" I was bent over lacing them up and since my back was turned toward her, she couldn't see my eyes roll. Under my breath, "I thought you said you didn't want to know how much they cost." "Boy, you better tell me how much those fucking shoes cost!" "Twenty-two dollars and ninety-eight cents." "Fine. You will pay me back every last red cent your daddy spent!" "Mumma, what are you talking about? *Da* bought 'em with *his* money." I never looked up, but I could *feel* her eyes burn through me. "You dumb ass. Don't you know your daddy's money *is* my money?" *No, I wasn't aware of that.* "How am I gonna pay you back?" "I don't know. That's your problem. You're always talking about how much money you make cutting grass, pay me back with *that!*" "But Mumma, that's *my* money!" That was the straw that broke the camel's back.

The Look often caused a physical reaction within me. Her anger sometimes sent me running for the bathroom not knowing if I would be doing "Number 1" or "Number 2" once I closed the door. It was a frightening experience when she was in that state of mind. I don't know how else to describe it. Some parents said they ruled by putting the fear of God in their children. I wasn't sure how that played out in other homes, but Mumma instilled *fear* in me. Throughout my life, I wasn't afraid of God, his son, Jesus, or something called The Holy Ghost. But the Holy Mother that was Jean Elizabeth Latimore Lewis Ferguson? I was always afraid of her.

The Look usually came with a spanking or a verbal assault or sometimes, both. It was close to 8:15, the time Miss Roberta Faucette's Bus No. 17 pulled up to take Bridgette and me to school, so Mumma took the verbal route. "Boy, you better march your black ass outta here and get on that school bus before I make you walk outta here in your *socks!* You have some God-damned nerve talking about *your* money when you and your daddy spent 22 dollars and 98 cents on a pair of sneakers that you won't even be able to wear in 6 months! You know yelling gives me a headache since I had my car accident and look at what you're making me do! Go get on that fucking bus!" She pointed to the front door. I headed out thinking, "You know what? I don't even like these shoes anymore. It wasn't even worth Da buying them."

When Da came home from work that evening, I was sitting on the front porch with my bottom lip poked out because of that morning's events. He asked, "What's wrong?" "Mumma said I have to pay her back for the sneakers." He thought that was funny, but I didn't. "I thought your mom might say something like that!"

Those shoes weren't very practical. I became afraid to stand near anyone at school because I didn't want them stepping on my blue suede shoes! I couldn't wear them to play basketball on dirt courts either because the dust and grime made them filthy (maybe I was slightly OCD like Da). It was funny how some things turned out in life. Things you couldn't wait to have sometimes were the things that you couldn't wait to get rid of. Well, at least that was how I felt about those sneakers.

It was amusing 40 years later, but it wasn't on that first day of school of 7th grade or the Saturday mornings that followed when I headed out to cut grass. I was essentially cutting each yard for free because Mumma wanted her money back before the green grass turned brown. My grass-cutting "business" came with a tight budget. I bought the gas for the lawnmower with my earnings, and I had little margin for error. My mother was cutting into my profits! To make matters worse, Da charged me 50 cents a week to use *his* lawnmower. He called it "depreciation." *Like I knew what that meant.* I felt as though he and Mumma were trying to run me out of business with their rules and regulations. Each Saturday evening found Mumma standing in the driveway waiting for me to putter in and hand over my grass money. I didn't know it then, but she was providing me a lesson in *gas money*. Money was not to be splurged. Hers, Da's or mine. I didn't understand all of that at 12 years old. I just thought Mumma was being mean. Eighth grade came and to make matters worse, Mumma was right again. My feet had outgrown those blue suede shoes!

CHAPTER 48

Each summer brought Aunt Virginia and Uncle Buddy and their kids down from Pennsylvania to stay at Grandpop Lewis' house. Faye, Portia and Michael liked seeing them and their kids, but they were not happy that Aunt Virginia and Uncle Buddy seemed to stay out fishing from sunup to sundown. Although Faye, Portia and Michael complained about that, Grandpop never did, and I guess that was all that really mattered. It was *his* house.

Aunt Virginia and Uncle Buddy liked fishing and crabbing out on the Rappahannock River down at Mr. El-ick's marina. Uncle Buddy kept a boat down there that he used for fishing parties. Aunt Virginia and Uncle Buddy were gone each morning before the window shades were pulled up and came back when we were pulling them down for the night. "All they ever do when they come down here is eat, sleep and fish. They oughta be ashamed of themselves," said one of my aunts, but I would never admit which! Faye was close to 26, Portia around 22 and Michael near 17. Me? I was 12 and a half! Of course I could parrot what they said, right? *I could not have been more wrong!*

Unlike her older brother, Portia made great hamburgers and french fries. I preferred the Richfood brand of crinkle-cut fries that came in a white cardboard box. I asked Portia to make them *every* day, but that was probably the only thing she wouldn't do for me. "Boy, you better leave me alone and eat something green out of Pop's garden!" Fridays, though, were usually burgers and fries for all of us at Grandpop's house. I was gobbling them down as quickly as Portia removed them from the frying pan. "You better leave some food for Buddy and Virginia. You know they'll be hungry when they come in from down at El-ick's." Portia was in the kitchen cleaning up while I continued stuffing my face at the dining room table.

(Insert "Almost Grown" by Chuck Berry) I let her know how I felt about Aunt Virginia and Uncle Buddy being gone from sunup to sundown, "Nobody told Aunt Virginia and Uncle Buddy to stay out in the river all day. They don't help out around here anyway. All they do is eat Grandpop's food and make a mess! I ain't saving nothing for them! If they wanted something to eat, they should've come home earlier!" I only repeated what I'd heard Faye, Portia and Michael say countless times, but couldn't understand why Portia wasn't giggling or responding to my outburst. *Why is she so quiet?* For that matter, why does it seem like the entire house is quiet? Unbeknownst to me, Aunt Virginia and Uncle Buddy were standing right behind me as I complained about their comings and goings. When I turned around in my chair to see the two of them, I thought I was going to pee in my pants! It got real ugly from that point.

Uncle Buddy folded his arms and leaned back against the dining room wall as Aunt Virginia let me have it! "*You* are a child! *You* have no opinion and if you do, it doesn't matter! If I want to stay out in the Rappahannock River for a week, that is *my* business! Who are *you* at 12 years old to be questioning what *I* do?" *Aunt Virginia, I'm almost 12 and a half!* "If I want to stay out in the river until the cows come home, I will!" *We don't even have any cows! What is she talking about?* "And there is *nothing* you can say about it. Since when does the opinion of a 12-year-old matter?" *Why does she keep saying I'm 12? I'm 12 and a half!* "You better learn to shut that big mouth of yours and respect your elders. You must have lost the little sense that God gave you thinking that you are gonna tell me and Buddy what and what not we should be doing on our vacation." And so it went for the longest five minutes of my life! I thought Portia would rescue me from Aunt Virginia's river of words. I knew she was going to say to her big sister, "Virginia, Troy *is* right! You *do* stay out in the river all day. And you *don't* help with the laundry or the cooking or cutting the grass. All you *do* is take advantage of Pop!" No one came to my rescue. I sank lower in my chair pushing my cold fries around on my plate. My appetite for burgers and fries went floating down the Rappahannock like Uncle Buddy's boat! At 12 years old, I learned a very important *gas money* lesson. I learned to make sure "the coast was clear" when verbalizing something about someone that I shouldn't have been, especially when it was my Aunt Virginia and Uncle Buddy!

Almost 30 years later, Da had Aunt Virginia, Uncle Buddy, Faye, Portia and Michael over for dinner during the Christmas holiday. They were recounting old stories, and at some point, a reference was made regarding my behavior as a little boy. I froze. I was 42 years old and still afraid of Aunt Virginia. Even more afraid she might repeat the "burgers and fries" story in front of Da because I was still afraid of him too! He never knew how much trouble I caused that day, and 30 years later, he would not have been happy with his now 42-year-old son! I tried minimizing what I felt Aunt Virginia was about to comment on. "Well, as a little boy, I did run my mouth a lot and probably said some things I shouldn't have." I was not prepared for her response. "Oh, c'mon. You were always such a good little boy. You were always so well mannered." Portia and I looked at each other from across the table. We smiled. Aunt Virginia forgot! We couldn't believe it! It was one of my most stressful childhood memories, and Aunt Virginia forgot all about it. Portia got up to get a drink of water from the kitchen, and I followed her. From the kitchen sink, Portia glanced over at Aunt Virginia and then back toward me. She whispered, "Oh Lord, she forgot *all* about it! I know you were sweating bullets on that one, my boy!" *Yes, I was!*

CHAPTER 49

Portia had a boyfriend named Kenny. I always felt that he didn't like me very much, and I wasn't too crazy about him, either. Whenever he was around Grandpop's house, I tried to be somewhere else. He was from "up the county," and his parents were Atlas and Otelia Payne, a handyman and a schoolteacher. Atlas was an unusual first name, and Mr. Payne was the only "Atlas" I ever met. One day when I was about 6 years old, Da introduced me to him while I was playing with the many buckets of nails within the Urbanna Lumber Company. Da took me with him to the hardware place two to three times a month, and I *lived* in the nail aisle! He called me over to where he and Mr. Payne were chatting. "Chopper, this is Mr. Atlas Payne." I shook his hand, "Hi, Mr. Payne." They went on talking, and I headed back to the nails. I liked the clanking sound they made when they fell from my hands into the bucket. Once Da's pickup was loaded with the lumber he needed, he yelled from the loading dock, "C'mon, Chopper. Put the nails down and let's go!" "Okay, Da." Heading to the pickup, I was thinking, "Isn't Atlas supposed to be a real strong guy? Didn't I read somewhere that he holds up the world?" I walked toward them. "Mr. Payne, can I ask you a question?" "Go ahead, son." "Do your arms ever get tired holding up the world?" Da and Mr. Payne stared at each other, then laughed. As we drove away, Da yelled back to Mr. Payne, "I never know what this boy is gonna say next!" *What was funny?*

I tried to prevent the marriage of Portia and Kenny. Pushing through the gathering crowd at Union Prospect Baptist Church, I found

Portia in a back room where final touches were being made to her hair and gown. I marched over and whispered in her ear. "Portia, I really don't want you to marry Kenny. He ain't never nice to nobody but you." The first thing she said to me was, "Boy, what on Earth are you doing in here?" I lowered my head. "I'm sorry." She recognized that I was down. I was sad because I didn't like Kenny very much, and I was sad because I felt like I was losing her to Kenny (I had a crush on Portia, too!). Then, she sighed and took a long look at me before she said, "You know you just used a triple negative in a sentence." *Huh?* "Don't worry, Troy Boy Tomato, it'll be okay. Now go back out there and sit with Jean and Bridgette."

Troy Boy Tomato was Portia's nickname for me. The produce section at Mr. Walton's grocery store carried a tomato with that name. I loved peeling the labels from the tomatoes and sticking them on my forehead every chance I got. When it was time for a bath, I wouldn't even scrub my forehead because I wanted the labels to remain stuck to my noggin! That was how I became known as Troy Boy Tomato! As she ushered me from the room, "I have to get ready, Troy Boy. Everything will be alright." I didn't sit next to Mumma and Bridgette. I went outside and plopped my rear end on the brick steps of the church entrance to toss pebbles at ants crawling on the sidewalk. *I'm not even going to watch!* Listening to Mendelssohn's "Wedding March," I pretended each ant that I picked off was Kenny. I was jealous of him! I wanted to marry Portia! I didn't care if she was my aunt!

(Insert "I Can Understand It" by New Birth) A few months before the wedding, Portia, Kenny and Michael couldn't stop talking about the big concert that was coming to the Richmond Coliseum. The concert featured The Intruders who had a big hit with "I'll Always Love My Mama," and New Birth, who sang "I Can Understand It," and a few other musical groups. Dee-jay Kirby Carmichael's commercials on WANT-AM told us that, "Everybody who's anybody is gonna be there!" I wanted to be one of those bodies!

WANT's signal was faint in Middlesex, but whenever Michael and I drove over to West Point in Portia's Beetle to pick up some lunch from The Golden Skillet we could hear WANT loud and clear. The

Golden Skillet was a fast-food chicken chain that we frequented about once a week. We were headed west and that brought us closer to the WANT signal. The Skillet offered a "Number 1" that came with a leg, a wing, fries and a biscuit for $2.79; a "Number 2" also had fries and a biscuit, but was $4.79 because the leg and wing were replaced with a thigh and a breast. Very seldom did Michael and I have enough money for a "Number 2!" The summer that Mumma was in the hospital, Tony and I stopped by The Skillet before we went down to see her. I guess he felt sorry for me because he told me I could get *anything* I wanted when we got out of his maroon 1972 Triumph Spitfire. I got a "Number 2" with an extra biscuit and a large Pepsi. I never forgot Tony's generosity that day, and any kid that was with me got to eat *whatever* they wanted!

Everywhere Portia, Michael or Kenny went during the summer, I was right behind them. I guess that's why Kenny couldn't stand the sight of me. I was a puppy yapping at their heels. The more they talked about the upcoming show at the Coliseum, the more I wanted to go. Did I care that Portia and Kenny were in college and Michael was in high school? No! Did I think they were too old for me to hang out with? No! Was I determined to go to the Richmond Coliseum with them? Yes! I was 12 and a half! I was almost a teenager! For weeks, I begged Portia to let me go with them, and finally she gave in. "If you can come up with your *own* $5 for the ticket, you can go!" "Okay!"

Maybe Portia figured I wouldn't be able to come up with the money in such a short amount of time. Five dollars was a lot of cash, and it was hard saving money with Da "nickel and diming" me with "depreciation!" Someone told me that Mr. Walton paid 5 cents apiece for empty soda bottles at his grocery store. I knew there were plenty scattered along 33 because anyone with eyes could see that. I wasn't ashamed to admit that I wasn't altruistic, but I was going to do my best to clean up Middlesex County for a few days! *I never understood why people littered.* The *Keep America Beautiful* ad campaign featuring the Native American "Crying Chief" with trash thrown at his feet from a passing car had a huge impact on me.

One hundred bottles would make an even $5, but I also figured I needed another $2 or so for popcorn, candy and a soda at the Coliseum, so 140 bottles became my goal. I spent each day walking up and down Middlesex County looking for them. I probably resembled a homeless man (or homeless boy) with a Hefty trash bag slung over my shoulder. *Not that I knew what a homeless person was.* We didn't have "homeless" people in Middlesex County. I wouldn't see a homeless person until I started working in New York City, and when I saw that, it really startled me.

Mr. Raymond Walton, who owned the grocery store in Urbanna, was one of the nicest people in Middlesex County, but I thought he was a "redneck" just because he had a tattoo on his arm. A lot of the people that I knew who weren't nice to black people in Middlesex County had tattoos, so I thought Mr. Walton was one of *them*. I was wrong. He hired Mumma as his first black employee in 1970. She became a cashier who memorized food prices as she walked up and down the aisles after the store closed on Friday nights. Even though each item came with a sticker price, Mumma wanted customers moving quickly through her line, so she memorized the prices. She wanted to show Mr. Walton that he made the right decision in choosing her. If she did well, it might be easier for other blacks to get hired. Some white people didn't like Mr. Walton's experiment, and even when her line had the fewest customers, they waited their turn at another register. But when they had the misfortune of being stuck in her line, some placed their money on the conveyor belt instead of touching Mumma's hand. She told me certain white ladies wouldn't budge from her line until they had compared the itemized receipt to each item in their grocery bags, and they didn't care how long they held up the line, either. Mumma stood watching patiently with a smile. Once satisfied that all was correct, they moved on, and Mumma politely said, "Have a nice day!" Mr. Walton watched from his elevated corner office and gave Mumma a wink to let her know she was doing okay.

A couple of years later, Mumma got a job down in Toano at the textile plant that paid a little more money, but she continued shopping at Mr. Walton's store. After she and Da broke up, making ends meet was difficult. All we had for income was Grandma and Grandpop Latimore's Social Security checks and Mumma's paltry check from the plant. Often when Mumma was about to hand over her cash or write a check for our groceries, Mr. Walton walked over from his corner office to ask Mumma how she was getting along. "I'm doing okay, Mr. Walton. Thanks for asking." While the items moved along the belt, Mr. Walton informed the cashier that, "Jean already paid. Her 'books' are clean." Then, he helped her take the groceries out to the car. "Mr. Walton, you don't have to help me like this. I'm getting by." "Jean, we can't have the kids going hungry now, can we?" Mr. Walton often gave free food to a lot of black *and* white families that were facing hard times, but I initially thought he was a mean, old "redneck" with a tattoo on his arm.

But when Da and I drove over in the Chevy pickup to hand over my 140 bottles, I didn't know anything about Mr. Walton's kindness because Da was still living with us. Outside of his grocery store, there were wooden soda crates set aside for the "empties." Mr. Walton came out to chat with Da, and he asked me why I had so many bottles. "I want to go to a concert at the Richmond Coliseum with my Aunt Portia this weekend. I think I have enough bottles so I can buy my own ticket!" He wished me luck and went back inside the store. Da and I filled up the crates, and I ended up with *143* bottles for a grand total of $7.15! *When state lotteries came along, I played 143 a lot!* Mr. Walton gave me an extra quarter and told me, "Have fun at the show!"

The Saturday evening of the show, I could not have been more excited as Da drove me to Grandpop's house to meet Kenny, Portia and Michael. *They didn't know I was coming!* I hopped out of Da's truck wearing tan double-knit cuffed pants, a brown and white checkered popcorn shirt with a butterfly collar and brown platform Thom McAn shoes. It was my favorite outfit! I thought I was the coolest kid in the county going to see his first concert. Portia wasn't nearly as happy as I was when I showed up with my $5 bill in hand. "I'm ready, Portia!" She had to be thinking, "Oh, Lord, now I have to take this child with me." She kept her word though, and I took a seat next to Michael in the back of Portia's Volkswagen. I don't remember much about that night, except Kenny complaining that we had to pay $2 for parking, and how different "live" music sounded compared to "recorded" music. The sound disappointed me, and kept me from going to another "live" concert until the year 2000 when Kat Peeler and I took Da to see Little Richard and James Brown perform at B.B. King's on 42nd Street in New York City. We ended up liking the Friday night show so much that we went back on Saturday night to see them do it all over again. It was the best money I ever spent! Who was Kat Peeler? She's another story!

CHAPTER 50

Let me formally introduce Horace and Grace Latimore, Mumma's parents. They were married on November 29, 1933, and stayed that way until Grandma died in 1996. They made it almost 63 years, and how Grandma put up with Grandpop for that long was a miracle to me. After Grandma died, I didn't think Grandpop would make it a week without her, but he proved me wrong for another 10 years.

While Grandma and Aunt Jenny were the kindest souls I ever met, Grandpop could be one of the nastiest. He was the epitome of a mean drunk. I found out there were plenty of them in the world, but back then, I thought *he* was the only one. Sober, he was the nicest person you ever wanted to be around, but when I was growing up, he wasn't sober very often. There might have been one sober day for every four intoxicated days. I never knew which day was going to be which.

Grandpop Latimore had six brothers and two sisters: Uncle Percy, Uncle Neal, Uncle Grant, Uncle Elmore, Uncle Carey, Uncle Eddie, Aunt Emma Lee and Aunt Edie. A kerosene fire killed Aunt Emma when she was 15 or so. A lot of people, me included, mistook Aunt Edie for Aunt Jenny because they looked very much alike. Sitting on Aunt Jenny's front porch one evening, Aunt Jenny admitted that Aunt Edie considered herself more attractive than Aunt Jenny, and Aunt Edie didn't like it when people said they couldn't tell them apart! I thought it was kind of funny that one 80-year-old aunt thought she was more attractive than the other. Aunt Jenny thought it was funny, too, and she told me to never repeat that story, but I couldn't resist.

"Why did Grandpop drink so much?" I never knew the answer to that question, and it wasn't like I or anyone else was ever going to ask him. Those types of questions weren't asked. Even if the question had been asked, his response likely would have been, "That's none of your *God*-damned business. Now shut the fuck up and leave me alone." All of us simply learned to live with his drinking, and we never discussed the reason behind it. As I said, he could be mean, but he never hurt anyone, except for the time he chased Grandma, Uncle Dee, Aunt Grace and Mumma up the road to Uncle Carey's house with a rifle around 1949.

Every now and then at the dinner table, Grandpop fell asleep and landed in the plate of spaghetti Grandma had prepared for him. Sharon, Bridgette and I stared, shook our heads and ate quietly. A few minutes later, Grandpop would wake up, wipe the sauce from his face and look at us as we stared back at him too scared to avert our eyes. "What the fuck are y'all looking at?" "Nothing, Grandpop." We went back to eating. His eyes shifted toward the kitchen. "Mom, I want some more spaghetti. Never mind, I'll get it my God-damned self." That was when we knew there would be no opportunity for "seconds." Once he staggered to the stove, instead of scooping food onto his plate from Grandma's spaghetti pot, he ate directly from the big tin pot. At least we got to eat before he dug in, so that made it a good night. Bad nights were when he ate from the spaghetti pot *before* we filled our plates. Those evenings became peanut butter and jelly dinners. In his drunken stupor, he ate and stared at us while we watched *our* dinner disappear into *his* mouth. I loved Grandma's spaghetti and hated Grandpop when he ruined it for us. He had his demons like anyone else, I guess. I had them, too. They caught up with me when I least expected it, but that's another story.

Grandpop's youngest brother was Uncle Eddie. He married Aunt Dot sometime in the early 1950s. He courted another lady and was close to marrying her, but she didn't like a couple of Uncle Eddie's friends. One was named *Johnny Walker,* and the other was *Jim Beam.* There was another buddy named *Gordon.* The names didn't really matter. They hung out with Uncle Eddie at his house all the time. The other lady was Mrs. Leuvenia Adkins, and she dated Uncle Eddie for some time in the 1950s, but Mumma didn't know this until they met on a train headed to Philadelphia. By that time, Mrs. Adkins was in her 80s when she looked at Mumma while settling into her seat and said, "You don't remember me, Jean Latimore, but I remember *you.* I used to date your Uncle Eddie a long time ago." That exchange began a 295-mile conversation from the Amtrak station at Williamsburg's North Boundary Street to Philadelphia's 30th Street Station. As the train navigated its way north, Mumma learned a lot about the Latimore brothers, and that was how I learned something that was *never* talked about, but I will get to that in a second.

Often I tried to learn more about Grandpop's family. *What was it like for him growing up?* In my 30s and 40s, I used to pick up Grandpop Latimore from Aunt Grace's home in Philadelphia to drive him down to see the handful of relatives and friends that remained in Middlesex County. I now liked spending time with Grandpop Latimore because he wasn't drinking. Drives down I-95 gave me the opportunity to learn more about his life. At times, we talked nonstop as I weaved around those who refused to get out of the left lane. Other stretches of the road found us both silent and not quite sure what to talk about next. He did teach me that Franklin Delano Roosevelt was the "greatest man who ever lived. I don't know what we would have done without him back during the Depression. That man put food on the table for my family." I became a Roosevelt fan, too and spent a weekend in 2011 visiting his Hyde Park home. I think Grandpop would have liked that.

I was amazed at the things that fascinated Grandpop when he was in his 90s. Living at Aunt Grace's house, he led a sheltered existence. He didn't participate in the technology changes taking place around him. Maybe that was the price of getting old. Cell phones fascinated him, and when I handed mine over to him to talk to Mumma or Aunt Grace or Pat-Pat, he always shouted. "Grandpop, you don't have to yell. Just speak normal. They can hear you." "This thing is so small.

I don't see how they can!" Every 50 to 60 miles, he asked, "Do you think we should pull over and check the oil?" "No, Grandpop. It's okay. Cars can drive a long way now before you have to worry about the oil!" He admired the convenience of E-Z Pass, "I can't believe you don't have to stop to pay the toll! That's crazy! Every time you go through the toll booth and hold up that little white square, I keep looking in the side mirror for the cops!"

We talked about his family and what it was like to grow up with them, but I could tell that his past was something he wanted to keep buried. As far as he was concerned, it was the *past*. He was more concerned about my life and what I was doing with it. But I always wanted to know more about his. I would ask for more information during each of our trips. "Tell me about this brother? Where did he live? What did he do? Did he ever get married? What were the names of his children?" He recounted as much as he could remember about Uncle Percy, Uncle Neal, Uncle Carey and Uncle Eddie. "Now, what about Uncle Grant and Uncle Elmore? What was their story?" He paused for a bit while staring at the highway. I thought he had forgotten what we were discussing. His voice softened as he said, "Grant and Elmore went up North and forgot everything Mom and Dad taught them. I guess you could say they sort of lost their minds." *I didn't ask what all of that meant.*

It was on the Philadelphia-bound Amtrak that Mrs. Adkins told Mumma what happened to Uncle Grant and Uncle Elmore. They were both killed for fraternizing with white women back in the 1920s or '30s, she couldn't remember the exact year. Word reached the family that one uncle died from pneumonia after being beaten by a mob and left for dead. The other was either beaten to death or hanged. Mrs. Adkins couldn't remember which. But they were indeed dead by the time they were in their mid-20s for seeing white women. According to Mrs. Adkins, that's what started the Latimore boys down the drinking path. I guess knowing your brothers were killed and there was nothing that you could do about it could lead you to drink. I started down that path for a period in my life for far lesser reasons, but everyone had their own motives for doing certain things. I know I had mine.

CHAPTER 51

Of Grandpop's brothers, Uncle Eddie was my favorite. His other brothers rarely said anything to me other than, "Get outta the way and be quiet. Do you ever shut up? Grown folks are talking." Uncle Eddie took an interest in me, and the more I talked to him, the more he talked to me. He liked sports and so did I, and sports became the focus of our conversations.

Uncle Eddie was a good-looking, slim man with wavy hair, a moustache and very smooth skin. Yes, he, too, was an alcoholic, but unlike Grandpop, Uncle Eddie was affable when drinking. A bottle pressed against his lips was accompanied with a smile, contrary to the constant scowl and dazed look seen with Grandpop. When Uncle Eddie drank, he was relaxed; when Grandpop drank, he was harsh and unpredictable. Uncle Eddie's intoxication allowed me to do most of the talking, and if there was one thing I was good at, it was talking!

Uncle Eddie was a sergeant during World War II and "Uncle Sam's" G.I. Bill gave him the chance to go to college, something no one else in Grandpop's family got to do except Aunt Edie. Uncle Eddie ended up teaching vocational and technical skills like auto mechanics, farming and carpentry to St. Clare Walker High School boys in the 1950s and 1960s. He also was the head coach for the baseball and basketball teams, and Butley's dad and Dickie Jackson played under him.

Grade school was as far as Grandpop and his other siblings got before they needed to find work to help their parents save money. Over time, they acquired almost 30 acres of Middlesex County soil. Great-Grandpop Carey Latimore was an oysterman, and he pinched pennies to buy as much land as possible for his children to have something when he was gone. Sometime in the 1930s, a stroke incapacitated him. He was dropped off at the Central Lunatic Asylum up in Petersburg, the first institution built in the U.S. "for colored persons of unsound mind." That was pretty much the end of him. I didn't know if he became a non-communicative "mute" or a "crazy" man who carried on conversations with the voices circling in his head. He was only 58 when he died in 1932. By the time I came along, he wasn't talked about, and I didn't know anything about him until I was in my 50s. It was like he never existed.

Uncle Eddie's property was adjacent to Grandpop's, and together, they leased out their property to Mr. Frank Moore for corn and soybean planting. A row of honeysuckle and shrubs separated Uncle Eddie's crops from Grandpop's, and that row ran about 1,500 feet all the way back to the woods behind both houses. As a boy during the spring and summer, Tony taught me how to use a Mason jar to catch bees over in that honeysuckle row. Holding the glass in my hand, I could feel the vibration and hear their collective whirr. An old fork was used to punch holes in the metal screw-on lid to give the bees some air, but they quickly became "goofy" when their air supply ran short. With their movements slow and labored, we unscrewed the lid and let them fly away. More often than not, a bee stung me to show its displeasure with being held captive. I ran back to the house crying, "A bee stung me!" Mumma yelled at Tony from the kitchen window, "How many times do I have to tell y'all to leave those God-damned bees alone?" She removed the bee's stinger with a set of tweezers, placed wet tobacco around the welt, and tightened it with a shoestring she kept in a cabinet drawer. That drawer contained hammers, extension cords, nails, candles, matches, glue, yarn, rags, pliers and about a hundred other items. You name it, and Mumma had it in that drawer. Many times she told me to "Go find it. It's in that drawer." *Are you kidding me? It's impossible to find anything in there!* After removing the stinger, she sent me back out to find more mischief with Tony. Eight years my senior, I don't ever remember him getting stung, but one summer when he was about 10 or so, a skunk sprayed him. Mumma soaked him in tomato juice for days and had him sleep on the back porch for nearly a week!

In 1st grade, Uncle Eddie taught me how to read box scores from the *Daily Press*. He let me know he was heading over to our place by standing in his backyard and yelling across the field, "Heww" before hopping into his car. "Heww" was my cue to get my "sports report" together. He pulled up in his 1964 purple Ford Falcon station wagon to sit on the wagon's gate, pour from a brown paper bag and find out how the Los Angeles Dodgers did last night. Most black people that I knew liked the Dodgers because of their signing of Jackie Robinson in 1947. By the time I was starting to understand what sports were all about, Mr. Robinson had retired, and I was a Baltimore Orioles fan. The Dodgers? They were all the way out in some city called Los Angeles. Like I was ever going there! I cared nothing about the L.A. Dodgers.

WNNT-FM carried Oriole games on the radio, and I thought that both *Brooks* and *Frank* Robinson were black because they had the same surname as Jackie. *All of the Robinsons that I knew in Middlesex County were related, why wouldn't Brooks, Frank and Jackie be, too?* Then, I saw my first World Series game at 9 years old on TV in 1970. I remember running from the school bus to catch the last few innings of the Orioles playing the Cincinnati Reds in the last World Series when all of the games were in the afternoon. "At bat, the left fielder, Frank Robinson!" *Ok, he's black.* "At bat, the 3rd baseman, Brooks Robinson!" *Brooks Robinson is white?* At the end of each inning, Uncle Eddie wanted me to come outside to give him an update. I kept trying to get him to come in and watch the game with me, but he was more content sitting on the gate of his station wagon under the shade of the elm tree.

Uncle Eddie taught me the importance of men like Jackie Robinson and Larry Doby, who broke the color barrier in the American League the same year that Mr. Robinson did in the National League. Because Jackie Robinson was the *first*, history wasn't as kind to Mr. Doby. I didn't know anything about Mr. Doby, and Uncle Eddie made me feel bad for not knowing who he was. "Son, you need to know who *everybody* is!" I went to the library, and Mrs. Barlowe helped me learn more about this Doby guy. I don't remember if Uncle Eddie ever got to see Jackie Robinson actually play, but he talked about him so much, he made it seem like Mr. Robinson played 2nd base for the Middlesex Blue Sox instead of up in Brooklyn. Many years later, I worked in Brooklyn, and I was never more disappointed to find out that all that was left of Ebbets Field (the former home of the Dodgers) was a 100-foot slab brick wall with a housing project hiding behind it.

Summer afternoons found me reading the *Daily Press* sports page to Uncle Eddie while he poured "brown water" from a paper bag into his miniature Dixie paper cup. He shared his "water" with his "real" drinking buddies, Horace King and Dick Cook, and I gave all of them a recap of the sports day even if his buddies didn't want it. Sometimes, Uncle Eddie gave me a nickel for my recap. Sometimes, he didn't. I didn't care. I just liked being around him. "Troy, who's leading the National League in hitting?" "Willie Mays, .363." "Stolen bases?" "Maury Wills, 88." "Strikeouts?" "Bob Gibson, 183." Speaking of Mr. Gibson, I met him when I was working at the record store in Nebraska. I was standing outside on my 20-minute break drinking a soda when I noticed a gentleman needing assistance with putting some Tru-Value boxes in his car. I didn't recognize who he was until he closed the lid to his trunk. *It was Bob Gibson, the man who posted a 1.12 ERA in 1968!* I wanted to tell him that my Uncle Eddie really admired him, but that he admired the Dodgers more, so I said nothing other than, "Have a nice day, Mr. Gibson!"

Uncle Eddie gave me a love of sports that lasted forever, and I never thanked him for it because he dropped dead from cirrhosis of the liver at 51 years old on his bathroom floor when I was 10 years old. I didn't go to his funeral because I was too sad. Instead, I went over to Christchurch and shot free throws while he was lowered into the ground at Antioch Baptist Church. Later on, I was mad that Uncle Eddie didn't make it to the Thanksgiving dinner when I ate the toothpicks. He would have stopped me from doing that because he always kept an eye on me. I got even madder when I was old enough to understand that it was Uncle Eddie's "drinking buddies" that helped dig his grave.

Uncle Eddie and his wife, Aunt Dot. 1960

CHAPTER 52

When Grandma and Grandpop Latimore left Mumma in 1958, they went to work for the Peddle family who had homes in Ardmore, Pennsylvania, and Avalon, New Jersey. Grandma and Grandpop's jobs were similar to the butler and maid roles Morgan Freeman and Esther Rolle portrayed in *Driving Miss Daisy*. The "hand-me-downs" from the Peddle children made Bridgette and me some of the "best-dressed" black kids in Middlesex County (or so I thought). They were each older than us by a year, so when their outfits were a little "too tight" for them, they were "just right" for us. Sometimes Mrs. Peddle purchased Mumma a new dress, coat or hat because she knew Mumma didn't have much, and fortunately, she did.

Before heading into any store, Mumma always made sure our appearance was perfect. If I had fallen asleep in the backseat, she dabbed some of her spit onto my face to wipe the drool from the corner of my mouth. I squirmed away from her. "Mumma!" "Now, stand still so I can get this mess off of your face!" My shirt had to be tucked in and my belt had to be aligned with my shirt and zipper. When I got to Air Force Basic Training, "gig" lines and a neat appearance were easy because Mumma had me working on that kind of stuff since I could remember! *Maybe Mumma was a drill sergeant in a previous life.*

Tying shoes was a difficult process for me because it required fine motor skills, and God never blessed me with those! I didn't perfect tying shoes until I was in the 2nd grade, so when Mumma was too frustrated to help me for the one hundredth time, I paid Bridgette a nickel to tie a knot for me. On the days I wasn't so nice to her, she would tease me before we fell asleep. "You were mean to me today. I'm not gonna tie your shoes in the morning unless you pay me a dime!"

Once my outfit and Bridgette's passed Mumma's inspection, she lined us up in the parking lot next to our GTO to give us our marching orders. "We're going in this store to do some Christmas shopping. If you touch anything, if you break anything, I will break your God-damned necks! Look with your *eyes,* not your hands!" And we knew she meant it so we didn't test her. Her lips barely moved as she delivered her threat. I often thought Mumma could have been a ventriloquist and wondered why she didn't try out for *The Ed Sullivan Show* because she was *that* good. I watched people as they passed us in the lot. I was pretty sure they were thinking, "Aren't they cute!" Bridgette and I knew otherwise because there was nothing "cute" about this scenario. It was serious business, and we had better pay attention to Mumma's instructions. As we headed into the department store, I struggled to open the heavy doors for Mumma and Bridgette. "A man opens doors for ladies." "Mumma, I'm not big enough to open this door! It's too heavy!" "You'll be a man one day, now shut up and open that damn door! Your mother doesn't have any arms!" Once inside, Bridgette and I remembered to keep our little hands folded behind our backs or stuffed in our pockets. Up and down each aisle we followed behind her like little puppies. Shopping with Mumma was never much fun at any age, except for the time the grapes fell through the bottom of the bag in Italy!

Mrs. Blanche Peddle was an attractive blonde woman in her mid-30s who I only met once when I was about 6 or 7 years old. She whispered something to me during that encounter that I never forgot. Mumma, Bridgette and I had driven up to Pennsylvania to see Aunt Grace and Uncle Dee. Later on, we stopped by the Peddle house to see Grandma and Grandpop for a bit, and Mrs. Peddle came out to the driveway as we pulled up. She gave Mumma a big hug, and I could tell she was genuinely happy to see her. I had never seen *anybody* hug Mumma, let alone a *white* person. Hugs weren't very popular in the 1960s. As I climbed out of the back of our Pontiac GTO, Mrs. Peddle came over to me and whispered, "You must be Troy. Well, don't you have the prettiest brown eyes!" I didn't even know what color my eyes were until she pointed them out, but from that point on, I never forgot! I was hooked on Mrs. Peddle for life! Anytime I filled out a form asking for my eye color, I checked the box marked "Brown" and could still hear Mrs. Peddle whispering in my ear.

From 1958 until about 1969, Grandma and Grandpop Latimore came back to Virginia about every two months or so. I was always happy to see Grandma, but couldn't wait for Grandpop to go back up North. He kept you on pins and needles with his up-and-down moodiness from drinking. He was scary. He yelled and screamed at anybody and everybody within earshot when he was drinking. The only person he didn't yell at was the insurance man who stopped by once a month to pick up his check. "Be quiet, it's the insurance man!" If sufficient funds were in Mumma's checking account, we opened the door. If her account was running low, the door remained closed, and we all remained quiet, even Grandpop. The insurance man had to know we were home because there were three or four cars in the driveway! Grandpop screamed at the Virginia Electric and Power Company (VEPCO) meter man who never made a sound other than closing his truck door. Or Sharon. Or Mumma. He didn't care who bore the brunt of his anger, but Grandma was his primary focus. When alcohol was in him, she did nothing right.

When we moved to Christchurch, I was glad that I wouldn't have to deal with his "crazy" visits anymore. However, in 1969, Grandma and Grandpop retired and moved back to Virginia. Then Mumma and Da broke up in 1973, and although we only lived with Grandma and Grandpop for about a year and a half, it sure seemed like a lot longer. At least every other night, he cursed me, Mumma, Tony, Sharon, Bridgette and Grandma for any infraction. It could be that the ice tray wasn't filled to his liking. We changed the channels too much. The TV was too loud. Or, the refrigerator door wasn't closed properly. He got up to demonstrate repeatedly, "Slam it nice and tight. Like this!" "Now, get up from that God-damned table and show me you know how to do it right!" The heat was too high. Too many lights were on. "That's right, leave all the fucking lights on. I'll just sign my property over to the VEPCO man when he comes by next month!" The dishes clanked too loudly. The phone was tied up too much. "Get off that damned phone! How will someone get through if there's an emergency?" Sharon, Bridgette and I looked at each other and thought, "What *emergency,* Grandpop? The only 'emergency' we ever have is when Aunt Jenny can't talk to Grandma about what just happened on *The Guiding Light.*" After repeated busy signals, she would dial "0" to tell the Operator that she needed to get through because of a family emergency. "This is the Operator, please hang up your phone to receive an incoming emergency call from Mrs. Virginia Latimore. Thank you."

Another source of aggravation for Grandpop Latimore was Tony's car, the Triumph Spitfire. After high school, Tony got a job at the Philip Morris plant in Richmond and bought the British two-seater. He put a muffler on it that everyone in the county could hear. Grandpop could hear it when it was at least a mile away. The noise riled him. "Here he comes with that ugly ass, loud ass car!" Grandpop was right on one account; it was very loud.

The way I saw it, none of Grandpop's sons got along with him very well, and I couldn't blame them. The drinking made him difficult to like. Tony, like the rest of us, never knew what to expect from Grandpop when the alcohol was swirling around in his brain. When Tony came home at 3 or 4 in the morning from a night of partying or hanging out with some girl, he turned his ignition off, coasted down the road and *pushed* his car into the driveway. I wished he had done that more often because it would have given Grandpop one less thing to complain about.

When my cousin/sister Sharon started dating in high school, she started seeing this guy named Arthur, and I liked him about as much as I liked Portia's husband. Arthur had a 1970 white Volkswagen that was almost as loud as Tony's Spitfire. Arthur used to wait for Sharon to come outside to get in his car, and while he waited, his VW idled outside of Grandpop's bedroom window, and that was a recipe for disaster. "You go outside and tell that bushy headed, yellow motherfucker to turn that God-damn engine off and come in here and say 'Hi' like he's got some God-damn respect!" Like me, Grandpop was not a fan of Arthur. Grandpop and I may not have agreed on much, but we did on that point!

When the sun rose in the morning and the alcohol had cleared Grandpop's system, it was as though the previous day's infractions hadn't occurred. I literally lived with *Dr. Jekyll and Mr. Hyde.* Grandma put up with him because she loved Grandpop. Plus, where was she going? Women didn't leave men in Middlesex County, at least none that I knew of. Men may have moved on, but not the women. They stayed. Grandma never cursed at Grandpop or anyone, but she did yell at him sometimes (but not enough for my satisfaction). The unkindest phrase she ever used was, "Oh, John Brown-it, Horace. Shut your mouth and go to sleep!" Their arguments continued throughout the evening until Grandpop fell asleep while Sharon, Bridgette and I lay upstairs giggling. Sometimes we laughed at the situation. Sometimes we were too scared to move. Every now and then, Grandpop fell out of bed, and the three of us went bounding down the steps to make sure he was okay. The scrapes on his face or forehead kind of scared me, but he did not like us seeing him in that state. "What the fuck are y'all looking at?" We closed his door and scrambled back upstairs.

When intoxicated, everyone and everything agitated him, with the exception of Faye. From time to time, we asked for her help in calming Grandpop. It was as though she was a 1970s-style hostage negotiator (not that any of us knew what a hostage negotiator was). But, as far as I was concerned, she was just that, a pacifier of emotions. Even with Grandpop swearing at the top of his lungs, Faye did not escalate his anger. She got him to laugh at himself and relax while he continued saying things like, "Shut the fuck up, Faye. You little skinny bitch!" Or, "Kiss my black ass, Faye. You may tell your husband what to do, but *you* don't tell *me* shit!" Faye would laugh, "Yeah, yeah, you're right, Mr. Latimore, now let's get you in the bed.

I'm gonna read you a bedtime story." And that would make them both laugh, and for the time being, all was okay. Faye was as cool as a cucumber. Seeing her pull up in our driveway was a comforting feeling. Once she walked into the house, I knew everything would be okay.

Grandpop Latimore could be in a nasty mood for any reason. It never took much to set him off. Back in the 1st grade, I was on the phone going over a homework assignment with Cleo Morris one evening. Cleo sat right behind me in 1st and 2nd grade. We were good at sneaking answers to questions to each other! The Latimore house had one phone in the living room that came with a "party" line (a line where two or more parties were connected to the same communication loop despite having different numbers). "Party" lines were shared with others in the community and were cheaper than "private" lines. We "shared" a party line with three or four other families who lived within 400–500 yards of us because we were too poor to have a "private" line. Aunt Dot and Uncle Eddie across the field had a "private" line. With Uncle Eddie being a schoolteacher and Aunt Dot having the Leggett's sales job, I considered them very rich. Their house had "running water" *and* a "private" line!

Our black, rotary telephone sat on a small table against the living room stairwell wall between two chairs. One chair was a purplish, blackish, upright wooden chair that was solid and uncomfortable. The other was a supple leather chair that you could really sink into, but Sharon, Bridgette and I weren't allowed to sit on it because that chair was for adults only. The telephone table kept an oversized, white leather family Bible. While going over my homework with Cleo, I placed one of my schoolbooks on top of the Bible. Grandpop noticed that, walked over and smacked me in the face so hard that the phone's receiver flew from my hand. Stars danced about my head as I searched for the phone's receiver. I located the receiver and managed to mumble, "Cleo, I'll call you back." Fighting tears, I looked at Grandpop. "What did I do?" He smacked me again. "Nothing goes on top of the Bible!" "I didn't know that!" He smacked once more. "Don't talk back to me!" I shut my mouth.

I learned a couple of lessons. First, nothing was placed on top of the Bible, and secondly, I shouldn't question Grandpop when I was 6 years old!

The next day found Grandpop in a better mood. He had sobered and came outside to sit next to me on the front porch steps as I watched the traffic pass our house. We sat there in silence for a few minutes until he asked, "What do you wanna be when you grow up?" *You knocked the shit outta me last night, and now you want to know what I want to be when I grow up? Okay, here goes.* "I want a million dollars, and I want to own a McDonald's!" *I had never stepped foot inside of a McDonald's, but I loved their commercials!* He stared at me for a while, then said, "Well, as long as you have your health, you've got everything." I thought that was the *dumbest* thing I had ever heard. *Why would anyone choose health over a million dollars or owning a McDonald's?* As I grew older, I came to realize just how wise Grandpop was. He deserved more credit than I gave him. Health was more important than money, and all I had to do was live a little to realize that.

CHAPTER 53

Grandma Latimore never swore, but her oldest grandson sure did (that would be me). My tongue worsened when I went away to college and even more so after I joined the military. I never used "bad" words around Grandma, but often I slipped and said "Jesus" or "Good God" or "Good Lord" when someone was in the left lane traveling 55 miles per hour. "Good Lord, why can't you get in the right lane and do that?" Grandma did not like me using that type of language as I drove her from place to place. "You better watch your mouth and quit using the Lord's name in vain, or you'll end up in H-E-double-L sitting right next to the Devil himself." "I'm sorry, Grandma."

During the college summer break, I held two jobs, one at Colonial Williamsburg and the other, waiting tables for Mr. Howard Johnson at one of his restaurants. I had fun making ice cream sundaes and getting to know people from all over the U.S. and the world. Evenings were the busiest of times for the restaurant, and one of those evenings I had an encounter with Jesus Christ himself!

I opened the lid to the front freezer bin to make a hot fudge sundae, and the most important of Mr. Johnson's 28 Flavors was missing! There was no vanilla because the day shift forgot to put out the required two tubs for the evening shift. I slammed the bin door shut to head for the large freezer in the rear to grab more vanilla. Under my breath, I swore, "Jesus Christ! How could they leave without putting out the vanilla?" A male customer standing near the cash register overheard my foul language. "You should mind your tongue, my son." I looked up and to my surprise, there stood Jesus Christ himself. He was about 30 to 35 years old, decked out in a white gown and a beaded necklace. He had long, brown hair, a full mustache and goatee just like the Jesus Christ that had been staring back at me all of my life from Grandma's living room wall. I froze and for a brief instant thought, "Jesus! Grandma was right! I died for using the Lord's name in vain!" I continued staring at Him while he handed over His money to the cashier. *It was a surreal, out-of-body experience.* I said to him, "I'm sorry, Sir." He smiled and calmly said, "It's okay my son, but you really shouldn't use the Lord's name in vain like that. You never know where you might end up if you keep using that type of language." "Yes, Sir. You're right." *I realized I was still alive!* "Sir, if you don't mind me asking, *who* are you?" "Oh, I'm the actor portraying Jesus in *Jesus Christ Superstar* over at William and Mary!" "Jesus Christ! You look just like the real Jesus!" He wagged his index finger because I swore again, but we both laughed. It was a spooky encounter. I quit saying "Jesus Christ" for a long time!

My third summer job was driving Grandma and Grandpop Latimore to the doctor's office, the drugstore in Urbanna, the grocery store, the Saluda Post Office, up to Aunt Jenny's, down to Aunt Maggie's, or anywhere else they needed to go. I resented doing all of that on my day off. *I'm 19 years old, I work two jobs, I get one day off a week, and I have to spend it driving Grandma and Grandpop all over the county. I hate this!* What I wanted to do was sleep in, or go down to Quarterpath Park and play basketball, or go over to some girl's house while her parents were at work or just do nothing. I was selfish. Looking back, I was ashamed of my self-centeredness, and even though I only had to chauffeur them three or four times a month, it seemed like it was a lot more. Mumma reminded me that she had a far greater responsibility at a much younger age than I. She had to do something for someone else *every* single day, but her life wasn't mine. At 18, 19 and 20 years old, it was hard for me to put myself in her shoes when she was my age. Fortunately, as I got older, I gained a better perspective on

Mumma's life. However, I never appreciated her sacrifices until I was closer to dying than living.

I didn't want to drive the 40 miles from James City County to Middlesex County to take Grandma and Grandpop wherever they needed to go. However, once they were in the car with me, it turned out for the best. Their banter was entertaining, and their genuine affection for each other was heartwarming, to say the least. Grandpop was the nicest guy in the world when he didn't have alcohol in his system, and although I wanted to be doing other things, in hindsight, running errands with them was where I was supposed to be. Our rides "up and down the county" provided me with insight into their relationship.

Grandma and Grandpop loved listening to "country" music on the car radio, and once a country station was located, that was where the dial remained. *"Country" was the last thing I wanted to hear.* But 30 years flew by, and one day I woke up, and I couldn't believe how much I loved the music they made me listen to. *I became my grandparents!* Buck Owens. Ray Price. Johnny Cash. Marty Robbins. Kitty Wells. Webb Pierce. Charley Pride. Patsy Cline. I couldn't get enough of those guys and gals.

(Insert "Let Your Love Flow" by The Bellamy Brothers) In the 1980s, The Bellamy Brothers had a hit with "Let Your Love Flow," and as soon as it finished playing, Grandpop caught my eye in the rearview mirror of Mumma's 1977 four-door sky blue VW Rabbit and said, "Man, try to find that song on WGH or WNNT, they might be playing it now!" *Good Lord! You want to hear that song again!* "Okay, Grandpop." After they died, hearing The Bellamy Brothers put me right back in Mumma's Rabbit with the two of them. Time taught me that my third summer job wasn't so bad after all. *I wished that I could go back and do it all over again. That would have been okay with me.*

CHAPTER 54

Other than Mrs. Pollock's ghost chasing me, the scariest moment of my childhood involved a ride with Grandpop Latimore in his four-door white 1965 Chevy Impala station wagon. If there was a time when I thought I was going to die, it was during that trip. I was about 9, and Bridgette and I were heading up to Pennsylvania with Grandma and him on a Friday evening. *I don't ever remember leaving the county with him other than that one occasion. It was the last time Bridgette and I got in the car with him.* It was cold outside so it must have been close to Christmas because I do remember that Bridgette and I didn't have school on Monday. We were excited to be leaving the county because that didn't happen very often. However, once we hit 17 North, the excitement changed to fear. At times, Grandpop hid his drunkenness well, and it was hard to determine if he was drunk or sober. *He had built up much tolerance over the years.* Once we got about 10 miles out of Saluda, I knew it was a "bad" night because he couldn't keep the station wagon on the road.

Campaigns against drunk driving were unheard of in the 1960s. In general, people laughed about it, and in my family, it was tolerated. Grandpop swerved from one side of the two-lane highway to the other. When he wasn't across the dividing line, he was on the shoulder. We got as far as Tappahannock before Grandma convinced him to turn around and head back home. If we thought the first 29 miles were scary, it wouldn't compare to what was about to happen. Maybe Grandma thought continuing to Pennsylvania for another 250 miles was ominous, but I doubt she thought heading back would be even more treacherous. *Trust me, it was.*

"Dammit I'm fine, but I'll turn around if that'll make you happy." Grandpop made a U-turn in the *middle* of 17, and that brought cars that had been cruising along at 60 miles per hour in both directions to a screeching halt as he swung the big Chevy wagon onto the right shoulder to begin his semicircular turn. U.S. 17 was a two-lane highway that left little margin for error. Approaching drivers did all they could to avoid slamming into us. *Bridgette and I were scared to death.* I guess we both thought we would die on that night in 1970 because something took place that had never happened before and almost 34 years passed before it happened again at Da's funeral. We held hands. *That's* how scared we were. With our free hands, we grabbed the front vinyl seat to peer through the windshield and watch the nightmare unfold. I often wondered what went through Grandpop's mind that night. *Did he care that he could have killed or injured a number of people, including me, Bridgette and Grandma? I later found out that when you had that much alcohol in your brain, you don't care too much about anything.* At some point, he must have felt Bridgette and me pulling on the front seat or breathing on the back of his neck because he shouted, "You God-damned kids better sit back in your seats and let me concentrate on the road!" We sat back and looked at each other. *Concentrate? Is he kidding?*

Grandma never learned to drive so she was of no help. Our lives were literally in Grandpop's hands and at God's mercy. I gripped Bridgette's hand tighter, rocked in my seat and silently prayed for His assistance. I only knew one prayer, and added a slight twist to it. "Now, I lay me down to sleep, I pray the Lord my soul to keep. If I should die *while I'm awake*, I pray the Lord my soul to take…"

Grandpop was pissed that oncoming drivers honked their horns at his crazy stunt in the middle of the highway. He said to no one in particular, "Shut the fuck up and just let me turn around!" Once he started southbound towards Saluda, it got even more frightening. The Chevy was off the road, on the shoulder, back on the road, and across the white dotted line that was supposed to keep drivers on the straight and narrow. Grandma and Bridgette cried and begged Grandpop to pull over. "Oh, shut up, I know what I'm doing!" Despite him dozing off every few minutes, the Chevy kind of took on a life of its own and kept itself headed back home like it knew where it was going. *Maybe God was hearing me.* When his head pitched forward, Grandma pleaded with him, "Horace, please wake up!" He lifted his head and held the steering wheel tighter. U.S. 17 was a lonely stretch of highway between Saluda and Tappahannock, and even if Grandma had convinced Grandpop to pull over, I wasn't sure what we would have done after that. Go knock on a stranger's door and ask if we could use their phone to place a "collect" call to "PL8-2876." I really don't think Grandma would have had the courage to do that. She would have been too embarrassed to admit to a stranger (and to one of her kids on the receiving end of the phone) that her husband was too drunk to get us home. I doubt if Grandma would have been able to explain where we were on 17 anyway, but none of that mattered because Grandpop wasn't going to pull over. It took about an hour to drive those 29 miles back, but somehow, he got us back home. How he managed to steer the Chevy Impala station wagon back into our driveway, I will never know. *All I knew was that I was home! Thank you, Jesus!* Grandma told everyone at the house that we turned around "because Horace didn't feel good." *Feel good? Grandma, are you kidding me? Horace almost killed us!*

I made a promise to myself that night I was going to learn to drive and soon! *I don't care if I am only 9 years old. This will never happen to me again.* No one ever told Da what happened that night, but a few days later, I pushed him to teach me how to drive. Over the next few Sunday afternoons, he showed me how to handle our Plymouth Duster on the back roads that surrounded our house down at Christchurch. Da thought that I just wanted to learn how to drive. I never told him about Grandpop Latimore almost killing us that night. I just wanted to be prepared in case I was ever in that situation again. I didn't mind my life being in God's hands, but I was *not* going to allow Grandpop's hands to determine my fate again.

Starting in the 7th grade, those driving lessons came in handy because I started driving all over Middlesex County when I was 12.

Why? Because I had to pick up Grandpop Latimore and bring him home. He often fell asleep in someone's lawn chair or on someone's back porch after hours of drinking. Sometimes people called the house to tell us where we could find him, and sometimes they didn't. Grandma stayed up all night drinking hot Lipton tea when he went missing. As evening turned into night, she wore out the dial on the rotary phone calling anyone that she could think of to ask, "Have you seen Horace?" Usually, he was passed out down at Dick Cook's house or Horace King's house or Robert Cook's house. He had a number of options to choose from. In the morning, Grandma would wake Sharon and me up around 7 and send us out on a search mission. "Go find your Grandpop!" We hopped in Sharon's 1970 two-tone brown Ford Mustang to search for him and his missing Chevy station wagon. What a pair we made, a 16-year-old and a 12-year-old on the prowl for a missing grandfather! "Silver Alerts" were nonexistent back then, and it wasn't like Grandma was going to call the Middlesex County Sheriff to say, "My husband is out drunk somewhere in his station wagon. Will you please go find him?"

Every now and then, we found Grandpop's car at Miss Pauline's house outside Urbanna. She was a character who walked around the town with a cane, a noticeable limp and an omnipresent, mischievous grin plastered on her face. Miss Pauline was a black woman about 70 years old who everyone said kept a gun tucked in her pocketbook. *No one was going to ask her if that were true because the assumption was good enough!* People steered clear of Miss Pauline. Women nodded and men tipped their hats in her direction, "How you doin' today, Miss Pauline?" All veered to her left or right when she came limping down the sidewalk. *I know I did!* She lived in what was essentially a wood shack atop Red Hill, a piece of land with about five or six black families on it. Red Hill was just on the other side of the sign that told you that you were no longer within the Town of Urbanna. *Remember, you had to be white to live in it.*

Miss Pauline became one of Grandpop's many drinking partners after he returned to Virginia, and we often found him lying asleep in the backseat of his station wagon in her backyard. "C'mon Grandpop, let's go. Grandma wants you to come home." "You

God-damned kids better leave me alone and let me sleep." "Ok, Grandpop, just lay there and go back to sleep. We'll take you home." Fortunately, most of the time, his keys were still in the ignition, and we didn't have to go searching through his pants for them. *I hated going through his pockets!* Once they were located, I hopped onto the seat cushions that lined his front seat to sit a little higher and closer to the steering wheel. "Just do what I do and follow me" were Sharon's instructions as I trailed her Mustang back to the house. "When I signal, you signal. When I turn, you turn." I became a pretty good driver at 12 years old.

CHAPTER 55

Grandpop Latimore was serious about television news, and when the clock ticked to 6:30 on a weekday evening, the TV had to be on the *CBS Evening News with Walter Cronkite.* Walter Cronkite was probably as important to Grandpop as was the A.B.C. store in Urbanna. David Brinkley and Chet Huntley were "those clowns over on NBC," and the ABC News was never even an option in his house. When Harry Reasoner left CBS in 1970 to join ABC, Grandpop labeled him a "backstabber," and even when he came back to CBS in 1978, Grandpop still didn't like him. He turned the channel whenever Mr. Reasoner's face appeared during a *60 Minutes* segment.

During the winter, Grandpop became enraged at the furnace when it kicked on, masking Mr. Cronkite's voice. Then, he staggered over to the thermostat to turn it off for half an hour. He was not going to be disturbed during those 30 minutes of airtime, not even by the heater. He could have cared less how chilly the house became because he hated utility bills. When the Arab Oil Embargo came along in 1973, nothing made him happier. OPEC gave him the opportunity to make the house even more frigid! "Grandpop, can we turn the heat up?" "No, and don't ask me again. Richard Nixon said the thermostat needs to be set at 68, and I'll make it even colder in here if y'all don't fucking shut up so I can hear Walter Cronkite!"

We only had three channels to choose from and 99 percent of the time the TV dials remained on WTVR/Channel 6, the CBS affiliate in Richmond. Each weekday starting at 9:00 a.m., Grandma watched *The Virginia Graham Show, Love of Life, The CBS Mid-Day News with Douglas Edwards, Search for Tomorrow, The Guiding Light, Love Is a Many Splendored Thing, As the World Turns, The Secret Storm,* and lastly, *The Edge of Night.* When Mr. Cronkite was "on the air" there was no time for fun and games. No phone calls. No playing around. No talking. Sit still, be quiet and watch Grand-pop's TV in the living room or Grandma's small portable TV that sat on the dining room buffet. When 6:30 p.m. rolled around, it was serious business. If you spoke, Grandpop shouted, "You God-damn kids better shut up and listen so you can learn something about the world." Seated at the dining room table, Sharon, Bridgette and I listened half-heartedly, in case Grandpop decided to give us a glob-al "pop quiz" during Mr. Cronkite's commercial break. It didn't matter his state of inebriation, Grandpop was aware of what was happening in Tel Aviv, Ho Chi Minh City and Washington, D.C. If one of us gave an incorrect answer, he shouted, "You dumb-ass kids better listen if you wanna be anything when you grow up. Now go sit in the kitchen and eat since you ain't paying attention. I'm tired of looking at your dumb asses."

Grandpop sometimes threw a spoon in my direction. It was never a knife or fork, but I didn't know if it was *always* going to be a spoon. That was the power a *crazy* person held over you. Fear. You never knew what they might do next. He might throw a glass filled with ice water at one of us when he was really pissed. *That* scared the shit out of me because it could occur so indiscriminately. A container of cold liquid cocked in his hand was a scary image for Sharon, Bridgette and me. We froze until he either calmed, fell asleep at the table or the wall clock ticked to 6:57 p.m., allowing Walter Cronkite to exit our home. An "Okay" nod from Grandma let us know that we could sneak from the table and take our plates to the kitchen. *That's just the way it was.*

Grandpop could be scary and mean, but he was also warm and caring. When I was about 5 years old, he and I were walking into Doc Marshall's Drug Store to pick up a few things. Grandpop must have said "Hello" to every single person that passed us on the sidewalk that morning. Most of those people were strangers to me, but Grandpop seemed to know each of them by name and a little something about them through the brief conversations that took place. Once we finally made it inside, I said, "Grandpop, why don't you just say 'Hi' to people instead of calling everybody by their name? That takes up a lot of time!" "Son, even a dog likes to hear his name, and why are you in such a hurry? It makes people feel good when you take time to talk with them and call them by their name. It makes them feel important." As we walked up to the counter, I thought about that, and how much our Boxer, Sam, liked to hear *his* name. Grandpop was right. A dog *did* like to hear his name! At an early age, I learned from him that people liked hearing their name. It *did* make them feel valued. He also taught me that it was important to know the significant events that were taking place around me and throughout the world. That was why he wanted us watching Mr. Cronkite. Attentiveness to the world and the everyday people who made up the world were just two ways Grandpop put *gas money* in my pocket.

CHAPTER 56

Grandpop and his middle son, my Uncle Ronnie, never seemed to get along well, and their relationship soured as the years went by. It was as if they were rams because they locked horns every chance they got. By the time Grandpop was in his 60s and Ronnie in his 30s, they had quit speaking to each other. No communication whatsoever. At the time, I thought it was unusual, but the more I learned about people, I found out that there were lots of fathers and sons and mothers and daughters who quit talking to each other for some reason or other. With Ronnie and Grandpop, there was no exchange of phone calls or birthday cards or anything. I thought it was kind of comical and kind of sad. No communication took place for over 20 years, but like anyone, Ronnie had his reasons.

While I was away at college, Grandpop either pushed or knocked or kicked Grandma to the floor one day. *Was that the only time? I didn't know, and I didn't want to think about it.* Varying accounts from various family members made it hard to determine what really happened, and understandably, no one wanted to talk about it. It was difficult for Mumma or Ronnie or Grandma to say out loud that their father or husband was physically abusive at any age, let alone in his late 60s. We were all conditioned to the verbal abuse, but the physical part was a whole new ballgame. Instead of physically retaliating against Grandpop, Ronnie chose to make him a "nonentity." His father had ceased to exist. *Poof! Grandpop was gone.* Even at Grandma's funeral, Ronnie's disdain for all things Grandpop continued. A nod acknowledging the other's presence was their only communication at her funeral. Their stalemate ended in a curious fashion, and I played a small role in resolving it, but that's another story.

After Grandma passed away, insomnia and Ronnie became fast friends. *When Da died eight years later, the same thing happened to me. I don't think I ever slept very soundly again after that, but that's another story, too.* Grandma's life wasn't the easiest, and Ronnie often wished that it hadn't been such a struggle. He was angry that Grandma had to deal with Grandpop's craziness for over 60 years. He was also saddened that Grandma's health was always an issue. She battled epilepsy throughout her life and at the end of her life needed a wheelchair to get around. Her epilepsy "spells" scared the bejesus out of me. Epilepsy caused her to stare at things that weren't there. Drool trickled from the corner of her mouth while Mumma or Sharon rushed to her side. When that happened, I usually ran upstairs or outside because I just wanted to get away. I didn't know if she was going to drop dead at the dinner table or start hallucinating or what the hell was going to happen. I just remember being scared. I did not like to see my Grandma staring at nothing.

Time took its toll on Grandma and Grandpop Latimore as they got older, and when they could no longer care for themselves, they moved in with Aunt Grace and her second husband, John, in Philadelphia. But when Grandma lived in Virginia and her legs were still good and the weather was, too, you could find her out in the front yard working on her petunias and gladiolas and begonias and rose bushes. On the front porch, she tended to her dieffenbachias, pewter plants, snake plants and prayer plants. From the ceiling dangled Swedish ivy and Wandering Jew plants that Sharon, Bridgette or I watered every two to three days. *Grandma, if these are your plants, why do we have to water them?*

In her 80s, Grandma's inability to use her legs was a constant source of irritation, and when I stopped by Aunt Grace's to visit, she stared out the large living room glass window that overlooked a quiet corner and watched her slice of West Philadelphia pass by. She had to be placed in a wheelchair to go anywhere within Aunt Grace's place.

She complained that her "old, useless legs" wouldn't even allow her to water the few philodendron plants she had scattered about the house. "Oh, it's okay, Grandma. I'll do it for you." *But we both knew it wasn't the same as her doing it herself.*

I think it was Ronnie's frustration with Grandpop that kept him awake. Grandpop was probably Grandma's biggest problem as far as Ronnie was concerned. More than likely, that was the real cause of Ronnie's inability to sleep. *He was still mad at Grandpop.* They never had much respect for one another. I was never really sure why. I think Ronnie viewed him as an "alcoholic," and that may have been an accurate description, but Grandpop was a lot more than that. I didn't think *one* adjective could ever be used to describe a person, let alone Grandpop Latimore. *A thesaurus was needed for that!*

Grandpop and Grandma Latimore. 1992

Grandpop provided for his family as best he knew how with his limited education and funds. He sent money every chance he got when Mumma was raising them and left property for each of them when he died. Could he have done better? Maybe. Who was I to judge my Grandpop or anyone else? With all of his faults, I think Grandpop did the best he could. Grandma Latimore truly adored Grandpop, and I guess that was all that really mattered. I think she was just happy to have Horace Latimore in her life. *I learned that you put up with all kinds of things when you truly loved someone.* Her affection for him was evident except when he was drinking, and even then, she only said, "Oh, Horace, hush!" She said that so often that when I was a little boy, I asked Da, "Is Grandpop's last name Latimore or Hush?" "Why are you asking me that?" "Because Grandma says Horace Latimore Hush all the time. Does he have *two* last names?"

CHAPTER 57

A few months after Grandma passed, another restless night stirred Ronnie from bed and sent him downstairs to his kitchen for a drink of water. After placing his glass in the sink, he headed back up to bed, but something stopped him dead (no pun intended) in his tracks. Hovering near his living room stairs was Grandma's spirit. She emerged from the brick-faced wall and floated for a while near the living room steps because she needed to tell her son something. Her voice was crystal clear, "Now Ronnie, you need to cut this foolishness out. Stop worrying about me. I am just fine where I am. This not sleeping silliness has gone on long enough. Now stop it and go to sleep!" Those were her only words. Ronnie climbed his stairs, got in bed and had his best night of sleep in months. "It was so good to see Mumma. I feel so much better. I still can't believe that happened. It was so real. She seemed really happy and at peace. I guess that's the important thing to take away from all of it. At least I don't worry anymore."

Grandma kept me from making my share of mistakes, and she stopped me from doing something really stupid when I was about 13. Grandpop was in an agitated, intoxicated state and complaining about something or other that didn't really matter. Grandma said to him, "Be quiet, Horace! You're as drunk as 'Cootie Brown.'" *At that time, I didn't know what the hell Cootie Brown was! I later found out it was a Southern metaphor for an inebriated person.* Grandpop's argumentativeness had been going on for what seemed like hours, and

I was tired of it. I wanted him to shut up. I wanted him to drop dead. I wanted Grandma to have the luxury of not dealing with *him* every single day. I looked at him, took a deep breath and was just about to say, "Oh Grandpop, will you just shut up!" I guess Grandma had taken a few mind-reading lessons over the course of her life because she quickly walked over to me, lifted her index finger next to her lips and whispered in my ear, "He's your Grandfather, *you* don't ever talk back to him even when *he* is like this. Just let it go. It's not worth it." Had I told Grandpop to "shut up," things would only have escalated, and although I didn't agree with her at the time, Grandma was right. As much as I wanted him to be quiet, it would have been very inappropriate and disrespectful for me to tell him to shut up! I don't ever recall *anyone* telling Grandpop to do that, not even Grandma. Instead she chose, "Be quiet" or "Oh, Horace, hush!"

Despite only having a 7th grade education, Grandma Latimore was sharp. When I was younger, I associated formal schooling with being smart, but I later discovered there were a lot of people with excellent educations who were pretty dumb, and many more with very little education who were plenty smart. *Grandma was one of the "plenty smart" ones.* She taught me how to use "cursive" script over one weekend in 2nd grade when all others' attempts had failed. She helped me understand multiplication tables and taught me how to use the two "guide" words at the top of each dictionary page when nobody else could. More importantly, she showed me how to respect the elders in my family (which I was pretty good at except for the day I was mean to Faye). Unlike, Ronnie, I slept easy after Grandma passed away because I knew that if there was a Heaven, she easily floated past St. Peter. How could she not be in Heaven? She went through Hell with Grandpop for 63 years! She had to be "In The Upper Room" with her favorite singer, Mahalia Jackson! How else could she have materialized from Ronnie's living room wall if she wasn't? Grandma Latimore was an angel who never stopped whispering in my ear, and I needed that because there were more than a few relatives I wanted to swear at over the years!

(Insert "In The Upper Room" by Mahalia Jackson) Grandma Latimore had a very nice singing voice. She loved to sing along with

Mahalia Jackson gospel albums on Sunday mornings while getting ready for church. When I was a little boy, I thought she sounded just as good, if not better, than the great gospel singer. One morning, over bacon and eggs, I mentioned that to Tony. He chuckled and said, "Boy, you think you're so smart! Don't you know your Grandma *is* Mahalia Jackson?" *I was shocked!* "She is?" He whispered, "You damn right she is. That's why Grandma and Grandpop live in Philadelphia because it's easier to make records up there because there are so many recording studios. There ain't none down here in Middlesex! She likes to keep it a secret so she lets that Mahalia Jackson lady take all of the credit because she doesn't want to be famous. Everybody in the Latimore family knows it, now you have to keep it a secret, too." I had newfound respect for Grandma. *She was a star!*

A few Sundays later, I was riding with Da over to Grandpop Lewis' house to pick him up and take him to church. During those times, all Southern radio stations offered only church service or gospel music on Sunday mornings, and a Mahalia Jackson song was coming over the airwaves from the GTO's radio when Da said, "Boy, that Mahalia Jackson sure can sing." I glanced over at him and could see that he was serious. *Maybe he didn't know the secret. Maybe the Latimores never told the Lewises! I couldn't keep a secret!* "Da, I'm not supposed to tell you this, but Grandma *is* Mahalia Jackson." He started laughing so hard that I thought he was going to choke. He swallowed hard and said, "What in the Devil are you talking about?" I let him in on the Latimore family secret. "Da, Grandma doesn't want to be famous so she lets Mahalia Jackson take all the credit. Grandma is the one who goes in the studio and does *all* of the singing." He laughed some more, and I started getting mad. "Chopper, who on Earth told you that?" "Tony." "He was just having fun with you. Your Grandma has a nice voice and all, but she is *not* Mahalia Jackson." I didn't care what Da said. *He was wrong.* We continued in silence while Mrs. Jackson continued singing on the radio. Now I didn't know whom to believe. Da or Tony? Tony had lied before. Like when he told me each morning before school that I had my socks on the wrong feet. *I'm never gonna figure this sock thing out!* Or the time he told me that if you count the number of cars in a funeral procession, your fingers and toes fall off when you're asleep. *I tried staying up all night after I did that the first time, but, thankfully, when I woke up, my fingers and toes were still attached!* His tale of James Brown's role in the murder of Otis Redding and the sabotaging of his plane had turned out to be false. *Maybe Tony had lied to me again.* I didn't know what to think, but I was sure mad at Da because he wouldn't stop laughing. My bottom lip was still poked out when Grandpop Lewis got into the car. He saw my lip and asked Da, "What's wrong with that boy?" Da explained the Mahalia Jackson story to him. We backed out of Grandpop's driveway and headed for church. Grandpop turned around in the front seat and asked me to come closer. He gave me a big smile, rubbed my head and said, "Well, I've always thought Mrs. Latimore had a beautiful singing voice." That made me feel better!

Grandma and Grandpop Latimore
and Aunt Grace. 1990

Grandma Latimore taught me how to play Solitaire when I was about 7 years old. I liked cheating at that game, though, especially when I needed a Queen of Hearts instead of a Queen of Diamonds. I peeked through the deck searching for the desired Queen. "You better stop it! You're only cheating yourself when you cheat." I sat across from her on the other side of the dining room table while she played Solitaire with her own deck. I was amazed at how she managed *two* decks of cards, hers and mine, while hardly glancing at me. Whenever I cheated at *anything,* I could still hear her saying, "You better stop it! You're only cheating yourself when you cheat." I thought both grandmothers watched out for me long after they were no longer on Earth, but I prayed that they didn't see everything their little boy was doing when he got older!

CHAPTER 58

I never saw Grandpop actually "drink" from a bottle. He hid that habit. In his bedroom or quick jaunts down to the basement or walks around the property was where his drinking took place. He had many locations for his bottles of alcohol. A bottle stashed underneath the seat of the riding lawnmower. Another bottle buried in dirt at the edge of the cornfield. One more could be found in a bucket filled with rags. Any hiding place sufficed as long as he thought Grandma wouldn't look in that spot. I found his bottles all of the time, but I never disturbed them. I was embarrassed when I stumbled across them, and I was even *more* embarrassed for him. As I got older, I found out that lots of people had things they wanted to keep hidden. *I became one of them.*

After Grandpop returned from one of his walks, events could take an unpleasant turn quickly. He would yell at Sharon, Bridgette or Grandma or me for some infraction while he was seated at the dining room table or lying in his bed at 7 or 8 in the evening. Grandma would come to our defense and say, "Oh, Horace, leave those poor kids alone! They aren't bothering you. You're making me sick." He shouted from the bedroom at her, "Then die and prove it!" *God, he loved saying that!* Grandma could be really mad at him, but sometimes, even she giggled at that remark!

In the summer of 2006, Grandpop Latimore was near the end of his life, and he and Ronnie still weren't talking. His body was simply running out of gas at 98 years old. Aunt Grace and John took care of him for 21 years and Grandma for 11 of them. John was an affluent man who owned an office cleaning business in the City of Brotherly Love, and he was much like Philadelphia's all-news radio station, KYW-News Radio, which boasted that it was "All News, All the Time!" Aunt Grace's second husband was "All Business, All the Time!" Despite his crankiness, I liked him a lot because I knew that underneath his tough exterior was a very nice man.

John and Aunt Grace met at a bus stop in West Philly around 1974. She was waiting for the city bus to take her home from work, and he noticed her as he drove by. *John knew a good thing when he saw one because Aunt Grace was (and still is) an attractive lady!* He pulled his car over to the curb, rolled down his window, and asked if she needed a ride. She declined. It became a daily ritual at 5:30 in the evening. "Do you need a ride?" "No, thank you. The bus will be along shortly." She continued declining for a few weeks until she finally relented and agreed to go on a date with him. She admitted, "I thought going out with him would be the only way I could get rid of him!"

While Ronnie maintained his silence with Grandpop, I often asked him when he planned on speaking with Grandpop again (it had been going on for over 20 years). "Ronnie, who am I to be giving you advice, I'm just your nephew. But Grandpop ain't getting any younger, and you do *not* want him to die without ever talking to him again. I'm telling you, you're going to feel bad about it. When people are gone, they are gone, and there is nothing you can do to bring them back. I really hope you decide to fix this thing with Grandpop. Good Lord, I got along with Da, and look at all the stuff he did. Yeah, there were things that he continued to do that pissed me off, but I just learned to let it go. It wasn't worth it, and Da wasn't going to change anyway. I forgave him and moved on, and when he died, I had no regrets. Not one." From the other end of the phone line, I could tell that my words were falling on deaf ears.

Finally, when Grandpop only had a couple of days left, his once sound mind had become disoriented. Ronnie went to see him at the Philadelphia nursing home where his body was shutting down. Ronnie called to tell me about his visit. "Good for you, Ronnie. How did it go?" He took a deep breath. "Daddy was asleep when I walked into his room, but he opened his eyes when he heard me approaching the bed. He looked at me as though he recognized me, but he had no idea who I was." "Okay. So what did you do?" "I took a seat in the chair next to his bed and said, 'Hi, Mr. Latimore. How are you doing?'" Ronnie took a moment or two to gather his composure. "Daddy didn't say anything for awhile, and I didn't know what to say, so I sat there watching him stare at the ceiling. Then, he turned his head toward me and said, 'You know, you look just like a son I used to have, but I don't know what happened to that boy. He got lost. I wish I knew where he got off to.'" "Wow, how did you respond to that?" I could hear the emotion in his voice over the phone. "I said to Daddy, 'Well, Mr. Latimore, your son may have been lost, but now he's found.'" "Well, Ronnie, I think that was the perfect thing to say, and I couldn't have said it any better." "Daddy and I went on talking off and on while he drifted in and out of sleep, but he *never* knew who I was, and I didn't care. He sure seemed happy to see me, whoever he thought I was. I'm glad I went to see him, and I'm glad you kept telling me to do it. We had a very nice conversation." It only took 23 years! Grandpop died the next day.

When the funeral arrangements were being made, Mumma told me that she and her siblings were having a hard time coming up with nice things to say about Grandpop for the service. I thought that was sad because I had plenty of nice things to say about him. I wasn't sure if any of them had spent the kind of time with Grandpop that I had. When Pat-Pat, Eddie, Darnell, Tony or Mumma visited Grandpop, there were usually so many other relatives around that it was hard to talk with him. Even for Aunt Grace, it was different. She took care of him each day, and she was busy managing the household and assisting with John's business. I wasn't sure how much time she was actually able to *talk* with Grandpop. I was a captive audience during the trips he and I took up and down I-95. I had learned a great deal about him. "Mumma, don't worry about it. I know exactly what to say about Grandpop tomorrow."

I didn't prepare anything, but I was confident with what I wanted to say. I turned to face those gathered at Antioch Baptist Church. "I want to thank all of you for coming out to show support for the Latimore family today because it really means a lot to us." I took a deep breath. "Grandpop Latimore." I looked at his children, my aunts and uncles, seated in the front row. I never thought I would start crying over Grandpop Latimore, but I did. It took me a few more moments to speak. "Well, what can I say about Grandpop?" I took another deep breath. "Grandpop was a complicated man, but, then again, aren't we all? I can close my eyes and still hear Grandpop calling out Grandma's name in the middle of the night, 'Mom, Mom!' Or, whenever I've dropped a glass in the kitchen and broken it, I can hear Grandpop saying, 'That's right, break it up! I'll buy another one tomorrow!' Or if there were too many lights on, I can hear him saying, 'That's right. I'll just give all of my money to the VEPCO man.' One thing was for sure, Grandpop kept us all entertained." His children and grandchildren nodded their heads and smiled. We were all too familiar with Grandpop's antics over the years. "When I walked up here to say a few words about Grandpop, I wasn't sure exactly what to say. But the more I thought about it, the easier it became." I pointed at myself. "I have a lot to thank Grandpop Latimore for because he put seven people in my life that were a positive influence on me. They are sitting right here in front of me. Aunt Grace, I'll start with you. Thank you for taking care of Grandma and Grandpop for the last 23 years. I know it wasn't easy doing what you did, and I know I could *not* have done it, so God bless you. The entire family appreciates all you did. I've always enjoyed your sunny disposition, and I tried to steal some of that from you. You showed me how to be a good child to your parents. Next, I want to thank my Mumma for just being Mumma. I could not have asked for anyone better as a mother, and if it weren't for Grandpop, you wouldn't be in my life, and only the Good Lord knows where I may have ended up without your discipline!"

I thanked each aunt and uncle for something small or large that they had done for me over the years. *They helped shape my life, and for that, no "thanks" was ever enough.* Most of Grandma and Grandpop Latimore's children could easily have been my older siblings, instead of my aunts and uncles. Pat-Pat was only 16 years older than me, and the youngest, Tony, was only separated from me by 8 years. Officially, they were my uncles and aunts, but I always considered them more like my brothers and sisters. I could never have thanked Grandpop Latimore enough for putting those good people in my life. Good people who taught me right from wrong when I was growing up. They smacked me upside the head when I needed it and took me for rides in a VW to keep me from crying. They impacted my life in a positive fashion. Letting each of them know how much they meant in my life was the most fitting way that I could think of to "thank" Grandpop on his last day above ground in Middlesex County. As I stood in front of those at the small Baptist church behind the Saluda Courthouse, the more I thought about it, the more I realized that Grandpop wasn't so bad after all. *It took me until July 10th of 2006 to finally understand why Grandma loved him so much.*

Grandpop Latimore and me heading to
Grandma Latimore's funeral. 1996

CHAPTER 59

There were many complicated people in my life, but I think Da was *the* most complex. Some people were hard to understand, and Da was one of them. William Franklin Lewis was born in Caroline County, Virginia on August 9, 1939, and he died in my arms on December 29, 2004. *An enigma if there ever was one.* Charming, witty, smart, brilliant were adjectives that could have been used to describe him. On the other hand, labels like evil, vile, mean or cruel could just as easily have been used to describe him. Da broke my heart on more than one occasion, but my love for him never wavered. I just didn't *like* him all of the time.

One of my earliest memories of Da took place on Christmas morning of 1966. I was 5 years old and Bridgette was 4, and Da had turned 27 four months earlier. That morning he took Bridgette and me outside to teach us how to ride our new bicycles that Santa Claus had dropped off during the night. There were two new Sears Radio Flyer bicycles under our Christmas tree that morning, an identical red in color. Bridgette's bike came with training wheels, and thankfully, mine did not! *I didn't need any training wheels because I had been waiting for this moment all of my life!* "C'mon Da! Let's go outside and ride! Please!" "Put your coats on!"

He showed us how to hop on and off and maintain our balance, but it wasn't a "merry" Christmas at all. Da's patience was thin that morning, as it was on most days, and sadly, what I remember most about that chilly Christmas morning with frost on the ground was that riding a bicycle was probably the easiest thing I had ever learned. For Bridgette, it wasn't. Even with the training wheels Santa Claus (aka Da) attached to her bike, she had a hard time maintaining her balance. She squeezed the handlebars' black rubber grips tight and held on for dear life. She was too scared to push one pedal ahead of the other. She just kind of sat in one spot of the driveway while Da made fun of her inability to propel the bike. *Me?* I flew around our dirt driveway like I was Richard Petty of Randleman, North Carolina, being chased by Bobby Allison from Hueytown, Alabama! *I was required to know NASCAR drivers and their hometowns like I had to know state capitals!* Bridgette froze, her balance remained wobbly, and Da did nothing to increase her confidence. He teased her for not picking it up as quickly as I did. At the time, I didn't care, but as the morning wore on, and I saw how much she was struggling, I began to feel bad for her. I was having fun, and it was obvious that she wasn't. I had been waiting since about August for Santa Claus to bring me that bike, but in a way, I wished Santa had left it behind at the North Pole. I had that bike for another two or three years, but *every* time I hopped onto it, I remembered Da's impatience. Besides the bike, he gave me some *gas money* as a Christmas present in 1966. He taught me *not* to be like him when teaching someone how to do something they had never done before. Be patient and show compassion. *That might have been an even better gift than the one Santa Claus left under the tree when I was 5 years old.*

Da never had much patience with Bridgette. On the other hand, neither did I. She and I were always oil and vinegar from the start. Mumma tried getting the two of us to "mix" all of her life, but that was to no avail. Da's final resting place would be in Virginia, and when we were piling into cars to head south from Pennsylvania, Bridgette said, "I'll ride with you." *Are you kidding me? This is going to be a long trip. What do I talk to Bridgette about? This is going to be the most time I have spent with her since 11th grade!*

(Insert "An Old Fashioned Love Song" by Three Dog Night)
Three Dog Night's "An Old Fashioned Love Song" played from the speakers of my silver 2003 Nissan 350Z as we sailed down the in-

terstate with other relatives trailing behind us. I was playing Three Dog Night's Greatest Hits CD when Bridgette said, "I always liked that song. That was out when we were living down at Christchurch." "Yup, it was." She fell silent for a spell. *Okay, now what do we talk about?* She ended our quiet a few minutes later. "Why do you think Da never liked me?" *Uh oh. I'm not ready for this conversation tonight or any night.* "I don't know, Bridgette. To be honest, I don't think Da liked too many people." I tried to soften the blow even though she and I both knew the truth. The truth was that he didn't like her very much, and over the years, that was pretty evident. *Shoot, I wasn't always sure he liked me.* Da always called me on my birthday, but for some reason, he could never remember to call Bridgette on June 13th. "Da, did you call Bridgette yesterday?" "Oh shoot, I forgot!" "Da!"

A few more miles rolled by before Bridgette asked, "Why do you think he liked you and Jennifer [his child with Sandra V.] *more* than me?" I was searching for the right response and not sure at all if I would find it. "I don't know, Bridgette. Da was just complicated, and it's way too late now to try and figure him out. We'll never know the answer to that one. I gave up trying to figure him out a long time ago." I tried to lighten the atmosphere. "But you know what?" "What?" "He liked Jennifer more than me and you *combined*!" She got a chuckle out of that and said, "You got that right!" The mile markers continued flying by us (or my Z-Car flew by them), and our ride became more enjoyable as the conversation turned lighter. *It was unfortunate our bicycle ride 38 years earlier wasn't nearly as nice.*

I often wondered why Da wasn't as nice to Bridgette as he was to Jennifer and me. I think Bridgette just reminded him too much of Mumma. Bridgette was feisty even as a child, and that made us quite different from the other. I liked smooth sailing; Bridgette embraced bumpy rides. I once asked Mumma if she used her connections at Rappahannock Central Elementary School to steer Bridgette or me away from certain schoolteachers when we were coming along. Some of those teachers were really good and some weren't. *Just being honest!* Judy's mom, Mrs. Kidd, prepared the class rosters, and she and

Mumma always had a good relationship. Mumma said, "No, I don't remember doing anything like that." A few minutes later, she retracted her earlier admission. "Uh oh, I forgot something." "What's that?" "There was one teacher that I didn't want *you* to have." "Who was that?" "Mrs. White." I thought about it for a few seconds and cautiously said, "Mumma, you have to help me with that one. If I remember right, wasn't she Bridgette's 1st grade teacher?" She said "Ye-sssss" so slowly and deliberately that it became two syllables. "Okay, then why was that lady good enough for Bridgette, but not good enough for me?" I was afraid to hear the response. "Troy, Mrs. White wasn't the easiest teacher to get along with. Strict as hell, but I knew Bridgette even at 6 years old wouldn't take any shit from her. You? You were different even then. *You* would have gone in a shell from that type of treatment." I gave that some thought. "You know what, Mumma? I guess you're right. That would have bothered me." "I know my kids. I knew Bridgette was different from you when Rev. Gayles gave her that baptism diploma that Sunday morning at Antioch. In front of the congregation, he pronounced her name as 'Brid-get,' and even though she was only 5 years old, she stopped Rev. Gayles in the middle of the ceremony and told him how her name needed to be pronounced." *I forgot about that!* "She stood up and told him, 'Rev. Gayles, *my* name is Brid-*gette*, not Brid-*get!* It is spelled capital B-r-i-d-g-e-T-T-e!' Now, Rev. Gayles was a 70-something-year-old man, and he wasn't used to that kind of talk from a child, but he apologized to her from the pulpit that day. That was how I knew she wasn't gonna take shit from anyone. Not even Mrs. White." "You're right, Mumma. If Rev. Gayles had called me 'Tony' Lewis instead of 'Troy' Lewis, I would have just left it at that. I would not have given him a spelling lesson, that's for sure!" *Bridgette never let anything slide. Ever. It wasn't in her nature.*

I think as far as Da was concerned, everything was a battle with Bridgette. From "What do you want for breakfast?" to "What did you learn in school today?" Sometimes, it was a chore to get a simple answer from her. *It was the same way with Mumma.* You had better have slid on your "kid gloves" when attempting a conversation with either of them because the wrong emphasis on the wrong word could set off a volley of cannons. *Who wanted that? Who needed that?* That was the price Da paid because he aided in making them both that way. When a person was mistreated often enough, they bit back every chance they got. *There's some gas money for you!*

I think Da tried *controlling* Mumma mentally and physically, leaving Mumma without much recourse. I know she loved him when they first married, but that turned sour after only a few years. Da did nice things for her like throwing her a surprise 30th birthday party. He also built her a new home, but that was just as much for him. I know she hated him when he beat her up or even worse, taunted her with snakes. Mumma was like Indiana Jones when it came to those slithery reptiles. She was petrified of them. Da knew that and used it against her. Sometimes, he placed one in her underwear drawer or put one in a shoebox in her closet to scare the shit out of her. At other times, he coolly walked into the house gripping one in his hand with a wicked grin spread across his face. C-Y told me when I was in my 40s, "You know, I couldn't stand Bill Lewis even when he and I were little. He used to get this stupid look on his face like he was up to something, and I wanted to smack it off! He was a sneaky little devil even then. Just a puny, little thing up to no good."

Mumma could be in the kitchen preparing dinner, and when she turned around to see a snake in Da's hand she screamed! Loudly. *Boy, did she scream.* By the time Bridgette and I made it up from the basement where we were playing, Da had released the snake in the backyard and was leaning against the refrigerator without a care in the world. The damage had been done. His mean side had reared its ugly head again. He pointed to a corner baseboard and said, "Your mother saw a spider over there in the corner. I stomped on it." The mischievous look on his face spoke something far more sinister. I wouldn't learn about his sick fascination with snakes until after the dirt had been thrown on him.

"Aw Mumma, I'm sorry Da was so mean to you." "It's okay." *No, it wasn't.* "My life turned out much better than his anyway. He paid for it in the end, and he's still paying for it because God don't like ugly." Tears touched Mumma's cheek, and I felt awful for her in that moment, but she was right about one thing. Her life did fare better than his. She invested well, never lived beyond her means and had a comfortable, enjoyable retirement. Da never saved a dime, bought things he really couldn't afford and would have needed to work every day for the rest of his life to survive. He *had* to die when he did because he couldn't afford to live. *Bill Lewis was one of the meanest people I ever met, but he was my Da, and I still loved him. After he died, I missed him every single day.*

The first time I heard the phrase "God don't like ugly" was from Grandma Latimore when I was a little boy. It was her way of saying, "That when you do bad things, God is watching and retribution will be His." Grandma was never more right. When we lived at Christchurch, Bridgette and I were going "across the road" to play with our friends one day. The two of us were arguing about something when I pushed her, and she fell and scraped her knee on the asphalt. She was crying and shouted at me, "You better leave me alone. You know Grandma always says that 'God don't like ugly,' and you're gonna pay for that!" I stuck my tongue out at her and in that very instant, a passing bird dropped some shit right onto my tongue! *That was disgusting!* Bridgette could not stop laughing, and I never poked my tongue in anyone's direction ever again. Bird shit on my tongue was *gas money* of a different nature!

While Mumma was with Da, she was stuck. Stuck with Middlesex County. Stuck with raising *her* kids and her *parents'* kids, stuck with her sister's child, stuck with getting punched around by Da, stuck with getting knocked around by life and stuck with having snakes thrust in her face. Just plain old stuck. "Did you ever think about leaving him?" It didn't take very long for a response. "Troy, where was I gonna go? Plus, Bill would never have let me leave if I tried to take you with me. And, I wasn't leaving *without* you *and* Bridgette, so I just dealt with it. Thank God I only had to put up with Bill for 13 years. Some people go through that shit their whole lives. Then, I caught your Dad in bed with Sandra Meredith and that solved that problem!"

"Stuck" was also the adjective Mumma used when she found out she was pregnant with me. "How did you tell Grandma and Grandpop?" She giggled, "Yup, I was stuck alright, and I never told her or Daddy. I never told anyone except your Aunt Grace. I just called Mom and Dad in Philadelphia and told them Rev. Lewis' son asked me to marry him. I think Mumma had her suspicions, but she never said anything." "Did anyone ever say anything to you because the '9-month math' didn't add up?" *They were married on October 15, 1960, and I was born on April 22nd of '61.* "I wish they would have! People didn't fuck with me. They knew I would tell them to kiss my ass in a heartbeat and go look in the fucking mirror and think about all the shit that was going on in their *own* God-damned family! Hell no, nobody better not have asked me no shit like that!" *I told you my mother could "snap" like a twig!*

Da, Mumma, Grandpop Latimore,
Grandma Latimore and Grandpop Lewis. 1960
Mumma's not even showing yet!

CHAPTER 60

It took many years for me to ask Mumma one question in particular. To be precise, I was 45 years old before I had the confidence to do so. Sometimes there were just some things you didn't want to know the answer to. Even worse, there were some things you were *afraid* of finding out what the answer would be. The question I wanted to ask Mumma was, "Did you ever fight back with Da?" *Did she ever punch him? Smack him? Kick him? Throw something at him? Spit on him? Anything?*

I was seated at the small table in the dining area where she and Gerald ate most of their meals, armed with my question. Seldom did they sit in the formal dining room of the ranch home they built in 1988; it was used only at Thanksgiving and Christmas. Before they moved into their ranch, Bridgette, Gentree, Mumma, Gerald and I lived in a "double-wide." Anyone who grew up in the South knew what a "double-wide" was – a mobile home. I started living there in July of 1975. The double-wide trailer was all Mumma and Gerald could afford after they got married. It was a far cry from what I used to live in down at Christchurch, and although it was only 40 miles away, it seemed a whole lot farther. The U.S. economy wasn't at its best in the mid-1970s when Mumma and Gerald married, and they struggled to make ends meet. Gerald had recently started working for the Chesapeake & Ohio Railroad Company, and when periodic layoffs hit, he was one of the first to go because of his lack of seniority. He might work for a month, then be out of work for a month. Things were so tight for us that we couldn't even afford a telephone. A telephone was considered a "luxury," not a "necessity," so we didn't have one for almost a year. When we had to make a call, we used the phone at Gerald's parents' house or the phone at his cousin's house about 50 yards away. I needed that phone to talk to my girlfriend, Brigetta.

I saved enough money from my after-school job to have a phone installed in our trailer when I was in 10th grade. If I remember right, it required a $100 deposit and another $75 for the telephone man to come out and run the phone line; after that, it was $12.98 per month plus long-distance fees. "Y'all are gonna have to pay me for your long-distance calls!" I even had the *Orr Dasidy* to charge Mumma for her calls, and she paid me for a couple of months until, finally, she had enough. One evening after school, I came home ready to wash my hands, brush my teeth and get something to eat from the refrigerator, but there was no soap in the bathroom, and my toothbrush and toothpaste were missing. "Mumma, where's my stuff?" "What stuff?" "My bathroom stuff!" "Oh, are you referring to the stuff that *I* bought? You'll get *that* back when I can stop paying for long-distance calls." *Uh oh.* "And don't even think about putting those dirty-ass hands in *my* refrigerator to eat *my* food!" "Okay Mumma, you win. Call whoever you want!" I was really self-ish when I was growing up. I didn't like sharing anything.

Brigetta and I didn't talk about much on that telephone, but we sure stayed on it a long time. We discussed our homework or what we ate for dinner or which one of our family members we were mad at that particular week. But most of the time, there was a lot of silence be-cause we ran out of things to say pretty quickly. Brigetta might say, "Ok, I'm gonna hang up now, we aren't saying much. I'm gonna go iron my clothes for tomorrow." "What? You don't wanna talk to me? Do you wanna go call somebody else?" I was extremely jealous at that time in my life, and that made me an unpleasant 14-year-old boyfriend. Brigetta conceded and stayed on for a little longer. I was afraid she was going to call some other high school boy who lived closer to her because we had a long-distance relationship of about 20 miles. The way I saw it, the longer I kept her on the phone with me, the less time she would have to talk with someone else. I had insecurity issues at 14, but was there a teenager who didn't? When I got older, I thought those issues would disappear, but they never did; they just manifested themselves in other ways. I discovered that I wasn't the only teenager or adult who had insecurities.

In high school, I was just a messed-up kid seeking direction in life. In retrospect, I was a 14-year-old kid who didn't fit in. My dress and appearance made it even more difficult to belong to any group at school. I had a huge Afro, and when it wasn't an Afro, my hair was plaited or braided. I wore baggy Levi jeans that were 32 inches around the waist and 34 inches in length, and those jeans hung loosely from my 140-pound frame. I should have been wearing jeans that were 28 inches in the waist and 30 inches in length. To top it all off, I wore Timberland boots that were always untied. *I had perfected the "urban" look in 1974 before that term and style even became fashionable!* I thought I was "cool," but no one else did. At that time, I didn't really care what anyone thought. I liked my "style." No one dressed like that at Lafayette High School in 1974; I was "urban" even though I lived in the "country." *I was different.* Brigetta's father was a college graduate, and I was sure he didn't think I would ever make it there. Even though I was a polite kid with nice manners, I still didn't fit what a lot of parents were looking for when their daughters started dating. I learned that it was hard for people to look past appearances. *Especially when those people were your 9th grade girlfriend's parents – or worse, an uncle!*

(Insert "Stairway to Heaven" by The O'Jays) The first time I met Brigetta's Uncle Frank, who lived a few houses away from her parents' place, the two of us were sitting on her front porch listening to The O'Jays sing "Stairway to Heaven." *God, I loved that song.* We tried holding hands, but her bratty sister, 4-year-old Rayette, did her best to prevent any physical contact. *I hated that little girl back then! In retrospect, Rayette was a human form of birth control for Brigetta and me, and that's what we needed. Who knew what kinda trouble we could have gotten in without her around!* That evening, Uncle Frank pulled into the driveway and parked his car. Brigetta whispered, "Uh oh, that's my Uncle Frank. I'm not sure how he's gonna greet you." I stood as he advanced toward us. "Uncle Frank, this is my boyfriend, Troy." I extended my hand and said, "Hi, Uncle Frank. It's nice to meet you." His right hand remained at his side as he examined me from head to toe for about 30 seconds. *This is not good.* Once his examination concluded, he walked right by me as though I was a ghost. It was a very uncomfortable feeling, and I never forgot his snub, but I understood Uncle Frank a lot better when I got older. He disapproved of my appearance, and in retrospect, I didn't blame him! But I promised myself that I wouldn't react like that with *anyone* regardless of how they looked.

CHAPTER 61

I finally asked Mumma my question. "Did you ever fight back? Did you ever try to get back at Da in *any* way for all of the stuff that he did to you?" Her reply came quicker than I expected. "Nope, I just dealt with it. I mean, what was I gonna do?" I didn't have an answer for her then, and she didn't have one 30 years ago. She went back to watching TV, and I went back to reading the *Southside Sentinel* on her table.

I was surprised Mumma never took some type of action against Da. It wasn't characteristic of the person who took no shit from *anyone*. I had hoped there was a *What's Love Got to Do With It* Tina Turner–like moment in the limousine with Ike. I was slightly disappointed. *Joshua 2:21* offered the phrase, "So be it." That was how I felt after Mumma told me she accepted his abuse. I dropped the subject.

Mumma looked across the table at me and said, "You know what? I forgot about something!" Her voice sounded happy. She startled me, but I didn't even look up from the *Sentinel*. "What's that, Mumma?" "You know how your Dad liked chopped ground beef fried in a pan with just some salt and pepper on it?" "Yeah, I remember." *This sounds interesting, so I placed the paper on the table and gave her my undivided attention.* "Well, I'm gonna tell you something and don't you get mad at me." "Oh, Mumma, please. I'm not gonna get mad." "Okay. He had pissed me off so bad one time that I sprinkled some d-Con in his ground beef and served it to him. Nice and warm like he wanted it with some mustard spread across the top." "You did *what?" This is crazy! That was crazy!*

d-Con was a rodent pesticide that caused internal bleeding. "Mumma, weren't you afraid Da might *die?* And if he did, weren't you afraid there might be some sort of investigation. Or, that you might go to jail?" Mumma explained, "Troy, there was only one sheriff in the county back then, and he knew the Latimore family. We had a really good reputation. I wouldn't have been suspected of anything, and it's not like we had people who investigated deaths back then, especially where black people were concerned. There was no coroner or nothing like that. We never had any murders in the county. The only shooting I ever remember was the one with Beaver Curtis, and nobody was ever arrested for that. Nobody performed autopsies, and nobody was gonna come all the way down from Richmond to investigate a black person dying. If they died, they just died. Nobody was going to care if a black man died back then, even if it was Rev. Lewis' son. They would have just thought he had some kinda stomach problem. Bad ulcer or something." I sat there stunned with a billion questions whizzing through my head, but I only asked one. "What happened?" Mumma laughed, "That bastard. He just got sick and threw up. I thought he was a mouse, but it turned out he was a fucking *rat!" That's a great line, Mumma! I wished I had come up with it!* Yes, my father was a *rat* at times. Yet, no one outside the Latimore family knew that Da sometimes crawled around on four legs. Everyone else in Middlesex County thought he was a saint, especially the Lewises.

A couple of weeks later I was talking with Sandra V. at Jennifer's house, and mentioned the d-Con story to her. *She found that hilarious!* In fact, she couldn't stop laughing. "Sandra V., when Da was mean to you, did you ever do anything to get back at him?" "Oh, no, Troy. I never did anything like that! I was scared of your dad. He was too strong for me to tangle with." We started talking about something else for a bit while I played with Jennifer's kids. About 20 minutes went by before she began to giggle. "Oh, my goodness! I remember something I used to do to your Dad. I totally forgot about it because I haven't thought about it in so long because I miss him so much." *Uh oh, it's an epidemic with Bill Lewis' women!* "What happened, Sandra V.?" "When your Dad used to hurt me, I was so mad at him that I didn't know what to do. Bill was strong, and I wasn't gonna try to fight him, but here's how I paid him back!" *Here it comes!* "I used to go in the bathroom, grab his toothbrush, take a seat and pee on it! It made me feel a whole lot better!" *Now, that's funny!* "Good for you, Sandra V.!"

Sandra V. and Mumma had a lot more in common than I ever realized. They both admitted, "Troy, your Dad could make you do some crazy things." *Sad, but true.* Mumma and Sandra never became friends, but I was happy that they were cordial to each other at weddings and funerals. However, after Sandra V. told me about the "toothbrush" incident, I called Mumma to pass along that story. I knew Mumma would appreciate that she wasn't the *only* person Da had nearly driven mad. "Put Sandra on the phone!" They stayed on my cell phone chatting and laughing and telling Bill Lewis stories for almost an hour. *I thought that was great!* My two "mothers" having a good time discussing Da's madness. I would never have guessed that the two of them would have an hour-long conversation laughing and giggling like schoolgirls, especially after what the two of them went through almost 40 years prior. Laughter often became the best medicine when discussing my father. Da inflicted scars on Mumma and Sandra V., but slowly, time allowed most of their wounds to heal. *Writing did a lot of that for me.*

CHAPTER 62

Da loved music. He played drums, bongos, guitar and the harmonica. He was also an excellent singer. I thought he memorized the bass line to *every* song ever played on the radio, and after he died, I hummed those same bass notes in his absence. He was a 1st tenor in his high school barbershop quartet that consisted of Mr. Billy Thornton, Mr. Edward Yarborough and Mr. Frank Sutherlin. They sang at a state competition that was broadcast on TV. Faye told me that she and Portia and Grandma and Grandpop Lewis piled into Grandpop's 1952 Pontiac to drive over to Mrs. Frances Johnson's (my piano teacher) house to watch Channel 6's broadcast of the program. Mrs. Johnson was the only person Grandma and Grandpop Lewis knew that had a television in 1956. Sitting on Mrs. Johnson's couch, they saw Da's quartet selected by the Future Farmers of America as the best barbershop quartet in the state of Virginia. *Well, it was the best "colored" quartet in the state, anyway!* As the years passed, Da's quartet continued to sing at their high school reunions until sadly, only Mr. Sutherlin remained.

Da was a talented guy who loved singing the "harmony" to any song. "Chopper, *anybody* can sing the lead to a song. Harmony? Now, that's the *hard* part. It takes real talent to do that." His keen ear was always able to find the "hard" part to any song. In the early 1970s, he formed a male/female gospel quartet that consisted of Faye, Mr. George Sutherlin and Mrs. Bessie Cauthorn. They traveled to local churches and summer gospel revivals to sing hymns on

Saturdays and Sundays. I was often forced to tag along with them, and I hated getting "dressed up" on a Saturday or Sunday evening. *Good God, isn't going to church on Sunday morning enough?* I wanted to be reading a *Sports Illustrated* or playing over at Christchurch or going up to Butley's house or, call me crazy, maybe stay in my room to do some homework! Anything was better than going to church. But with the passing of time I sometimes wished that I could return to 1972 to hear them sing their songs again for a couple of hours. Seeing them decked out in their light brown double-knit slacks with cream-colored turtlenecks and brown blazers would have been nice because I never fully appreciated their skills when I was 11 years old. Their harmony was "tight," the word Da used to describe close harmony chords. **(Insert "You're All I Need to Get By" by Aretha Franklin)** The intro to Aretha Franklin's "You're All I Need To Get By" was a song he thought possessed "tight" harmonic chord structures that were sung with precision. He was correct on that one!

(Insert "Sweet City Woman" by The Stampeders) Da tried his best to demonstrate the differences between "harmony" and "lead," but my ear wasn't as finely tuned as his. When The Stampeders came out in 1971 with "Sweet City Woman," Da considered it the perfect song for his little boy to hear what went into three-part harmony. Da bought the 45 RPM to teach me. Singing harmony could prove difficult at any age, let alone at 10 years old. Da said, "C'mon, *you* pick one of the harmony parts to sing, and I'll sing the lead." "Okay, Da, I'll try." No matter how closely I listened, my young ear and voice could only locate the "lead" section. "Da! I can *hear* it, but I can't *sing* it. Just let *me* sing the lead. *You* sing the harmony parts!" He was wasting his time on me at that age!

From performers like Lester Flatt and Earl Scruggs to Buck Owens and Roy Clark to Bill Withers and Al Green to Curtis Mayfield and Sly and The Family Stone, Da knew them all and taught me to appreciate all types of music. Ray Charles was his all-time favorite performer, and Kat and I took him to see Mr. Charles perform at Avery Fisher Hall at Lincoln Center in New York City one year. Da acted like a kid in a candy store!

(Insert "War" by Edwin Starr) In June of 1970, Edwin Starr released the song "War", and it became one of my favorite songs to sing. Not because it was a song of protest, but simply because I thought it had a good beat! I had a hard enough time trying to understand what was going on in Vietnam (and I wasn't by myself because most of America couldn't either). All I knew about Vietnam was that Mr. Cronkite gave body counts each evening on the *CBS Evening News*, and my buddy, Carlton Reed, was over there. He's another story.

In our living room, I shouted with Mr. Starr as the 45 record spun on the record player. The lyrics contained six "Good God" references, and I knew exactly when to shout each of them because I played that song about 50 times a day. I screamed and stomped like I imagined Mr. Starr might have done if he were on stage. I pretended I was auditioning for Mr. Dick Clark because that was what I wanted to do one day, make it onto the *American Bandstand* show. Unfortunately, I knew that would never happen because I wasn't a good dancer, but I thought I still had time to learn because I was only 9! I continued singing "War" for the 51st time at the same time Da pulled in the driveway and parked his truck. I was unaware that Da considered the "Good God" phrase "swearing." Because it was contained within the song, I thought it was okay to repeat it. I continued strutting back and forth across the living room "stage" until I saw my own "stars," and it wasn't Edwin Starr! Da backhanded me so hard that I felt like Wile E. Coyote after The Road Runner had the ACME Construction Company drop an anvil on his head. I lay on the living room floor crying. "What did I do?" "You swore!" "I didn't say a 'bad' word." "Yes, you did." "What?" Another smack came because I said "What" to an adult. "'Good God' is swearing and don't you talk back to me!" "I didn't talk back to you. All I said was 'What' and I didn't know saying 'Good God' was 'bad.'" Tears streamed down my face. "Well, you do now! Take *that* song off and don't play it again." He went outside to wash his truck, and I swore that if I ever got to meet this Edwin Starr guy, I was going to smack *him* right in *his* face. He should have known better than putting a "bad" word in a song that kids would sing!

(Insert "Bridge Over Troubled Water" by Aretha Franklin)
When I first heard Aretha Franklin's remake of Simon and Garfunkel's 1970 hit, "Bridge Over Troubled Water," I told Da, "Aretha sure messed up that song! I like Simon and Garfunkel's version a whole lot better!" "Boy, you don't know good music when you hear it! Have you listened to the harmony in her song compared to what Simon and Garfunkel did? There ain't no comparison. Simon and Garfunkel ain't bad, but Aretha knew what she was doing with their song!" Da was right; I didn't know good music when I heard it! The three artists were awarded Grammys for their versions of the song in 1971 and 1972.

(Insert "Ode to Billie Joe" by Bobbie Gentry) Da liked quizzing me while we spent time in his Chevy pickup truck listening to the AM radio. Bobbie Gentry's hit song came from the dashboard speaker. "Chopper, what's the name of that song?" "Umm, 'Ode to Billie Joe.'" "Who sings it?" "Bobbie Gentry!" "Okay. Now what's an 'ode'?" "Da, I don't know!" *I knew what was coming next.* "Now what's the point of singing a song if you don't know the meaning of the words? I think you should look up 'ode' in the dictionary before we have supper tonight." *Who was he kidding? "Should" wasn't a suggestion. Why can't I just listen to the radio without an exam breaking out?*

When we made it home, Da reminded me, "Don't forget what you have to look up." *Yeah, yeah, I know. How could I forget?* I flipped to the "O" section of our red, hardback *Webster's Dictionary. Okay, now I know what an "ode" is!* "Da! Where are you?" "I'm down in the basement." "Okay, I'm coming down. I looked it up. An 'ode' is a dedication to someone." *He and Mumma got mad when I didn't use "an" in front of a vowel. They didn't always follow that grammar rule, but I had to!* "Good, now you won't forget what a ode is." *Yup, you're right, Da. I'll never forget.* "Chopper, what's the name of the bridge she talks about in that song?" "Da, I'm gonna go back upstairs to get the dictionary and bring it down here with me because I feel a bunch of questions coming on!" "Why is that?" "Because I know what questions are coming. 'What state is the bridge in?' 'What river runs underneath the bridge?' 'What kinda name is Tallahatchie?' Right?'" "Yup." Because of Da's incessant questioning, I eventually learned the backgrounds to many songs from the 1950s, '60s and '70s. I stored that information away forever: who wrote it, what year it came out and the back-up vocalists and so forth. It was stuff that Da and I appreciated long before *trivia* became a popular term. I thought it was neat to know the origins of a song. But it wasn't neat watching Da get older. When a song came on the radio that I thought for sure he would remember who sang it and who wrote it and who the backup vocalists were, *I* now asked *him* questions, and he didn't have the answers anymore. Although he made a full recovery from his stroke in 1996, his brain was not quite what it used to be. The stroke took much of his memory. Da was now in his late 50s and early 60s and his mind wasn't as sharp. That made me very sad. *I never thought Da would forget anything.*

Mumma and Da gave me a thirst for knowledge at a young age. They were good at creating tasks that forced me to do some research. When I couldn't find the information in the dictionary or the newly purchased encyclopedias, I knew Mrs. Barlowe would help me at the school library. "Hi, Mrs. Barlowe. Mumma and Da are making me look up stuff again, will you help me?" I hated learning new stuff, but each time I flipped a page I started reading about something else and thought, "This research stuff isn't so bad after all!"

Mumma and Da showed me how to navigate the United States and the world using maps. Mumma constantly bought new and improved versions of them. At 6 years old, I knew how to navigate from Maine to California with my eyes closed! I knew each state that I would pass through. Many times she said, "Maps will take you anywhere and everywhere." She wanted me to dream about going places that I never thought I would get to see. She had more hope for me than I did, but I thought she was nuts with her ridiculous assignments. "When I come back from hanging up clothes on the line, I want you to tell me what interstates I should take to get from Richmond, Virginia, to Albuquerque, New Mexico, and tell me how many miles it is. After leaving Albuquerque, I'm coming back to Virginia, but I wanna drive through Chicago on Route 66 because I like that Nat 'King' Cole song. Is Route 66 an interstate or a local road? About how many miles will be added if I go through the Windy City?" "Mumma, what's a windy city?" "That's for you to figure out! Get to work!" *Why does she give me this stupid stuff to do? I ain't ever going to no Al-bu-quer-que!* But I did, and I knew exactly how to get there.

Sometimes it seemed Mumma's and Da's lessons would never stop. *Good Lord, will y'all just let me read a book or listen to a song or see a road sign without a pop quiz associated with it? Please!* I thought their attempts at making me think about what was going on around me were more of a nuisance than anything else. I resented it, but then in elementary school and high school and college and as an adult, I was amazed at the stuff some people didn't know! *I worked with people who didn't know who Nelson Mandela was, for God's sake!* But, when you're 6 or 7 or 8 or 9 years old, do you really care where Bobbie Gentry's Tallahatchie Bridge is? Much later, I learned that the river that flowed under the Tallahatchie Bridge was where 14-year-old Emmitt Till's body was found in 1955.

I wasn't sure where Mumma and Da found money to buy our major source of information, the *World Book Encyclopedia* set, but I didn't care because those books fascinated me. All kinds of information could be found in those volumes. I felt like I could find the answer to any question in the world in "Volumes A-Z". Mumma told me, "Every summer, college kids drove around the county trying to get people to buy those encyclopedias. Each year when one of them knocked on the door, I said, 'Maybe next year.' Finally, around the time you and Bridgette were ready for school, I figured it was a good time to buy them, so I signed up for a $10 a month payment plan with one of those college kids. That's how y'all got 'em. I think they were about $300 or $400. God knows how long it took me to pay that off!" As she described picking up the boxes at the Saluda Post Office in 1966, she found it hard to conceal her excitement thinking about something that happened 40 years ago. "I bought them for you and Bridgette, but I wanted to read them just as much as y'all did! Probably more. When Mrs. Anton called me from the post office, I flew up there in the GTO to pick them up. I had to use a dolly to get them out to the car because they were so heavy!"

It was funny to see the jubilation on Mumma's face as she recalled picking up those boxes. I remembered my own excitement when we unpacked them and placed them in the little bookshelf in the living room. Our *World Book Encyclopedia* set was thick, white leather bound books engraved with green letters along the spine, and the pages were trimmed with *faux* gold gilded edges. In a way, they *were* gold because they expanded the horizons for me, Bridgette, Sharon, Eddie, Ronnie, Darnell and Tony. When the *World Books* arrived, all of us were still in school, and those books helped us a lot. *I think Mumma got a good return on her investment!*

Me and Da. 1970
*The picture over my head was the man with six
names, Rev. Dr. Martin Luther King, Jr.*

CHAPTER 63

As a little boy, Da shined shoes on the streets of Urbanna, worked on oyster boats for Mr. El-ick, and when he got a little older, worked at Les Newbill's Texaco gas station "up the county" after graduating high school in 1957. Da became a self-taught mechanic and carpenter. Using his smarts, he constructed a wooden clock from scratch, and it hung on the dining room wall when we moved down to Christchurch. *I often wished I still had that handmade clock, but Mumma threw it out in the trash when she and Da broke up!* Da didn't have a lot of material things when he was growing up, so once he was able to afford them, he took meticulous care of them, especially his vehicles. Starting in the 1980s, he was a street-rod enthusiast and restored a 1939 Chevy Coupe, a 1946 Chevy pickup truck and a 1958 Buick Roadmaster. The Roadmaster was still being worked on in his garage when he died, and it was the same model and color as the one I selected for the cover of *Gas Money*. *In a way, it was sort of like he picked it out for me.*

Da's first car was the 1959 VW Beetle that he bought in 1960 right before I was born. He sure loved that car! Mumma used to have a 1953 Ford Custom Line Coupe when they got married, but Da made her get rid of it to better control her comings and goings. He washed his cars and trucks every day of his life, except for the day he had his stroke and the day before he died. I think he kept them clean to remind himself that he wasn't as poor as he once was. He hated a dirty car! You had to close his car doors with an elbow to avoid fingerprint smudges on the door panel. If you didn't, he shot you a look that made you want to crawl in a hole.

Visiting Grandpop Lewis' house was tricky when rain had fallen. Da was not about to drive his clean VW down that dirt lane and get mud on his car. Instead, he parked the VW where the pavement ended down near C-Y's house, and made us walk the remaining quarter of a mile to Grandpop's. Thankfully, the Virginia Department of Highways finally paved that road around 1969, and we didn't have to walk down the muddy lane that led to Grandpop's house anymore.

Da traded in the Beetle for a new, red 1965 Pontiac GTO that cost $3,643.79. Equipped with a 389 cubic inch engine and 335 horses, it was a very fast vehicle. Mumma loved driving Bridgette and me on the back roads of Middlesex County to "open her up!" Dips in the highway made our stomachs roll, but from the backseat, we still begged Mumma to go faster.

One of the scariest moments of my life came when the GTO wasn't even moving. It was stuck in the mud in Grandpop Latimore's cornfield. How Mumma managed to get the GTO stuck was something we never figured out. *She was too good of a driver for that to happen.* I was about 7 years old, and it was the first and only time I *ever* saw Mumma nervous. We knew Da was coming home soon, and if he saw his GTO in the *mud...* well, none of us wanted things to get to that point. Mumma tried rocking the GTO by shifting from 1st gear to Reverse and Reverse to 1st, but the more she pressed the accelerator, the deeper the car sank. The chassis was almost even with the ground, and the spraying mud made the red GTO almost orange in color. Mumma joked about the situation, but I could tell she was scared to death that Da would get home before we got it out. Ronnie, Darnell and Tony pushed and rocked that car, but it wouldn't budge from its resting place. They put wooden boards under the tires, and that didn't help. At one point, they literally tried to lift the car from its quandary. That didn't work either. My eyes constantly darted from the car to the driveway to Mumma's face. I prayed Da wasn't barreling down 33 in his 1965 light brown Chevy pickup. If he came home and saw the GTO in that condition, it would *not* be a pleasant evening for Mumma.

Da was abusive, but he was a "smart" abuser. He wouldn't leave visible bruises. He never punched her in the face because that would have made *him* look bad. Punches or kicks to the stomach and ribs were more to his liking. And Mumma kept that to herself. I never *witnessed* his violence because Da was too clever and secretive for that. But I knew he beat Mumma often because I *heard* the blows in the middle of the night that caused her to move slower in the morning. With the GTO sinking deeper, the knots in my stomach made it feel like Da was punching *me* instead.

Mumma called the gas station over in Urbanna where C-Y's husband, Arthur, worked. "Arthur, can you come over to the house to help me? I'm stuck in the mud." "I'm on the way!" He was there in five minutes, and I don't remember what he did, but somehow he freed the GTO. My uncles washed the car and scrubbed the tires with Ajax and Comet and anything else that was lying around, and when they were finished, they washed it again. It was a nervous day for all of us, especially a 26-year-old mother and a 7-year-old little boy. *Thank God Da never found out.*

Not knowing each day what might set someone off was scary. It was even scarier when it was your mother who lived with that kind of fear. Little things brought on Da's wrath. If she left a dirty glass in the sink, if she fell asleep on the new couch, if she forgot to buy him chocolate ice cream or if the bed wasn't made properly. He might punch her in the stomach while she was in the basement doing laundry, leave her in the fetal position sobbing on the cold cement, grab his truck keys and head on over to the Urbanna Lumber Company to buy some two-by-fours for tomorrow's job like nothing ever happened. *That was my Da.* Mumma never talked about it until I started writing about it. Nobody talked about abuse. That kind of stuff was kept "hush-hush." People were ashamed of it back then as they are today.

Da and Grandpop Latimore having a "discussion" next
to Mumma's 1953 Ford Custom Line Coupe. 1960
Two of the worst "listeners" ever assembled!

Da's 1959 Volkswagen. 1962

CHAPTER 64

It was around 1963 or 1964 when Da began working for Mr. Floyd Jones. Mr. Jones was a white man who ran a small home-building business over in Remlik, about 5 miles outside of Urbanna. Da told me Remlik was named after someone whose last name was Kilmer. *I never found out if that was accurate or not, but when spelled backwards, it made sense to me!* Mr. Jones dropped Da off in front of our house around 6 each evening, and the slamming of Mr. Jones' Chevy van door was the cue Bridgette and I needed to run from the front porch to jump into his arms. *I thought Da was the strongest guy in the world when he picked the two of us up!*

A couple of years later, Da got a job with Mr. Charles Garnett, a black man from King & Queen County, and together, they built our house at Christchurch. Da gave me small jobs like sweeping, or running out to the pickup trucks to fetch tools. (I did the same things for him at 18 that I did at 8! My mechanical ability hadn't improved in 10 years!) One evening, though, proved to be a far tougher job. He needed my help finishing the backyard well that would be our source of "running water." He wanted to remove another 5 to 10 feet of dirt. Ronnie, Darnell and Tony had gone to a basketball game or a dance or something, so I was Da's last option.

It was November of 1969 when Da rigged up a generator in the basement to provide light for the two of us while we dug that night. I sat on the mound of dirt that had already been removed from the hole in the ground, and watched Da assemble our trade tools for the evening. He dropped buckets, a ladder, a spade, a shovel, some rope, a couple of flashlights and a pulley next to the well. *What am I gonna contribute to this situation!* "Chopper, here's what we're gonna do. I'm going down in the well to fill up the buckets with dirt. You're gonna use this rope and pulley to bring them up, then go over there and dump the buckets on the dirt pile you're sitting on. After you dump 'em out, you're gonna send 'em back down to me. Understand?" "Yes, sir." *Da, this seems pretty simple, but I hope I don't mess this up or you're gonna be really mad.* He dropped about 10 buckets down in the hole before stepping on the wooden ladder to go down. He used the spade to dig and the shovel to fill. I tried pulling up the buckets as quickly as possible, but I wasn't strong enough to keep up with Da's pace. As soon as I emptied one bucket, it seemed like Da had four more buckets ready for me to pull up. Each bucket held about 25 to 30 pounds of dirt, and I wasn't the strongest 8-year-old in the county. I peered over the dirt rim to see that Da was running out of space to maneuver. He yelled at me from the bottom of the well all that evening. "Good grief, I can't believe how slow you are! C'mon boy, go faster!" *It was awful.*

CHAPTER 65

Robert and Sandra Meredith came to Middlesex County a couple of years after we integrated in 1969. I believe it was 1972 when they moved "down the county." Mr. Meredith became the new principal at St. Clare Walker Middle School after Mr. John Whitley took a new job somewhere. *I often wondered if Mr. Meredith wished he'd never heard of Middlesex County.* I liked Mr. Whitley. But he didn't believe that I was capable of doing something, so Mumma had me show him that I could.

For a while, Mumma was a teacher's aide at St. Clare Walker Middle School, where I was headed after 5th grade. Standardized test results had recently returned for the elementary school students. Mr. Whitley took an interest in my score because Mumma was constantly telling him how well I read. My math score was average for a 5th grader, but my reading comprehension score was pretty good. It showed that I was reading at a 12th grade level. He thought that unusual and summoned Mumma to his office. He wasn't a "mean" person like some whites were in 1971. In fact, Mumma told me that Mr. Whitley taught her a lot about how to get along with people, white *and* black. However, he did find it hard to believe that I could read and understand material that 12th graders could. Mumma wanted me to show him that my test score was an accurate one.

She marched across the road to Rappahannock Central and pulled me out of Mrs. Carrie Peterson's class. "C'mon and go with me!"

Uh oh. What did I do this time? We walked back in silence to the middle school where she sat me down in Mr. Whitley's office. "Mr. Whitley, you can grab *any* English text book you want from your bookshelf, and Troy will read it and then explain to you what he just read." He grabbed a Charles Dickens novel. I read, "It was the best of times, it was the worst of times, it was the age of wisdom, the age of foolishness, it was the epoch of belief, it was the epoch of incredulity, it was the season of Light, it was the season of Darkness..." He asked for my interpretation of Mr. Dickens' prose. I provided my 11-year-old analysis of the 19th century novelist's writing. I softly asked, "Do you want me to read some more?" "No, thanks. I've heard enough. You can go back across the road." He smiled. Mumma smiled. I smiled.

Mumma walked me back to Mrs. Peterson's class. When Miss Roberta Faucette's Bus No. 17 dropped Bridgette and me off from school that afternoon, Mumma was in the kitchen making my favorite meal – hamburgers and french fries. She was standing over the stove when I walked through the kitchen. "I was really proud of you today so it's hamburgers and french fries tonight, and it's not even Friday!" That was 1971 and I didn't hear those words from her again until 1992 when I received my bachelor's degree. I think she was proud of me at other times in my life, but it just wasn't her nature to voice it. Maybe she didn't want to, maybe she didn't know how. Maybe I didn't give her many things to be proud of. *She wasn't perfect and neither was I.*

Over the summer and into the fall of 1973, Da remodeled the Meredith house that overlooked the Deltaville Marina and Boatyard when the short-lived affair between Da and Sandra was discovered. "It was meant to be..." is the way Mumma explained it to me when I was 48 years old.

Mumma had awakened from a dream on the Tuesday morning of November 13, 1973, after working the midnight shift at the textile plant down near Williamsburg. "I forget what I was dreaming about, but I jumped up because I remembered I needed to go make a house payment down at the bank. I was in a really good mood that morning, and you know that never happened." *Yeah, I know.* "I had to go down to the Bank of Middlesex branch down in Deltaville. I felt so good that day that I decided to make a hot lunch for your dad and was gonna drop it off for him after I stopped at the bank. You know, I don't ever remember taking a hot lunch to your dad before. I always packed his lunch box for him at night before I left for work." She thought about that for a while as her mind drifted down memory lane.

(Insert "The House of the Rising Sun" by The Animals) Mumma shook her head and sighed. "I pulled in behind your dad's truck in the Meredith's driveway, got out and knocked on the back porch door and waited for Bill to come out." *And, she waited. And then, she waited some more.* Cautiously, I asked, "So what were you thinking?" "Oh, I remember exactly what I was thinking, 'If Bill's truck is here and Sandra's car is right in front of his, why is nobody opening the door?' Something about this shit ain't right."

Mumma reached for the porch door and crept in. "Bill? Sandra?" No response. "I walked in through the kitchen and off in a little side room, I saw Bill and Sandra scrambling to get their clothes on." "Oh, Lord." "Troy, it was okay. I wasn't even angry. At that moment, to be honest, I was kinda relieved." "Huh?" "I knew that now I was gonna be free of Bill Lewis' ass. I wouldn't have to deal with his shit anymore, and people in Middlesex County were gonna stop thinking of his yellow ass as a fucking saint! In a way, I was happy!" *I didn't expect that to be her reaction, but it made sense to me.* "I walked over and snatched Sandra's underwear as 'evidence' and started laughing. Shoot, I was headed back to the car until Sandra tried talking me into staying inside to work things out."

"What was Sandra gonna say to you?" "I have no idea. She just wanted me to sit down and talk. I guess she thought about all she was about to lose. Her marriage. Her kids. Who knows? I didn't give a shit." Mumma saw this as her chance to get away from Da. "You know, she kept asking me to give back her underwear, but I told her she better get the hell away from me. Then she had the audacity to try and snatch them outta my hand!" *Imagining Mumma at that moment in 1973 was surreal.* "Good Lord! So what did you do? Did you give them back?" "Yeah, right! After she swiped at them, I punched her and that got Bill mad. Then he ran over and gave me the hardest punch I ever took from him. It hurt so bad I thought he had split my head open again. Remember, I had only been out of the hospital from that car accident a couple of months." "Yeah, I remember." "I was calm until he punched me. It pissed me off even more that *he* was defending *her*. After that, I went kinda crazy!" *Da's punch was the proverbial straw that broke the camel's back.*

Mumma began trashing the Meredith house by tossing dishes and lamps. She overturned chairs and tables. She flung books at Da and Sandra while laughing hysterically. Maybe she was thinking, "What is Robert Meredith gonna think when he comes home from school today and sees this mess?" Maybe she was thinking, "Bill Lewis ain't hitting my ass anymore." Maybe she was thinking, "How am I going to make a house payment and a car payment and buy groceries and clothes for my kids *without* Bill?" Maybe she was thinking, "How close am I to literally losing *my* mind?" *I don't know what she was thinking, and when I thought about it, I didn't want to know.*

"Troy, I just lost it! I looked your Da right dead in his eye and said, 'I've got you now, muthafucker!'" She took the hardest blow Da had ever delivered, literally and figuratively, but *smiled* because she was now a free woman. Freedom from Da was what she had been seeking since about 1964 or so, and now, it was hers. No longer would Da be able to say how "bad" Mumma was. Now she had *proof* that Da wasn't the "good" person everyone thought he was. "I stuffed her underwear in my bra and started smashing up stuff, I just didn't give a shit. Your Dad and Sandra stood there watching me. I think they were too afraid to move because they could see I had become a certifiable crazy woman. After I ran outta shit to break up, I got in the car and drove up to the middle school to tell Arnetta (Mrs. Kidd, the middle school secretary) that you and Bridgette needed to take the bus up to Mom and Dad's house instead of going to our house at Christchurch. I was afraid that if you went home, Bill would hide you from me." "Well, I definitely remember Mrs. Kidd coming into 6th period gym class to tell us to take Mrs. Hammond's bus instead of Mrs. Faucette's. I couldn't figure out why we were going to Grandma's on a Tuesday. I just kept shooting basketball." "You know, it's funny. I even stuck my head in Mr. Meredith's office to say 'Hi' to him." "You did what? Why?" "I guess I just wanted to see if I could face him. I don't know. I just needed to know that I could have a conversation with him, that's all. I know. Weird, right?" "Nothing is crazy to me, Mumma."

Mumma's life had become more complicated a couple of years earlier in 1971. I think she began seeing someone. Things got even more complex when she became pregnant with my little brother, Gentree. When he was born in 1972, I didn't think he looked like me or Bridgette or anybody else in our family. I thought he resembled the guy that Mumma became friendly with, but what did I know? I was only 11. *It was all speculation on my part, and there was no way I was ever gonna question Mumma about that!* After Gentree was born, people in the county really started whispering. "Why would Jean cheat on Bill? He's so good to her. He built her that nice house down at Christchurch. She oughta be ashamed of herself!" Mumma wasn't ashamed of anything. Ever. Was she perfect? No. Were any of us? No. She knew no one would believe her about Da, and the abuse she had endured for the past 13 years, so she kept his mistreatment quiet. *Even if she had voiced it, no one was going to do anything about it anyway.* The whisperers were mistaken about what went on in our house.

Da was charming, good looking and conniving. He may have been a great guy on the outside, but on the inside, he could be a terror. I knew what he was capable of, and many years later when I tried to convince certain family members about his behavior, they refused to believe me. Some even got angry. "Oh Troy, you gotta be exaggerating. You were too young to remember anything like that." *I can remember everything else accurately, but I've got Da's ugly side all wrong? I don't think so.* I doubt Mumma gave much thought to what others said about her. Mumma only cared about the opinions of two people, C-Y and Eveleen. As long as they remained her friends, Mumma felt the rest of the county could "Kiss her black ass!" *Her quote, not mine!*

Mumma was human. She probably needed attention, and not the kind that Da offered. I was pretty certain he pushed her to the brink of insanity at times. Throw in his countless affairs with women from surrounding counties, and I could see why Mumma did what she did. *She was sick and tired of being sick and tired.* Seeing someone else was probably the only way Mumma knew to retaliate against Da. I wasn't going to pass judgment on either of them. We all had our reasons for doing things. *I know I did.* Passing judgment was reserved for the man who told me to "mind my tongue" when I was running low on vanilla ice cream at Howard Johnson's Restaurant. Of course, I never witnessed anything that went on down in Deltaville; I was in 6th period gym class shooting basketball. Over the years, Mumma offered glimpses of what transpired at Mr. and Mrs. Meredith's house that November, but as much I wanted to know more, I could tell she wanted to discuss it even less. I often wondered, if Mumma thought lunchtime was crazy, did she think it would get even wilder that evening? *Trust me, it did, and I witnessed that.*

By the time Bridgette and I stepped off Mrs. Hammond's Bus No. 18 at 3:30 p.m., Mumma was sitting at Grandma's dining room table waiting for us. She didn't provide much information other than saying, "I've decided to leave your Dad." *She may have said more, but that was all I remembered.* She then went upstairs for a nap in the bedroom that I used to share with Eddie, Ronnie, Darnell and Tony. Grandma fixed Bridgette and me something to eat, but we were too numb to put anything in our mouths. I pushed my food around on her "china" plates. *I once asked Grandma if her plates came from Beijing, and she looked at me like I was nuts.* Grandpop didn't eat much, either. He was on his best behavior that evening and sat at the table waiting for 6:30 and Walter Cronkite to show up. Around 6 o'clock, Da pulled his Chevy pickup into Grandma and Grandpop Latimore's driveway, and Grandma took a deep sigh before she got up to let him in the front door. "How you doing, Mrs. Latimore? Is Jean here?" "Yes, she's upstairs resting." "Thank you. I wanna go up and talk to her for a second." I guess Da went up there thinking his charm and personality would make things better. Maybe his smooth words had worked in the past, but they wouldn't on that day. We all sat at the dining room table staring at the plastic tablecloth and not knowing what to say. Grandma, Grandpop, Bridgette and I each found an object on which to fixate. It was a tense situation until Mumma's scream pierced the silence.

"Get the fuck out!" Her scream sent a jolt through all of us. I walked a few feet toward the living room before I froze. Da was slowly backing down the stairs with his hands held high, and Mumma was holding him at gunpoint. A .22 pistol was pointed at his chest. *Mumma's gonna kill Da right here on Grandma and Grandpop Latimore's living room steps.* Grandma pushed me aside and lodged herself in between the two of them. *It was the only time in my life I saw Grandma move quickly.* Grandma always had good instincts, and she knew Mumma would *never* shoot her, but maybe she felt Mumma just might pull the trigger if Bill Lewis was the target. Grandma demanded, "Jean, put that gun down." Mumma screamed at Grandma, "I'm gonna kill him! Get him the *fuck* outta here!" Mumma's left hand (she was a lefty like me and Tony) was still aiming at Da. Grandma's back was jammed against Da's chest, and she put her arms behind her to wrap them around him. *The .22 didn't scare me nearly as much as Mumma's mouth.* Mumma never cursed in front of Grandma. Not ever. Once more: Not ever. Mumma was close to being featured on an episode of *Snapped*, but that television show wouldn't be created for another 31 years. Has she lost her mind? Only Grandpop cursed in front of Grandma. *What is wrong with her?*

"Jean, you need to calm down and put that gun away," said Grandma, in the most convincing manner she could. "I *will* calm down as soon as he gets the fuck outta here!" *Whoa! Mumma's losing it. That's three f-bombs in front of Grandma.* Grandma got Mumma to go upstairs, and told Da to wait in Grandpop's bedroom. Grandpop sat at the dining room table waiting for Walter Cronkite to come on, Bridgette buried her head in her arms, and Da pulled me into the bedroom with him.

I sat on the edge of Grandpop's bed and looked at my father. "Da, what is going on?" I *never* forgot his response. "I've done something wrong, and I hope you never do what I've done." He said he was going away. *Going away? What do you mean? Where are you going? You can't go away.* I asked him, "Am I ever gonna see you again?" Da lifted me from the bed and placed his hands on my shoulders. He said, "I don't know." *What do you mean, "You don't know?" You've been here my whole life.* But I never said a word. I just listened. From upstairs, I could still hear Mumma sobbing and then screaming, "I'm gonna kill him." Grandma was "hushing" her. Da was saying "goodbye," and there I was at 12 years old in a world that would never be the same. *That was life. It often changed in an instant.* Only 10 minutes earlier, Da had asked, "Is Jean here?" Ten minutes later, the lives of many would be forever changed. Da took me from the bedroom and sat me next to Grandpop at the dining room table. "From CBS News Headquarters in New York, this is the CBS Evening News with Walter Cronkite." And like the snakes Da often toyed with, he slithered away.

I watched Da get in his Chevy pickup with the 8-track player. *Would I ever hear The Chi-Lites with him again?* He headed out of the driveway, got on 33 and was gone. *Where was he going?* Mumma calmed down once he left. She came downstairs and took Bridgette and me into Grandpop's bedroom. She told us that she and Da were breaking up, and with those words, Bridgette began to cry. Mumma turned to look at me, and I said, "As long as you're happy, I'm happy." That was all I remembered about that day in November of 1973: Shooting basketball in 6th period gym class, taking Bus No. 18 to Grandma's, Mumma pointing a .22, Grandma pushing me out of the way, Da saying goodbye and me wanting Mumma to be happy. I wasn't glad she and Da had parted, but I felt that things would get better for Mumma.

I never liked thinking about Mumma going on a rampage that day. The image of a 31-year-old mad woman laughing hysterically while tearing one house apart and holding Da at gunpoint at another made me sad. I always thought Mumma could handle any situation. *But I would have bet good money she came close to losing her mind on November 13th of 1973.*

My little brother, Gentree. 1973

CHAPTER 66

Mumma left to work the midnight shift at the textile plant later that night. "I had to go to work. What was I gonna do? Sit at home and cry? I knew I couldn't depend on your Dad anymore." *Wow, I didn't remember that.* "Mumma, how do you think the news spread so quickly around the county? It seemed like everybody at school knew what was going on the next morning." "I don't know, Troy. People liked spreading bad news, and I'm sure the phone lines were burning up that night!" The following day was when I began surrounding myself within the "walls of protection" that stayed around me for another 38 years, but that's another story. Many of the boys at school whom I used to consider friends, now snickered when I walked down the hall or they cupped their hands over their mouths to point, laugh and say nasty things about Mumma or Da. *I was 12 years old when I quit trusting people.*

There was probably only one person in Middlesex County who didn't know about Bill Lewis and Sandra Meredith. That was Reverend John Joshua Lewis. No one had the heart to tell Grandpop Lewis. He found out the following evening, and as Mumma explained, it was a pitiful scene. Faye asked Mumma to go with her to tell Rev. Lewis that his oldest son had gone "up the county" for good. Faye didn't want to deliver that news alone. Forty years later, Mumma still cried when she described how Grandpop Lewis took the news. "Rev. Lewis shook his head and said, 'Not my William, he wouldn't do that' over and over again. It was awful. I felt so bad for him. It was the *only* time I ever saw Rev. Lewis cry. I don't wanna talk about this anymore." *And we didn't. I never asked her another question about the circumstances surrounding their break-up.*

Mumma was right. The thought of Grandpop Lewis sobbing was awful. I doubt if Da or Sandra ever considered the ramifications if they got caught. *How would they get caught anyway?* Mr. Meredith was at school, and Mumma never went to the Meredith house. *Who would catch them? Fate* would. Fate woke Mumma up that morning and put her in a good mood. Fate had her prepare lunch for Da that day. Fate sent her "down the county" on Tuesday instead of Monday to pay the mortgage. *Well, at least that was the way I saw it.*

Da and Sandra headed to Pennsylvania that night with no plan and very little money between the two of them. Faye told me Da stopped by her house for what she could spare. "I gave him about $23 and handed him a banana! It was all I had on me! Bill kept saying that he and Sandy were leaving and I kept thinking, 'Who in the hell was Sandy?' I just didn't get it. It never crossed my mind that something was going on between him and Sandra Meredith." They ended up staying with Aunt Virginia and Uncle Buddy in Ardmore until they saved enough money for an apartment. My cousin, Lynette, told me they stayed there for about a month, and Aunt Virginia never let them sleep in the same bed! *I thought that was funny!*

We quit living at our house down at Christchurch because "ugly" people kept making crank calls threatening us. Grandpop Latimore was afraid they might do something stupid, so we just stayed at Grandma and Grandpop Latimore's from then on. It wasn't the life that I had become accustomed to at Christchurch, but at least I had a roof over my head and food to eat. *Lots of people weren't as fortunate.*

That first weekend after Da left, Bridgette and I stayed with Ronnie and his wife, Sabrina, in Richmond. *Mumma needed a break.* They took us to see a Richmond Robins minor league hockey game with a bunch of their friends. I had never seen a hockey game, and after I saw my first, I had no desire to see another. However, I was on my best behavior, and I acted like I enjoyed the contest because I thought Bridgette and I were being "shopped around" to another family. On Sunday morning, Ronnie asked me to help him put our things in his light blue 1972 Volkswagen for the ride to what I thought would be a new destination. Ronnie closed the front lid of the VW and I asked him, "Who are we gonna go live with now?" "What are you talking about?" "Well, you had all of your friends at the hockey game on Friday night. Which couple liked us? Mumma can't afford to take care of both of us anymore. I know Bridgette and I are going to be given away." Like Da did earlier that week, Ronnie placed his hands on my shoulders and said, "Troy, as long as I'm alive, *that* will never happen. Now, go get your sister and let's go back to Middlesex." His words made me feel a lot better, and as much as my family got on my nerves, I didn't want them to get rid of my feisty sister or me. I never thought November 12th would be the last night we slept at our house down at Christchurch, but it was, and despite all of the craziness that went on within it, I always missed that place.

(Insert "Walk Away From Love" by David Ruffin) Da snuck back into the county about a month later. His brother, Michael, came over to pick me up to go play basketball with him at the Middlesex High School gym. "Hi, Jean. How you doin'? I came by to pick up Troy so we can go play some ball." "No, he can't go. He's got some homework he needs to finish. Have fun." *Mumma can be so cold. Why can't I go play with Michael? He's never come by to get me before.* Michael left, and Mumma told me to put my coat on. She drove me to Grandpop Lewis' house. "Get out and go in there to see your Dad. Tell him the next time that he wants to see you, he can come by Mom and Dad's to pick you up and not get his little brother to do his dirty work. I'll be back in an hour." *How did she know Da was home?*

I went inside, walked down the hall and Da stepped out of Grandpop Lewis' bedroom. "Hey, Da!" I hadn't seen him in over a month. His first words were, "Have you heard David Ruffin's new song? That thing is tight, ain't it?" "Yeah, it is. I love that song!" Music was always our connection, but it seemed strange he chose those words to be our first verbal exchange after not seeing each other for a long period of time. I guess Da went with what he was most comfortable with. Music. He was never good with words. Plus, he was only 34 years old. In many ways, Da was still a kid. I don't remember anything else about that hour-long conversation, and I wouldn't see him again for nearly a year.

Ronnie and me. 1963
*My uncle had been looking out for me since I was an infant,
and when I thought I was about to be given away,
he let me know that I wasn't going anywhere.*

CHAPTER 67

Thirty-one years after almost losing his life on the wrong end of a gun barrel, something far less sinister, but equally as threatening, took Da's life. He entered the hospital on December 28, 2004, complaining of chest pain. The physicians diagnosed his discomfort as GERD-related (gastro-esophageal reflux disease, or heartburn) and kept him overnight for observation. Jennifer called me the next morning when I was heading out for lunch to meet my old boss and a coworker, Mike Labat and Donnie Lucas. "Hey, Troy. It's your sister, Jen." "I know who it is, ya clown! The caller ID tells me that! What's up?" "I just wanted to let you know Da was put in the hospital yesterday, but they think he's gonna be okay." "What's going on?" "He's got some pain in his chest, but they think it's a bad case of heartburn. They increased his heartburn medication, and I think he's gonna be released this afternoon." "Okay, thanks for letting me know. I'll call ya later." I hung up, and called Donnie to let him know that I was running late. "I'm still gonna meet y'all for lunch. Tell Mike I'll be there in 20 minutes." Donnie said, "Boy, you better go see your dad! You never know." *Donnie had been providing me with good advice since 1999.* "Yeah, I guess you're right."

I made my way from New Jersey down to Da's hospital room in Pennsylvania. Over the years, Da and I had developed a routine. Whenever we saw each other, he greeted me with, "Hello, my son!" I replied, "Hello, my father!" *I don't remember how or when that started, but it had been going on a long time.* Da was lying in bed flipping through the channels when I walked in. *He was also dying, but neither of us knew that at the time. Well, maybe he did.* "Hello, my son!" "Hello, my father!" Jennifer, seated at the foot of his bed, rolled her eyes and stepped out to take a phone call as I slid into her chair. Da was 5'11", 160 pounds and in pretty good shape physically. His contracting business kept him active and in constant motion. Internally though, he was a far different story. He was a stroke survivor with high cholesterol and hypertension and was smoking again! *Da was a ticking time bomb at 65 years old.* Over the years, I pestered him about his poor eating habits (who was I to talk about that) and to quit smoking those nasty cigarettes. *Like Da was going to listen to me!* I said to my 65-year-old father, "What am I gonna do with you?" "Oh boy, be quiet! I'm hungry. The food in here is awful. I think they are trying to kill me! Go down to the gift shop and get me a couple of Three Musketeers bars!" "Da! That's not food!" I left to get them. *Anything Da ever asked me to do, I tried to do it for him, even when I was mad at him. He was my Da.*

We talked about the college bowl game on TV and the Philadelphia Eagles chances in the playoffs (they went to Super Bowl XXXIX a month later, but Da wouldn't see it). Silence crept over us until he said, "You know. I'm really sorry I yelled at you that night when we were digging the well. You were doing the best that you could. I should have been more patient." "That's okay, Da. You just wanted me to go faster." *I should have known the end was near. Da was apologizing, and that was something he never did.* More first downs were exchanged and more silence lingered. "And I'm sorry I smacked you for saying 'Good God' when you were singing that "War" song. You didn't know what you were singing was bad." I smiled. The game was in the third quarter when he said, "You know, I shouldn't have embarrassed you in front of Mrs. Thornton at the 'tuna'-ment. That was wrong." "Oh, Da. It's okay. That was 40 years ago."

Released at 4:00 p.m., Da asked me to follow him and Sandra V. back to their house. I declined. "Nah, Da. Since I'm down this way, I'm going to see Grandpop Latimore in Philadelphia. I gotta beat the traffic." "Come spend some time with your Old Pop!" "Da, I gotta go!" He looked disappointed, but ugliness crept into my heart.

Da never really had time for me, so why should I have time for him?

We got into our cars and headed out of the hospital parking lot. Da and Sandra V. sat at the red light with their right turn signal flashing red and west toward their home. My signal flashed left and east toward Philadelphia and Grandpop. I caught Da's reflection in the passenger side mirror of their 2003 white Toyota 4Runner. *I should have known something was really wrong when he was in the passenger seat. Da never let anyone drive him anywhere.* His face appeared sad. I could tell that he was upset that I had rejected his offer to follow them home. When I visited Da in the past, he never said much and neither did I. Mostly, we watched the Eagles and let the television do the talking for us. I couldn't tell if he was happy that I came to see him or not. *I never knew what Da was thinking.*

I sat at that signal light with many thoughts running through my head, but when the light changed, I turned right to follow them. The side mirror showed Da smiling! *It would be my last night with him.* He, Sandra V. and I watched TV for a while, but it was evident that he was worn out from the past two days. At 7:20 p.m., he said, "I'm gonna go get in the bed. I'm tired." "Okay. I want to show Sandra V. how to do something on the computer for a little bit." He got up from the couch and walked down the hall to their bedroom. Five minutes later, Sandra V. and I heard a thump. "Go back there and see what your Dad is up to." "Okay, I'll be right back." I headed to their bedroom to find an unconscious Da on his right side sprawled on the bathroom floor. His last few moments alive were accompanied by the "death rattle." *That snorting sound was one I never wanted to hear again, but I often did when trying to fall asleep.* Da's labored breathing sounded much like a horse clearing its nostrils. His body was fighting to live. His lungs did all they could to seize more air, but it was a futile effort. I knelt on the floor next to him and rubbed his left shoulder. I thought he would regain his strength and say, "Old Pop had you scared for a minute, didn't he?" I whispered, "It's okay, Da. I'm here with you. You're gonna be okay. It'll be alright." But much like flipping a light switch, Da was gone. The death rattle lasted about 20 seconds. An aneurysm in his dissecting thoracic artery stopped him from breathing. Nothing could have been done to save him. I stared at his now limp body with one thought, "God, Da. Was it all worth it? All of that meanness at times. Was it all worth it?" It all happened so quickly. I heard Sandra V. walking toward the bathroom. She walked in and asked, "What are you two doing?" I looked up at her and said, "He's gone." Her bottom lip began to quiver as she stood there looking down at the two of us. We were both in shock. Despite her being scared, she was still strong. "What am I gonna do without him?" I said, "I don't know, but you know I'll help you any way I can. We'll get through this." She looked so sad, and I felt so bad for her. I didn't think we would ever get through it, but over the next few weeks and months we made it through together. Later on that night, I called Mumma to tell her the bad news, and it took longer than I anticipated for her to respond. "Mumma, you okay?" An even longer period of silence followed. "Mumma?" "Troy, I never thought Bill Lewis would die. I know it's crazy, but I thought he would outlive us all."

A right turn to follow the 4Runner was the "right" turn for me. I was glad Donnie convinced me to get on the New Jersey Turnpike that afternoon. "Boy, you better go see your Dad. You never know." It was as though I was supposed to be there when Da took his last breath. *Fate* showed up once again. It was Mumma that pointed out the significance of a "right" turn years later. Regardless of how smart I thought I was, she was always smarter. "Troy, it wasn't just a 'right' turn, it was right for you to follow him home. Bill probably knew something wasn't right with him, and he wanted you to be right there with him." I often thought about that night and how bad I would have felt if I weren't there. Da would have died on that bathroom floor all by himself. *I thought everyone wanted someone with them at the end, including me, but that's another story.* I was glad Fate selected me to go check on Da instead of Sandra V. Had she gone back to the bathroom to find him dying on the floor... well, let's just say I never liked that thought. Had I not made that right turn, she, too, would have been alone that night. All alone with a dead man on the bathroom floor. *It was often strange the way things could "turn" out in life.*

An estimated 600 people showed up for Da's funeral on January 2, 2005. It was 5 degrees that morning when Sandra V. and I and the rest of the family made it from the parking lot to the inside of the much warmer church. Seated in the front pew, Sandra V. and I looked at each other and said at the same time, "Where did all of these people come from?" Da's street-rod buddies were there, his contractor buddies were there, his church choir buddies were there, and his favorite buddy, Dickie Jackson, was there. After the minister asked if anyone wanted to say a few words, Dickie was the first to step forward. He explained how close he and Da were as high school students and elaborated on their 50-year friendship. Then, another man offered his condolences and described how Da helped with a challenging construction job. Another man gave an account of how Da fixed the carburetor on his street rod. One by one, various people came forward to offer perspectives about Da's kindness over the years. I had no idea he knew so many people or had touched so many lives. Many were very emotional as they tried to explain the impact Da had on them. *I knew Da could be a really nice guy, but it was also hard for me to forget about the really mean guy.*

While people continued reminiscing about Da, Sandra V. nudged me in my ribs and motioned for me to lean in closer. "What's up, Sandra V.?" "I got a question for you." "Um hmm?" She nodded in the direction of where Da rested. "Who's in the casket?" We both giggled softly. *Good question!* Who *was* in the casket? Neither of us recognized the kinder, gentler Bill Lewis being described that morning. But those who spoke of him did, and maybe that was all that really mattered.

No one was more surprised than I that Grandpop Latimore attended Da's funeral. Da was *persona non grata* with many of the Latimores after he left Mumma and us with no choice but to move in with Grandma and Grandpop. Judging by the looks on many faces, they were equally as shocked. Many drove from Middlesex County to Pennsylvania for the funeral, so they were well aware of the history between Da and Grandpop. As my 96-year-old grandfather slowly took his seat, I turned around to watch and read the lips of many, "Wow, it's Mr. Latimore." Several in attendance hadn't seen Grandpop in 20 years, and they certainly didn't expect to see him on *that* day. Years later, I mentioned to Mumma, "I thought it was very nice that Grandpop came out to Da's funeral." She sighed deeply. "Troy, Daddy wasn't showing respect for Bill, he was showing respect for you and Bridgette." *I hadn't thought about it that way, but I guess she was right. Again! Was Mumma ever wrong?*

Da and Sandra V.'s house in Pennsylvania. 2004

CHAPTER 68

If there were one adjective to describe the relationship between Mumma and me, "tenuous" may have been the best choice. We had good days and more bad ones. Quite honestly, the first 30 years or so were wrought with a lot of animosity and much contempt, but after we got past those 10,950 days, it was smooth sailing!

Those first 30 years were very unpleasant at times. Mumma was too mean for my taste. According to her, she was tough on me because she felt that would make me a better person in the long run. Maybe it did, but when I was on the receiving end of her anger, I often thought of matricide. So, when I told her that I wouldn't be around the evening of her 42nd birthday, I was surprised at her reaction. "What do you mean you're leaving tomorrow? You've always been here for my birthday." I was taking an 8:00 a.m. flight to San Antonio on June 21st of 1984, a trip that would prove unpleasant for a couple of reasons: Basic Training awaited me once I stepped off the plane, and I had an earache that wouldn't quit. But on the bright side, I was getting away from Mumma.

Gerald dropped me off that morning at the Military Entrance Processing Station in Richmond in his red 1979 Ford F-150 pickup truck, and it was an awkward sendoff. We weren't close then, but on the other hand, I wasn't close with anybody. Neither of us knew what to say as we sat in his pickup staring at the windshield. "You take care of yourself, listen to your sergeants and don't volunteer to do shit. You hear me?" "I hear you." I hopped out of the F-150 and headed off into the wild, blue yonder to start my new life at age 23. It was a liberating day because as I hit the airport entrance I distinctly remembered thinking, "Drill sergeants can't be all that bad. I've been dealing with Mumma all of my life!" After landing in San Antonio, I was mad at the US Airways pilots who flew me halfway across the country. I felt that they had done an extremely poor job of pressurizing the cabin (not that I knew anything about pressurization, and I certainly didn't know that all I had to do to "fix" my ears was "pop" them). *How would I have known that? It was my first trip on an airplane!*

(Insert "The Tennessee Waltz" by Patti Page) However, during my college years before leaving for San Antonio, Mumma and I shared some fun times together. In looking back, they were my fondest memories of her. On Saturday nights, we went out on a "date" while sitting in the living room listening to WGH-FM. Gerald was usually out rolling dice down at Mr. Robert Piggott's garage, Bridgette was brooding in her bedroom or on a date, and Mumma and I were listening to Roger Clark's *Big Band Radio Show*. His show started each Saturday night at 11:00 p.m. After Mumma fell asleep, I went out looking for girls at the dance clubs down in Hampton, Newport News, and Norfolk. But before I headed east on Interstate 64, Mumma and I sat in the living room of the double-wide listening to Mr. Clark. He spun songs like Patti Page's "The Tennessee Waltz" and Benny Goodman's "Don't Be That Way" while Gentree sat in front of the TV playing something called "Pong." Why on Earth he played a "game" on a TV, I could never understand. A game where you didn't run around outside? What kind of game was that? You only exercised your fingers! The times were a-changing, but I was caught unaware that kids would one day welcome the opportunity to "sit" and play. That was a totally foreign concept to me in the 1980s.

Mumma loved music as much as Da, but unfortunately, she wasn't blessed with much of a singing voice. That never kept her from singing, though! I was never more surprised when she knew all of the words to "The Tennessee Waltz" as it played on WGH one Saturday night. Mr. Clark informed me that Ms. Page's version of the song hit the airwaves around 1950 when Mumma would have been 8 years old. "How do you know the words to this song?" "Oh, I loved this song when I was a little girl." I was 20 years old before I ever thought about Mumma being a child. Before that moment, she was just *Mumma*.

I had never heard Mumma sing along to a standard because Mumma was more of an R&B person. I was sitting on the floor next to Gentree watching him play Pong when I received another shock. Mumma got up from the couch, walked over to where I was sitting and told me to stand up! *What did I do this time?* "Hold your arms out straight!" *What is she doing?* "It's time you really learned how to dance." "Mumma, I can't dance to *that* song!" "You don't dance to it. You *waltz* to it! Now, follow me!" *Mumma knows how to waltz?* Our hands interlocked, and we ambled about the living room floor for about a minute in three-quarter time. Gentree even stopped playing to watch us move about the living room. He had to be thinking, "Mumma and Troy are dancing?" She counted off, "One, two, three. One, two, three. One, two, three." I followed her lead until I became too embarrassed and cut our dance short. Gentree couldn't stop laughing. Neither could Mumma and I. We stood there in the middle of the living room floor staring at each other, grinning from ear to ear. *Why couldn't we get along like this all of the time?* Our first dance maybe lasted 60 seconds, and it was the best 60 seconds of my life.

Once Mr. Clark signed off, I was off to some club to meet the girls who screwed up the college opportunity Sandra V. worked so hard to get me. *Really it was my fault, but I liked blaming girls for my academic shortcomings.* Most college students may have been able to handle the freedom that college offered. *I wasn't one of them.* I showed up to class when I felt like rolling out of bed and only worked hard in the classes that I liked. I was irresponsible, but I had the best 5 years of my life at Shippensburg State College. *That's right, 5 years with no degree.* I was so ashamed that I lied to Mumma and told her that I graduated, but she was too smart for that. She let me continue that lie for many more years. I thought getting on that plane to San Antonio would prove to be a better option for me, and it was. The military provided much needed structure and even more discipline to my life. I met quite a few people who gave away *gas money* like it was free! *And you know what? It was!* However, my real reason for joining the Air Force was because I was much like Richard Gere's character, Ensign Zack Mayo, in *An Officer and A Gentleman*. I had nowhere else to go.

When Mumma said to me, "What do you mean you're *not* gonna be here for my birthday? You've always been with me on my birthday," I hadn't thought of that. I had been with her on every one of her birthdays since 1961. I headed back to my room, sat on the edge of my bed and thought, "Oh my God, *she* is gonna miss *me*?" That was the first moment that I thought Mumma actually liked me. Despite all of the nice things she'd done for me throughout her life, she did some mean things as well and those proved harder to forget than the nice things were to remember. She was verbally abusive, and a lot of what Da gave her, she dished out to me. We had a complicated relationship, to say the least. Internally, I made excuses for her animosity toward me. I thought it was *my* fault when she said ugly things, and it took Lori to point out the unhealthiness of the relationship once we began dating.

Lori and I had left the double-wide and were heading to her apartment one night when she said, "Why does *she* talk to you like that?" "What do you mean?" "Troy, it's as though *she* doesn't even like you, and it's really sad that you don't see it." "Lori, you're nuts. Of course, Mumma loves me. Look at all of the stuff she's done for me." "I don't care what she's done *for* you. *How* she treats you is all I care about, and it's plain to see there is no love there. That lady despises you." We drove on in silence. I was mad at Lori. *How dare she attack my mother who had done so much for me throughout my life?* Once we made it to her place, I didn't even pull in to park. I wanted her out of the car. "Don't you wanna come in? We could *do* something!" I fumed and lied, "Nah, I don't have time. Mumma needs the car back. I'll call you when I get back home." Getting back on I-64, I thought, "For years, I thought *I* was the only one who thought Mumma didn't like me. One minute she likes you and in the next, she turns on a dime and says or does something really ugly. What did I ever do to make her hate me?" I had been having those thoughts ever since I could remember, and finally, Lori validated it for me. Sometimes, that was all it took – another person to validate your feelings. I was elated to be getting away from Mumma. I was happy to be leaving for the Air Force because for the first time in my life, I felt like I would *not* be the *only* one getting yelled at.

I was 31 years old before Mumma and I started on the road to a "healthy" relationship. Things began to change for the better when she came to Omaha for my college graduation in 1992. After having lots of fun at Shippensburg State College, but never graduating, an Air Force supervisor helped me get my act together and forced me to get my degree, but she's another story. After the graduation ceremony, Mumma put her arms around me, told me how proud she was of me and that she loved me. *It was the first time anyone in my family had ever told me they loved me.* Later that night, I told Lori about it, and she said, "It's about fucking time!" Mumma stayed with us for about two weeks, and her visit went far better than we expected. We kept waiting for the "other shoe to drop," but surprisingly, it never fell. Each morning, we woke up about an hour or so before she did for breakfast. Seated across from each other at our tiny dining room table, I said, "What is *wrong* with her? She is nothing like the lady I remember." "Troy, I don't know who that lady is upstairs sleeping, but she is *not* your mother! *That* lady is really nice." "I know what you mean. Whoever she is, let's keep her!" When Mumma came down to join us, she greeted us with a cheerful, "Good morning! What are we going to do today?" *Who is this person?*

For the two weeks Mumma was in Omaha with us, I saw no evidence of the volatile mood swings. She was no longer the crazy person who was mad at the world. She had mellowed, and if there was one word I thought I would never use to describe Mumma, it was *mellow*. I guess that was something she never had a chance to do because she had been responsible for a sister and four brothers, two husbands, two sons, a daughter, a niece, and others her entire life. *Mellow* never got a chance to be part of her vocabulary, and that was the reason I kept my distance from her when I was an adult. For the first 30 years of my life, I feared Mumma, so I chose to be around her as little as possible. I chose *mellow* as my disposition, instead. After Mumma finally mellowed, I wanted to be with her as much as possible.

Mumma at my college graduation. 1992
The happiest day of my life.

CHAPTER 69

The person who mellowed Mumma was Gerald Leon Ferguson. He was a pleasant, but stern guy who served a couple of years in Vietnam. He did us the biggest favor in the world by asking Mumma to marry him, and I never appreciated all that he did for us until I was older (and even then, I wasn't sure that I showed him enough appreciation). Bridgette, Gentree, Mumma and I didn't deserve him, but thank God, he stuck with us. He could easily have walked away. Had I been in his shoes, I would have because the four of us could be real jerks at times.

An unintentional act of deception persuaded Gerald to pursue Mumma. He was 25 years old and 6 years Mumma's junior when he started seeing her in 1974. They met at the textile plant where they both worked, and he thought that the Chevy Caprice Mumma drove was indicative that she had a little money. *He was correct about one thing; she had very little!* Growing up, Gerald was probably poorer than both the Latimores and Lewises, and if there was a chance for him to improve his economic status, he was going to do just that. *Poor guy, he didn't know what he was getting himself into.*

Like a lot of combat veterans, I think Gerald saw things in Vietnam that he wanted to forget. He never talked about what he saw, and I only asked him about what he did over there once. I was about 15 years old, and we were tinkering around with one of the "fix 'er up" automobiles he'd recently bought. Those vehicles were constantly in need of repair from his ample-sized hands. Gerald was a "Ford" man if there ever was one, and a big supporter of the man from the State of Michigan. Not the one named Gerald R., but the other guy named Henry. We went through at least six Fords and one Chevy in a three- to four-year span that I could remember: a '64 Falcon, a '68 and '69 Torino, a '68 Galaxie, two Ford F-150 pickups and a '65 Impala. Most of them were headed for the bone yard by the time he bought them, but that was all he could afford. Gerald worked under the hood while I watched him fix the water pump or the fuel pump or the carburetor or the timing chain or anything else that needed to be done to keep them running. I had a simple job while I watched him work – keep the flashlight focused on his hands and don't touch anything! "Hey, Gerald, did you ever shoot anybody over there in Vietnam?" "Keep the light still, boy!" "All right." No response. "Gerald, I asked you a question." "I heard ya." He kept working and kept his mouth shut. *I guess that was my answer.* He wasn't going to talk about anything that happened "over there," but he did have a Bronze Star with four Oak Leaf clusters to show for his two years in the Vietnam Conflict. Gerald was cited for bravery on five separate occasions, and I thought that was pretty impressive. The "Bronze" was awarded for "acts of heroism in a combat zone," and after I served in the Air Force, I knew those weren't given to just anyone. Forty years later, Gerald hadn't said a word about what he did to receive those awards for his time in Vietnam, but when I looked back at his sacrifices for my family, his "star" was never brighter. Gerald Leon Ferguson was a beacon of light for my family. *I should have given him a thousand Oak Leaf clusters.*

Gerald let me drink my first beer when I was 13. *This guy is nothing like Da!* He and Mumma had just started dating when Gerald took me with him to the Richmond Dragway in Sandston, Virginia, for my first visit "legal" drag race. *I had been watching Mumma do that kind of stuff illegally for years!* Coming home in Gerald's white two-door 1965 Chevy Impala, we pulled into the Three Gables Restaurant parking lot in New Kent County to grab a bite to eat. Three Gables wasn't a true "restaurant" – it was more of a "juke joint" where black people went for burgers, beer, fries and fun on a Friday or Saturday night. It sat in the median of U.S. 60 about halfway between Williamsburg and Richmond. There was plenty of parking all around the wood building that was painted white with green shingles.

(Insert "Tired of Being Alone" by Al Green) Gerald and I took a middle booth near the Wurlitzer jukebox that informed everyone with ears that Al Green was tired of being alone. A few people were sitting at the bar watching professional wrestlers Rip Hawk and Swede Hanson battle Chief Wahoo McDaniel and Paul Jones on the TV, while others shot pool and a few couples grinded on the makeshift dance floor. *Da would never have brought me to a place like this!* Gerald and I ordered cheeseburgers, fries and a bottle of Miller High Life for him and a Coke for me. The waitress asked Gerald if he wanted his beer "in a glass or a bottle?" He said, "Beer in a glass is for girls." *I always liked that line, and I borrowed it from him for the next 40 years!*

As we waited for our food, a loud-talking, brash guy sporting a light-blue double-knit leisure suit, a flowered popcorn shirt with an open butterfly collar and platform shoes came strutting through the front door. *If he missteps in those things, he's going to break his ankles was my first thought!* He made his way through the crowd, talking to any and every body that he brushed against. "Hey, girl, how you doin'? Umm umm umm!" "What's up, man? I got next. Rack 'em up, chump!" *Uh oh, he's headed this way! Oh my God, this guy knows Gerald?* He slid into our booth, pinning me against the wall. "Scoot over, man. I need some room!" "Troy, this here is my brother, Buddy."

He was Gerald's older brother, Thomas Harry Ferguson, Jr., but no one called him that. He was "Buddy" to everybody! "Hey, Gerald! Whatchy'all doin' in here!" Gerald was low-key and quiet, even shy at times. Buddy was the complete opposite. "Oh, we just stopped in to grab a little something to eat." Buddy looked at me, "What you drinking?" "A Coke." "A Coke? How old are you, boy?" "13." "Aw, man, that's old enough." He waved the waitress over, "Gimmee two Miller High Lifes, a cheeseburger and some fries." *Wow, Buddy has a drinking problem. Two Miller High Lifes?* The beers came. He slid one bottle over to me and tilted his for me to clink like I was Humphrey Bogart. I looked at Gerald. "Go ahead, but don't you tell Jean!" I had my first sip of beer and thought, "Wow, this stuff is overrated. I'd rather have a Coke." I wouldn't admit that to Gerald and Buddy, though. *It tasted just fine!*

Our burgers showed up and we were having a good time, but suddenly, that all changed. Ladies screamed and ran. Pool cues dropped to the floor as men bolted for the front door. Waitresses put down their trays and slowly backed out. Everyone, Gerald and Buddy included, headed for the parking lot until only three people remained inside: A black guy in his mid-20s drinking his own Miller High Life, a black woman about 30 or so with vengeance on her mind. And 13-year-old me! The woman sent everyone scrambling after she removed a hatchet that had been tucked under her blouse in the waistband of her blue jeans. Her outfit reminded me of Elly May Clampett from *The Beverly Hillbillies,* but she wasn't nearly as sweet as *Elly May;* she was more like *Granny!* Mesmerized, I watched her pull that hatchet from her blue jeans. In the booth opposite mine, the young black guy never budged as Hatchet Woman stood over him gripping her small axe. His eyes showed no emotion while he stared directly at me. I stared right back with eyes opened wide in amazement. Only six feet or so separated him and me as Hatchet Woman towered over him about to strike with the swiftness of a cobra. She screamed at him, "Muthafucker, if you ever lay a hand on my little sister again, I will use *this* on you, and they will *never* find your black ass!" He kept staring straight ahead at me. "Do you fucking understand me?" His hands remained wrapped around his beer bottle. We continued our staring contest. "Yes, I do." "Yes, *what* muthafucker?" *Uh oh. She was like Mumma. I hope he has good manners and says, "Yes, ma'am!"* "Yes, ma'am. I understand," was his reply as his eyes finally broke away from mine. He craned his neck to now stare directly into her brown eyes.

At that instant, Gerald crept back in and worked his way around to where I still sat hypnotized by the action. Hatchet Woman cocked her head to look at him and said, "Who the fuck are you?" "Excuse me, Miss. I don't want no trouble, I just want my boy here. I'm gonna take him outside and get him outta your way." He yanked me up by the back of my shirt collar and marched me outside with the others. "Boy, you better get your dumb black ass out here! What the fuck were you thinking?" "I don't know. I never saw anything like that in Middlesex County!" He, Buddy and I shared a good laugh until Hatchet Woman strolled out fierce and confident that she had put the fear of God in that guy. The parking lot crowd parted to give her plenty of room. It was as though she were a female Moses striking the Red Sea with her own version of a staff, only it was a diminutive axe from which she drew her power. She peeled out of the parking lot in a white 1970 Dodge Charger, leaving the smell of burnt rubber in the air and tire marks on the asphalt. Moses freed his people, and I liked to think that she gave her abused sister some freedom on the evening I tasted my first beer. We all went back inside, and that guy was still sitting there holding his beer and staring straight ahead.

On payday Friday nights, Gerald spent time down at Mr. Piggott's garage. Mumma hated when he stopped by there *before* coming home because she knew that he might possibly arrive later that evening with more money, but sometimes, it was less. Later that night, Gerald might stumble through the double-wide's rear door, toss his greasy work jacket onto the washer-dryer combo, grab a bite to eat and head for the living room floor. Often, it was after midnight. He grabbed a cushion from the couch, tossed it on the floor, placed it under his head and went to sleep. There he stayed, too tired and possibly too intoxicated to get up and, probably too afraid of what Mumma would do if he tried to join her in their bed.

While he napped, Mumma sent Bridgette over to search his coat pocket for his Chesapeake & Ohio Railroad Company paycheck with the hope that there might be a little extra cash in there from shooting dice and playing cards. Bridgette had no problem searching his pockets, but I considered it an invasion of privacy. When Mumma asked *me* to do it, I declined. "I'm not going through his pockets, you do it." I was of the opinion that whatever was or wasn't in Gerald's pockets was his business, not mine. His pockets were private property, and I refused to be a trespasser. Instead, I scooped up his jacket and handed it over for Mumma to rummage through his pockets. Regardless of the pocket picker, it was a quiet night when at least the paycheck was located. On the Friday nights when Gerald's paycheck didn't make it home because it was left on Mr. Piggott's dice or poker table, it was a long night for all. When he came home with little to nothing, Mumma started in on him. "Why do you throw your money away like that? How am I gonna buy groceries tomorrow? Gentree needs a new coat. You know that furnace is dying. What are you thinking about?" Gerald had a lot of shit he thought about and a lot more shit that he probably wanted to forget. I didn't blame him for having a good time down at Mr. Piggott's garage. Could Gerald have made better choices? Probably. But I understood even then, that Gerald was self-medicating with whiskey and gambling, and I saw nothing wrong with it. *Never did I think that I would start my own form of self-medication some 35 years later.*

Gerald's response was often silence and that pissed Mumma off even more. Just like when her foot was on the accelerator, Mumma went from "0 to 60" quickly, as did her emotional state. Once her internal tachometer hit "Red," she usually came out swinging. Sometimes, my crazy-ass sister, Bridgette, joined her! They "jumped" Gerald as he lay snoring on the floor. Their blows weren't the strongest, but they weren't gentle, either. Sometimes, they nicked him up pretty good and drew a little blood. *Mumma and Bridgette were crazy!* One of them might kick him softly in the side, while the other screamed in his ear. It didn't happen every payday Friday, but had I known I was going to one day write about their exploits, I would have maintained a better record of their Friday night fights!

Gerald never fought back. He was a gentle guy and could have hurt them if he had a nasty side, but instead, he chose to swat Mumma and Bridgette away like they were flies. "Y'all leave me alone while I try to get some sleep. I ain't bothering nobody." He defended himself by curling in the fetal position, and waited for Gentree and me to get out of bed and walk over to lay our bodies over his to stop their attack. "Y'all leave him alone, he's just trying to sleep. He's tired!" Mumma yelled, "You and Gentree always stick up for him!

Who sticks up for *me* when I have no fucking money, and there's no God-damn food in this house? He does this shit all the fucking time, and I'm *sick* of it!" *I get your point Mumma, but kicking him in the ribs ain't gonna help.* Sadly for Gerald, payday Friday was probably the only day he had money because once Saturday morning arrived, it was all gone to take care of us.

(Insert "Devil Woman" by Cliff Richard) Gerald's calm demeanor was a blessing, and he often found humor in the "beatings" he received from Mumma and Bridgette. After one of those Friday night fights, Gerald said to Gentree and me, "Y'all hear that?" I looked at Gentree, and he looked at me. "Hear what?" Gerald never listened to any rock music that I knew of, but he started singing the lyrics to "Devil Woman." Gentree and I thought that was funny, and Mumma threw a bedroom slipper in our direction to shut us up. "He's not funny!" *Yes, he is!* Our laughter only encouraged him. **(Insert "Witchy Woman" by The Eagles)** "Hold on, I got another one!" He then offered his impression of Don Henley singing "Witchy Woman." "Somebody hand me a broom so your Mumma can fly around on it!" Even she laughed at his impersonation and that night became a good one, but there were a bunch of bad ones.

Gerald was a guy a few years removed from war who married a woman with a lot of "baggage" and three kids to boot. I didn't blame him for drinking and gambling on paydays. He needed a little excitement in his life because there wasn't much of that in our double-wide. *I think staying out for a while on Friday nights gave him something else to think about besides Vietnam and the four of us.* Eventually, he helped make Mumma a nicer person, and in turn, she settled him down and provided him with a good home. They grew to understand and accept each other for their strengths and shortcomings. All I ever wanted for her was a little happiness in her life. Gerald made that happen for her. *I always knew Mumma was more than just a devil woman with evil on her mind.*

Gerald, Mumma and me. 2012

CHAPTER 70

I often thought about the "hats" Mumma wore. Angel, devil, disciplinarian, motivator, intimidator, educator and guidance counselor were many of the characters she portrayed in my life. She took on even more roles for her sister, brothers and the "strays" that she took in over the years. The fact that her life was so difficult was what I think made Mumma bitter for nearly 50 years. As I learned more about her, I finally began to understand why she was in a bad mood more often than not. At 16 years old, Mumma managed the lives of Pat-Pat, Eddie, Ronnie, Darnell and Tony and anybody else who happened to be staying at our house. I was barely responsible for myself at 16, and there was no way I could have prepared a 13-, 11-, 10-, 8- and 5-year-old for life each day for the next 11 years. In fact, one summer when I was home from college, Mumma made Gentree and two of my younger cousins, Territa and Calvin, my sole responsibility. They were 12, 11 and 6 years old at the time, and I thought I was going to lose my mind. Each evening I had to cook for them, color with them, create homework assignments, have them brush their teeth, run their bath water, have them say their prayers before tucking them in and lastly, read them a bedtime story. Mumma did that forever! I did it for 3 months and nearly lost my sanity!

I can't imagine what that strain was like for Mumma as a rising junior at St. Clare Walker High School in 1958. Each morning, her brothers and sister needed to be scrubbed, cleaned and presentable for school without the aid of indoor plumbing. She had to cook something to put in their tummies before the school bus came. She had one of the older boys walk 5-year-old Tony over to Aunt Dot's house at 6 each morning. Before Aunt Dot got a job at Leggett's, she drove a school bus for the "colored" schools. Aunt Dot dropped Tony off at Aunt Maggie's house down at Cook's Corner where he stayed until school was over. *I could barely get myself out of bed at 16, and even less so when I was in college. Mumma prepared 6 people for school at the age of 16!*

With no car, Mumma was always dependent on others to give her a lift when she needed to go somewhere. People like "Miss Beck" Burrell, who lived way "down the county," gave her rides to the grocery store on Saturdays, and long before he became her father-in-law, Rev. Lewis gave her rides to Doc Marshall's Drug Store or Bob Bristow's Hardware Store in Urbanna. "Why did Grandpop Lewis help you? You weren't even part of his family then." "Well, Rev. Lewis was a minister, and even though I didn't go to his church, he still knew I needed help, so he helped me." Mrs. Holmes took her to P.T.A. meetings and parent/teacher conferences to discuss the progress of her siblings and their studies. Those P.T.A. meetings and one-on-one teacher sessions continued for her until Tony graduated high school in 1971. Mumma was 28 years old when she went to her last P.T.A. meeting for one of her brothers. She had been a parent for all of them since 1958. Her chance to be a high school kid with no worries had long since passed her by, and I think that was one of the reasons she resented me. From her perspective, it may have appeared that I didn't have a worry in the world. *Had she known what was going on inside my head, she would have thought differently. I had been contemplating suicide since Mrs. Pollock scared the shit outta me back in 5th grade.*

Even the simplest of tasks were complicated at the Latimore house that Mumma ran. Bathing required "drawing" buckets of water from the well out in the backyard. "Drawing" water was the process of dropping a tin bucket attached to a rope into the well, and using a rope and pulley to "draw" it up. Dropping that bucket in the well was done about 30 to 40 times a day to get enough water for the 10 of us to take a bath. *That didn't even take into account the water needed for cooking and laundry.* With no "running water," Mumma "drew" water from the well throughout the day and night as needed until her brothers were strong enough to do it themselves. To bathe, she warmed the nearly freezing well water on their only source of heat, the kitchen's wood stove. Chopping wood was her job until she trusted her younger brothers to use the crosscut saw and axe. Once she felt they were big enough to handle those tools, she took them down in the woods behind the house to show them how to select the best trees for firewood. "Mumma, how did you learn to do all of that?" "Trial and error. I taught myself."

When the water reached the simmering point, it was poured into small plastic tubs that were large enough for one person to stand in at a time and "wash up." After one person had cleaned, the water from the tub was tossed into the cornfield, and the "wash up" process started all over again for the next person in line. "Okay, who's next? Get your butt in here!" It was a routine that took place every night for Mumma until she was "rich" enough to have "running water" installed in 1969. She lived in that house from 1952 to 1969, 17 years of drawing water. The well water was needed for everything from bathing to house cleaning to cooking. And for washing laundry, Mumma did all of that by hand every two days. She told me, "I didn't have a choice. We were poor. We didn't have that many clothes to wear so I had to wash them every other day!"

From the back porch, Mumma washed clothes, towels and sheets in a large tin basin using a washboard and hung them on the backyard clothesline to dry. She laughed when she remembered how the damp clothes froze during the winter. *But I bet she wasn't laughing back then.* Those frozen clothes were brought in and placed next to the wood stove on a wooden clothes rack to thaw out. Mumma said the worst part of the winter, though, was waking up to a cold house because they couldn't fall asleep with the fire roaring in the stove. "Why not? Why didn't y'all just put enough wood in there to last all night?" She looked at me as though I'd lost my mind. "Troy, wood stoves weren't safe back then, you idiot! You'd be crazy to fall asleep with a fire burning all night. We put it out before we went to bed." "So how did y'all stay warm?" "We didn't. We shivered a lot under the covers!"

Other than washing and ironing clothes, giving baths, fixing bee stings, attending P.T.A. meetings, monitoring homework assignments and patching up clothes, Mumma's life was pretty easy! The amount of organization, responsibility and discipline needed was inconceivable to me. From how much toilet paper would get them through the week to how many cans of preserves would get them through the winter to fitting cardboard in the bottoms of shoes that were worn out to what got planted in the garden in the spring to praying that the check from her Mom and Dad would arrive sooner than later were constant concerns. Then, by the time she turned 21, there was a husband, a niece and two kids of her own to oversee along with her siblings and "uncles" Danny Lee Davis, Tommy Thornton and Carlton Reed. We needed all of the space that Grandpop Latimore's house provided, especially when those "other" uncles stayed over. My uncles and I slept head to toe in four twin beds that filled one of the upstairs bedrooms. *Mumma ran her own version of a shelter before I even knew what a shelter was.*

I loved going upstairs to listen to them talk about girls, cars, shining shoes, The Four Tops versus The Temptations or Russell versus Chamberlain. When I was five years old in 1966, I had seven "uncles" that were between the ages of 13 and 18, and they were my heroes. "What are y'all talking about?" "Boy, you better go back downstairs before Jean fusses at you. You know she wants your head stuck in a book all the time instead of hanging out with us!" "But, y'all are more fun than some ole dumb book!" Mumma yelled from downstairs. "Troy Ferrand Lewis, what are you doing up there?" "Nuthin'." "Nuthin'? That word is pronounced 'nu-thing.' Put the 'g' on the end, dammit." "Yes, ma'am." "Anyway, aren't you supposed to be reading a book down here before you go to bed?" "Yes, ma'am." "Have you finished it yet?" "No, ma'am." "Then, get your butt down those stairs and leave those boys alone. They ain't talking about nuthin' anyway!" *How come she doesn't have to put a "g" on the end?* "Yes, ma'am." "Uncle" Carlton Reed looked at me, "We told you to get outta here!"

I didn't spend much time with Mumma's brother, Eddie, because he caught the Greyhound bus that stopped at the Esso gas station in Saluda and took off for the Army in September of 1966. But when he was still at our house, I liked being around him because Eddie was "smooth," much like his oldest brother, Uncle Dee. Eddie was also a good-looking guy like Uncle Dee, and from what I recall, he had his fair share of females who probably agreed with my assessment. One in particular was a young lady named Ruth Ann Fitchett. *I never forgot about her!* Eddie was shocked when I mentioned her name at the surprise party we threw for Mumma when she turned 70 years old. "If I remember right, when you were in high school you dated a girl named Ruth Ann, right?" Eddie graduated from St. Clare Walker in 1966, and the look on his face when I mentioned her name more than 45 years later was pretty funny. "Boy, how old were you then? Five?" *Yes I was, but I never forgot the good-looking ones!*

A slew of Eddie's buddies stayed with us when I was growing up. Danny Lee, Tommy and Carlton were the ones who seemed to be at our place the most. They were around our house so much that I thought they were part of my family, and in a way, they were. Years later, I learned they stayed with us more often than not because in their homes, they weren't treated very well. Mistreatment by a parent or grandparent or aunt or uncle or whoever was raising them occurred every now and then, so Mumma had them stay with us from time to time to give them a break.

I once asked Mumma if Carlton was related to us and her reply was, "No, he just stays with us a lot." "How come?" "Does it matter?" "No, ma'am, it doesn't." "Then, why are you asking?" *I didn't ask again.* Carlton never played jokes on me like my "real" uncles. He treated me like I was a long-lost brother, and I clung to him like a puppy does to its mother. The way everyone explained it to me, his dad was a mean, old man with a real nasty side. Mr. Mezzie Reed used his children as punching bags because he could and nobody was going to stop him. One day, he went too far and little Arthur Reed ended up dead hanging from a wall hook in their basement. Carlton's older brother by two years was dead at the age of 7 in 1951. "How did he get away with that?" "Troy, *they* certainly didn't care how *we* died back then and sometimes, *they* don't really care how *we* die now!" "Wow! How did Carlton's mother deal with that?" "Mrs. Reed just kinda lost her mind after that boy died. She was never the same. She was only 44 when she died. Carlton was around 12 or 13 when she passed away, and that's why I had him stay with us so much. I tried to keep him away from his mean-ass daddy as much as I could. He was always an asshole!"

Carlton joined the Army around the same time that Eddie did. I wasn't sure what happened to Danny Lee. He moved up to Philadelphia and sort of disappeared. Tommy died while serving in the Army, and, sadly, so did my buddy, Carlton. When "Uncle Sam" gave him furloughs though, Carlton often came back to Middlesex to stay with us. Sometimes, I slept next to Carlton with him at one end of the twin bed and me at the other. He usually brought home a gift for Bridgette and me. One year, he brought me a black nylon, lightweight zippered jacket from Vietnam with my name on it. My years of service in the Vietnam Conflict were sewn across the front left breast pocket. It read: "Troy Lewis. Vietnam. 1966–1968." Across the back of the jacket, was a stitching of a snake wrapped around a wooden pole that was accompanied with the word *Saigon* spelled out in red, black and yellow letters. I loved that jacket and wore it even when it was 90 degrees outside!

The last time I saw Carlton, he, Bridgette and I were sitting on the brick flowerbed that Ronnie laid around the front porch for Grandma Latimore's petunias. Carlton was taking the Greyhound headed for Richmond, and then a plane headed to someplace that Bridgette and I couldn't pronounce. He placed a 50-cent piece in our palms, kissed us good-bye and marched out to 33 with his olive green Army duffle bag slung over his shoulder. In his Army dress greens, he stuck his thumb out to hitch a ride to the Saluda bus terminal, a patch of dirt next to the Esso station. I shouted, "Hey, Carlton! I'll see you next time!" He dropped his bag near the spot where Mr. Miles nearly ran me over earlier in the year to jog back toward the house. I ran out to meet him halfway. "Troy, I ain't coming back. I won't be seeing y'all no more." "Yeah, you will. You'll be back!" *He was right.* A few months later, I was in the backyard playing with my yellow Tonka dump truck when I heard the phone ring and Mumma scream. He was gone. Many times I stopped by Carlton's grave at Antioch Baptist Church to say, "Hey, Carlton! I'll see you next time!" When things went "dark" in my life, I spent a lot of time at his grave talking to him. *I loved that guy.*

Robert Carlton Reed in Vietnam. 1968

CHAPTER 71

Was Carlton an angel looking out for me from above? I wasn't sure, but *somebody* was looking out for me one night in 1998 when I was driving home from Brooklyn, New York, to my place in New Jersey at 2:00 in the morning. It was about a 60-mile drive and halfway into it, I began dozing off. I pulled my red 1998 Pontiac Grand Prix over onto the right-hand shoulder of the southbound New Jersey Turnpike that ran alongside Newark Airport and watched red eye flights touch down before closing my eyes. *In 5 minutes I'll be okay.* It was exactly 2:00 a.m. when I fell asleep because I remembered hearing the 1010-WINS-AM News Radio top-of-the-hour station identification. *"This is 1010-WINS. All-News, All-The-Time. You give us 22 minutes, we'll give you the world."* Eighteen minutes passed before I sprang from my nap and felt rested enough to drive the remaining 30 miles. Signaling to get back on the Turnpike, I reached to place the gearshift in "Drive." That was when I realized that wasn't necessary because the car was still in "Drive" with my foot resting on the brake pedal. I had been sleeping for 18 minutes with my foot on the brake and the car in "Drive!" Often, I thought there were angels looking out for me, and many other times, I thought no one gave me a second thought. One thing was for sure, *something* or *someone* kept my right foot resting on that brake pedal for 18 minutes. *I didn't know how else to describe it.*

Mumma and Da enjoyed driving fast on any stretch of highway, and so did I. There were many speeding tickets between the three of us to prove it! When I was stationed in Nebraska in 1993, a state trooper pulled me over for going 104 mph in a 55 mph zone. *I'm going to jail for the first time.* I steered my teal 1991 Honda CRX onto the right shoulder and prayed! I handed over my driver's license, registration and proof of insurance to the trooper. He stared at me. I stared back. *I know this guy from somewhere!* He was thinking the same. "I know you. You're the 'Auggie Doggie' from the Transportation Squadron over in Germany!" He laughed. "You gotta be shittin' me. You're Sgt. Lewis from the SP Squadron!" As it turned out, he and I were stationed together in Germany from 1984–87 when I was a Security Policeman. During base exercises, I always requested that particular "Auggie Doggie" (or augmentee) from the Transportation Squadron to be on my "Fire Team" while we patrolled the base searching for the "enemy." An augmentee was a person who wasn't assigned to the SP Squadron, but it was part of their "extra duties" to support my squadron during "time of war." I always wanted that guy to ride around with me in the "deuce" troop truck because he knew what to do during "enemy" skirmishes when a lot of augmentees didn't. So I kept him in the warm truck cab with me while the other augmentees on the Fire Team sat in the freezing, open-air troop section of the "deuce." I liked that guy, and now that he was a Nebraska State Trooper, I hoped that he would remember how I looked out for him during those three years of exercises! He returned my credentials. "You know, Sgt. Lewis, you always took care of me when it was cold as shit over there, and thank God you never put me in one of those freezing-ass foxholes. But hey, where in the hell are you going in such a hurry? In this little-ass car, if you flipped it over, there'd be nothing left of you. Slow down man!" "I've got no excuse, I just like driving fast, that's all." "Here's what I'm gonna do. I'm gonna give you a warning this time, but if I catch you going this fast again, I'm gonna have to take you to jail, so don't make me do that!" *I was glad I never put that guy in a foxhole!*

Only once did I fight a traffic ticket because only *once* was I "Not Guilty." I was driving back to New Jersey from Brooklyn in the company car owned by my pharmaceutical company around 7:00 p.m. in January of 1999. I pulled out of an Exxon station on the corner of Pennsylvania Avenue and Linden Boulevard to head to-

wards the Belt Parkway and back to New Jersey. I made a left onto
four-lane Pennsylvania Avenue to head toward the Belt. The bumper
of my 1998 Grand Prix hung over the double yellow line that divided Pennsylvania Avenue by about 10 inches. In Brooklyn, and
any other borough of New York City, minor traffic infractions were
an everyday occurrence. Everyone pushed the limit with traffic eti-
quette, but a member of New York's Finest considered my maneuver
inattentive driving. He cited me for "impeding the flow of traffic,"
"reckless driving," "making an illegal left turn," "expired registration" and "failure to provide proof of insurance." I explained that
the car was insured and registered with my pharmaceutical company,
but the paperwork was late arriving in the mail. "I was only over the
line by *this* much, there weren't even any cars coming." *He wasn't
buying it.* When I handed over my identification, I made a point to
show my former military I.D. card to the officer because, generally,
a lot of police officers might cut you a "break" when they saw the
card that identified you as a present or former member of the military. Many former military members went on to become civilian
law enforcement officers. *This* particular policeman would not have
cared if I were Bronx-native General Colin Powell. I received five
citations. *Count 'em! Five!*

Each time a court notice was mailed to my apartment requesting
my appearance in Brooklyn traffic court, I checked the box that
gave the option of choosing a later date. The more I delayed my appearance, the better I felt my odds were that the policeman would
miss traffic court to present his side of the story. Living in New Jersey, Macedonia Baptist Church in Trenton had become my adopted
church and was led by the very charismatic Rev. Keith Marshall.
Each of his sermons left me with a clear, positive message to consider during the week. *Even When the Lord is Late, He's Still On Time*
was the theme of Rev. Marshall's sermon the day before I was to
appear in traffic court. "God doesn't work on *your* time, you work
on *His* time, and even when *He* is late, *He* is still on time" was the
message that Sunday. Throughout the Sunday morning service, I
was praying that Jesus would be "on time" Monday morning when
I was to make an appearance at the downtown Brooklyn Traffic
Court. *Please God. Help me get outta this one!*

Walking through the halls of the traffic court, there were many police officers waiting to testify that morning. Fortunately, I didn't see the officer who had written my tickets. I was confident that my "delayed appearance" plan was going to work! He was going to be a "no-show!" Maybe he was caught in traffic. Maybe he was sick. Maybe he was out on Pennsylvania Avenue giving someone else a ticket. I didn't care where he was as long as he wasn't in court! I located my name on the case docket schedule, took a seat and watched the other poor souls plead their cases.

A middle-aged Jewish judge with the disposition of TV's *Judge Judy* would hear my case. Her Honor was conducting the court's business swiftly that Monday morning. "Bailiff, call the next name on the docket!" *Judge Judy's* twin was running her traffic court in an efficient manner, and most of those who stood before her left her courtroom defeated. I hoped that I would not be one of them. "Mr. Troy Lewis, Case Number, 12345, please come forward." I faced the Bench feeling positive that the officer would be a "no-show" because I hadn't seen him. *I was mistaken.* From out of nowhere, he was standing next to me. *Where did he come from?* At that instant, I literally thought that it was the policeman who was "on time," not Jesus. Standing in front of the judge, I looked up to the ceiling and muttered under my breath, "Thanks, Jesus. *You* really helped me out this time."

The officer and I stood in front of the judge to present our cases. He presented his version of events first. Then, it was my turn. The judge spun her chair to the left, peered over her glasses, pointed at me and said, "So Mr. Lewis, what do you have to say for yourself?" I was afraid. Afraid she wouldn't believe me, afraid I'd lose my job because of how these five citations would affect my driving record (my company wasn't going to allow me to keep their car with a poor driving record), and afraid I would blunder in front of a big-city judge. I had never been in a courtroom in my life. I began my explanation: "Ma'am, I've drawn up a diagram which I think captures what happened that night. I was a Security Policeman while I was in the Air Force, and I disagree with the officer. As you can see here, I made a left turn onto Pennsylvania Avenue. Granted, my rear bumper hung over the yellow line, but in no way did I impede the flow of traffic. There wasn't even any oncoming traffic because the light held them up on the other side, and there's no right turn on red for anyone else. I wouldn't consider my driving 'reckless' in any fashion. Also, it's a company car that has insurance. I brought the latest insurance card and a brand new registration that I tried to explain to the officer was coming. It was late arriving in the mail, that's all." She paused, leaned back and swiveled to her right. As she held up her thumb and index finger leaving an inch between the two, the judge asked in her Brooklyn accent, "So Officer, was Mr. Lewis' bumper hanging over the double line about this much?" He replied, "Well, Your Honor, it was over the line a *little* more than that." She abruptly replied, "Then *that* one's out!" Another question. "Officer, did Mr. Lewis explain that the car was indeed owned by the pharmaceutical company that he worked for, and he *did* have a registration and insurance card, but they were expired?" "Um yes, your Honor." "So you *did* know the car belonged to the pharmaceutical company?" "Uh, yes ma'am, I did." She gave a wry smile, and before I knew it, she dismissed all five charges against me. My court case took all of 5 minutes. From her bench, she looked down at me and said, "Mr. Lewis, I apologize for the Borough of Brooklyn taking up your time today. Thank you for coming in, you're free to go. Have a good day!" I gathered my notes and headed for the courtroom door. She swiveled back to her right and focused on the officer. She went after him much like Mumma did when Gerald failed to bring home his paycheck. "The next time you come into my court, your case better be a lot stronger than that one! How could you write five tickets for a borderline violation? That gentleman didn't do anything wrong and you know it." The judge was so hard on him that I almost felt bad for him, but not *too* bad! I looked up to the ceiling again and said aloud, "Jesus, I will *never* doubt you again! *You* are always on time!"

CHAPTER 72

Mumma answered many questions for me throughout my life. *God knows I had plenty of them!* Another question I needed answered was how she felt when she graduated from high school on June 7th of 1960. On that Tuesday afternoon in the hot St. Clare Walker High gymnasium *sans* air conditioning, she received two documents: The customary high school diploma and another certificate that was inscribed, *"Special Diploma for Duty Above and Beyond."* The school acknowledged her for raising her sister and brothers while managing to finish school at the same time. The school principal, Mr. Charles I. Thurston, signed her certificate, and he wasn't known to be the nicest school administrator in Middlesex County history. Years later, I learned that when we integrated in 1969, Mr. Thurston was offered the position of *assistant* principal at Middlesex High School after having been a head principal for 19 years at St. Clare Walker. Yet, the white principal that was hired only had three years of experience. Mr. Thurston chose to retire. I never knew him, but I developed a soft spot for the man that many of my aunts and uncles cursed over the years because he was so tough on them.

I often wondered how Mumma felt as she walked across the stage with the two certificates Mr. Thurston handed her that afternoon. Was she thinking, "I'm glad I'm done raising these damn kids. Patty can take my place and raise the boys. She's going on 16 now. I started when I was that age, so can she. Maybe I can go off to Philadelphia like Dee and Sister (Aunt Grace) and find a job. Maybe I can scrounge up some money and go to Virginia State College or Virginia Union University. Maybe Mrs. Holmes and Mrs. Cameron can use their connections to help me get away from *here*." But that didn't happen. I always felt like something held her back much like circumstances kept George Bailey in Bedford Falls. But then again, sometimes I thought, wherever anyone ended up in life was where they were *supposed* to be. George's father died and that kept him in Bedford Falls. Mumma got pregnant with me and that kept her in Middlesex County. Pregnant by Bill Lewis just a couple of months after she graduated. She and Da got married in October of 1960 and I came along in April of 1961 and Bridgette, 14 months after me. *Mumma wasn't going anywhere.*

Mumma's Senior Class picture. 1960

I wanted to know what Mumma's plans were when she headed home after leaving her graduation ceremony. On the other hand, I was afraid to hear her response because I felt that *I* was the reason she didn't have the opportunity to mellow earlier in life. I finally asked her in 2012. "Troy, my only thought was, 'What am I going to do tomorrow?' I had laundry to do. The house needed to be cleaned. I needed to go buy some groceries. Shoot, Tony was only 7 when I graduated. What was I gonna do? Leave him behind? Turn my back on my sister and brothers? They couldn't have done it by themselves. I wasn't gonna let Mom and Dad down." After taking care of her sister and brothers through her junior and senior years of high school, Mumma was still interested in their welfare. She was in it for the long haul. "Did you ever think about going in the military to get away?" "Back then, women didn't just go off and join the military like they do today. It was a different time. I figured I'd just stay in Middlesex and see what happened." Many adjectives could describe Mumma; selfish wasn't one of them.

CHAPTER 73

When Sharon, Bridgette and I were coming along, Mumma *never* allowed us to leave the house with a spot on our clothes. "I will *not* have dirty kids leaving my house." If butter fell from toast onto my shirt as I was collecting my books to walk to the school bus, I was not allowed to leave the house. "Go right upstairs and change. Hurry up. The bus is coming! I don't care how poor we are, I will *not* have dirty kids leaving *my* house." *I know Mumma. I've heard it 4000 times before.* I became just like her when I grew up. I introduced Mumma to the people who ran my dry cleaners in New Jersey, and they all came from behind the counter to hug her. "Your son finds spots we never see! He gives us plenty of business!" *I was a reflection of her.*

But our mother/son relationship was tumultuous and remained so for a long time. At times, I thought she was only proud of me on *two* occasions in my life: When I showed Mr. Whitley my reading comprehension skills, and when I finally finished college. I think my mother showed her love through encouragement and support. No matter how much any of us screwed up in life, Mumma was there for us. *Trust me, we screwed up a lot!* When we were younger, if any of us complained about a piece of homework we couldn't decipher, her oft-used reply was, "There is no such word as 'can't!'" But what she was really saying was, "You can do it!" *Exhibiting* love through hugs and kisses just wasn't her strength. Then again, I think her being tough on me was her way of loving me. She prepared me for life. Unfortunately, sometimes I just wasn't as strong as I needed to be, and that story is coming.

I was pretty certain my mother never read a book on how to be a "mother." I doubt if any mother, black or white, was reading one of those in Middlesex County in the 1960s and 1970s. What was Mumma going to do? Read a book on child rearing that discussed how spanking is *not* a good form of discipline for a child? *I don't think so!* What was some Ph.D. with no kids who'd written a book on child rearing going to teach her? When I was growing up, I didn't know any mother who *didn't* spank their child, and often, they used a *switch!* For the fortunate individuals who didn't know what a switch was, it was a small branch from a tree. It wasn't quite large enough to be considered a limb, and it definitely was not small enough to be coined a twig. A switch, at least for me, was reserved for *severe* misbehavior. For being a smart mouth, crossing the road without permission or using one of the "new" words Darnell or Tony had taught me. Mumma yelled, "Go find me a *good* one and bring it back. Hurry up, God-dammit!" A *good* one should not have been too dry because it might snap on contact with flesh and bone. It also couldn't be fresh because it might prove flimsy and not deliver the proper sting. Mumma wanted it to be just like it was for Goldilocks. "Just right!" If I didn't have the guts to pick a "good" one from a tree, that really pissed her off, resulting in a worse beating. I preferred to get it over with the first time, so *most* of the time, I tried to pick ones I knew would be to her liking. Spankings made Bridgette and me cry but not my cousin, Sharon. *She* was tough. She wouldn't give her Aunt Jean that satisfaction. I don't ever remember Sharon crying. Not once. Butley said, "Sharon Latimore was the only girl I was ever afraid of in my life!"

One night when Mumma and Da were at a P.T.A. meeting for Sharon, Bridgette and me, the three of us were chasing one another in the house, and we knew that was a "no-no." Playing in the house wasn't allowed. "If ya wanna play, take your asses outside," Mumma always said. Well, we *were* playing in the house, and somehow, one of us toppled Mumma's large vanity mirror. *Uh oh.* Ronnie, Darnell and Tony came running into the bedroom when they heard the breaking glass. I think it was Darnell who said, "I don't know how y'all are gonna explain that one to Jean, but the three of y'all would be better off dead!" *He was probably right*. When Mumma and Da walked in, they could tell something was wrong by the looks on our faces. Seeing the broken glass, she asked, "Who did it?" Sharon, Bridgette and I had forgotten how to speak. "That's just great. Now all three of you get a beating." It was too dark outside to go searching for a switch, but Mumma always had a backup plan. A belt, a flyswatter, a bedroom slipper or a loafer. It didn't matter. She just wanted something that would sting! Her favorite option was the wooden Heat for the Seat paddle. We always tried hiding that thing from her, but she usually found it. "Go line up against the couch and stick your butts up in the air!" Sharon and Bridgette came up with the brilliant idea to stuff toilet paper in their underwear to lessen the sting. "Y'all are crazy. Mumma's gonna find out. She's gonna see that toilet paper sticking out of your pants, and then y'all are really gonna get it!" *I took the honest route*. We knelt against the couch and lifted our buttocks as she whaled the paddle against our rear ends. She went back and forth between the three of us. Sharon and Bridgette were screaming and begging her to stop, but I could see their faces. They were smiling! I wasn't. I was crying like a baby! Once finished, Mumma said, "Now, get your black asses in bed!" We marched upstairs. Sharon and Bridgette were giggling like they'd just come back from the carnival that was across the road from our place every August. They teased me until we fell asleep. I think that was the only time any of us ever outsmarted Mumma. *Well, at least Sharon and Bridgette did it once!*

Mumma was difficult, and patience wasn't her strong point. So when I failed to grasp something as simple as learning to tie my shoes in 1st grade, she got annoyed. I became afraid to ask her how to do something, especially if she had already shown me once or twice. I didn't want to hear, "Are you stupid or something?" As Gentree got older, sometimes he, too, didn't want to listen to her, so he tuned her out. He chose a rocky path, and every time I came home from the Air Force, Mumma said to me, "Go find your brother and talk some sense into him." I wanted to say to her, "Mumma, Gentree is 'out there.' You can't save him." But I didn't. I didn't have the heart to hurt her with those words. *She never gave up on anybody.* Gentree did once say to me, "I can't believe you went off to the Air Force and left me here with her!" "Gentree, do yourself a favor and listen to *what* she says, not *how* she says it. Mumma has nothing but good intentions. She has your best interest at heart, but it's her tone that will drive you nuts. She only wants what is best for you." He didn't want to listen to me, either. I felt sorry for him because I knew she could be unbearable at times. I understood his frustration. That being said, I tried not to disappoint her with *my* life choices. I learned to forgive her. I forgave Da for all of the shit he did. I could certainly forgive Mumma. What was the point of being angry for 50 years anyway? Was she a perfect mother? No! Was I a perfect son? Absolutely not! Everyone had imperfections; that's what made us human. And when I really gave it some thought, I would not have wanted anyone else to be my mom or my dad. They both tried their best. They did some things well and some things not so well. *Didn't we all?* I learned to be like them in many ways and unlike them in others. Often, I made the same mistakes they did.

I thanked Mumma every day of my life for all of the positive things she taught me. "There's no such word as 'can't.'" Definition: "You can do it. Don't give up!" "Mumma has no hands." Definition: "Always open the door for a lady." "Books will take you anywhere." Definition: "You don't have to actually visit a place to have knowledge about it." "Pay your bills and you'll be able to buy anything." Definition: "Good credit gives you freedom." "Get your mind off of those girls and in those books!" Definition: "Not applicable to me!"

The infatuation with young ladies began when I was 5 years old. The Panthers from Ruthville High School of Charles City County were visiting the Wolverines of St. Clare Walker for a basketball game. Darnell and Tony took me to the crowded gym and planted me in the bleachers with a Coke and popcorn. It was my first time at a high school game or any game, for that matter, and they left me sitting there while they went off to do whatever they did at 15 and 13 years old. I watched our guards Oscar Fitchett (my first hero who died from cancer after inhaling fumes for 20 years while working in the Lincoln Tunnel) and Stanley Redmond (who was killed in

Vietnam right after he graduated) get one layup after another while the numbers were posted on the scoreboard. They were a tough backcourt and led the Wolverines pretty far in the "colored" state basketball "tuna"-ment that year. The scoreboard displayed "Home" and "Visitor," and I kept forgetting if the Wolverines were "Home" or "Visitor." *I wasn't very sharp at 5 years old!* I asked one of the girls cheering for Ruthville to tell me who was winning. She picked me up and sat me on her lap to explain. *I can die right here!* She had a sister sitting on her left and right. They were "stairsteps." A senior, a junior and a sophomore. Each of them "fought" over me to become their "boyfriend." Darnell and Tony came to check on me at some point and when they saw my "women," they tried flirting with them. *I was jealous for the first time in my life.* I thought the girls would be interested in my uncles since they were closer to them in age. To my surprise, the girls told Darnell and Tony they already had a "boyfriend" and his name was Troy. They sent my uncles away!

After the game, one of the sisters said, "You have to come to Ruthville next week. We're gonna play y'all again in the 'tuna'-ament. The pep bus will only be $1. You should come. We'll be waiting for you!" I had no idea where Ruthville was, but that wasn't going to keep me from trying to get there! *I would walk if I had to!* It was 40 miles away. "We hope you can make it! We'll wait for you in front of the school when your bus pulls up!" I said, "Okay, I'll tell my Mumma!"

When Mumma picked Darnell, Tony and me up after the game, I told her that I needed to bust my piggy bank for four quarters or ten dimes. "First of all, it's burst, not bust!" *Huh?* "Why do you need to burst your piggy bank for a dollar?" "My 'girlfriends' want me to come to Ruthville for the game next week." She laughed and asked Darnell and Tony, "What's that boy talking about now?" They told her that I met some "older women" who wanted to see me again. On the drive home, Mumma said, "Troy, those girls were just being nice to you. They were teasing. You can't believe *everything* girls say." "No, they weren't! They *promised* they would wait for me." "Okay, we'll make a *compromise.* Do you know what *that* is?" "No, ma'am." *Great, another word I'll have to look up in the dictionary when we get home.* "You can go to the game next week." *Yeah!* "But, you can't break your piggy bank." *Shoot!* "You are not spending your money on girls at 5 years old." *Mumma!* "You can earn money this week by doing extra stuff around the house." *No problem!* "And in case the girls aren't waiting for you, I'll go on the bus with you to Ruthville." *Fine with me, you'll get to see how pretty my "girlfriends" are!* I did the extra chores and Friday finally arrived. On the long bus ride to Ruthville, Mumma warned that the sisters wouldn't be waiting. "Troy, those girls were just having fun with you." But when the bus pulled in front of the brick building that was the Ruthville High School, I peered from the bus window searching for the three sisters. They were jumping up and down on the sidewalk waiting for me! At the time, I was missing some teeth, but that didn't keep me from smiling! I turned to look at Mumma and said, "See, I told ya!" She was shocked! *I wasn't!* I hopped off the bus and walked over to "my" girls. One of them said to Mumma, "Thanks for bringing your little boy to the game. We'll take care of him!" And off we went! I sat in the Ruthville cheering section and could have cared less about Oscar Fitchett and Stanley Redmond. I caught Mumma's eye as she sat across the gym from me with those who came over on the pep bus. She smiled and shook her head back and forth in amazement. *I was 5 years old, and I had 3 women!* I think St. Clare Walker won the game, but the score wasn't important. The girls returned me to Mumma for the trip back to Middlesex, and they thanked her again for bringing me to the game. I took my seat next to Mumma on the school bus and beamed. She smiled at me and said, "Those sure were some pretty girls." *Yes, they were!* "What am I gonna do with you, boy?" I had no answer. *I wish I could remember their names!*

Me (hiding my missing teeth), Bridgette and Sharon. 1967

CHAPTER 74

Mumma once told me that life was a test every day, and she was certainly right about that. Life would test you. I failed a bunch of its examinations, but each time, I learned from the mistake. Like an Air Force colonel once told me, "Experience was what you got when you got what you didn't want." Grandpop Lewis' funeral in 1994 taught me another lesson. It was desperation that led me to steal money from my place of employment. It was *only* $50, and I felt I needed it more than my employer did. Like I said, I was desperate. Fifty dollars was plenty of gas money for a round trip from Nebraska to Virginia for Grandpop's funeral. I was making about $17,000 a year in the Air Force, so an extra $50 was a great deal of money. I had a part-time job at Homer's Records and Tapes for about three years and loved working there, but I was angry that management wouldn't increase my minimum wage salary. I wanted a 25¢ increase, and since they refused, I wanted to get even. *Life was testing me.*

Grandpop Lewis was three years short of 100 when he died, and I was going home to say goodbye to the man who used to give me and Bridgette Barnum & Bailey Animal Crackers. At 89¢ a gallon, I knew my teal 1991 Honda CRX could make the round trip on $50 with plenty of gas left in the tank. *God, did I love that car!* Before taking off to Virginia for the 23-hour one-way trip, I worked the late shift with the Homer's assistant manager, Marc. He was a nice kid about 20 years old and was the biggest Prince fan I'd ever met.

When he turned 21, he drove from Omaha to Prince's club in Minneapolis for his first legal drink!

On the night that found Marc and me missing $50, we scoured the Ticketmaster machine in the rear of the store, the main register up front and the four aisles between the wooden shelves that held CDs. Everywhere. We couldn't find that $50 bill. We remembered a customer handing over one that was placed under the cash tray. So we looked there. Nothing. "Where did it go?" "I don't know!" We knew our manager would not be happy that we were "short." We continued looking for about another 15 to 20 minutes after we locked the front doors, but we couldn't find it. Marc went to the rear of the store to start the nightly accounting paperwork before he and I deposited cash and checks in the First National Bank of Omaha night drop-box about 100 feet away. (I had to follow him in my car like I was a security guard.) While he crunched the numbers, I swept and vacuumed before taking garbage and cardboard boxes out to the dumpster we shared with other strip mall occupants. Below each cash register, there were two small plastic trashcans, one under the Ticketmaster register and another below the front register. I dumped trash into a Hefty bag before heading outside to the dumpster. While pouring the front register's trashcan contents into the bag, a $50 bill gently floated into it. Somehow it had fallen out of the register. Was it good luck? Divine intervention? Or Fate? *I wasn't sure, and I didn't care.* Marc was in the back. He wouldn't know. I had the gas money I needed to get on Interstate 80 and Interstate 29 and Interstate 70 and finally, Interstate 64 before pulling into Mumma's driveway. *I learned this route a long time ago on one of Mumma's maps!* I debated doing the right thing for about two seconds before slipping the $50 bill into my pocket.

I slung the Hefty bag over my shoulder and headed to the dumpster feeling vindicated. As I lifted the dumpster's lid, though, my conscience said to me, "Troy Lewis, your Mumma and Da didn't raise you to steal anybody's $50 no matter how much you need it. Are you really going to drive to your minister grandfather's funeral on stolen gas money? That just doesn't seem like a good thing. You could show up at the funeral and say to him in his casket, 'Hi,

Grandpop. I made it to your funeral all the way from Nebraska, and I filled up for free! Aren't you proud of your grandson?'" I closed the dumpster lid, walked back inside of the store and said to Marc, "Dude, I found that $50. It fell in the trash." "Thanks, dude." And that was that. We punched out, and I followed Marc to First National as we dropped off the cash and checks and headed home.

During the short drive home, I cursed my existence. *I didn't even have enough money to go home for a funeral.* I was angry for not making more money, for not studying harder when I had the chance in college, for *not* stealing the $50 bill, for having to use a credit card to pay for gas to go home. I didn't like my life. I hated my life. But the saddest part of my drive home was the realization that my life and its circumstances were all the result of my actions. That was a sobering thought. *If I had just kept the $50, I wouldn't be having this uncomfortable conversation, at least not tonight anyway.*

I parked the car and walked into the Base Housing home where Lori and I lived and headed upstairs to shower. As I undressed, Lori asked, "What time are you leaving in the morning?" She knew I would drive 23 hours straight to Virginia. It was a game for me. I always liked driving while trying to outsmart state troopers and battling fatigue. I liked to imagine that I was a racecar driver participating in the 24 Hours of Le Mans. I liked to drive fast. It was what I saw Mumma and Da do; I think it was part of my DNA. Mumma slowed down when she got older. Da never did. Driving or living. *Me neither.* "Oh, I'll get up and leave around 6:00." "Well, hurry up and take your shower and get in the bed." The shower was running when Lori yelled from the bedroom, "I forgot to tell you. There's a letter on the dining room table from your mother." "Ok, I'll look at it when I get out." *Mumma wrote me a letter? What is that about?* Out of the shower, I threw on a tee shirt, a pair of shorts and ran downstairs to see what she'd written. The short note read: "Hi, I thought you might need a little help in coming home for Rev. Lewis' funeral. Enclosed is $50. Love, Mumma." *Are you kidding me?*

I often thought that if I *had* taken that $50, Fate might have had Lori forget to tell me there was a letter downstairs, or maybe Fate had the mailman place Mumma's letter in our mailbox the *next* day when I was already on I-80 and I-29 and I-70 and I-64. I often debated about which was my companion in life, *Destiny* or *Fate*. The former dealt with the "finality of events," while the latter dealt with "predetermination." I never figured out which accompanied me on my journey. I did know that I didn't always enjoy the ride. *Did any of us?* But on the night before I drove to Grandpop Lewis' funeral, *I* made the decision to do the right thing. Then again, maybe it wasn't *I* who made the decision to hand over the $50 bill to Marc. Maybe it was listening to Grandpop Lewis preach on the radio when I was 6 years old about sin or Grandma Latimore teaching me the game of Solitaire while scolding against "cheating myself" or Technical Sergeant Michael Wentling teaching me when I was an Airman in Germany that once you become a Sergeant, "*You* set the example. Who cares what everybody else is doing?" Maybe *I* had nothing to do with it after all. *Or maybe I did.*

Mumma didn't recall the note or the money when I mentioned it to her many years later, and I said to her, "How could you remember *all* of the nice things you've done for me?" "You know, Troy, life will test you every day. It puts a lot of pressure on you. Sometimes you fail, sometimes you succeed, but you always have to do what is right." *Sometimes I succeeded. Sometimes I didn't.*

CHAPTER 75

As I got older, I was fortunate to have a number of supervisors that showed support and offered encouragement at various points in my life. There were also a few who simply weren't good people and went to great lengths to make things difficult for me and other subordinates. A few didn't have my best interest (or anyone else's for that matter) at heart, but I was fortunate to learn from both sets of people. Some people woke up thinking, "How can I help someone today?" Many others woke up thinking, "Whose life can I make miserable today?" Fortunately, most of the people I met were "helpers," not "immobilizers." One supervisor, who didn't have my best interest at heart, encouraged me to apply for a new position because it would be "a great opportunity!" Twenty minutes later, she told my good friend and counterpart to not apply for the same position "because it's a step down and you won't be able to grow in that role." There were three open positions performing the same role. Why was it "good" for me, but "bad" for my friend? That supervisor was not a "helper!" She was an "immobilizer!" But the more and more I learned about people like that, I saw their pettiness and often wondered how bitter and miserable they must have been on the inside, and at times, I felt sorry for them. Other times, I didn't! *Why wouldn't you just want to help someone? I never understood why people didn't want to do that.*

Captain Theresa Meyer was a "helper," and she changed my life. She was the O.I.C., Officer in Charge, of the Current Intelligence section when I was stationed in Nebraska. I worked the 3:00 a.m. to 11:00 a.m. shift in an area known as "The Watch" at U.S.A.F. Strategic Air Command Headquarters. We monitored global hotspots, and at 3 in the morning, it was my responsibility to review intelligence message traffic and compile a two- to three-page intelligence summary for General flag officer review. Capt. Meyer reported to work at 6:00 a.m. to review and critique my summary. After a few days had passed, she pulled me aside and said, "You know, Sgt. Lewis, what you write each day is really pretty good. I only make minor changes to what you've put together." "Thank you, Capt. Meyer." "How did you learn to write so well? Did you go to college before you came in the military?" "Yes, ma'am, I did, but that was a while ago. I'll probably never go back. I'm too busy now. I like coaching sports and coming to work and just living my life."

With her next sentence, she took my life in a totally different direction. Up to that point, I was content to stay in the military for 20 years and get my pension. I really had no desire or intentions to do anything else. Get up, go to work, coach youth league sports, coach my squadron basketball and softball teams, play flag football and just live my life. "I'll tell you what, Sgt. Lewis. If you don't go back to school, it'll reflect on your A-P-R." An A-P-R was the Air Force's Annual Performance Report. "Capt. Meyer, you can't do that! I don't have to go to school." With a playful grin, she said, "You're right, you don't. But I'm your O-I-C, and I can pretty much do anything I want when it comes to your A-P-R, and there isn't much you can do about that now is there? How do you like those apples, Sgt. Lewis?" I stood there puzzled. I knew I should go back to school to finish my degree, but I was having too much fun enjoying life. I was married to Lori, and we were getting along very well. Bear came over on Friday nights to stay with us through the weekend, and there was *nothing* like "weekend" child rearing because we got to give him back to his parents on Sunday night! The only real complaint I had was that I didn't make a lot of money. *Often, I thought that God would provide me with what I needed. No more than that and no less than that.* However, at that time, I was still *lying* to Mumma by telling her that I had graduated from Shippensburg State College years ago. That was shameful, but from my perspective, telling her the truth was even more shaming. *Maybe Capt. Meyer in my life was a good thing.* By the way, Mumma knew all along that I hadn't graduated. She told me years later, "I just liked watching you squirm whenever the topic came up!" "Mumma!"

Captain Meyer said, "Sgt. Lewis, the military will pay for everything, even your books. You really have no excuse not to go back. You're obviously smart enough to do the work." Every few days, she asked if I had registered for school, and I'd shrug my shoulders. "No, ma'am. Not yet!" "That's fine. It's your A-P-R. But you know the military frowns on people not trying to better themselves." The military wanted good citizens. People who tried to improve themselves and help others in the community, by working with Boy and Girl Scouts, senior citizens or volunteering at a local hospital. It didn't matter what it was as long as it was positive. I felt that coaching youth sports was good enough for me, but Capt. Meyer said to me one day, "Sgt. Lewis, coaching sports is great, and I know you're having fun coaching Bear and the other kids. But in the long run, where is that gonna get you?" *This lady is serious about me going back to school, and I think she will make it reflect on my A-P-R. She isn't going to drop this college thing. Shit!*

Captain Meyer's persistence forced me to sign up for classes, and it only took me about a year and a half to graduate with all of the credits that I had accumulated at Shippensburg. Going back to school indeed changed my life because a couple of years later, a "RIF" (Reduction-in-Force) order was issued by the Clinton Administration, and I needed to find a job within *two* months. Thankfully, I had a college degree to begin a job search, and had it not been for Capt. Meyer "forcing" me to sign up for classes, I wasn't sure what I would have done. It was like she gave me the *gas money* I would need for the rest of my life.

After signing up for classes, there were two people that helped me with the *one* math class I needed to graduate. By my calculation, they were two of the least likely candidates to do so because I barely knew either of them. Since Capt. Meyer had "strong-armed" me into completing my bachelor's degree, I was now attending the University of Nebraska-Omaha, where Nebraskans were fond of saying tongue-in-cheek, the "N" stood for Knowledge! One algebra class was required to complete my degree, and that subject scared the shit outta me. After 7th grade, math became more and more difficult, so whenever possible, I avoided it. *My brain just wasn't meant to do anything other than basic arithmetic.* I needed a "C" or better to graduate. On the day before my first Saturday morning class began, I was discussing my math inadequacies with coworkers on "The Watch" when Lieutenant Roland Darey walked over and said, "Hey, Sgt. Lewis, I'll help you with your class. I was a Math minor at the Air Force Academy." I had never said anything to Lt. Darey other than "Good morning, Lt. Darey" and now, he was going to be my new best friend! Lt. Darey was *gas money*!

After the first day of the algebra class, I spoke with the professor and discussed my shortcomings with all things mathematical. I don't remember his name, but I let him know that I would never miss a class, that I would be there promptly every Saturday morning at 8, and that I would try my best to do well in his class, but algebra really intimidated me. Algebra and chemistry were always tough subjects for me because equations were involved, and sometimes my brain just froze when it was time to solve them. In the relaxed atmosphere of the classroom, I could usually figure them out or raise my hand to ask for guidance, but put an exam in front of me and give me an hour to answer 20 questions, and I froze like a deer in front of a tractor trailer. I worried that I would forget certain steps and you know what? I usually did. It was really sad. It truly was. It made me feel dumb.

The math professor didn't make any promises. His only comment was, "Best of luck to you this semester." *That didn't sound promising.* I was there every Saturday morning at 8, and I never missed a class. Lt. Darey helped me throughout the semester, and I grew anxious as "Finals" week approached. I had an "A" or a "B" in my other classes, but the algebra class? I had a 68 average going into the final exam. A low "B" or high "C" would allow me to graduate, but a low "B" probably wasn't likely. That would be akin to thinking *21 Jump Street's* and *Hangin' with Mr. Cooper's* Holly Robinson Peete would want to spend time with me!

(Insert "Just The Two of Us" by Grover Washington, Jr. and Bill Withers) I had a huge crush on her when she was on those TV shows in the 1990s. Then, a few years later I got to hang out with her with at the 2003 Atlanta NBA All-Star game because my girl-friend, Kat, worked for a company that was hosting a cocktail event for the game. *Just kill me now!* Holly was doing promotional work for Kat's company, and Kat introduced me to her! There I was sip-ping wine and making "small talk" with Holly for about 10 minutes while Kat "worked the room." *Just the two of us! Holly and me! Was this Troy Lewis from Middlesex County hanging out with Holly Robin-son Peete sipping Pinot Grigio at a cocktail table at an NBA All-Star game party? Crazy!* Of course, Holly and I never dated, but I could tell Butley that she and I had spent a few moments alone together! The following day, it got even better!

I was on the Ritz-Carlton hotel elevator going down to get a Pepsi for breakfast. *Don't tell Mumma I was having a Pepsi for breakfast!* At one floor, former NBA All-Star Tim Hardaway, creator of the "killer crossover" move got on. *Wow! What am I doing here!* Next stop, Amar'e Stoudamire, 2003 NBA Rookie of the Year got on. *Unbelievable!* There I am on the elevator with two big-time NBA names and when the elevator doors opened again there stood Holly. She hopped on and said, "Hey, Troy! What are you up to today?" "Oh, I'm just going down to get something to drink from the gift shop. How's your day going?" Out of the corner of my eye, I saw Tim and Amar'e stare at each other. *Who the hell is this Troy guy!*

The algebra exam was the "take-home" variety and could be picked up on Friday morning at 8:00. My classmates and I had 24 hours to work on the 20 equations, then, show up Saturday morning with a blank piece of paper to demonstrate that we could actually do the work. Lt. Darey walked me through the unraveling of each problem. Then he showed me again. Then it was my turn to show him. We worked on the equations through Friday night into Satur-day morning. Lt. Darey made solving math problems look as easy as Mrs. Johnson playing "Home on the Range!" We worked on those 20 questions until I felt comfortable. *Well, I was never really "comfortable" because it was math!* My coworkers on "The Watch" laughed at my anxiety. "Sgt. Lewis, you'll be fine. You've got it now! Go home and sleep on it." No way was I going to sleep! A nap might cause forgetfulness. I couldn't take that chance. I might forget what "*x*" equaled!

Around 7:30 the following morning, I thanked Lt. Darey for his patience during the night and throughout the semester. I grabbed my backpack to head over to the old Martin bomber plant that built the B-26 *Marauder* and B-29 *Superfortress* aircraft during World War II, but now was a 1.7 million square foot multifunctional office building called "Building D." I was slightly confident when I walked into the makeshift classroom to grab a blank exam from the professor's desk at 8:00 a.m. for my hour-long exam. I took my seat and began solving the equations. *I know this stuff! I've been working on it all night!* I answered the first five questions with ease and then panic set in. *Uh oh. I'm gonna forget a step.* I froze. I sat there praying that the steps Lt. Darey had shown me just a few hours ago would return to my thought process. But they marched right out of my head. Sadly, once again, I was inept when it came to math. As the clock slowly ticked to 9, I sat there wondering if I'd ever graduate. I answered 5 questions out of 20. I placed my exam on the professor's desk. *Nope, I'm never going to graduate. I am dumb.* At that point, it was the absolute saddest day of my life.

Lori was making breakfast when I stepped inside of our duplex. "So how did it go?" I slid into a dining room chair, placed my head on the table and cried for about 20 minutes. I sobbed while Lori rubbed my neck and kept asking, "What happened? What's wrong?" I couldn't say anything intelligible. Finally, I lifted my head to wipe the snot from my nose with the sleeve of my shirt like a child. *At that point, I had no shame.* "Lori, I swear to God, I am so fucking stupid. I'm never gonna fucking graduate. I only answered 5 questions. I'm gonna have to do this shit all over again next semester." I probably cried off and on for about 2 hours. *I felt worthless.* Lori, forever the optimist, said, "Well, maybe something will work out. Miracles do happen." "Lori, did you hear me? I answered 5 fucking questions outta 20. I'm done. Lt. Darey is gonna be so disappointed. I let Mumma and Sandra V. down again. I'm a fucking idiot."

"Well, Troy, you're not an idiot. You just got scared that's all. You do that sometimes. It will be okay." "Lori, ask me who won the first Heisman Trophy in 1939. Ask me who won the first Triple Crown in horse racing in 1919. Ask me the only U.S. President to serve non-successive terms. Ask me to interpret Charles Dickens. Ask me the 14th Amendment to the U.S. Constitution. But ask me to solve 20 simple algebra questions, and I can't do it because I'm a fucking idiot." "Look, you said the professor will post your scores at noon, right?" "Yeah." "So, go back at 12:00 and see what you got. You never know." "Whatever." I fell asleep on the couch watching a VHS tape of Carolina beating Duke (that always made me feel better), and Lori woke me at 11:50 a.m.

Why am I even driving over here? Building D was about a one-mile drive and the posted speed limit at Offutt AFB was 25 miles per hour. *That gave me even more time to think.* The bulletin board outside of the classroom held the final grade scores using a personal code. I ran my index finger down the sheet of paper and located my score. Next to my code was a "C+." *That can't be right!* I pulled the computer printout page from my backpack to confirm my code. "8888." *That's the right code.* I looked at the bulletin board again and blinked. There was still a "C+" next to my code. I walked into the class to speak with the professor who was still seated at his desk going over paperwork. "Excuse me, sir. I think you gave me the wrong grade. I know I didn't pass." "Yes, you did." "No, sir, I don't think so. I only got 5 questions right. The other 15, I just stared at 'em for an hour." "Sgt. Lewis, you passed. You showed up every day. You always participated. You had a great attitude, and you tried. Now, take your 'C+' and go graduate from college." *Oh, my God. I don't believe he just said that.* That Saturday morning began as one of the worst days of my life, and now it was probably the happiest of my life. I was going to graduate in 1992 after beginning college in 1979. I was 31 years old and a soon-to-be college graduate. Mumma raised a bunch of us, but only Sharon and Ronnie graduated from college. *Now, I could walk across the podium like them.*

CHAPTER 76

The more I thought about my life, the more I realized I never really planned any of it. Maybe that was shortsighted on my part. *Who knew?* Lots of people I met and worked with had goals they wanted to reach. They spent each day thinking about the "next" job. Some of them were rather ruthless and even worse, devious and scheming. I never understood that type of behavior. I always felt that when you were old and gray and near death, would you remember the "jobs" you had and what you did to get them, or would you remember the "people" you worked with and "how" you treated them and "how" they treated you? Did you help them? That was all I ever wanted to do. Help people. I wasn't saying my thought process was correct. It was just what worked for me. I wasn't in a constant search for the next rung on the corporate ladder. All I ever tried to do was help others like so many had done for me. *My only work aspirations were to keep helping people and getting paid every other Friday!* I came to see that it was the random people in my life who provided me with *gas money* from the time I was a little boy until I was in my 50s. I tried to do the same. In fact, it was a random person that I met in a parking lot who led me to getting a job in the pharmaceutical industry.

While I was in the Air Force, I also worked as a UPS part-time loader of boxes. *I loved that job because you got to "work out" and get paid for it!* I parked my Honda CRX in the same spot every evening, and each evening I saw the same guys and girls in business suits driving the same cars, Chevy Luminas. *Why do these people all drive the same car and why aren't they dressed like me in shorts and a tee shirt and boots? I'm dressed like a bum! Why aren't they?* One evening while walking into the facility, I asked one of the guys who had just pulled his Lumina into a parking spot, "Who are you guys and girls who drive the same car and wear suits every day?" "Oh, we're sales representatives." *There are no sales reps in the Air Force. What the hell is that?* I asked him, "What's a sales rep?" "Well, all of those boxes that you guys load, sales reps go out and set up contracts with those companies to convince them to use UPS instead of somebody else." "Okay. I didn't know that's the way it worked. I have one more question." "Sure, go ahead." "Why is it that all of y'all drive the *same* car?" "Oh! *Those* are company cars. UPS gives them to us." "They give you a fucking car? Are you fucking kidding me?" He wasn't. That UPS sales rep gave me *gas money* that day because I now knew what I wanted to do if I ever got out of the Air Force. I was going to find a job where you got a "free" car, and that's what I ended up doing.

I never was quite sure where I was going, but I slowly began to realize: What was the point in worrying about that? So far, a lot of things had worked out for me. I also used to worry about Mumma and Da and Gerald growing old all the time. Honestly, I worried about that pretty much *every* day once I turned 30 or so. Thoughts of them growing old and feeble haunted me. None of them took the best care of themselves (not that I was a perfect physical specimen, but I was younger than they were, so I had years on my side). I worried about them a lot more than I did myself. Despite all of the disagreements I had with Mumma, Da and Gerald over the years, all I could think about was their care as they got older. *That* worried me for about 14 years or so. Then Da collapsed in his bathroom and died in about 20 seconds. When I was following the ambulance to the hospital, I was thinking, "I sure spent a lot of time worrying for nothing." God had his own plan for Da. From that point on, I quit worrying about stuff. *What was the point? Worrying wouldn't change a thing.*

CHAPTER 77

One of my first district managers was Mike Labat. A wiser man, I never met. I really liked Mike, but I wasn't alone because *everyone* liked Mike. He was the only person I *ever* worked with that I never heard anyone say a negative word about. He tried to help people every day, always saw the big picture and hated B.S.! Mike was a black guy in his 60s from New Orleans, and a more dapper dresser, I never met. From head to toe, his attire was impeccable. Then I met his wife, Connie, and I thought, "Good God, this guy really possesses excellent taste in *everything.*" One year, I gave Connie a black ceramic angel to place atop their Christmas tree, but I told her it should have been her up there instead because she was prettier than any angel I had ever seen! *She liked that!* Connie looked at Mike and said, "He's a good salesman!" Mike replied, "That's why I hired him!"

The first time Mike gave me *gas money*, we were attending a dinner program that our company sponsored and after dinner concluded, all I wanted to do was get home. The dinner was held in Manhattan's Roseland Ballroom, and it was followed by a night of ballroom dancing. *What the hell am I doing at an event where there's going to be ballroom dancing! There was no ballroom dancing in Middlesex County! Get me outta here!* I headed in the direction of the coat check closet before Mike stopped me. "Where are you going?" "Aw, Mike. I don't belong in this place. What the hell do I know about ballroom dancing? I'm gonna take off." "Nobody said you had to dance. Just watch. It's the experience that counts. Let me tell you something, you're gonna be in a bunch of situations with these doctors where you'll think you don't 'belong.' I'm gonna give you a piece of advice: In *any* situation, 'always act like you belong.'" He continued, "And, if you keep doing that, pretty soon, you'll start to think that you do 'belong.'" I never forgot that. *Always act like you belong.* Going forward, when I found myself in awkward situations, I remembered Mike and the Roseland Ballroom, and it made me feel more comfortable.

It was Mike and a handful of others who helped me meet Kat when I was too afraid to introduce myself. *Pretty girls intimidated me, and she was pretty!* Mike, Donnie and I were having dinner at B. Smith's Restaurant on 46th Street in Manhattan with a few physicians. Across the way from us was a table of four, two guys and two girls. It looked like a double date to me, but Mike and Donnie were always smarter than I. They kept saying, "She's not on a date. That girl is checking you out." "No, she's not! Y'all are crazy!" They didn't know it at the time, but I hadn't initiated contact with a female since 1984!

(Insert "Caribbean Queen" by Billy Ocean) When I was stationed in Germany, there was a dance club that I liked go to on the weekends – Ka-zar-bra's, in the city of Kaiserslautern. Many Friday and Saturday nights, I saw a young black lady there who I thought was gorgeous. Every now and then we made eye contact and smiled at each other. Finally, after a couple of Fridays had passed and maybe a few more Saturdays, I said to myself, "I'm gonna ask her to dance!" I really thought her frequent smile indicated that she was interested in me. I walked over when Billy Ocean's "Caribbean Queen" came on. "Would you like to dance?" She declined. "Okay, I'm confused. I thought we had been checking each other out for a while?" She took a deep breath and said, "No, not really. I only keep looking at you because I hope that you'll quit looking at me." *Ouch!* I never approached a female again. Until Kat Peeler.

My group had been at the restaurant for some time while Kat and I continued to make occasional eye contact. At one point, one of the physicians jokingly suggested, "If you don't go over there and speak to that young lady, then you'll no longer be welcome in my office!" Mike said, "Boy, you better get your ass up from here!" A few minutes later, Kat headed to the rest room. I followed her. I waited by the wall pay phone near the rest room to make my move! *And yes, it was slightly stalker-like!* I held the phone receiver to my ear and pretended that I was using the phone when I saw her emerge from the Ladies Room. Beaded perspiration danced on my forehead as I asked, "Are you checking me out or am I checking you out?" She giggled and said, "I think we both are!" We exchanged business cards and thus began our relationship. I often wondered why I had been pushed to pursue Kat that evening. *Life was funny like that, I guess.* There was no way for me to know it, but our chance encounter would later have a huge impact on my life. But, then again, I *never* realized someone was placing *gas money* in my pocket until much later.

As sales reps, Donnie and I were pretty much inseparable (although Mike wanted us working apart). We had a lot of fun working as a two-man team and did quite well in our Brooklyn, New York territory. However, there was a time when Donnie and I thought Mike was going to terminate the two of us for exercising poor judgment. We took some clients out to a Manhattan steakhouse, and allowed them to go overboard with the wine list. Our tally was well over our monthly budget by at least $3,000, but we thought it would be okay because he and I were generating a lot of revenue for the company. *Wrong!* It was a typical Friday morning and Donnie and I were riding together when his cell phone rang. He answered. Screaming came from Donnie's phone, and it sounded like Mike. Donnie took the phone away from his ear, and I heard Mike's voice say, "Put me on speaker! I know Troy's ass is with you, and I told you two clowns to work separately anyway!" *Shit! How does he know?* We looked over our shoulders to see if he was following us! We pulled over on Flatbush Avenue. "One of y'all needs to explain to me why in the hell I have a $3,000 receipt for one freaking dinner? Do y'all realize I have to explain this shit to the regional director?" Silence. "I usually can't get either one of you to shut up and now all I hear is crickets." More silence. "Speak up!" Donnie went first. "Uh, Mike.

See, what happened was that the doctors were having a good time and..." "Shut up! I don't wanna hear that! Both of y'all meet me at the Brooklyn Diner in an hour." *Uh oh.* Donnie, who had a wife and three young kids, said, "How am I gonna tell my wife I got fired?" *We are screwed.* We got to the diner ahead of Mike and worked on our story. When Mike walked in, we smiled and stood to shake his hand. "Hey, Mike!" "Oh, now the two of y'all can talk? An hour ago, y'all were deaf mutes." *This is not gonna be good.* He ordered a sandwich and told us to get something from the menu. Neither one of us had an appetite. We felt like it was our version of *The Last Supper.* Mike gobbled down his meal while Donnie and I picked at our burgers in silence. We finished, and Mike asked for the check and stood to leave. Donnie asked, "You aren't gonna fire us?" "No, but don't you two clowns ever pull that again!" A few days later, I asked Mike, "Why didn't you fire us the other day?" "Hey, I might fuss and cuss at y'all for doing something stupid. But, I'm not gonna fire y'all for making a mistake. The first time, it's an accident. The second time, it's a pattern. Now, if you and Donnie do something dumb like that again, I *will* fire your asses!" *The first time, it's an accident. The second time, it's a pattern.* Throughout our diner meal, Mike didn't say much. He didn't have to. Donnie and I knew we had messed up, but we never did that again.

CHAPTER 78

A missed phone call from another district manager took my life in another direction. Sales reps made their own schedule, and the Friday of the missed call found me already at home by 4:00 p.m. *C'mon, it was Friday. You had to beat New York City traffic!* Terry Pompey was my district manager with a new company. He was a black guy who was about 6'8" and 260. He played college football at the University of Delaware. I ran outside to my apartment complex parking lot to return his call and prayed that cars would pass by to make it sound like I was still in Manhattan! "Hey, Terry. Sorry I missed your call. I was in a doctor's office." *No, I wasn't!* "What's up?" "No problem. Quick question. What are your thoughts on going in the Training Department?" "Oh, I don't know, Terry. My numbers were better last year than this year. Why, do you think I should try to go in there?" "Well, I think you'd be a good fit for two reasons. One, you're good at making complicated things simple and reps need that kind of simplicity. Two, you care about people and always try to help others, and the Training Department needs that. That's why I think you'd be a good fit. Think about it over the weekend and call me on Monday and let me know what you think." "Okay." I hung up. I had never considered doing that job. Ever. Then, all weekend, it was all I thought about. I was having fun being a sales rep, going from one physician's office to the next. *Who wanted to sit in an office cube all day? What made Terry think that I'd be a good teacher? That was a funny thought. Me? A teacher?* The more I thought about it, the more I came to the conclusion that it might be a good step for me, and it became just that. Terry forever changed my life with that phone call. Like Mrs. Prater, I guess he saw something in me I didn't.

Once I started the new job, I had no clue what I was doing and no one took the time to help me. Except one person. A guy named Brian Bauer. Although he and I only worked together for eight months, I felt as though he was intentionally placed in my life. As a sales rep, I tried to use my personality and relationship building to sell to physicians. As a trainer/teacher, I needed to improve my clinical knowledge, and I wasn't ashamed to admit, I didn't possess much of that! That's where Brian helped me.

At the time, Brian and his wife, Suzanne, had recently had their first child and were living in Easton, Pennsylvania. For Brian, it was about 140 miles round-trip to our job in Parsippany, New Jersey, each day. Our training workday usually wrapped up around 5:00 p.m. and Brian tried to get away from the office as quickly as possible to avoid traffic. He could see that I was really struggling with the clinical stuff, so he offered to stay after work and help me. He had to do that a lot. *Because I needed lots of help!* Brian went over the nuances of atherosclerosis, dyslipidemia and clinical trials. *And, trust me, it took a while for me to understand that!* Brian became a confidante who never judged me, even when I forgot concepts that he had just gone over with me the night before. I'd tell him, "Just go over it one time with me, and I won't forget it," but I would still forget. He teased me and started calling me, "Troy 'One-Time' Lewis!" *I couldn't help it, sometimes my brain went into panic mode and I forgot!* But, much like Lt. Darey, Brian just wanted to help, and I appreciated his patience. I came to lean on him for advice and friendship, but I guess the thing that Brian impressed upon me the most was the importance of giving new employees confidence with newly learned concepts. He said, "Don't judge them for what they don't know or haven't already figured out. Just *help* them! That's what we are here for. That's why it's called the *Training* Department!" Brian Bauer helped me in my new role when no one else did, and for that, I was forever grateful to him.

CHAPTER 79

When I was a little boy, Tony loved watching black and white movies from the 1940s and 1950s on Sunday afternoons. He was an Edward G. Robinson fan, and I became one, too. *"Yeah, see, I'll hit you right in the kisser!"* When Turner Classic Movies was launched in 1994, it became my favorite TV channel. Like many things that took place in my life, some things were meant to be, and one of them occurred when I woke up at 10:34 on the Saturday morning of January 4, 2014. After flipping to CNN to make sure no terrorist attacks took place while I slept, TCM was usually the channel I went to next. Reruns of *The Tonight Show Starring Johnny Carson* interviews had become a new feature on TCM, and whenever Johnny was on, I watched him because Mumma wouldn't let me watch *The Tonight Show* when I was a kid!

Tony referred to Mr. Douglas as "Cool Kirk" the first time I watched *Gunfight at the O.K. Corral* one Sunday afternoon with him, and anytime I saw Mr. Douglas in a movie thereafter, as a tribute to Tony, I always said, "There he is, 'Cool Kirk!'" That Saturday morning, a broadcast of Mr. Carson's interview with Mr. Kirk Douglas from 1988 was being replayed. Mr. Douglas was promoting his book, *The Ragman's Son,* and Mr. Carson asked him what made him decide to write a book at that point in his life. His explanation went like this: "Well, you know John, I was filming on the set of *Spartacus* one day when someone, I forget who it was, asked me what I was doing after the shoot that evening. I said, 'I'm tired. I'm going to drive home and go to bed.' He looked at me and said, 'You're going to drive? You're Kirk Douglas. You're a star. You should go home in a limousine!' And, you know what, John? I got to thinking about that remark, and I thought, 'He's right. I *am* Kirk Douglas! I am a star. I should go home in a limo!' So I arranged for one to pick me up the next day because I needed to head up the coast for a golf tournament on Saturday morning that was about 2 hours away. I'm not going to drive that far! I'm Kirk Douglas! I'm a star! So the driver picks me up and puts my bags in the trunk and I get in the car, still in my *Spartacus* outfit. That's right, John. I'm still in my *Spartacus* outfit!" Mr. Carson and the audience laughed at that visual.

Mr. Douglas went on with his story, "I'm tired from filming all day so I lay down in the backseat and took a nap. We were about an hour or so into it when I felt the car slow down, and the driver pulled over. I sat up and asked him, 'Is something wrong?' He said, 'No, Mr. Douglas, I just need to go to the rest room' as we pulled into the parking lot of a gas station. He got out of the car, and I laid back down for a spell before I decided that I wanted something cool to drink. I remembered that I had some change tucked away in my *Spartacus* outfit so I get out of the car and walked in to buy a soda. The guy behind the counter, his eyes were popping out of his head as he gave me the once-over, and I paid for my drink." Mr. Carson and his audience laughed. "So I head back out to my limo and you know what, John? It's gone! The driver thought I was still lying in the back. So now what am I going to do?" "What did you do, Kirk?" "I went back in and asked the guy behind the counter if I could borrow a dime? Hey, I didn't have any more money! So I called the limousine company, and they apologized and promised to have the driver return to my location once he reached the hotel. But I wasn't going to wait that long. So I headed out to the edge of the highway and what did I do, John?" "What?" "I stuck out my thumb! That's what I did. There I was, John, in my *Spartacus* outfit, standing alongside the highway, and oh, about 30 to 40 cars slowed down and gave me a double take, but none stopped to give me a ride, until finally, this young kid in a pickup truck stopped, and I slid in next to him. He looked at me and said, 'Do you know who you are?' He and I both laughed, and he gave me a ride all the way to the hotel, but as we drove, John, I really began to think about that kid's question. 'Did I know who I was?' And the more I thought about it, John, the more I realized, I didn't like who I was. I was a bitter, angry man, and if you looked back at the majority of my films, I played bitter, angry characters. So John, I never forgot that kid saying that to me in 1960. He really made me begin to think about who I was and why I was so angry. I had everything I could ever want, but I wasn't happy. I wanted to learn about who I was and writing it all down removed a lot of that anger. So, John, that's why I wrote this book. It helped me understand who I am." *Do you know who you are? Did I know who I was? That was a damn good question.* And, until I started writing *Gas Money*, I didn't know who I was and I didn't like who I was. I was much like Kirk Douglas, bitter and angry at life and at everything. "Cool Kirk" had his reasons. I had mine.

From the time I was a child to a teen, when Mumma was in one of her rages, and I had done something to displease her, she screamed at me, "I wish you'd never been born!" You hear that often enough and it made you wish that you hadn't been born. She didn't say that every day, but she said it often enough for me to never forget it. Sometimes, I even asked her, "Well, why didn't you just have an abortion then if you hate me so much?" "Oh, shut your smart-ass mouth." Knowing that she sometimes wished I'd never been born messed me up for many years. I never quite believed that *anyone* liked me. I became paranoid. Even when people acted as though they liked me, I never believed it. I felt that they were faking it. I tried to make those negative voices and thoughts go away, but they never really did. *How does anyone like you if your mother, of all people, wishes you'd never been born?*

Writing lessened a lot of the anger and pain I harbored over the years. Putting it all on paper began a healing process for me. Mumma's hurtful words never left my psyche, but I learned to accept my life and my relationship with her. Maybe she was tougher on me because I was the oldest. *I didn't know.* I do know her toughness kept me from doing any *crazy* shit because I *knew* if I did do something illegal, *she* would have fucked me up. *I don't think Bridgette* or *Gentree ever had that fear. Or, on the other hand, maybe they were fearless.* But not me, when it came to Mumma. *I was fearful of that woman, forever.* As Gentree got older, he had legal troubles that he brought on himself, but I don't think he ever really had the same fear of her that I did. I never had any legal problems (other than speeding tickets) because I was always afraid she would kill me if I did. If there was one thing in life I was serious about, it was that. As an adult, Mumma and I had many disagreements over Gentree's choices, but I eventually realized I wasn't going to change her mind about anything. It was hard for a mother to not do as much as she could for a son. One thing Mumma never did was to turn her back on anyone, not even Gentree when he was in and out of jail. I was often angry that she sided with him because I felt the stress he gave her was taking years off of her life, and that made me angry. *I wanted her around as long as possible.* But one time she told me something that shut me up, and I learned to keep my thoughts to myself after that. "Troy, if I'm not there for Gentree, who will be?" *Okay, Mumma you made your point.* When she raised me, I felt that everything was black and white, and with Gentree, everything was grey. *Since when did things become "grey" with her?* That bothered me, but Mumma was Mumma. Nothing I said was going to change her. She was who she was, and who was I to tell her anything. She had been taking care of people since she was 16. Me? I could barely take care of myself.

For the first 50 years of my life, I hated *me* every time I looked in the mirror. Mumma's hurtful comments didn't make seeing my reflection any easier. *I always heard her saying, "I wish you'd never been born."* When I flossed, I heard her. When I brushed, I heard her. When I had an Afro, I heard her. When I went bald and shaved the few hairs that remained, I heard her. It got to a point where I could never stop hearing that phrase every time I looked in a mirror. Only now, instead of hearing Mumma saying it, it was my own voice wishing that I'd never been born. Those voices coupled with life's disappointments when I looked back at 50 years worth of "roads not taken" became too much for me to handle. I visited a deep and dark place for about 9 months the year that I turned 50. I no longer cared about any of the *gas money* I'd been given in life. Like George

Bailey, I, too, lost faith in life and in me. I was at the end of my rope. It took the love of four people, as well as writing and reflecting on the 50 years of *gas money* that had shaped my life, that kept me from leaping from the metaphorical Bedford Falls Bridge. Who were those four people? Well, they are part of the forthcoming story.

During the months that preceded and succeeded my 50th birthday, I began to take a hard look at my life, and I didn't like what I saw. For nearly 9 months, I cried every day about the mess that my life had turned into. At that time, I was unable to shut out the voices in my head that told me I was worthless, ignorant, stupid, unattractive, fat and unsuccessful. Even *I* wished I'd never been born, and that sentiment had been part of my fabric ever since I could remember. I decided to do something to quiet those negative voices.

Milestone birthdays offer an opportunity to reflect on life's accomplishments, and I felt that I hadn't done anything positive. I reached the conclusion that I had "a good run." I had been to places I never thought I would get to see. I owned some property. I had a good job. Yet, much like Kirk Douglas, I was a malcontent. A disappointed, angry person dissatisfied with life was an accurate description of me. I felt like I had no reason to continue living.

CHAPTER 80

Despite all of the "good" that was in my life, sadly, I never appreciated how fortunate I was. As I got older, I forgot what the nice people in my life had offered me with their kind words or deeds. I didn't care about any of that or them around the time I turned 50. I guess I went through a mid-life crisis, and I turned away from people because of my dissatisfaction with who I was. Even at 50 years old, I was still a lost, little boy longing for affection and acceptance and a better life than the one I had. I didn't see a "better" life coming, so I took my life in a different direction. It was a path that wasn't for the best, but it sure seemed so at the time.

I never liked *me*. I just was never content with who I was. In elementary school, I wanted to be Larry South because *all* of the girls loved Larry South. He was a light-skinned kid with a perfect Afro like Coach McCleary's, and he had green eyes. *God, the girls loved his eyes!* I didn't know what happened to Larry South, but I never forgot how envious I was of him! In high school, I wanted to be Andre Hopkins, but 20 years later, hard times found him and when I saw his appearance I was shocked. In college, I wanted to be Magic Johnson because I knew he made a lot of money, and I thought he had a pretty good life. I remember a 1980 *Inside Sports* magazine cover that featured Magic and his salary structure. According to the article, the manner in which his contract was set up at the time, Magic would make $42,000 a month for the rest of his life. *I hated Magic! All I wanted was to make $42,000 a year!* I wanted *his* life! But Mumma had always warned me to "be careful what you wish for."

I first started thinking about suicide in 5th grade when Mrs. Pollock's ghost chased me all over Middlesex County. *I guess it was crazy for a 10-year-old to think suicide was a good option, but it's what I thought. I never said I was sane.* Back then, I was trying to escape life at the age of 10, and 40 years later, nothing had changed. Some felt that only cowards killed themselves, but I felt it took a brave individual to stick a gun in his or her mouth or jump from a bridge or swallow a bunch of sleeping pills. I felt unloved and unwanted at 10 *and* at 50, and I was tired of feeling that way. Maybe I was crazy at 10 or maybe I was just delusional at 50. I was a half-century old, closer to dying than living, unhappy with life and full of self-doubt and self-hatred, so I had nothing to lose, but my life.

Negative voices bounced around in my head since childhood. *Not good enough. Not smart enough. Not attractive enough. Not rich enough.* I felt there was no hope for me. Yet, hope was precisely what I sought. A beacon of light. I guess I had been searching for a little hope since I was a little boy, *something* that would bring me true contentment. *Wasn't that what each of us wanted?* Mrs. Barlowe gave me a book on lighthouses in 4th or 5th grade and from that point on, I wanted to become a lighthouse keeper. I thought that livelihood would be ideal because of its isolation. I supposed lighthouse keepers could distance themselves from society, yet their role was still needed by ships and the men who steered them in to port or out to sea. With my insecurity, a lighthouse keeper seemed like the perfect occupation. *Regrettably, no one gave me gas money to get that job!* But I did visit over 100 of them, and I was like a little kid whenever I saw one! However, at 50 years old, that little boy lost his way and ran out of optimism in life. Not even visiting lighthouses brought him joy anymore. Saddened by life's disappointments and failed relationships and poor life choices, he gave up. His spirit was broken. *My spirit was broken.*

I wasn't ashamed to admit that I wasn't as strong as the two strongest people I knew, Mumma and Butley. I finally reached the point where I said to myself, "Fuck it. I'm *not* Mumma or Butley. Who said I had to be as strong as them? Let's get this life over with." I had no reason to get up in the morning, so why get up? I lost my way. When you don't care anymore, you really *don't* care anymore. Losing the will to live was an awful state of mind. I became a person with no purpose. I was apprehensive about what awaited me on the "other side" after I took my life, but I was willing to take that chance. It was hard to concentrate at work and at some point of each day I found myself sitting in the parking lot in my car crying and wondering, "What the fuck happened to me?" *I didn't have an answer.*

Matt Siegel was a guy I once worked with, and his favorite phrase was, "Attitude is a choice." Each day at work, even when things were going well, I was a grump before 8:00 a.m. *Couldn't help it, just didn't like talking to people that early in the morning!* Matt felt that I could have been more pleasant, and I probably could have, but I chose not to. I *chose* to be standoffish instead of amiable. Indeed, it was a choice. Sadly, I chose to look at my life in a negative manner without recognizing the positives. I allowed negative voices to play a greater role than the positive ones. Instead of looking ahead at life, I continually looked backwards and at poor choices I made. Not studying. *That hurt no one, but me.* Cheating. *Grandma Latimore was right when I snuck a card at Solitaire.* Lying. *Ditto, I broke a few hearts and a few more tossed arrows that punctured mine.*

I admired Matt. He found a cute girl (trust me, he overachieved) and stuck with her, had two boys and never looked back. But his lifestyle was never good enough for me. That kind of life was boring, from my perspective. I often sought change and with that came drama. I should have been more like Matt. My choices weren't always smart. When I turned 50, one of my poorer choices became Absolut vodka, and I wanted more of that as often as I could get it. About 20 shots of it in the morning and another 20 shots in the evening made me feel better when I went "dark." *Hey, I wanted to sleep and forget about my life. Absolut and Ambien helped with that, and I wasn't ashamed to admit it.* The Latimore curse caught me, too, and at that point in my life, I didn't care. Before I turned 50, I used to average about 4 six-packs of Miller High Life a year (I liked

Miller beer because that's what Gerald's brother, Buddy, let me have the evening we met Hatchet Woman), but in 2011, a bottle of Absolut became my new beverage of choice. *Who was this person that I turned into?* I didn't know, and I didn't care. What I did care about was that I became good friends with the people at the local liquor store. I knew they liked me! Every other evening, they greeted me with, "Hey, Troy!" when I made the bell that hung from their door chime. *Yes, I went through one liter of vodka every other day. I was Horace Latimore.* While I was trying to kill myself and my liver and kidneys, I became what every business needed to survive, a repeat customer. There I was heading to the liquor store trying to forget about life and remembering the hand that Fate had dealt me. *Or maybe, it was the hand that I had dealt myself.* Once I made it up the stairs to my condo, I became Grandpop Latimore and Uncle Eddie and Glo and Uncle Dee trying to forget about life. I used to judge them, but after I started drinking, I never judged anyone again. *I thought it was rather funny as I stumbled from room to room at my place.* Some nights I bounced into a wall. Another night, it would be the refrigerator, but I recovered and made it back to my bed just like when I used to watch Grandpop Latimore stagger from the dining room to his bed when I was a kid. *I had the bruises to show for it.* Closer and closer I was to George Bailey teetering on the Bedford Falls Bridge, only I wasn't seeking God's help to keep me from jumping. I just wanted my pain to end. I wanted to die, but it never crossed my mind that there would be so many Clarences preventing me from ending the misery that my life had become.

On May 23rd of 2011, I decided to end it all. I swallowed 20 shots of Absolut (or maybe it was 21) and a couple of Ambien. I grabbed Peter Rabbit, walked down to my garage and closed its door behind me. Next, I duct-taped a newly purchased hose to the exhaust pipe of my charcoal grey two-door 2008 Honda Accord. *That took a while because I struggled with all things mechanical!* I ran the hose to the driver's side, looped it through the window and into the interior of the car. *I had been waiting for this day since the 5th grade, and now it was finally here.* Google suggested that I place towels around the base of my garage door (I did) to keep the carbon monoxide from escaping. The search engine told me I'd be dead in 10 to

40 minutes if the seals around the exhaust and garage were pretty secure. *For once in my life, I had done my homework!* I slid the key into the ignition and turned it clockwise. As always, Honda engines were reliable and quiet. Mine "started like a charm," which was one of Grandpop Latimore's favorite phrases when he and I cut the yard at his house. He took great pleasure in saying, "She started like a charm" after I had pulled on the starter rope of his *Lawn-Boy* push mower for the 16th or 17th time! "No, it didn't Grandpop!"

(Insert "The Sounds of Silence" by Simon and Garfunkel) Other than the purr of the Honda engine and my breathing, there was only silence in my garage. My chest rose and fell and I thought about Simon and Garfunkel's "The Sounds of Silence." Music was important to me throughout my life, but I wasn't listening to any as I sat there waiting to fall asleep for the final time. In fact, I had quit listening to music months ago. In my head, though, I could hear the Queens, N.Y., duo chanting the opening to their song. Calmness comes over you when you've made up your mind to end it. *I know it did for me.*

I texted my supervisor, Darla Boatman, to thank her for trying to help me through my depression, for being a good friend, and an even better supervisor. When times were good, I borrowed the tune of Handel's "Hallelujah Chorus" to sing "Dar-la Boat-man, Darla Boat-man" to her each morning when she walked by my desk. That made her giggle! *I was going to miss Darla's laugh.* She never responded to text messages quickly, so I figured that on that particular Sunday evening when she got around to reading mine, I'd already be dead. I texted her so that one person would know where to find my dead body. *Or, maybe I was reaching out for help.*

Peter Rabbit was seated next to me in the passenger seat just like he had been on so many solo trips along U.S. interstates. *Only this time, it would be a totally different destination for us. Where we were headed wasn't on any of the maps Mumma bought for me as a kid.* I picked him up, placed him against my chest and reclined the driver's seat. *Wow, Peter, we've been together since 1966. That's a long damn time for any relationship!* I closed my eyes. Lots of things flash through your mind when you are about to die. I thought about how sad Mumma might be when she got the news, but I knew she would be okay because she was always strong. She persevered when Da beat her up for 13 years, and after they broke up, he continued beating her up emotionally for another 20. *Mumma and I knew firsthand what the psyche could do to you.* She survived seeing Gentree go to prison for a total of 16 years. She endured raising four brothers and a sister at 16 years old. *Surely, she could live with me dying.* But I never thought she or *anyone* really cared about me anyway, so I thought no one would miss me. Sitting there, I thought about being a little boy and how I was never really happy then, and how I wasn't happy now. Despite all of the nice things people had done for me over the years, I just never felt *wanted.* I felt I was a nuisance to everyone. When someone reaches their lowest point, it's hard for them to find any positives.

My eyes had been closed for about 10 minutes. Sleep was slowly coming. I thought back to the time I was driving back from Virginia in 2004 and began falling asleep in Maryland. Pulling into a rest stop on I-95 at 1:00 a.m., I put my Nissan 350Z in Neutral, pulled up the emergency break and reclined to take a nap. At that very instant, my cell phone rang. *Who in the hell is calling me at 1:00 in the morning?* It was Butley! "Hey, Butley! What's wrong?" "Nothing. I was just checking on you. I know you left your mom's late, and I figured you might be getting sleepy about now." "Wow, I just pulled over to go to sleep. I can't believe you called right now! That's crazy!" "We've always been brothers from different mothers." *I was sad knowing I'd never talk to him again, but at that time in my life, I wasn't talking to anyone. I had become a recluse.*

Light-headedness was coming over me. I didn't know if that was the result of the carbon monoxide or the Absolut or the Ambien. It didn't matter. I just wanted to go to sleep for one last time. *Bang! Bang! Bang!* I opened my eyes! *What the fuck was that?* "Mr. Lewis, if you are in there, you need to open up! We are the New Jersey State Troopers, and we'll tear this door down if we have to!" *Shit! Darla read my message and sent the troopers over! I can't even fucking kill myself right!* I wanted to stay in the car, but I didn't want them to tear down my garage door! If they had gotten there 30 minutes later, that would have been their only option. Then Mumma and Gerald would have been responsible with paying the Condo Association for the damages, and I didn't want that. At my condo development, Wells Fargo and I owned the interior, but the Condo Association owned the exterior and the garage door!

"Jesus Christ!" *I'm sorry Grandma Latimore. I know I shouldn't have said that, but where I'm trying to go, Jesus won't be there.* I couldn't believe Darla read my text that quickly. I was more afraid of raising the garage door to face the state troopers than I was of dying. I turned off the ignition, ripped the duct-tape and hose from the exhaust, threw them in the trunk and closed the lid. *Hide the evidence!* I scooped the towels from the garage floor and tossed them in a corner. Next came the hard part: Opening the garage door to lie to the state troopers. Up came the door. "Are you Troy Lewis?" "Yes, sir. What's going on?" "Mr. Lewis, we received a call that you might be trying to harm yourself." I looked at them and at the neighbors peering from their windows. Not that I cared what the neighbors thought, I had lived there for four years and knew not one of them, but it was still embarrassing to have policemen in my driveway. "Are you okay, sir?" "Yes, sir. I'm fine. Not sure what this is all about." *What was I going to say? Yup, you caught me. I was in the garage trying to kill myself. Take me to the nearest hospital and the loony bin. I learned in the military to "Deny, deny, deny!"* The other trooper asked, "Mr. Lewis, can you explain why we could hear your engine running with the garage door down?" "Oh, that? I was just sitting in the car before I hit the remote to open it, that's all." "Well, Mr. Lewis, I have to be honest with you. Most people I know don't sit in a closed garage in the middle of May and run their engine. Can you explain why you were?" *Fuck! I can't answer that one, Officer! I just stared at him like he was an algebra equation that I had no chance of solving!* The other trooper was on his cell phone talking to someone. "Yes, ma'am. He seems to be okay. We are gonna stay here and talk to him for a bit." He looked at me and handed over his phone. Darla was a smart, attractive blonde from Tennessee with the cutest Southern accent and an even more pleasant personality. She and Capt. Meyer were the best people I ever worked for. Twenty years apart, they rebuilt my work confidence after the two supervisors who preceded them went out of their way to make things difficult for me. I sat on my condo steps talking with Darla while the troopers leaned against their vehicles staring at me. *I was sure they had more important things to do than babysit a 50-year-old man who wanted to kill himself.* They couldn't have been nicer to me. Darla made me promise her that I wouldn't harm myself that night, and she again encouraged me to take it one day at a time. "Okay, okay." *I said whatever I could to get her off the phone. I was mad that she called 9-1-1. When people are at the "bottom," they are often angry when someone tries to help them. They were ashamed of their plight, ashamed there was a problem and really ashamed people were seeing them at their lowest point. I know I was.* We talked for another couple of minutes. "Troy, if you need to take time off from work, you can do it. I'll take care of it." "No, Darla, I'm fine. Plus, I have to fly to Phoenix this week and train the new hires out there. I'm okay." *I wasn't okay, but I didn't want "higher-ups" at work to know how "sick" I was.* I didn't want her explaining that to them. I was too private for that. "Darla, I'll be in tomorrow. I promise I'll see you in the morning." *I lied to her, too. I had no intention of seeing her in the morning.* I hung up and handed the trooper his phone. He said, "Mr. Lewis, we aren't gonna leave here if you're going to harm yourself. We'll take you to the emergency room." "Officer, I am fine. I think my supervisor overreacted." *I lied one more time.* I wanted to end my life with as little fanfare as possible. I sent the text to Darla to thank her for being my friend, and now, cops were involved. *I just wanted someone to know where my body could be found.*

I guess I shouldn't have sent her the text, but she ended up saving my life. I convinced the troopers that it was a misunderstanding, and I was barely able to hold it together while they continued sizing me up. After about 30 minutes of questions and answers, both officers prepared to leave. One took off in his cruiser and the other was about to follow his partner, but put his vehicle in "Park," got out and walked back toward me. "You know, Mr. Lewis, it'll be a real damn shame if you do something to yourself later on tonight, and we have to come back here. You know why?" He answered his rhetorical question. "Because you're really gonna hurt that lady that was on the phone with me. I could tell she really cares about you. So my advice to you is, whatever you're thinking about doing, don't do it." "Yes, sir." He left me standing in front of my open garage door staring at my Honda.

My relationships with the opposite sex were always of a precarious nature, and that was always a result of my actions. Needless to say, Kat and I had split up a few years earlier, but Darla made contact with her anyway because she knew I didn't have *any* friends in New Jersey. Kat was the only person she knew to call. My cell phone rang. I looked at the caller ID. *Good God, it's Kat.* "I just got a call from Darla a few minutes ago." *Oh, boy.* "You know I don't have a car, but I'll find a way to get out to your place if I have to. It would be a lot easier if you came into the City. Will you do that for me?" "Okay." *Why do people even fucking care about me? Just let me die. Please.* Now I had committed to seeing her.

It was about an hour's drive to Kat's Harlem brownstone. *It was the commitments and promises that were keeping me alive.* I rang her buzzer and walked up to her 3rd floor apartment. I sat on her couch, and she planted herself in the leather swivel chair across from me. She leaned in, putting both elbows on her knees with her hands cupping her beautiful cheekbones. I always thought she was a pretty girl. *What the hell did she see in me?* "What is going on?" It was the saddest expression I had ever seen on her face, and at that point, we had known each other for 11 years. I didn't know where to begin because there were so many demons spinning in my head. "I don't know, Kat." She continued. "Troy, I don't know what is happening, but I'm here to help you in any way I can. I don't care if we aren't together anymore, but whatever is bothering you, it will be okay. I'm here for you." *No, it won't.* I wasn't even seeing her anymore, and she was still nice to me. I was pathetic. She was heroic.

It was a lengthy process. For months, I thought about returning to my garage *every* day, and that would have been easier than the struggle to continue living. Every waking moment found me thinking about suicide and how much easier it would have been to take that route. I forced myself to keep my mind active, but when only one thought consumed your brain, it was hard to think of anything else.

Brian Gathen (who challenged me to the state capital quiz once and only once) called each morning at 7:30 to check on me. Only he, Darla and Kat knew how close I was to dying. Each time I saw his number on the caller ID, I fumed. *Why the fuck does he keep calling me?* I was traveling for work all over the country. I rotated between the Chicago, Phoenix, Dallas and Atlanta regional offices of my pharmaceutical company. Being on the road and in the air gave me lots of time to think, but regardless of the time zone, Brian called like clockwork. Every morning at 7:30. "Hey!" "Hey, Brian. How are you?" "I'm good, just calling to check on my buddy." "Thanks, Brian. I'm fine." "You're gonna keep living for me, right? You promised me." "Yeah, I know. I promised you, Brian." I had given him my word that I would keep trying each day, but what I really wanted to do was kill *him* and *me* because he never stopped calling! But my promise to him kept me going. *I didn't want to let him down.* The state trooper's parting words kept me going. *I didn't want to hurt Darla.* Kat's words: "It'll be okay," kept me going. *I didn't want to disappoint her, either. No matter how selfish I was, I had given them my word that I would keep trying.* They pulled harder for me than I pulled for myself. The more I wanted to not fail them, the more I found myself trying to live for them. *I* had become secondary to *them. They* were more important than *me.*

I started seeing a therapist weekly, Diane Kolodzinski, whose desk placard read, "H-O-P-E." The first time I sat in the chair across from her, she asked, "So what brings you in to see me today?" I pointed at her placard and said that I had none. I sobbed like a baby for almost my entire 60-minute session. *I felt like such a loser crying in front of a total stranger.* But I was at the point where I had nothing to lose so what did I care? Crying in front of a stranger was certainly easier than crying in front of someone you knew. Diane encouraged me to discuss anything and everything, and initially, I didn't see the point of that. However, over time, the more I talked about the things that bothered me, the less they seemed to matter. The less burdensome those negative emotions seemed and the less burdened I became. Diane urged me to call her anytime that I felt I was in an agitated, "not safe" state of mind. I felt "not safe" plenty of times, but only had to reach out to her once. During our weekly therapy sessions, H-O-P-E became more of something I began to want for me than it was something I thought I had no shot at. *When I was "at bottom," I never thought that I would have H-O-P-E again, but I did. Maybe I was better at predictions like Mike Tyson remaining undefeated. Oh, I forgot, I wasn't good at that, either!*

The more time that passed, the farther I distanced myself from sitting in the garage with the door pulled down. The more I kept busy with helping others, traveling and writing, the more I began to heal. Each week, leaves fell from my branches until I was a barren tree for all to see. I became transparent. I was no longer embarrassed that I tried to kill myself. I liked sharing that with anyone willing to listen, and I was amazed at what others were willing to share with me. English naturalist John Ray said, "Misery loves company," and I think he was right on that one. The less private and isolated I held my emotions, the more others were willing to bare their souls to me. *I guess they thought, "What do I have to lose sharing stuff with this guy? He's already admitted that he tried to kill himself!"* Day by day, I got a little better. Diane wanted me to quit living for her because of a promise and for Kat because of a promise and for Darla because of a promise and lastly, for Brian because of a promise, but she wanted me to live for *me*. I never thought that would happen, but it did.

After many months passed, reflection offered a more tolerant perspective of the life that was mine. I slowly came to the realization that maybe, just maybe, my life wasn't so bad after all. *H-O-P-E was coming back.* I wanted to hear music again. I hadn't listened to *any* since Simon and Garfunkel played in my head on May 23rd, and there I was 35,000 feet in the air returning from Dallas on September 23rd of 2011 ready to listen again. I stared out over the wing from my United Airlines seat in Row 21F. *Loved that seat, extra legroom!* I was scared to hear music again because music offered strands of hope and pangs of disappointment and the joys of love gained and the misfortunes of love lost. Music was the soundtrack to my life. I wasn't sure if I was ready to listen to those echoes. But I took a chance. I was ready to press ahead.

My index finger teetered over the power button to my iTouch as I searched for a song to begin my comeback at life (it was my fourth iTouch, the previous three were lost during various Absolut and Ambien-induced comas). It powered on. *Scroll, scroll, scroll. There it is! I had found the perfect song after refraining from music for nearly 9 months.* It was the Chairman of the Board, Ol' Blue Eyes himself, who I was first introduced to by Mark Fratterole when I was a college sophomore and Fratterole was a year behind me. Mark called Mr. Sinatra "The Big Frank" as he eased himself into his beach chair outside of his Mowrey Hall Dormitory Room No. 232 and played Sinatra albums on Friday nights before we went out to party. Fratterole sat there smoking a pipe or cigar in his bathrobe and listening to *anything* Sinatra. *I could close my eyes and still see him!* Any time I heard Sinatra, I thought about Mark Fratterole and how I never thanked him for introducing me to "The Big Frank." "Fratterole, turn that old guy off. How can you listen to that shit?" "Froy [his nickname for me], there's nothing more awesome than 'The Big Frank!'" You don't know good music when you hear it!" I was 19 and he was 18, and it took me 31 years to fully understand how accurate Fratterole was. *Music didn't get much better than Sinatra.* He was an artist, not an entertainer, which was what I felt happened with much of the music that came after him, a bunch of entertainers with no artistry. In the early 1990s, I was a fan of The Notorious B.I.G. and his ability to "sample" music from another era. Da heard me listening to that and said, "Yeah, your friend, Biggie, can teach Smokey Robinson a lot about song writing." I stared at him and thought, "I guess Da is right on that one." I quit listening to rap music that day.

(Insert "I've Got You Under My Skin" by Frank Sinatra) Flying back from Dallas while that September evening turned to night, I was ready for music again. I chose Sinatra's live version of "I've Got You Under My Skin." I could not have picked a better song to listen to for the next 937 miles, and that's what I did. *The same song for the 3 hour and 20 minute flight back to Newark.* Thank you, Fratterole, for bringing me peace in September 2011. Thank you, Kat. Thank you, Darla. Thank you, Brian. Thank you, Diane.

Gas Money began as a collection of stories about my life. Never did I think it would provide insight into what made me, me. Never did I think, like Kirk Douglas, that I would begin to understand who I was and accept who I was. All of the self-doubt, self-hatred and disappointment that had been "under my skin" had departed. I was finally satisfied with just being *me*. Kat was right after all. I was going to be "okay." I had plenty of *gas money* to get to wherever I was going.

Darla and me. 2014

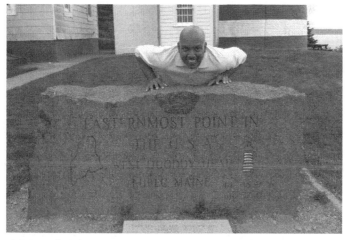

Me visiting the West Quoddy Lighthouse and loving my life. 2012

THE LAST CHAPTER

Darla and Brian and Kat and Diane were blessings in my life. The same went for Mumma and Da and Gerald. So were Grandma and Grandpop Latimore and Grandma and Grandpop Lewis and everyone else in my family. Even my "nemesis," Butley, was a blessing because he has been a friend ever since I can remember. Pretty much every person I ever encountered was a positive influence. *How many of us could say that?* I think sitting on the couch and watching *It's A Wonderful Life* with Towanda was a blessing. Over the years, the movie gave me much to think about. *What if I had never been born like George Bailey?* Having wished for that to happen for so long, I was now happy to be alive. It only took 50 years to reach that conclusion. I hope I impacted others in the positive fashion that so many others had influenced me. Hearing Kirk Douglas that January morning on TCM helped me start to realize who I am. Finally, I became thankful for just being me.

I began doing volunteer work for a suicide prevention hotline because I felt I had a lot to contribute since I was a suicide attempt survivor. I felt like I was making a difference in someone's life when they had run out of H-O-P-E. I could listen and that was what most people needed during their "dark" moments. I knew, firsthand, what it was like to be stuck on the shoulder of the highway called Life with no Hope in sight. I now had a lot to live for.

I finally told Mumma about my suicide attempt on Mother's Day of 2014 during one of our late night conversations. She got up from the little dining room table that had set the scene for so many of the discussions that helped in compiling *Gas Money*. She put her arms around me, kissed me on the top of head, and said, "Troy, I love you so much. I depend on you for so much. Please don't do that to me. I'd be lost without you." *That* was best the present I ever received from *anyone,* and I swear that all of the hurt she had *ever* caused me vanished once she put her arms around me.

I had far more positive people in my life than those who weren't, and in the big scheme of things, what else could I ask for? *Mrs. St. John, God rest your soul, sometimes it's hard not to end a sentence with a preposition.* I never knew how good my life was going to be until *after* I turned 50. I was no longer George Bailey thinking about the life that could have been and roads not taken. I grew into Troy Lewis, a person who never knew how good he had it until he gave up on life. He didn't have to jump from a bridge to come to that understanding, but instead he leapt from his Honda Accord while sitting in his garage. Fortunately, there were people in his life who cared about him and helped save him from self-destruction. He could not have done it alone. He had people supporting him all along, and it took an attempt at ending his life for him to realize that he had all of the *gas money* he ever needed.

Mumma, my Number One Favorite Girl. 2013

Kat Peeler, my Number Two Favorite Girl. 2013

(Insert "Way Back Home" by Junior Walker and the All-Stars)

Acknowledgments

I owe debts of gratitude to the many people who helped me in creating *Gas Money*. To those who read a chapter or chapters and offered their candid feedback, I cannot thank you enough. Kat Peeler for constantly telling me "to quit talking and start writing" and for having faith in me. Lori Lewis for believing in my story and remaining my friend through "thick and thin." Josie O'Hana for listening to my stories and selecting the perfect title for my book in less than five minutes. Gretchen Fritz for rearranging stories and maintaining a keen eye. Herbert Van Patten for always encouraging me to "get that book done!" His voice constantly rang in my ears, and even more so on the days that I didn't feel like writing. Diane Kolodzinski for helping me find H-O-P-E again. Darla Boatman for caring enough about me to call the New Jersey State Troopers when I was at rock bottom. Brian Gathen for checking on me when he had more important things to do. Mick Wieland for bringing my book to life with his interior design and for making a billion adjustments to the manuscript. Dave Kramer for making even me look good in a photo, and Nicole Ganz for creating the perfect book cover. Thanks to all of you for being such an important part of my life and providing me with the *gas money* that I needed to get to my next destination.

Made in the USA
Middletown, DE
01 September 2016